WAR
REPORT

WAR REPORT

From D-Day to Berlin
AS IT HAPPENED

Compiled and edited by Desmond
Hawkins, with additional material by
Mark Jones

BOOKS

1 3 5 7 9 10 8 6 4 2

BBC Books, an imprint of Ebury Publishing
20 Vauxhall Bridge Road,
London SW1V 2SA

BBC Books is part of the Penguin Random House group of companies
whose addresses can be found at global.penguinrandomhouse.com

Penguin
Random House
UK

Text © British Broadcasting Corporation

First published by Oxford University Press in 1946
Revised edition edited by Desmond Hawkins published by BBC books in 1994
Revised hardback edition published by BBC books in 1994
This edition published by BBC books in 2019

www.penguin.co.uk

A CIP catalogue record for this book is available from the British Library

ISBN 9781849907774

Printed and bound in Great Britain by Clays Ltd, Elcograf S.p.A.

Penguin Random House is committed to a sustainable future for
our business, our readers and our planet. This book is made
from Forest Stewardship Council® certified paper.

MIX
Paper from
responsible sources
FSC® C018179

PICTURE CREDITS

akg-images/Mondadori Portfolio: 482
BBC: 30, 45, 209, 421, 461
Corbis: 83; /Hulton-Deutsch Collection 303
Getty Images: 97, 143, 366 /AFP 233; /IWm/Conrtibutor 283;
/Life & Time Pictures 315

Maps by Bill Donohoe: 41, 70-1

Contents

Part I: 'And Now – Over to Normandy'

Part II: Normandy to the Rhine

CONTENTS

Part III: The Rhine to the Elbe

In Memoriam

Kent Stevenson
Missing from a raid on NW Germany by RAF Lancasters
22 June 1944

Guy Byam
Missing from an Eighth US Air Force daylight raid on Berlin
3 February 1945

Note On The Present Edition

It is now almost seventy years since the first transmission of War Report, on the evening of 6 June 1944, immediately after the nine o'clock news. The programme broke new ground for the BBC, delivering authentic sounds from the second front with a descriptive immediacy that only the eyewitness can bring. It is tempting with hindsight to make corrections of omission or inference, but this would certainly interfere with the veracity of the spoken and recorded dispatch. In this edition of *War Report* we have followed the example of Desmond Hawkins in his editing of the 1994 edition. The aim has been to respect the integrity of the original report but to amend or clarify where necessary by adding an italicised comment in square brackets.

Several new dispatches have been added, confirming the range of the programme. They contain the voices and experiences of fighting men as well as correspondents in unusual situations. Above all these reports form an authentic and very human picture of a total war entering its seventh year.

Mark Jones, 2014

Introduction

by John Simpson

It was the front-line correspondents in the Second World War, more than anyone else, who gave the BBC the reputation for honesty that it has enjoyed ever since; not just in Britain, but through much of the wider world. The afterglow of their reporting, seventy years ago, is only fading now; and for most of my career I have been able to profit from it.

In Russia, in Burma, in the Czech Republic, in Poland, in Belgium, in Norway, as well as in Germany itself, people have helped me in my work simply because I was from the BBC. In 1985 I wanted to film an important debate in the French National Assembly, but was told it was strictly forbidden. Then the deputy speaker, who had been in the Resistance forty years earlier, heard we were from the BBC, and took it on himself to smuggle my camera crew and me into a prime position in the gallery. 'You understand,' he said, 'I owe you such an enormous debt of gratitude.' Not me personally, of course: he meant the organisation I worked for, which had told people in Nazi-dominated Europe the truth about what was happening in the war, when every other national broadcaster was filling the air with lies.

Winston Churchill was often infuriated by the way the BBC sometimes seemed determined to report British reverses even before the Axis powers could do it themselves. Yet when the tide of war turned, in 1943, people who had heard the BBC tell them honestly and frankly about Dunkirk and the fall of Singapore and the sinking of the *Prince of Wales* and the failure of the Dieppe Raid knew they could believe it when it reported the fall of Stalingrad, the victory at El Alamein, and the successful Allied landings in Sicily. An old man in Berlin who had listened faithfully to the BBC throughout the war once put it to me succinctly: 'We knew that if you didn't lie about the bad things, you must be telling us the truth about your victories.' Eventually even Churchill saw the force of the argument.

The correspondents whose dispatches are published in this book gave the BBC that enviable reputation. Men like Richard Dimbleby, Wynford Vaughan Thomas, Frank Gillard and Howard Marshall faced all the dangers of the front-line soldiers, sailors and airmen they followed into battle, and their reporting has all the sharpness and actuality of the action they witnessed.

Here, for instance, is Guy Byam, jumping with the Paras on D-Day:

'We're over the coast now and the run in has started – one minute, thirty seconds. Red light – green and out – get on, out, out, out fast into the cool night air, out, out, out over France – and we know that the dropping zone is obstructed. We're jumping into fields covered with poles! . . . And then the ground comes up to hit me. And I find myself in the middle of a cornfield.'

This is Robert Dunnett reporting from Paris on 27 August 1944, as General de Gaulle, newly returned, drove victoriously through the Paris streets:

'I've been trying to get to the microphone, but it's been very difficult because there's been some shooting broken out from the – one of the buildings – I think it's in the neighbourhood of the Hotel Crillon. . . . [*confusion of voices – French and English*] the tanks massed in the square are firing back at the hotel, and I'm standing looking just straight across at it – smoke – smoke rising, and whoever opened up on the crowd from the hotel is [*several voices speaking in French*] . . .'

And this, most famous of all, is Richard Dimbleby at the liberation of Bergen-Belsen concentration camp, 19 April 1945:

'I picked my way over corpse after corpse in the gloom, until I heard one voice raised over the gentle undulating moaning. I found a girl, she was a living skeleton, impossible to gauge her age for she had practically no hair left, and her face was only a yellow parchment sheet with two holes in it for eyes. She was stretching out her stick of an arm and gasping something, it was "English, English, medicine, medicine", and she was trying to cry but she hadn't enough strength...'

The men (and at this stage in broadcasting history it was only men) who did the BBC's front-line reporting were taking part in a great national crusade. The wartime government understood the value of allowing journalists to work with the front-line troops and tell people back home what it was really like. It hadn't been like that at the start of the war; there were no BBC or newspaper journalists on the beaches at Dunkirk, partly because the system still hadn't been properly organised, and maybe because the British military authorities were nervous about the effect of negative reporting on morale at home.

Slowly they realised that people could be trusted to absorb bad news if they believed the basic cause was worth fighting for. The head of BBC News, R. T. Clark, had understood this right from the start. In September 1939, shortly after war was declared, he told his staff in a memo, '. . . the only way to strengthen the morale of the people whose morale is worth strengthening, is to tell them the truth, and nothing but the truth, even if the truth is horrible.'

Often it would indeed be horrible: yet honesty and truth were powerful weapons in the war against totalitarianism, and in the end they helped to win the war.

Seventy years after these dispatches were written, how much has changed? In the three big wars of recent times, two in Iraq and one in Afghanistan, the British and American governments knew that public opinion was deeply divided about the wisdom of the whole business, and did their utmost to control the reporting. The only journalist who managed to get television pictures of the major action in the first Gulf War did so by masquerading as an officer in the Grenadier Guards (it helped that he had indeed been one a few years before).

In the second Gulf War journalists were 'embedded', which meant that with some notable exceptions they only saw what they were allowed to see. Those who opted to report the war from no man's land found themselves in serious danger, mostly from American fire; their casualty rate was high.

But in contrast with 1939–45 these were little wars, fought against what we used to call Third World enemies. The Second World War involved the might of eight or nine of the world's most advanced countries, pitted against each other. By comparison with the kind of journalists whose work is quoted here, and with people like Martha Gellhorn or her one-time husband Ernest Hemingway, or Ernie Pyle, or Ed Murrow, the work of the journalists of my generation has mostly been done in the shallows of warfare.

And yet the odd thing is, how little has changed in terms of the way journalists do their work. By comparison with today's technology, the BBC journalists whom I quoted earlier had some pretty primitive equipment to work with: field phones and the infamous wire recorder.

But the work itself is much the same. There we saw Robert Dunnett fighting his way back to his engineer and the BBC phone to describe (with interruptions) what the hell was happening in the Place de la Concorde, without understanding any of it. And we saw Richard Dimbleby and Guy Byam, going through the most harrowing experiences, jotting them down a few hours later and reading their dispatches over a phone line. It's precisely the same today. If they, or Howard Marshall, or Frank Gillard were suddenly brought back to life and told to report for today's 'News at Ten', they would only need a brief session in some convivial bar about the changes in technology to be able to construct a perfectly creditable broadcast.

Such men seem like giants compared with today's television reporters, and yet they, like us, were thrown into the middle of things and expected to get on with it: journalism's habitual way of operating. But the things they had to report on were so much grander and more dreadful than most of the things we have seen since, that their experiences elevated them to the status of heroes, despite themselves.

As a young sub-editor at the BBC in the mid-1960s, I knew some of the figures whose dispatches appear in this book: Godfrey Talbot, Robert Reid, Dimbleby himself. I admired them, of course; but now, after fifty years of reporting myself, I admire them even more. There is a decency, a freshness and an honesty about their words which I find very affecting, and their courage, wholly unstated, shines out of every sentence. From the distance of seventy years, it's a real honour to be able to salute the BBC's Second World War correspondents in the way they deserve: through their own words.

Foreword

It gives me much pleasure to write a foreword to this record of dispatches broadcast by the BBC's War Correspondents. These dispatches give an interesting and vivid account of the progress of the campaign in North-western Europe from the Beaches of Normandy to the Shores of the Baltic; and, when the history of these times comes to be written, they will prove of great value and importance.

I think it is right to say that the keynote of this campaign was the Crusading Spirit, which inspired all ranks of the Allied Expeditionary Force, and which enabled them to face up to the great and often continuous demands which were made on their energy and enthusiasm and courage. This Spirit had many and deep sources, and the BBC was one of the means by which this Spirit was fostered. In this way these Correspondents made no mean contribution to final victory.

(sgd) B. L. MONTGOMERY
Field-Marshal, Commander-in-Chief, British Army of the Rhine
HEADQUARTERS, BRITISH ARMY OF THE RHINE
1 November 1945

Retrospect

by Frank Gillard

21 August 1944 was a day of unbounded euphoria in General Montgomery's Army Group. The protracted, exhausting battle of Normandy had at last been decisively won. The German Seventh Army had been annihilated. I sent the BBC a dispatch (see p. 204) which was broadcast extensively. Our victory was of such dimensions, and of such significance, that on the following day I ventured to offer a follow-up recording, amplifying my first account and adding new information. This story was firmly rejected by my editors in London. Not only did they decline to use it: they sent me a service message politely suggesting that yesterday had had its fling, and that what mattered now was today.

So, in the BBC's War Reporting Unit, we lived from day to day, and if yesterday's news passed swiftly from us into history, equally the future was not much in our sights either. Certainly it never occurred to any of us that our reports had survival value, and might be heard again after decades, and even appear in print. Such an awareness might have been disturbing. We had no time or opportunity to polish our material. The on-the-spot commentaries were unscripted and impromptu, often recorded in hazardous conditions, and for our written dispatches we were always working against the clock, in circumstances where every minute counted. The audiences of the time must have realised this; it was evident from the speed with which our stories reached them. One hopes that readers forty years or more later will grant us equal indulgence.

The BBC's thanks to Field-Marshal Montgomery, printed alongside his own Foreword to the 1946 edition of this book, were something very much more than just a nominal or formal acknowledgement. It was largely because of Monty's endorsement that our War Reporting

Unit went into Normandy in such strength, and, for the first time in the war, with adequate equipment. Monty sensed the importance of keeping the public at home, and the worldwide audience, in day-by-day and even hour-by-hour touch with the progress of his armies. He also saw how he could himself make use of broadcasting. Morale, he used to say, is the greatest single factor in battle. Morale would be strong if the soldiers had confidence in their leadership. If they could feel that they actually knew their Commander-in-Chief, that would be half the battle. So Monty went to great lengths to move around and be seen, and through the BBC he made certain that he was also heard. Whenever he issued an Order of the Day, I was invited around to his caravan so that he could record the message. The BBC was always delighted to broadcast it, on its news value. Thus these occasional Orders went out not only in printed form; the soldiers of Twenty-first Army Group actually heard them, in the Field-Marshal's own voice over the air, in War Report and news bulletins. In his mind Monty was speaking directly to them, and that is how they received his words. In other broadcasts he was thinking of wives, families and parents back home. He sought their confidence too, by radio, knowing that their attitudes would be reflected in the letters they wrote to their men, and that this, again, would help to sustain morale.

Monty and I had many talks about the role of broadcasting in our circumstances. To him it was clearly an arm of warfare – a minor arm, of course, but valuable. That was why my colleagues and I enjoyed his strong support. In all this the Field-Marshal always respected the BBC's editorial independence. He indicated willingness to broadcast from time to time, but never insisted. There were occasions when I thought it best that he should not go on the air, and he accepted my decision without quibble.

I remember, too, turning down a request of his of rather a different kind. During the early days in Normandy I went down with a bout of malaria – having picked up the bug a year or two previously in North Africa. Through a feverish haze I saw one of Monty's ADCs by my camp bed. He said that 'the Master' hoped I would soon be OK again, and that he wanted me then to get a puppy for him. But why me? 'He thought you might just mention it in your next broadcast,' said the ADC. Of course, any such mention (supposing it got past my editors) would have produced thousands of puppies, with ghastly consequences. So I sent back a message that I would guarantee Monty a puppy – he was a great animal lover – but not by the means suggested. As soon as I was on my feet again I scoured our narrow beach-head, and eventually, in the devastated little village of Douvres, almost under the German guns, I discovered a Frenchman with a Scotch terrier pup for sale. Monty received the animal with delight, and instantly named him Hitler. As far as I know, Hitler was the only tangible reward the Field-Marshal ever received for the massive assistance he gave the BBC during the entire campaign. This Hitler, too, did not survive the war. He ran under a tank in the final advance. But during his short life I know he gave companionship to a man who, inwardly, was rather a solitary person and who was carrying a monumental burden of responsibility on behalf of us all.

I still possess the signed photograph which Monty gave me of himself with the dog. Another of my trophies is the cheque I received from the Field-Marshal, in payment of a bet to which he had challenged me and which I won. He endorsed his cheque with these words: 'In full settlement of a bet, made on 17 December 1944, that the German war would not be over before 30 June 1945 – Bernard L. Montgomery.' That is the sort of cheque one cannot possibly pay in at the bank, so Monty did not really lose his bet after all. I suspect he knew well what he was doing when he wrote that endorsement.

These, of course, are exceedingly trivial incidents, seen against the colossal, heroic, military drama in which our forces were engaged. But they serve to illustrate the kind of relationship which could develop in this war between a war correspondent and the Commander-in-Chief. It was crucially important to a correspondent that he should be recognised and trusted as a member of the Army family, even though he could never allow the Army to use or manipulate him. This delicate relationship was greatly strengthened if it was seen that the correspondent was approved of in the top ranks of Command. But the information, and the human stories, rarely came from the Generals. At any headquarters one paid a quick courtesy call on the CO, if he happened to be around, and this usually included a perfunctory briefing. But it was in the less exalted ranks that the detailed, less inhibited guidance, and the true nuggets of news, were to be found. The correspondent found, too, the value of building two-way relationships. He was able to roam the front at will, but the officers and men he met were anchored to their particular sectors, often keenly anxious to know what was happening on their flanks and how an attack was developing as a whole. The more first-hand news a correspondent could supply, the more he was likely to receive in return.

Even the Field-Marshal's texts had to bear the censor's stamp of approval before they could be transmitted, though the censor who would change one word of the C-in-C's script had yet to be born. Every utterance by a correspondent, and every interview he conducted, had similarly to be scrutinised and approved. Earlier in the war, censorship had been a heavy burden. In Cairo, in Eighth Army days, a script or a recording was required to go through four separate censorship offices for approval, and all too often it emerged ultimately in a sadly mutilated condition. But now, in this final campaign in Europe, we in the BBC team actually had our own small censorship unit attached to us. Its members received their instructions direct from Army Intelligence, and we could discuss sensitive matters freely and speedily with them, and reach agreed solutions within the limits of their discretion. Moreover, with experience we became self-censors, recognising forbidden ground in advance and keeping well clear of it. In areas of doubt one sometimes prepared alternative versions of a story, hoping that one or the other would meet the censor's objections if they arose. The censors always had the last word, of course, but they were on our side right up to the limits of security. None of us wanted to utter anything on the air that would put a single fighting man in peril!

It is ironic that the dispatch of mine which is most frequently heard on the air forty years after the end of World War Two was not chosen, back in 1945, for inclusion in this book – and I had a hand in that selection. This is the report, relayed to London over our transmitter MCP from Twelfth Army Group HQ in the heart of Germany on 26 April 1945, announcing that the armies of the Western Allies and those of the Soviet Union had finally joined hands at Torgau, on the River Elbe. I could hardly keep the jubilation out of my voice. 'East and West have met,' I proclaimed, and in seconds those words had been flashed around the world. What a privileged moment for a broadcaster, and what a memory to treasure! Actually, some other correspondent might have been first with this supreme, transcendent and long-awaited statement. There were four reporters at Twelfth Army Group that day, all Radio people. The other three were Americans. Our only outlet to the world was MCP, and because it was a BBC transmitter I claimed the right to speak first. Naturally the Americans protested. We were all brothers-in-arms, of equal standing, they asserted. We asked the Chief of Staff to give us a judgement of Solomon, and he ruled against me. So, in an electric atmosphere of tension, we tossed up for it, and I won. The release time was 1800 hours, and I was on the air, live, at that exact moment. When, three hours later, the BBC repeated my dispatch in War Report as the lead item, followed immediately by messages of triumph recorded by Churchill, Truman and Stalin, I could hardly contain my exhilaration. That, indeed, was the climax of my war.

PART ONE
'And Now – Over To Normandy'

Broadcast War Reporting

War Report was first broadcast in the BBC's Home Service after the nine o'clock news on D-Day, 6 June 1944. In the months that followed it was listened to daily by ten to fifteen million listeners in the British Isles, and in addition by a considerable audience across the Channel. It was a link between the civilian and the services, a window on the war through which the combatant and the folk at home could catch a glimpse of each other. Those who spoke in War Report knew that they were talking simultaneously to a family round a London fireside, to a little group in a Midland pub, to a party of soldiers gathered round a radio truck in Normandy, to merchant seamen plying between England and the Continent, to Frenchmen and Belgians and Dutchmen listening secretly under the shadow of the Gestapo. To so vast an audience there was no special appeal other than the simple, human, honest account of what one man had seen and heard. Unlike the news bulletin, which it followed and to which it was complementary, War Report was essentially personal and informal. It took the microphone to places where things were happening, and let it listen – as one would oneself like to listen – to the sounds of battle, to the voices of men just returned from the fighting-line, to observers who had spent that day touring the scene of action.

In 1939 there were very few precedents in the field of war reporting. There had been Edward Ward's excellent dispatches from Finland, to recall one example, but the technique of those days was very different from what was to be evolved during the latter stages of the war when correspondents landed side by side with the troops, in gliders, by parachute, in assault-craft, talking into portable recording-machines or sending their dispatches by one of the mobile transmitters which followed the advancing armies. War Report represents this fully developed method as it was applied to the Western Front from D-Day onwards, but the singling out of this programme – outstandingly successful though it was – might give a misleading impression of the whole course of the BBC's reporting of the war. The improvements in organisation, in equipment, in general method, which contributed to the success of War Report, were the results of the experience gained in earlier campaigns. Long before D-Day a hundred dispatches a month were being broadcast and many of these would figure prominently in any general selection of reporting throughout the war. Further, War Report was only one of a group of closely related programmes designed to transmit material from the various fronts. The correspondents were not individually attached to a particular programme or department: their dispatches and messages were handled by a central organisation which 'fed out' the material to Combat Diary in the Allied Expeditionary Forces programme, to Radio News Reel which went all round the English-speaking world, and to other overseas services as well as to War Report in the Home programme. Outstanding dispatches would probably be carried by all these programmes in much the same form; others might have a specialised appeal for one particular audience and would be treated accordingly.

The event which had the greatest influence on the BBC's war reporting was, naturally enough, the prospect of what was incorrectly called a 'Second Front'. A successful invasion of Western Europe would put beyond doubt that turning of the tide which had begun at Stalingrad and El Alamein. In a more intimate sense for the British people, it would mark the recoil of war from their islands after the years of partial siege. The 'Second Front' carried with it the most profound hopes and anxieties of the nation; the responsibility which it placed on the BBC's news service was correspondingly heavy. To match the greatness of the occasion it was necessary to plan a much larger service of spoken news than had ever been taken from a single front and to solve the special problems which arise in reporting a combined operation of all three services on a gigantic scale.

In March 1943 a military exercise – 'Spartan', as it was called – was held in Southern England to test the new methods and equipment which were being prepared by the British Army. These manoeuvres offered realistic material for experimental reporting, and two groups of BBC people were attached to the opposing armies. Engineers recorded an elaborate sound-picture of the sham fighting, commentators gave eyewitness accounts, feature-writers set to work to reconstruct and dramatise particular scenes, and news dispatches were flashed to Broadcasting House, where the whole mass of material was censored and condensed into dummy newsreels and bulletins. Everything was done exactly as if the battle had been real – even to the extent of rushing bulletins through precisely at the scheduled times.

The BBC's principal innovation in the reporting of 'Spartan' was the collaboration of departments which had hitherto worked independently. This was, for the first time, a united effort – an attempt to blend all the talent the BBC could command into a versatile team. The various methods now brought together were highly diverse: there was the 'sound photography' of the recording unit, reproducing every noise and every word in a given scene, there were the descriptive dispatches and situation reports of the news correspondents, eyewitness running commentaries, and dramatised 'documentaries'. By combining them it was hoped to give a fuller and more graphic picture of a battle than had so far been achieved, and each method was therefore represented in the teams which covered 'Spartan'.

When the results of their work were played back to the Secretary of State for War and to the Commander-in-Chief, Home Forces, they agreed that the BBC must have the fullest cooperation of the Army – indeed of all three services – in the forthcoming invasion of Western Europe. The next step within the BBC was to set up a War Reporting Unit, transcending departmental boundaries and controlling all radio reporting on the Western Front. It was the task of this unit to select and deploy the correspondents and equipment necessary to supply dispatches, recordings, and material suitable for documentary treatment, to all the programmes engaged in presenting war news. Here the first essential was to secure adequate facilities from those in command of the armed forces: the goodwill of the War Office had been assured, but the appointment of General Eisenhower as Supreme Commander and the establishment of SHAEF (Supreme Headquarters, Allied Expeditionary Force) meant that all negotiations had to be started afresh. The facilities offered to all the various news organisations working for print or sound were limited, and there was a natural disposition in SHAEF to regard the BBC as simply one claimant; and it was necessary to show and to insist, indeed, that the BBC was not the equivalent of one American radio network, but was in fact the source of a worldwide radio service working through not less than a dozen organisations. For in addition to the multitude of transmissions from London in English, beamed to the Empire, to British forces in the many theatres of war, and to English-speaking people in occupied and neutral countries, there was the vast wartime range of foreign language broadcasts – ranging from French and German to three separate dialects of Chinese. For millions of people London was the voice of freedom – and very often the only voice. The prospect of a great liberating attack launched from Britain emphasised the prestige and importance which London already enjoyed as a news-centre. And, in radio, 'London' meant the BBC.

Looking back on it all it is easy to forget the astonishing wartime growth in the function of broadcasting. Such was the novelty of eyewitness descriptions of scenes of combat that there was angry criticism of a recording made at Dover in 1940, during the Battle of Britain. Many people felt that an eyewitness's account of a dog-fight overhead between RAF fighters and the Luftwaffe was not a proper thing to broadcast. The contention was that an incident in which men were losing their lives was being treated as if it were a cricket match or a horse-race.

Public opinion had changed radically by 1943. At the Trades Union Congress that year Sir Walter Citrine reinforced an appeal for increased production by referring to Wynford Vaughan-Thomas's commentary recorded in a bomber over Berlin – a striking example of the part that broadcasting had by then come to play in wider terms than the bare reporting of fact.

It would be ludicrous to suggest that there is any equivalent to direct experience of the hardships and hazards of battle. But at least broadcasting does help to diminish the gap between the combatant and the civilian – and not merely in the details of battle but also in those lesser items of song, of slang, of tone of speech, which are a not inconsiderable part of the measure of an army's exile from the homeland. If Caen and Arnhem seemed less remote psychologically than were Mons or the Somme thirty years earlier, it was largely because of the power of broadcasting to act as an immediate link between the battlefront and the home. Every fireside could entertain the voices, the personalities, of men in action, of men stepping out momentarily from the smoke and confusion of battle to talk in those intimate terms of informality – as between two or three people – which are peculiarly the gift of radio.

In the resistance of the occupied countries broadcasting played a unique part; it was the one means of general and widespread communication that the enemy could never silence. To loyal allies all over Europe the voice of London brought hope and encouragement. The oppressed peoples were to watch the beaches of Normandy with an anxiety no less than ours; and for news of how that crucial battle went they depended on the BBC.

To assess the value of broadcasting at such a time, to decide what facilities to give it in the field, and what difficulties to accept for the sake of using it well – these are important military considerations where things like shipping space and transport are not unlimited but must always be paid for by the exclusion of something else. If an army in the field carries correspondents, it must also carry censors, to make the correspondents' material safe before it starts out on its homeward journey. But news is important for civilian morale, and from a more narrowly military point of view there is an even more forceful consideration: troops in the field are able to listen and make immediate comparisons between their own experiences and the reports they hear broadcast.

This means that a modern army cannot afford to be indifferent to the way it is reported by radio, if only because of the possible ill-effects on its own morale. In broadcasting there can be no question of 'shooting a line' for civilian consumption only. Wherever there are radio sets the army has a complete, instant and wholesale check on the way it is reported. And no army thrives on hearing itself misrepresented. Woe betide the radio correspondent who fails to hold the confidence and goodwill of the fighting men with whom he is working. They provide his material: they individually appraise his treatment of it. If he introduces a false note, if he seems – however unwittingly – to sentimentalise or smarten up or patronise, then the soldiers will withhold from him that responsiveness which is the life-blood of reporting.

No less important than the quality of the correspondent is the factor of speed, which is one of the dimensions of accurate news.

For example, a report that 'the battle is going well' may be true when it is forwarded to GHQ, but if, because of poor facilities, the dispatch is outpaced by a change in the tide of battle, the result may be deplorable. To crown a day of desperate and unsuccessful fighting with the sound of a cheerful voice insisting that the enemy are on the run is not the kindest encouragement that a high command can give its forward troops. Yet more even than that, a report which is a true summary of the situation over the whole front may still not sound very good in some particularly unpleasant sector. No one who has taken part in patrol activity is likely to regard it as quite so 'slight' as do those who merely chronicle it.

These, then, were the factors involved in the negotiations between SHAEF and the BBC. These were the potentialities of war reporting by radio. In some ways they embodied new ideas which had been discovered gradually. The whole thing was comparatively new, and it was still growing. No one, whether in the BBC, in the services, or among the listening public, would claim to have foreseen exactly what was possible and what was not. From 1939 onwards there were mistakes and false conceptions in all three quarters; but on the whole the responsibilities and opportunities of broadcasting, and their recognition, developed more or less in step with the war's progress. Those who listened to the war correspondents' reports from Africa, from Greece, from blitzed London, and from other theatres of war before 1943 – not forgetting the earliest war dispatches from Spain and Finland – already appreciated the excellent work that had been done by individual reporters. They had fostered an audience for the eyewitness account, the personal story of the man on the spot told in his own way and in his own voice. They had taught us all to 'move with the microphone' – to move along the dive-bombed roads of Greece, to move over the mountains of Abyssinia to Keren, to go wherever the fighting was, to listen and to 'see'. The formal news bulletin gave an objective statement of major facts: the roving man with the microphone gave the authentic context, the setting, the mood, the significant small incident, the very stuff of reality, as it was known and experienced by the men who fought across a particular meadow under enemy fire, and were sometimes scared and sometimes brave and often hungry and often tired. He was there and could tell what he saw. He was not an official statement: he was two human eyes and a voice talking. The distinction is no mere phrase-making but a difference that was real to an audience which came to expect the eyewitness and saw a cardinal importance in hearing his *actual* voice.

Apart from the question of how many correspondents were to be allowed and what facilities they were to enjoy, the BBC's War Reporting Unit had to select its team and equip them with everything from transmitters to typewriter-ribbons. The number of experienced correspondents was inadequate to cope with the 'Second Front' while still covering the other fronts, so new ones had to be trained. The recruits came from the various departments concerned in war reporting, and in the following months they went through an intensive course of special training. To begin with, a physical training instructor toned up what he called his 'BBC Commandos' for life in front-line conditions, and they were instructed in gunnery, signals, reconnaissance, aeroplane and tank recognition, and map-reading. They went on assault courses and battle courses, they crossed rivers on ropes and ducked under live ammunition. They learnt how to live rough and how to cook in the field. Some were attached to regular army units and shared every exercise with their unit. They ran cross-country against men maybe fifteen years younger, and they finished the course. They often finished last, but they finished – and the army didn't like them any the less for that.

Perhaps that was the greatest benefit of the months of preparation, the winning of the army's respect and friendship. When the invasion

The general group from whom war correspondents were selected.
Back row from left: Stewart McPherson, Major Bonus, C. Angell, F.B.
Thornton, W.H.E. Lindop, H.O. Sampson, Robert Barr, Captain Castle.
Middle row from left: Colin Wills, Robert Dunnett, John Glyn-Jones, Richard
North, Sgt Weston (instructor), Harvey Sarney, Ian Wilson, Pierre Lefèvre.
Front row from left: Stanley Maxted, C. Hindson, S. Gore, D.G. Snell,
H. Shirley Long, R.D. Sigler, D.H. Fairley.

came, the correspondents were no longer meddlesome civilians in a
kind of khaki fancy-dress; they knew the army jargon, and the army
ways. They were men of the army who happened to have an unusual
and specialised job. This is worth stressing because it was new. The
army accepted the BBC correspondents as an informal extension of
its own public relations system. It trained them with the greatest
thoroughness; and when they had qualified it gave them complete
facilities to do their job in the most efficient way. They were briefed,
when possible, in secrecy on how an assault would take place.

In addition to military training the correspondents had to master
the special technique of radio reporting. In the first place they had

to learn enough of each other's trades to become interchangeable in emergency. If, for example, a recording engineer were wounded or unfit, the correspondent with him should know enough to keep his machine working. The man trained to documentary or dramatic writing had to be able to send a straight news dispatch, and vice versa. Then again, there were lectures by news editors as to the sort of material they wanted for their particular audiences. The Forces listener does not need so much factual 'background' as does the civilian; the requirements of the Latin American audience or the European are different again. The neutral, the occupied country, the ally, the soldier, even the enemy – each has to be supplied with what is significant news to him.

Censorship was another art to be studied, so that correspondents should learn how to avoid trouble. It is easy enough to cancel a word here and there in a written dispatch, easy enough for a subeditor to rewrite a phrase or a sentence. In a recording the only person who can rewrite even a single word is the original speaker; and deletions are much more difficult to handle once they are on discs than they would be in print. To demonstrate this, correspondents were taken to a plausibly 'German' HQ where a plausibly 'Nazi' Intelligence Officer played over some specially prepared recordings, made by a British correspondent, and then converted their innocent-seeming remarks into significant military information. The censorship necessary on those discs would have made them virtually useless. A course in military intelligence was the appropriate sequel, in which the correspondents learnt how to avoid the kind of things that any censor would unfailingly cut out.

As the last months before D-Day passed away the BBC's correspondents had their final tuning-up in special manoeuvres. They tested new equipment, they settled into army routine, and then they were ready.

Meanwhile there had been engineering and editorial problems to solve. The demand for news and eyewitness reports on D-Day would clearly be insatiable. Every phase of the departure from Britain had to be covered, in both speech and sound recordings; a substantial task normally, but now dwarfed by the difficulty of devising rapid transmission of news across the Channel in the first hours of the battle for the beaches. The landing of a quarter-kilowatt transmitter was planned to take place about a week after the first assault; until then correspondents would have to use a variety of methods to communicate with London. There might be opportunities to use the three operational transmitters which the army hoped to establish on D-Day. Secret transmission-points in the south coast area were held ready for correspondents returning to Britain with eyewitness stories. The recording units were installed in ships, and there was a service by military couriers for written dispatches and recordings made on land. Until the close of the African campaign all recordings in the field had been made with gear which weighed about 500 lbs and was carried in trucks; but as the first recording-truck was not scheduled to go ashore until at least a fortnight after D-Day some other means had to be found. This had been foreseen; a portable midget recorder, designed by BBC engineers, had already been tested in action at Anzio, and it was to prove its value on the Western Front.

This portable recording-unit, weighing only 40 lbs, was the lightest in the world. It carried twelve double-sided discs giving a total of more than one hour's recording; a microphone on a spring clip could be attached to anything from a branch of a tree to the rim of a steel helmet, and the detachable dry-battery unit was ready-wired to plug in with a single connector. Operation was so simple that anyone could use it without the assistance of an engineer – unlike the truck unit, which needed a technician.

One of these midgets was later used under enemy fire near Maltot by Chester Wilmot to record the sound of German multiple mortars. Bearing in mind the delicacy of recording machinery it is remarkable that the midget stood up so well to such a severe test. Wilmot's running commentary, broadcast in War Report, will be found on page 170. His personal account of how the recording was made gives a vivid picture of the midget in use and of the way in which correspondents performed their dangerous and exciting job:

'By the morning of 10 July the main city of Caen was in our hands, and west of Caen the Second Army had strengthened its bridgehead over the river Odon, which joined the Orne at Caen. From that bridgehead on this morning the 43rd Division with the 4th Armoured Brigade was to break out and drive up the western side of the Orne Valley. Although we didn't know it at the time, this was a feint to distract German attention and armour from the east bank of the Orne, where Field-Marshal Montgomery was preparing to attack the following week.

'It was certain that the Germans would react strongly to this new move for they had been making strenuous efforts to keep us in the Odon bridgehead ever since we established it at the end of June. And so for me the day's obvious task was to follow this new attack. At 8.30 in the morning I went to the usual conference at VIII Corps Headquarters and wrote a short situation report as a lead to a long dispatch on Caen which I was to broadcast direct to Australia at a quarter to ten. Then I set off in search of the battle – as usual with a midget recorder in the jeep, but not with my usual driver, George Brown. In his place was a driver, Bill Ball, whom I did not know and who had yet to hear a shot fired in anger.

'He was soon to hear plenty. The 43rd Division had dug itself an underground headquarters right in the middle of its main gun area and the 25-pounders were making such a row that even in the dugouts you had to shout to be heard. But here I happened to meet the Corps Commander, General O'Connor, and from him I learned the general form. The attack, he said, was going well but slowly. Our troops had taken the high ground between the Odon and the Orne and were in Maltot, about half a mile from the Orne; but the enemy were preparing a counter-attack. "Maltot is the place to watch," he said.

'It was early afternoon when we crossed the Odon at a shallow ford which the engineers had made by laying some heavy steel netting over a bed of stones. This was the healthiest place to cross, for the Germans were still occasionally shelling the regular bridges. We paused at Brigade Headquarters where the Brigade Major said to me, "You won't get into Maltot today, it's rather unhealthy. The Hampshires got in this morning without much trouble, but ever since the Boche has been mortaring the place to hell; he's left some chaps hiding in the ruins and whenever the mortaring stops they come out and make things awkward. No – don't go into Maltot – but if you follow up this road you might see something. Right here," he said, pointing to the map at a spot where a hedgerow ran over a slight rise 600 yards from Maltot, "here we have an artillery OP. You can go there, but keep your head down."

'We "jeeped" on . . . up the hill on the far bank of the Odon and along a sunken lane strewn with branches slashed from trees and with tiles and rubble blasted from houses. At one point a big fallen tree barred the road, a sign said "Mines", and white tapes marked the track that led off through a cornfield and back to the road further on. There machine-gun carriers of the Middlesex Regiment were lined up nose to tail for a quarter of a mile. Ball edged the jeep past them but we halted at the leading carrier.

' "What's doing?" I said to the platoon commander.

' "Nothing much," he replied, "we're waiting to go into Maltot but we can't get our carriers over the skyline. Jerry's come up on that flank and he can machine-gun the road up there where it runs along just below the crest."

34

' "Oh . . . I wanted to get to the OP in the hedgerow over there where this road meets the main one."

' "Well, I'd wait a bit; we're getting some Vickers guns in along this hedge and we're going to fire over the ridge."

' "Over the infantry's heads?"

' "Yes. Wait till we've shot them up a bit."

'While we waited I set up the midget recorder in the back of the jeep and worked out a short interview with the platoon commander. He told me that so far their main task had been to follow through behind the infantry mopping up. But one section, he said, helped the infantry to clear this road this morning. "Our main job was to move on the flanks and spray every farm and thicket with our machine-guns to clear out any snipers that Jerry might have left behind."

'It was raining slightly by the time we'd finished this recording, and down the road from the OP came a jeep. I waved to the driver and asked him, "Can you get through to the OP now?"

' "*We* did, sir," he replied with a hint of scorn in his voice and drove on.

'We packed up the recorder and I said to Ball, "Well, we'd better go on."

' "Suits me," he said as he climbed in.

'Shells were whining low overhead as he drove the jeep up the narrow road, but they were ours. Somewhere over the crest machine-guns were firing – ours or theirs? We'd know when we turned into the 500-yard stretch that ran along under the lee of the crest to the hedgerow and the OP.

'On that stretch we wasted no time but as we turned off the road and into the field behind the hedgerow there wasn't a sound of shot or shell. I felt a little foolish, as one always does when fears prove groundless, but I felt a little better when I saw that along the bank of the hedgerow infantry were dug in and were manning weapons that they had mounted on the bank. In the field behind, and almost on top of them, were four tanks with their guns brushing the branches and pointing towards Maltot.

'The Commander of the nearest tank called out: "I wouldn't leave that jeep there. Stick it behind my tank. They machine-gun this hedge."

'We tucked the jeep away; Ball found himself a trench, and, midget-recorder in hand, I moved along behind the tanks to the corner of the field where three hedgerows met. There the OP officer was dug in at the junction of the hedgebanks and I slipped down into the ditch opposite him.

' "What the hell have you got there?" he said, nodding towards the midget.

'I told him and said that I wanted to set it up and make some recordings. "OK," he said, "you ought to get plenty to talk about. The Boche is counter-attacking Maltot and my guns are shelling the area beyond it. Here's a shovel – dig yourself in a bit."

'That wasn't really necessary, for there was a hedgebank on two sides and a Sherman tank right behind me with its gun jutting out over my head. But I did need to cut away the bank to make a flat place for the midget, and it was soon ready. By this time the OP officer's headphones were crackling as the infantry called for more artillery support to stem the counter-attack, and the tank commander put his head out of the turret to shout to the OP: "My forward troop reports that some Mark IVs are coming up the road into Maltot – map reference so-and-so – can you get your chaps on to them?" "OK," said the OP officer, picked up his phone and called up his battery.

'Then the tank commander looked down at me and called: "I'm afraid you'll have to move if I need to fire – it's no fun down there under the muzzle when this 75 goes off. But I'll give you some warning – if I can."

'I started recording and looked out across the broad flat stretch of Normandy cornfield between us and the scraggy wood around Maltot. By now the wood was enveloped in smoke – not the black smoke of hostile mortars but white smoke laid by our guns as a screen for our infantry who were now being forced to withdraw.

'We could see them moving back through the waist-high corn, and out of the smoke behind them came angry flashes as the German tanks fired from Maltot. But even as the infantry were driven back another battalion was moving forward to relieve them – supported by Churchill tanks firing tracers over the heads of the advancing men. They moved right past our hedge and out across the corn.

'The Germans evidently saw them coming, for away off on our right flank machine-guns opened up and then the nebelwerfers – those many-barrelled mortars that put down the rocket-propelled bombs with the high, wailing sobbing note. From this they've gained their various nicknames – "The Sobbing Sisters", "Moaning Minnie", and "Wailing Winnie". But at least they do announce their coming unmistakably.

'I had just finished my second disc when I heard the wail of a coming salvo. With fingers none too steady I picked up another disc, put it on, and swung the cutting head into operation. But I'd spoken only a few words of commentary when the mortars began thumping down along another hedge about a hundred yards behind us.

'There must have been several nebelwerfers firing, for three distinct salvoes came over in quick succession. I talked on through the first, though my voice was completely drowned, but when the second began bursting rather closer I left the midget running, clipped the mike to a branch and dived for the bottom of the ditch, shoving as much of myself as possible into an old German dugout.

'When the last salvo had finished bursting I got up and looked at the midget. The second salvo had blown it "off the air". The cutting head had jumped and the sapphire point which actually cuts the groove had gone so deeply into the disc that it had stopped. If the midget had been fully wound at the start it might have continued cutting, but I realised then – too late – that in my haste I had forgotten to rewind it fully after the previous disc.

'I just had time to wind the midget and fit a new sapphire and another disc before the next warning wail. I set the recorder going and sought early refuge in the bottom of the ditch. The midget recorded perfectly right through the bursting salvo, for the mortars landed a little further away; and so, for the first time, we had a recording of the German weapon which our troops most disliked.

'By now our counter-attack was in full swing and our guns were already searching for the German mortar positions and soon the nebelwerfers were silent. Fortunately most of their bombs had gone over the heads of our infantry, but they had done some damage. The OP phone rang and word came from the battery that another officer in the OP a few hundred yards along the hedge had been killed.

'By now, however, the OP officers in the hedgerow could not give the gunners much help, for the cornfield and Maltot were obscured by the smoke of battle. Already the infantry had disappeared into the smoke and all we could see was the flash of the tanks' guns and the flare of their tracers and, away to the left, the blazing hulk of a tank that had been hit.

'Then over the radio from the forward infantry came the news that they had driven the Germans out of Maltot again, and they called for artillery concentrations on the wood beyond the town from which the Germans had launched their counter-attack.

'There were evidently some Germans, however, still this side of Maltot, for every few minutes we heard the crack of a machine-gun and bullets zipped through the hedge a few feet above our heads. But by now it was time for me to leave if I was to get back in time for the broadcast for War Report. With the midget I worked my way back along the hedgerow till I found Ball and the jeep, which by now was standing nakedly in the open, for the tank that had been shielding it had moved. As we got to the jeep that machine-gun opened up again and we crouched down. It seemed that this time the stretch of road along the crest might be unhealthy.

'As we got up I said to Ball, "Would you like me to drive?" And he shot back the answer "Not on your bloody life. This is my jeep – I'll drive it . . ." and he drove like the wind down that 500-yard stretch, his head bent low over the wheel.

'He didn't lift his head or his foot until he had swung the jeep around the corner and under the shelter of the skyline.

'An hour later we were back at the BBC Headquarters in a château near Creully. It was half past seven and I just had time to write a brief news dispatch for the nine o'clock bulletin, but as reception in London was bad that evening it was no use trying to relay the discs from our mobile transmitter – MCO.

'Next morning the circuit was clear. We played the discs to the censor and then played them over to London before dispatching them by air. Thus we could give War Report an early copy of the text and the editors could decide – even before the original discs arrived by plane – how the material was to be used. But that night they used something more than the censored discs – something which made the story rather more pointed. In relaying discs we were always allowed by censorship to say briefly what was on each disc and to explain any technical faults before playing, without submitting these comments to censorship. On this occasion I described what had happened when the nebelwerfers opened up, how I had sought refuge in the ditch (much to my humiliation), and how the midget had stopped. I was giving – I thought – merely service information, but London recorded it all, and used these comments in that night's War Report . . . uncensored.

'When we listened to this War Report the chief censor Major Gilbert Cubitt was with us. When the "ad lib" passage came over the air, he turned to me and said with a smile – "I don't remember *that* in the discs I censored this morning; it must have been drowned by the nebelwerfers!"'

Deployment for D-Day

The correspondents and the equipment were ready. Two things – two very difficult things – had still to be done. The correspondents had to be deployed so that they could immediately cover every phase of the landings; and they had to be supported with a very complete and reliable plan for getting their dispatches and messages back to Broadcasting House. The preparations for D-Day were naturally secret, and it was impossible to entrust such a momentous secret to even one more person than was absolutely essential. A sudden concentration of BBC personnel in Portsmouth or Harwich or Dover might in itself give a valuable clue to the enemy as to the direction of the offensive.

On the other hand it was imperative that the BBC's War Reporting Unit should know where its correspondents would be so that it could arrange routes by which the news could come through. Elaborate arrangements to cope with returning correspondents at Hull or Newhaven would be worse than useless if they came flocking in to Plymouth. And the movements of correspondents outside Britain were to be controlled by the services, who would transport them how and when and where it was convenient.

Suffice to say that the BBC contrived to be right on the spot to deal with the Normandy landings. On the other hand, the preliminary preparations seemed to be designed to cover a possible invasion anywhere from the French Atlantic coast to Norway – though in fact some of these preparations were designed more to mislead the enemy than to be used.

The disposition of BBC War Correspondents on D-Day

The dispositions for D-Day provided for a full range of spoken, as well as written, dispatches. Discs from the midget recorders would be carried back to Broadcasting House by the service couriers, by air or by sea. Recording units were covering naval and air news. Special correspondents went into action with paratroops, gliders and bombers. There was the prospect of using military transmitters on the beaches during a lull in operational messages, and certain correspondents were to be ferried back to special transmission points in Britain where they could send their messages (either recorded or in 'live' voice) 'up the line' to London.

In Broadcasting House recording channels were held open day and night to take these messages. In addition there was a telediphone unit constantly ready to convert verbal messages into typewritten scripts for censorship and for circulation to all news departments and programme editors concerned. The telediphone is a dictaphone which works from a telephone line. It records the words spoken on a wax cylinder, which is played back to a typist. The transmission-point which carried the bulk of this traffic was in the Portsmouth area, on a hillside near Fareham. Here, in a small field, there were a brick hut, two wireless masts, a large recording-van helping out the transmission facilities, a miscellaneous collection of vehicles ranging from jeeps to mobile recording units, and a couple of tents where the operating staff had their meals and slept – when there was time. For many days they were dealing, almost literally from minute to minute, with a continuous stream of British and American reporters driving in to send their stories through to London. Cars waited at the ports to bring the correspondents in, but a great deal of improvisation was necessary: one correspondent, who had come up-Channel with a convoy to a point three miles off-shore, managed to reach the Isle of Wight by ship's picket-boat; there he persuaded a Wren running a motor-launch to take him across to Hamble, and from there hitchhiked to Fareham. Despite these devious methods his dispatch was ready in London for transmission about two hours after he had left his ship.

This early use of voice recordings raised the greatest security difficulties, as it meant that uncensored material must pass from the battle-zone to England. Later, when transmitters and censors were established in France, it was a simple matter to censor a dispatch before it was transmitted to London. But in the first stages of the invasion such arrangements were impossible; fortunately the military authorities were by now sufficiently persuaded of the importance of radio reporting to permit recordings to be handled in Broadcasting House before submission to the censors. As the messages came 'up the line' they were recorded, telediphoned, and sent as scripts to the censors. After censorship, new recordings were made without the censored passages, and the original discs were then stored in conditions of secrecy. This measure of trust in civilian discretion is a remarkable tribute to the BBC's War Reporting Unit, and it was well justified. The transmission of news on and immediately after D-Day was much faster than would otherwise have been possible, and there was no leakage of secret information.

It is proper to add here that the benefit of these concessions, which had been sought by the BBC for purely technical reasons, was instantly made available to all Allied radio services and to the press in general. If a British and an American correspondent wished to use the same recording channel at the same time, they tossed for it.

So long as the armies were fighting to gain and consolidate a foothold in Normandy, Broadcasting House was the only source of supply of spoken news dispatches to the world – apart from enemy broadcasts. The concentration of news there, as has been explained, had to be achieved by all sorts of means. Everything had to be ferried back across the Channel, by either sea or air. This applied to the

Americans as well as the British, and the BBC can look back with pride on the service it was able to render to its American colleagues. The immense amount of work involved, however, was too great to be handled permanently by the BBC's limited means, and in any case it was desirable to establish transmitters in France as soon as possible. In due course some of the European broadcasting stations were to provide alternative studios and long-range transmitters, but apart from them the BBC wanted to establish its own mobile transmitters for sending correspondents' messages through to London.

A week before D-Day the first of the BBC's mobile transmitters, known by the code-name of MCO or 'Mike Charlie Oboe', was mounted in a 3-ton truck and moved towards the south coast in readiness for embarkation. It had originally been mounted in a truck which was forbidden to embark because the clearance of the chassis was too low, and the engineers worked frantically to transfer the equipment at the last moment to a new truck. Into the truck went transmitters, power generator, amplifiers, microphones and aerial equipment – everything necessary for direct broadcasting from the beach-head. The truck moved from waterproofing areas to assembly and marshalling areas, and so finally aboard ship and out into the Channel, where by ill luck it was caught in the tail-end of the heavy gale which raged during the second week after D-Day. On the night of 17/18 June MCO's transport put in at Arromanches and began to discharge its cargo. In darkness, lit only by bomb bursts and ack-ack fire, the tank ahead of the transmitter-truck lurched forward over the edge of the ramp and seemed to disappear into the sea. MCO followed, plunging into four feet of water, but managed to keep going and came safely up the beach. It arrived in the nick of time as the gale had so disrupted cross-Channel communications that, on the following day, the army transmitter which the BBC had been allowed to use was regretfully but firmly reserved for operational messages

War Reporting Unit staff put up camouflage netting on a
Mobile Recording truck in June 1944. The first Mobile
Recording Unit, codenamed Mike Charlie Oboe, was landed
at Arromanches on the night of 17/18 June, and made its first
successful broadcast on 20 June.

only. In a matter of hours, however, MCO's aerials were erected
and the engineers were on the air testing and checking reception.
From a studio, which was merely a tent to keep out the wind, the
first dispatches were broadcast direct to London where engineers
were waiting anxiously for whatever signals could be picked up from
the beach-head. In spite of its rough passage across the Channel,
and the enforced haste with which it was put into operation, MCO's

debut was a great success. The transmitter in Broadcasting House flashed back the words 'Reception quite satisfactory'. Exactly a fortnight after the first assault the BBC had its own speech-link with Normandy.

The next day the tent gave place to a more substantial studio in a fourteenth-century castle at Creully near Bayeux. There a tower room with a vaulted roof, narrow slit windows and a worn stone floor became one of the busiest studios of the BBC, and an endless procession of broadcasters passed through it during the day – the reporters of the Canadian and American radio networks often speaking in the small hours of the morning; BBC correspondents speaking not only for the Home Service and the General Forces Programme, but also broadcasting at odd hours for Africa, for the Pacific, and for other short-wave programmes; then Pierre Lefèvre, speaking in French by way of London to his fellow-countrymen, and other broadcasts specially aimed at Nazi-occupied Europe lying just over the front line, which was so near at hand that the windows of the studios had to be shut tight to keep out the noise of the guns and the aircraft.

Larger transmitters were crated in readiness to follow when the Allied armies pushed inland – the first, a 5-kilowatt transmitter, being installed at Le Marais, near Bayeux. This, however, was left high and dry by the speed of the great hue and cry across the Seine into the Low Countries, and MCO had to take to the road and chase after the pursuing armies, hugging the Channel coast all the way because of its necessarily small signal-strength. The speed of the advance led to all kinds of improvisations in order to get the news through quickly. One of the strangest transmissions came from Chester Wilmot in newly liberated Brussels, speaking on a secret transmitter fitted in a suitcase and dropped by the RAF for the use of the Underground during the German occupation. The wavelength was outside the BBC's normal channels and was therefore not monitored at Broadcasting House;

but the message was picked up by an Army receiving station and passed on. During the Arnhem fighting the Belgian authorities courteously interrupted the Belgian Home Programme to allow Frank Gillard to broadcast an urgent dispatch (see p. 265).

With the stabilisation of the front after Arnhem the high-power transmitters MCN and MCP ('Mike Charlie Nan' and 'Mike Charlie Peter') came into full use. By recording direct from their transmissions London received correspondents' messages immediately they were ready. If the quality of reception was good enough, these recordings made in London could be used for broadcasting without waiting for the original discs to arrive by air, for most of them were forwarded to London by courier after their first transmission. In any case, the War Reporting Unit in London had immediate direct contact with the correspondents in the field: this meant that it was possible to plan programmes with a full knowledge of what was likely to be available at any given time. Further, if important news 'broke' just as a London programme was going on the air, it was possible – given reasonable conditions – to relay the correspondent's voice in any programme to any part of the world. The immense value of this, in speed of news circulation, was well emphasised by Chester Wilmot in MCN's final broadcast on 25 May 1945:

'MCN is closing down. The war in Europe is finished and its job is done. But before it transmits its last words, I want to say something about that job.

'MCN came to the Western Front last August to take over from the small but highly mobile and efficient transmitter that had carried our dispatches from the Normandy beaches – the transmitter known as MCO. MCO had landed on the beaches on 18 June and had given us magnificent service from the beach-head. But now, as the triumphant march of the Second Army was carrying us further away from London, we needed a more powerful transmitter; and even before the break-out from the beach-head the BBC had MCN, a transmitter many times more powerful than MCO, ready to take up the main task with the forces driving inland, leaving MCO to follow the Canadians up the coast. But, at the start, MCN was unlucky. It landed just as the great drive to the Seine and Brussels was beginning, and its 3-ton trucks, towing 7-ton trailers, had no chance of overtaking the armies. In the attempt some of its vehicles broke down, and it was late in September before it was eventually on the air near Brussels.

'I first broadcast from Mike Charlie Nan on Sunday 24 September. Since then it's transmitted thousands of dispatches, not only by BBC correspondents, but by reporters from American, Canadian, Australian, French, and Belgian radio stations. Out from its aerials have gone dispatches for the BBC's European and Overseas Service, in German, French, Spanish, Dutch, Norwegian, Afrikaans, Flemish and Arabic. Its masts have truly been Towers of Babel.

'Most of the dispatches from MCN have of course been recorded in London for replay later, but it's also put out hundreds of live broadcasts that have been relayed simultaneously from coast to coast, across America or Canada or Australia. This live broadcasting service was one which I appreciated perhaps more than most. For, from MCN I was able to speak three times a week direct from the Continent to my own country and to my family in Australia. Of all the live broadcasts, perhaps the ones you'll remember most were those made by Frank Gillard "live" into the Christmas programme, and our contribution to the Victory programme when some of Montgomery's men spoke almost from the battlefield immediately after their Commander-in-Chief. And do you remember the Dutch woman who broadcast in the Christmas programme with her family direct from her sitting-room in Eindhoven, through MCN to London and out to every corner of the world? Then there was the story of the start of the Reichswald offensive. That was released half an hour after midnight on 9 February. BBC's Radio News Reel was due to go on the air to North America at that time and so we arranged to broadcast the news straight from MCN in Eindhoven, direct into Radio News Reel and out on a coast-to-coast hook-up across North America; and so listeners in Canada and America learned the full story of the Reichswald offensive before the newspaper flashes were on the agency tapes; and they learned it thanks to MCN. Thanks to MCN again, the BBC got the first full story of the German capitulation at Lüneburg. Though on this occasion, you'll remember, when we were relaying into War Report the recordings made that afternoon, MCN cut off the air for half a minute, and London thought we'd broken down. We were sorry to fail you at that critical moment – but we did get the recordings through, and a few minutes later the BBC Home Programme was broken into to bring you the full story that MCN had relayed.

'And then, last night, came MCN's last operational broadcast, the story of the death of Heinrich Himmler, told by a Sergeant-Major who was in the room when Himmler committed suicide. Thanks to MCN we were able to get a world scoop for that story. The release time was eight o'clock. We were on the air at eight to the minute with the full story, far ahead of any other means of communication.*

---

* The text of the broadcast was as follows:

24 May 1945. 'This is Chester Wilmot speaking from Lüneburg where Himmler committed suicide last night. One of the men in the room at the time at 31 Oetzemerstrasse was Sergeant-Major Edwin Austin of Mortlake in Surrey, and I've brought him to the microphone to tell you what happened:

' "Before he arrived, I didn't know it was Himmler; I was only told there was an important prisoner whom I was to guard. As he came into the room – not the arrogant figure which we all knew, but dressed in an army shirt, a pair of underpants, with a blanket wrapped round him – I immediately recognised him as Himmler. Speaking to him in German, and pointing to an empty couch, I said, 'That's your bed; get undressed.' He looked at me and then looked at an interpreter and said, 'He doesn't know who I am.' I said, 'Yes I do; you're Himmler, but still that's your bed; get undressed.' He tried to stare me out, but I stared at him back and eventually he dropped his eyes and sat down on the bed and started to take off his underpants. The doctor and the Colonel then came into the room and started to carry out a routine inspection, looking for poison which we suspected he probably had on him. He looked between his toes, all over his

'That's a perfect example of the service that's been rendered by MCN and MCO and their younger brother with the American 12th Army Group, MCP, from which my colleague Frank Gillard has made so many fine broadcasts. And now with perhaps the last great war story broadcast from Germany, MCN is packing up and going back to England.'

These broadcasts were, of course, usually intended in the first instance for reception in Broadcasting House only, but no doubt many listeners here and abroad occasionally picked up one of the 'Mike Charlies'. In Eindhoven, for example, Frank Gillard met a Dutchman who had been enjoying a preview of the correspondents' dispatches, and at the same time had gained some insight into the private life of Chester Wilmot:

'A few days ago Chester Wilmot had a little trouble over his typewriter and when he was sending a dispatch to London by radio he tacked on a message at the end asking Mrs Davis of our office in London to send him another typewriter. Yesterday morning, in Eindhoven, a Dutchman came running across the street to me and said "Is it true that you're Frank Gillard?" and I said "Yes", and he said "Well, tell me, has Mrs Davis sent out Chester Wilmot a new typewriter yet?" You really have to meet these allies of ours in France and Belgium

---

body, under his armpits, in his ears, behind his ears, in his hair, and then he came to his mouth. He asked Himmler to open his mouth. He did, and he ran his tongue around his lips quite easily, but the doctor wasn't satisfied. He asked him to come nearer to the light; he came nearer to the light and opened his mouth. The doctor tried to put two fingers into his mouth to have a good look inside, I suspected, and Himmler drew his head away and, clamping down on the doctor's fingers, crushed the phial of poison which he'd been carrying in his mouth for hours. The doctor said, 'He's done it,' and the Colonel and I instinctively jumped to him – the doctor held him by the throat as he was falling and tried to make him spit out the poison which he was swallowing, and the Colonel and I held him. After a struggle lasting a quarter of an hour in which we tried all methods of artificial respiration under the direction of the doctor, he died; and when he died we threw a blanket over him and left him."'

and Holland to realise what the London radio has meant to them in the last four years. Their whole lives have revolved around it, the broadcasts from London have been everything to them. Thousands of them say that they couldn't have kept up their hopes and their resistance without it. They listen in their own languages and to a very great extent to the Home Service in English as well, for there are vast numbers of people over here who can understand English even though they can't speak it. And they turn their dial, anxious not to miss a single word, even when it's just Chester Wilmot asking for typewriter reinforcements. And they go over past broadcasts with you, that Sunday morning service when General Montgomery read the lesson while the airplanes roared overhead, and that time in War Report when John Snagge said "Over to Normandy", and then there was nothing but silence because there was nobody to speak at the other end. "We were very worried about that, you know," they say to us, "it was a big relief to hear some of you talking again the next night." People crowd in upon us to express their thanks, and there's one thing they invariably say, "We listened to the BBC, and we trusted the BBC, because it always told the truth." '

The use of these mobile transmitters, advancing in the wake of the armies, marked a new phase in radio reporting. Their importance in the success of War Report cannot be overstressed, but it must be added that there were hundreds and thousands of things besides transmitters to be planned. It is impossible to describe in detail the whole organisation that was necessary, so some random examples must suffice. The movement of correspondents and transmitters required, in miniature, the strategy that deploys armies. The correspondents had to be placed where the next big news was likely to break, and at the same time they had to have quick access to a transmitter. The next moves of the opposing armies had somehow or other to be foreseen accurately – otherwise correspondents and transmitters would be chasing crosscountry when their messages were most urgently needed. Then again, the kind of material correspondents would be likely to send had to be matched with the needs and special requests of programme editors. One broadcast which many listeners will remember – the open-air church service from the Normandy beach-head – originated as a request from the Religious Broadcasting Department, and at that stage of the war seemed at first to be too difficult to handle. Frank Gillard, who arranged the broadcast, has described how it was done:

'I thought of all the problems involved in broadcasting a church service at home in Britain, where church, preacher, choir and organist were ready and willing, and where telephone lines, amplifiers, microphones and technical assistance were there for the asking. Here in Normandy every problem would be multiplied tenfold. We were a small team, our hands already more than full with the day-to-day job of reporting the war.

'Yet it was unquestionably part of our work to be a link between the men at the front and the people at home, and here was a unique and very worthwhile opportunity of bringing home and front together. Later that morning I put the idea to General (as he then was) Montgomery. Monty was enthusiastic. He saw at once what it would mean to the troops to be joined with their families in such a broadcast. "You must do it," he said, "and do it soon. Do it now while we are building up and while things are comparatively quiet in the line. I am behind this. You can use my name over it, to get all the help you need."

'And so it was settled. Messages passed between us and London, and the broadcast was fixed for the following Sunday morning at 9.30 in the Home Service. The Deputy Chaplain-General, Canon Hughes, although a little scared of the microphone himself, agreed to preach the sermon, and he brought in the Assistant Chaplain-General of Second Army, Padre John Steele, to make the general arrangements.

'The first thing to do was to fix a location. It was to be a simple, open-air service, representative of all the hundreds of similar services held up and down the front each Sunday. We picked on an overgrown garden – almost a field – adjoining a château just a few hundred yards away from one of the main supply routes leading from the beaches to the front. The Chief Signals Officer of the Second Army willingly undertook to lay cables from this garden up to our improvised Control Room and studio in the tower of Creully Castle on a hill a mile away.

'So far, so good. Now what about microphones and amplifiers? We had, of course, none of the elaborate apparatus commonly used by BBC engineers at home on such a broadcast as this – but here we reaped yet another benefit of the wise planning which had foreseen our needs, for the equipment of our recording trucks, powered by the batteries carried in the trucks themselves, would serve equally well.

'We were anxious to have some powerful instrument to accompany the singing, for – particularly in the open air – voices tend to sound rather thin and half-hearted unless they are well led. Hughes and Steele could only produce the usual small portable harmonium, but then Steele had a brilliant idea. He arranged to bring along one of the Army's loudspeaker vans, used normally for speaking to the enemy across no-man's-land. With its microphone set up beside the harmonium, this van amplified the reedy notes of the little instrument into something as forceful as a cathedral organ.

'So we went on with our planning. An Order of Service was drawn up. Hymn sheets were duplicated. We made rough estimates of timing. Transport was arranged to bring in men from all parts of the front, for the Army and the Air Force were entering fully into this project and each major formation of our men serving in Normandy was to be represented at the service. Censorship had to be settled. The entire service had to be typed out and submitted, and, in addition, since this was to be a "live" broadcast (and anything may happen unexpectedly in "live" broadcasts), provision had to be made for a censor to sit in the Control Room on the Sunday morning, with his finger on a switch which would put us off the air if he judged that to be necessary.

'The Security people were worried about another angle. Movements of the Commander-in-Chief were a close secret. Yet here were we, proposing to announce that the Chief was attending this service. Indeed, we were proposing to put General Montgomery on the air with a live broadcast, for he was to read the lesson. It was – said the Security Officers – an open invitation to the Germans to come over and bomb the locality of our transmitter (whose whereabouts they were believed to know well enough) and possibly to do a lot of damage, in the hope of finding the Chief himself. We got over that difficulty by drafting an opening announcement which laid emphasis on the fact that this was an *outside* broadcast, coming, not from our normal studio, but from "somewhere in Normandy", and thereby hinting to the Germans that if they had any unpleasant intentions they would have to search the entire beach-head to find the location of the service.

'There was a good deal of activity on one part of the front on the Saturday night. The British Second Army put in a powerful local attack to improve its positions and that meant that most of us had to be up and about for most of the night, seeing what was going on. However, soon after seven o'clock on the Sunday morning, we were preparing for the service. Harvey Sarney and H. O. Sampson, our two recording engineers, were getting their trucks in position, putting out their microphones, and – as the troops arrived in groups – checking over every detail. By nine o'clock Padre Steele was conducting a hymn practice, for none of these men had sung together before.

'So far things were going well. There was one doubtful factor remaining – what would reception in Britain be like?

'At nine-thirty sharp, London said: "Over to Normandy." Then, from our studio in the castle tower, I read the carefully prepared opening announcement, ending with the cue words "Over to the Service". At that moment Howard Marshall, sitting unobtrusively with a microphone, in a car drawn up alongside our recording trucks, described the scene so that listeners could picture the setting, and the service began. And we knew that fortune was with us, for we, in the studio in Normandy, listened on a receiver tuned to the Home Service and we heard the broadcast, clear as a bell, coming back to us from Britain.

'To the liturgy itself there were added other sounds, unexpectedly, which gave this broadcast an unmistakable meaning and reality. Our fighter aircraft, taking off on a sudden call from an airfield only a few hundred yards away, roared so low overhead that General Montgomery was obliged to pause, during the reading of the lesson, until they had passed. Scarcely had their sound died away when the bells of a shell-shattered village church, the little Normandy church of Creully, began to call the villagers to morning worship. Their sound – clear and sweet in the background – travelled across the world that Sunday morning. And when they had ceased and when Canon Hughes was preaching his sermon, his voice came to us accompanied by the song of the chaffinches perched in the branches of the tree only a few feet above the microphone.

'It was a deeply satisfying broadcast – satisfying alike to those who were present at the service, and to those on each side of the English Channel who shared in it by radio. The service was recorded in London and that night we heard extracts from it being repeated in War Report. Many listeners wrote to say how much they were moved by it. One man, writing to the *Radio Times,* said that in his view it ranked among the three outstanding broadcasts of the war.'

*

To come to lesser matters – equipment of many kinds had to be prepared in advance and located where it would be needed. The Army had planned its supplies and transport with remarkable thoroughness: those who worked with the Army had to plan in the same way, with the added precaution that they necessarily had neither the authority nor the military information that the Army enjoyed. Anyhow, in war all plans are subject to circumstance, and intelligent anticipation is the most that can be done.

The provision of non-military transmitters in the zone of operations was not only an innovation in war reporting but a most striking testimony of the ambitious scale on which radio 'cover' was planned. In all, the BBC had committed a massive amount of equipment to the reporting of the war. The Army authorities, for their part, had abandoned their most cherished traditions of security in order to accommodate this new technique, for it was impossible to censor the esoteric conversations in which engineer calls to engineer – addressing each other by such happy *noms de guerre* as 'Mike Charlie Oboe' and 'Jig Easy Sugar Queen', and exchanging technically significant pleasantries in the vein of 'There's a lot of QRM today', and 'Four, three, two, one, WOOF!' In these circumstances it was imperative that there should be no shadow of doubt about the discretion of every engineer, and there was the greatest consternation when a BBC transmitter, MCN, was heard calling a colleague, MCO, to say 'Winnie's coming today – about lunchtime' – on the very morning that Winston Churchill was due to arrive, in greatest secrecy, in Paris. It looked for a time as if all BBC transmitters in the war zone would be closed down, but the apparent indiscretion turned out to be an innocent reference to a public relations officer attached to BBC transmitters, a Captain Wynyard, known to his friends – unfortunately, on this occasion! – as 'Winnie'.

The Machine at Work

When the engineers and correspondents had done their part, and the recorded and scripted messages were available in Broadcasting House, the various war-reporting programmes had to be prepared for transmission. Here it may be interesting to trace the course of a dispatch from the time it was transmitted from, say, MCN at Eindhoven to the moment when it went on the air as part of War Report, and to see what things had to be done in Broadcasting House before the finished material was ready for broadcasting. This dispatch had been censored before it began its journey, of course. First, MCN's signal was picked up at a receiving station somewhere in England and passed on by line to Broadcasting House. Here it was split. By one line the spoken message passed to a recording room, where a recording of it was prepared on discs, much like ordinary gramophone discs. By another line the message passed simultaneously to the telediphone unit. This intake of messages had of course to be planned by the War Reporting Unit in such a way that the flow was as even and steady as it could be without delaying correspondents unduly at their transmitters on the other side of the Channel.

The next step was to check the telediphone script against the actual recording which had been made of the correspondent's message, and then to duplicate nearly a hundred copies of the corrected script for general circulation. This process of receiving and circulating messages was continuous round the clock, for there were news transmissions to one part of the world or another in every hour of the twenty-four. Each War Report programme was prepared in a twelve-hour shift, from 9.30 in the morning until 9.30 at night, so that in the morning the editor would be met with a great heap of scripts accumulated during the night. Those that seemed promising he would mark 'Hear', and those that did not seem to fit in with a probable plan for the day would be marked 'No'. An intermediate class were marked

'Hold'. He might very easily find at this stage of the day that there was already some sort of shape emerging from the overnight messages. But if he were short of material dealing with some particular point which he thought of importance, he would send messages to the most appropriate correspondents asking them to cover in the course of the day the particular subject he had in mind. In addition he would have to consider whether he could make good any gaps by means of material gathered on this side of the Channel. He might need the story of a particular air operation which was of interest, or he might have news of a soldier returned from the front with an unusual experience; and it would be his business then to speak to the service department concerned and ask them if they could send the man along to Broadcasting House. Sometimes this meant bringing pilots from remote stations to London, but considerable efforts were made by the service departments of all the Allies to help the BBC in getting speakers quickly to the microphone.

Meanwhile the work of War Report went on. Both the producer and the scriptwriters would make themselves acquainted with the news of the day and the correspondents' dispatches, and would consult with the editor over the probable shape of the night's War Report. The afternoon was devoted to the hearing of all the discs, including those received during the morning. By this time it would be likely that any speakers specially booked in this country would be arriving at Broadcasting House. Sometimes instead of one speaker it might be found that five or six had to be interviewed. And here in this process it was difficult but important to make sure that the actual observations of the speaker were written down in such a way that the material came naturally to his way of speaking. Men engaged on operations cannot be spared for long periods, and it was necessary therefore to do this work with the greatest rapidity and to secure censorship at high speed also; for the speakers had to wait in Broadcasting House until their scripts had been cleared by the censors before they could safely record what they had to say. Many parties of gallant men brought by air from a bombing raid over Germany or a battlefield in France or Holland, at no more than half-an-hour's notice, and rushed through this process of extraction, scripting, censoring, and recording, have spent time patiently waiting in Broadcasting House, when they might have spent their unexpected leave in a theatre or a restaurant, simply in order to give to listeners the latest, fullest and most vivid account of an action in which they had been involved.

The most arduous part of War Report's day was still, of course, to come. A second meeting at six o'clock was the last official editorial meeting, and it decided, roughly speaking, the shape of War Report for that night. From about seven o'clock onwards the scriptwriters would be consulting about the phrasing of the links to be read shortly by the announcer, whose task was to provide the explanatory comment which set the context of each recording as it was introduced.

The editorial headquarters of War Report was an underground room in Broadcasting House which had formerly been the artists' Green Room. In the early days of the blitz the Green Room became the home of the News Talks Department, and it had its own installation of bunk beds. The most conspicuous furnishing in the room was an enormous walnut table, ten feet long and about two feet wide, with lockers below. This was the chief furnishing of War Report, for on this table the team could lay out the piles of script in order, and there were times when it was covered from end to end with a double row of scripts. It was indeed a happy moment for the editor when the prospect was so clear that he could go down the banks of paper and throw out all the material which was not required, thus reducing two hours' broadcasting time into about twelve minutes. This table formed the stem of a capital T whose top was the desk occupied by the scriptwriters. When they had finished work on any particular script, taking out the unwanted passages, their 'master' copy would be handed to one of the secretaries who would correct in exactly the same manner fifteen other copies of the dispatch.

During the afternoon a great deal of work had been done on the texts of the dispatches themselves. Whole paragraphs were removed, not only from the beginnings or ends of the dispatches but from the middles. Sometimes a sentence might need to disappear, or even at times a word.

For a newspaper this operation is simple, but when the material is recorded on a disc it is a little more difficult. The principle, however, is easily understood. From the disc which you wish to edit you take the first passage you want and record it on a second disc; from the same original master disc you make a copy of the next passage you wish to use, recording it on a third disc; then you play the desired passages consecutively on to a fourth disc. This process had been used by the BBC for many years, but never so continually as during the eleven months of War Report.

During the whole of the day the loudspeaker in the Green Room was connected with the transmissions from correspondents overseas, and at any moment during the day it might be necessary to break off in order to listen to the correspondents as their messages came through from transmitters in the war area; or to listen perhaps to the engineer at a transmitter calling London to give a booking or a service message. The necessity of listening to these transmissions during the late hours of the day was even more acute; because, however wisely plans were laid beforehand, it was the last hour which was critical. This last hour might bring an outstanding dispatch which would upset the whole order and design of that evening's War Report.

Momentous news could 'break' as easily at 9.20 pm as at 2.20 pm, and War Report had to be capable of change up to the last minute.

There were desperate moments when material was put in and other material taken out after the programme had started. Perhaps the most striking and the latest of all such insertions was Chester Wilmot's description of the surrender of the Northwestern German Armies to Field-Marshal Montgomery on 4 May. The very last dispatch in that night's War Report had already begun to go out when the editor, who had been listening to the transmitter which accompanied 21st Army Group, came into the studio and scribbled a pencilled cue for the announcer to read; War Report went over to Germany for the great news, and Wilmot came up in good quality. Unhappily the transmission from Germany failed soon after he had begun, and it was not until 10.35 that night that the complete recording of Field-Marshal Montgomery was heard. Still, the news had got through.

Radio transmissions of this kind are susceptible to all sorts of hazard, and editors are inclined sometimes to think that the hazard increases just when the news is most interesting. It was on Sunday 24 September 1944 that the news came of the great fight for the bridge at Nijmegen. The American correspondent Bill Downs of CBS came through with a first account of what had happened. Chester Wilmot had been pursuing the story with great persistence and was delayed on his way back. The Germans had cut the road behind the Nijmegen party; but finally Wilmot, using a jeep and an aeroplane, got through to Brussels. It was late in the evening and he still had to get his story censored, and when it was censored the only transmitter he could use was the BBC's transmitter MCN, which had just finished its transmission test. MCN was silent and resting and nobody was listening for its voice in London. Wilmot therefore broadcast on a medium wavelength audible to ordinary listeners in this country, asking them to let the BBC know that he was desperately trying to come through. Within five minutes the BBC was inundated with telephone calls from Scotland Yard and from listeners scattered from Northumberland to Devon, but, by

the time Broadcasting House was receiving him direct, War Report
had finished. The excitement over Wilmot's message, however, had
been so immense that quite a party of people had gathered in part of
the Control Room to listen to him. The quality was appalling, but
everyone's enthusiasm was so great that finally one of the senior BBC
engineers seized the Morse transmitter key and himself started to
instruct direct on the technical changes that might be successful. The
following evening War Report was able to give listeners the full story
of Nijmegen bridge in all its detail (see p. 276).

The production of a broadcast like War Report in peacetime
would of course be a matter for careful and accurate rehearsal. When
War Report began, the teams had a not very strong hope – but still
some sort of hope – that rehearsal would be possible. And one night,
indeed, an attempt was made to rehearse. It was the only time any
attempt was made. For all the rest of those 235 nights of War Report
not one was rehearsed.

The programme was produced in a suite of rooms known as 'L1
and mixer'. This consisted of a studio, a recording room, and between
the two the actual mixer, which contained the controlling panel and
six gramophone turntables, over which the selected discs were ranged
in racks. The rooms were separated by glass panels, and it was thus
possible for the engineer at the control panel to look into the studio
where the announcer would be ready to read the material linking the
stories. Operations in the mixer were in the hands of the programme
engineer who switched from the studio at his right hand to the bank
of gramophone turntables at his left hand, according to the complete
script he had in front of him. The working of the turntables was the
job of a junior programme engineer. And it was on the artistry of
these three collaborators – the announcer, programme engineer, and
the 'jeep' – the familiar name for the junior programme engineer –
that the fine points of the production depended.

The Result

This, then, was the organisation the BBC had prepared in readiness for D-Day, founded on the experience gained earlier on other fronts, adapted to the special conditions of a grand-scale assault by sea and air, expanded to include and co-ordinate every technique of radio presentation, and equipped and staffed in the realisation that this was the biggest task the BBC had ever undertaken and that its accomplishment must override every difficulty and every other consideration whatever. This was an all-out effort to prove the unique value of radio in modern reporting.

And then the moment came at last when General Eisenhower murmured 'Let her go', and everyone began to realise that the long months of preparation had come to an end. At 5.30 pm on 5 June an RAF officer warned Stewart MacPherson that the briefing of fighter pilots would start at eight o'clock. At Harwell Richard Dimbleby began recording the take-off of the first paratroops, among whom was a BBC correspondent, Guy Byam, who was to jump with them. With the gliders went Chester Wilmot. By dawn next morning Air Commodore Helmore was shouting against the combined background of a static storm and his Mitchell's engines to record the sight below him – a great armada approaching the Normandy coast. At 1 pm his story was on the air in the first eyewitness accounts broadcast from London. At 7.15 pm Howard Marshall, fished out of the sea after his craft had sunk, was sitting in the studio at Fareham recording the first eyewitness account from the beaches. In Broadcasting House scriptwriters, news editors and producers edited and prepared the mass of first-hand material that came pouring in hour after hour. Volunteers of all kinds tackled whichever jobs needed doing next. At 9.15 pm on D-Day the announcer, Joseph Macleod, presented the inaugural edition:

'War Report! Night by night at this time this programme will bring you news of the war from correspondents and fighting men; it will contain live broadcasts and recordings made in the field, special broadcasts from forward areas, and dispatches and expert comment; to give the latest and fullest picture of the war on all fronts. Here is John Snagge to introduce tonight's War Report.'

On D-Day about 725 radio stations throughout the United States rebroadcast BBC invasion news. The 'actuality' recordings, in particular, made a deep impression in the United States. Before the Normandy campaign American radio had relied entirely on observers' commentaries recollected in the comparative tranquillity of a studio, so the sounds of warfare and the voices of servicemen on the job came as a novelty, and incidentally won this tribute from the *New York Times:*

'The service of the BBC, as D-Day listeners know, was not less than superb . . . exemplary in its presentation and especially fine with its actuality broadcasts. Time and again throughout the day they came over bringing a sense of reality and on-the-spot realism beside which the contrived studio program seemed virtually static.'

American radio tradition had been nourished on the skill of the professional reporter in evoking scene and atmosphere by the vividness of his narration, which was made directly to his listeners without the interposition of a recording. This meant that he could not bring back contemporaneous material from the front. In contrast with the 'virtuoso' method, as it might be called, the BBC used the radio medium as a 'sound-camera' aiming at facsimile reproduction, combined with the personal story of the eyewitness and the added comment of the expert critic. The BBC's editors had for years listened with respect to the American method, and the compliments which now came from the United States were therefore all the more pleasant.

There is no doubt that the British use of recordings speeded up transmission from the front line and gave editors at home the chance to broadcast material at any time. The reporter did not have to return from the front for his fixed 'spot' in a studio programme; he could make recordings and flash them back at any moment right round the clock from field-transmitters – or else fly the discs to London by plane. The extreme flexibility of this method was probably encouraged by the great number of war-reporting programmes radiating from London. The personal 'live' appearance of a correspondent at a fixed time daily is feasible enough in a single radio network, but if the BBC correspondents had 'come up live' in each transmission of War Report, Combat Diary, Radio News Reel, and similar programmes, they would certainly never have had time to see a battle and they would probably have been too busy ever to sleep or eat. An important dispatch might be broadcast, whole or in part, ten times in as many hours. The only practicable way of doing this was by recordings. Using a midget, a recording truck, or a mobile transmitter, the correspondent could devote the maximum time to covering the active fronts; and a steady hour-by-hour flow of 'hot' news was assured. In addition this highly developed skill in the use of recordings brought great benefits in the authenticity inherent in sound pictures made under enemy fire, and in the recorded speech of individual soldiers, sailors and airmen. Here were a spontaneity and a documentation that only radio could provide.

It was fortunate that William Haley, appointed sole Director General in March 1944, was able to oversee the development of War Report. As Editor-in-Chief he had already shown himself adept at sorting out difficulties between correspondents and their military commanders on the front line.

Understanding corporate rivalries, he wasn't afraid to use his authority to bring together the disparate programme and production elements necessary for the success of an operation like War Report. His closeness to the programme and its aims was reflected in a note to senior colleagues on 6 June. 'Congratulations on putting over this morning's historic programme. No one hearing it will have realised the alarms and excursions we were subjected to up to the very last moment. The programme matched the occasion.'

The primary criteria of War Report were those of journalism and moreover journalism of the voice, not of the written word. Much that fulfilled those conditions cannot survive apart from them, but there is also much that retains an obstinate liveliness. The object of this book is to select the best of these items and to present them in the durable form they deserve.

PART TWO
Normandy To The Rhine

A Note On The Text

The chronicle which follows illustrates the course of the invasion of Normandy and the destruction of the German armies through France, Belgium, Holland and Germany, with material broadcast in War Report. Other fronts are excluded (for the sake of simplicity), although they were represented in the series of nightly broadcasts.

DURATION
War Report began on D-Day, 6 June 1944, and continued until 5 May 1945 with one substantial gap. It was suspended from 4 February until the crossing of the Rhine on 23 and 24 March, the period in which the Allies were accumulating men and material for the final assault. The events which occurred during the suspension are summarised at the opening of Part III, on pages 364–5.

MATERIAL
The material is almost all taken from informal first-hand reports, selected and set in order by Desmond Hawkins. They are reproduced as they were spoken at the time in all their freshness and with the imperfections of extempore speech. The editor's task has been to cut them where necessary and set them in a coherent framework. He has not attempted to produce a full-scale consecutive history. Some comment has been retained, to explain situations, and for the same reason one or two messages have been used which were not broadcast, either because of delay or poorness of transmission quality.

DESIGNATIONS

Most of the reports came from BBC correspondents and are signed with their names. Other speakers are identified by the initials CBS (Columbia Broadcasting System), NBC (National Broadcasting Company), CBC (Canadian Broadcasting Corporation), or by the name of the network, agency or newspaper concerned. In the first stage of the invasion all messages from all correspondents were pooled, and some correspondents are therefore described as 'Combined Press Correspondents'. Much other material came from men in the Services, whose names and ranks will be found following the quotations.

DATES

The dates given with the quotations are all the dates of actual broadcast, not the dates of origination. Messages were occasionally delayed by censorship or transmission difficulties, and were broadcast later than the editors would have wished. In the chronicle such messages have been restored to their proper places, although they may have been broadcast late. This explains apparent inconsistencies which the reader will find in the dating of quotations.

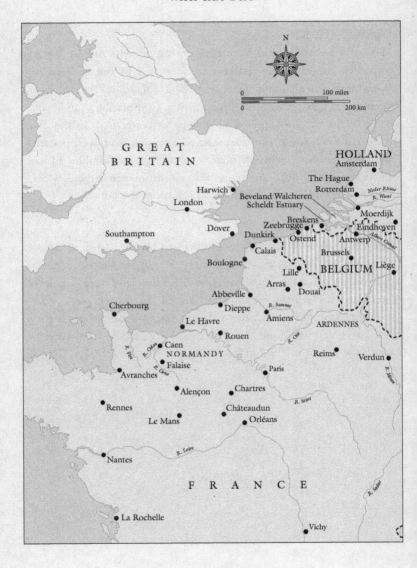

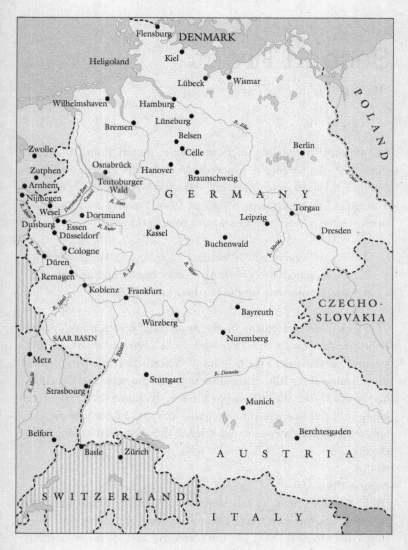

Western Europe

CHAPTER I
Second Front

'Well, this is it, boys'

On 4 June British and American troops entered Rome and thus eliminated the senior, if less redoubtable, half of Fascism. The celebration of this news, however, was shortlived, for the best of all reasons. A single sentence broadcast from London next morning swept the fall of Rome off every front page in the world:

> 'Under the command of General Eisenhower, Allied Naval Forces supported by strong Air Forces began landing Allied Armies this morning on the northern coast of France.'

This brief announcement from Supreme Headquarters, Allied Expeditionary Force, was followed by a personal message from General Eisenhower to the peoples of Western Europe. Throughout the morning every BBC transmitter repeated the news that the Allies had struck in the West. At 1 pm the first eyewitness accounts were going out, and listeners at home heard how, as H-hour approached, fighter-pilots had listened to the briefing they had been waiting for – the big show:

6 June 1944
'Well, this is it, boys. D-Day is tomorrow; and H-hour, when the American and our own forces go into the Continent, some time early tomorrow morning. Now our job tomorrow and for the succeeding few days is to maintain a complete air superiority over the assault area,

so that the Army and the Navy can get on with their job, and sort of get on – establish a beach-head – bridgehead – and go right on unmolested.'

STEWART MACPHERSON

For these fighter-pilots there was still time to snatch a few hours' sleep; on other airfields paratroops had already put on their war-paint and taken off into the darkness:

6 June 1944
'Their faces were darkened with cocoa; sheathed knives were strapped to their ankles; tommy guns strapped to their waists; bandoliers and hand grenades, coils of rope, pick handles, spades, rubber dinghies hung around them, and a few personal oddments, like the lad who was taking a newspaper to read on the plane. As they knelt round their padre in prayer, with bent heads and on one knee, the men with their equipment and camouflaged faces looked like some strange creatures from another world.'

ROBERT BARR AND GUY BYAM

The night sky throbbed with the engines of one great armada. Off the English coast another began to move through the waters of the Channel:

6 June 1944
'Up on the tiny flagdeck a senior naval officer stands beside the skipper, a microphone in his hand. Behind him is the trumpet of his loud hailer.

'It's coming up to time. Not zero hour yet, but zero hour minus.

73

The moment when the assault craft are to set off from their assembly area for the beaches.

'Astern of us, the assault craft have assembled. You know that they are neatly marshalled there, in formation, but you can only make out the leaders. The loud hailer checks them over. Voices reply faintly out of the darkness.

'The Naval Commander is looking at his watch. He puts the microphone to his mouth. "Off you go then – and good luck to you.'"

FRANK GILLARD

The first eyewitness account of what was happening over the other side came from an Air Force observer flying in a Mitchell bomber, and recording his commentary on a midget recorder. The RAF was out strafing on a grand scale:

6 June 1944
'We're going across to bomb a target which is a railway bridge, which may help those good fellows down below in those boats. I know that it's what they do today that matters, but every little bit that the RAF can do to help is going to mean something.

'We're coming down right low to attack our target; it's a pretty job, we're looking out for the markers now. I don't think I can talk to you while we're doing this job, I'm not a blinking hero. I don't think it's much good trying to do these flash running commentaries when you're doing a dive-bombing attack. I can see flashes where the Bomber Command stuff is falling down: a lot of Bomber Command are pounding this invasion spot like hell, doing their best to tear it to pieces.

'I've just heard the navigator say "OK. On it". Now we're getting our nose down, and we've got to go down and give this bridge the works. We're in a colossal static storm at the moment which is rattling in my ears like mad – what with the engine noise I can't hear myself speak at all. We're losing height rapidly – we're just going in. There's something ahead of us there – do you see – do you see that light? Oh, I thought I was talking to the pilot, I recorded that. There's a funny light, I thought it was the markers going down – instead of talking into the intercom I talked into the record. I just heard the navigator say, over the intercom, "We're over there", and I also heard the bomb-aimer say "Shall I give it a cosh the moment I see it?" And the pilot said "Yes".

'We're just going in to drop our bombs; it's a very tense moment – just the dawn of the moment when our troops are going in on the French beaches; I've seen them with my own eyes, practically in the act of touching down on the beaches. I feel it a great privilege to be here. I'll be glad to get home all the same. Never mind, we're just getting ready to go in and bomb, and I'd better shut up. Hold it! My God, there's some bloody nasty flak round this place – very nasty flak, blast it!

'Never mind, I heard the bomb-aimer say just now, "Go in and do your stuff. Righto." Ah, he hasn't let them off, I hear him telling the pilot to go "straight and steady, straight and steady". Oh, there they go – my God, what a good lift, what a good lift up into the air! We feel much lighter now. The best thing is to get out of here. We're pointed the right way round now anyway. Hello, the rear-gunner's reported – or the bloke at the back rather – has reported a night fighter after us. I hope we make this cloud ahead of us. I don't feel very belligerent. We're heading for the coast now. There's been a constant traffic of aircraft coming to and fro. Bomber Command's been out, we've passed a lot of them. There's great open patches in the cloud through which one can get a pretty good view. Now I can see the invasion craft out on the sea, like a great armada attacking

France. This is history; it's a thing I can't be eloquent about in an aeroplane, because I've got engine-noises in my ears. But this really is a great moment for us, and to feel that I sit here with this weird means of telling you about what I'm seeing gives me a feeling of witnessing a strange pageant – something unreal. I feel detached, and that awful feeling that the great history of the world is unfolding before us at this very moment.'

AIR COMMODORE W. HELMORE, CBE, RAF

Besides bombs, something else was swooping down on Normandy during the hours of darkness before H-hour – paratroop and glider formations, with their stores and equipment:

8 June 1944
'In the plane we stand pack to breast, I am jumping one but last of my stick. And as we stand in the plane, for there is no room to sit, we feel the tremendous vibration of the four motors as we start down the runway. And all around in the coming darkness are other great planes and row upon row of gliders.

'And the plane is airborne and in the crowded fuselage all you see in the pale light of an orange bulb is the man standing next to you.

'And you fly out over the Channel and the minutes go by, and the stick commander says that the pilot has told him we are over a great armada of naval ships. And then it is something else he says – something that gives you a dry feeling in your mouth – flak – and the word is passed from man to man. The machine starts to rock and jump. Ahead of us a comforting thought. Lancasters are going for the flak and a coastal battery is one of our objectives.

'We're over the coast now and the run in has started – one minute, thirty seconds. Red light – green and out – get on, out, out, out fast into the cool night air, out, out, out over France – and we know that the dropping zone is obstructed. We're jumping into fields covered with poles! And I hit my parachute and lower my kitbag which is suspended on the end of a forty-foot rope from my harness. And then the ground comes up to hit me. And I find myself in the middle of a cornfield. I look around and even with a compass I can't be sure where I am – and overhead hundreds of parachutes and containers are coming down.

'The whole sky is a fantastic chimera of lights and flak, and one plane gets hit and disintegrates wholesale in the sky, sprinkling a myriad of burning pieces all over the sky.

'The job of the unit with which I jumped was to occupy the area and prepare the way for gliders – we were to rendezvous near a copse, but I can't find it, so I go to a farmhouse and ask the way of a farmer and his wife standing on the porch of their house. It's a tricky business this moving about the enemy countryside at night. But we are well in hand and at the most I shall only meet my own patrols. I find the unit after having been sniped at once and challenged a number of times. They are assembling under a hedge.

'Like a tentacle into the air was the radio-set aerial, and the major was signalling.

'Allied soldiers talking to each other through the night.'

GUY BYAM

One of their first jobs was to prepare for the gliders to follow them in – gliders bringing more troops and heavier equipment:

6 June 1944
'I was in at the start of the invasion in the second dicky-seat of a glider tug. As we gathered round the leading aircraft on the runway

just after midnight, the Americans were going out in close formation. Somebody – he must have been a navigator – said: "Why don't they give us pretty lights like these to steer by?" We saw plenty of pretty lights a little later, but not to steer by. Take-off was fine and to the second. Visibility was good and the wake of the odd naval craft we spotted shone like silk in the clear moon. The Popeye voice on the intercom croaked: "This is going to be a piece of cake." And so it looked, until just short of the enemy coast we began to run into dense cloud. We went through that and came out facing the coastline. And there were the pretty lights. Hundreds of thousands of them, and all of them tracer. The enemy seems to go in for fancy tracer. Maybe it's to keep his gunners amused. There it was ahead of us like the Blackpool illuminations, and when it seemed obvious to us that we should call it a day and go back, the pilot put the nose of the aircraft into it as if it were confetti. Every now and then he called on the intercom: "Okay, glider pilot?" The voice always came back: "Okay, skipper."

'We had to skirt belt after belt of this flaming stuff to bring the glider exactly over the zone it was to land on. It was a trying time for any aircraft, but for a tug and a glider linked by a strand of rope it looked to me like suicide. There was no question of casting off and getting out of it. The skipper said: "Glider pilot, are you all right? Okay? Great! Well, hold on, son, there's a lot of stuff around here, but we'll get through it. . . ." Then the tough little glider sergeant-pilot's voice: "We're all right, carry on."

'We dived into the cloud. We could see nothing. The glider pilot could see nothing. All he could do was hang on to his controls and follow us about in the murk. The skipper kept on talking to him and always the gruff little voice came back: "Okay, skipper." The rear-gunner yelled suddenly: "The glider's hit." The skipper said: "Glider pilot, glider pilot, are you all right?" There was a short pause, and then the voice came again: "All right, we're with you."

'The navigator all this time had been working with his maps and his rulers. He was shouting to the skipper, and when we came out of the cloud and away from the flak, why there was the landing zone just as we had been studying it on maps for days and days. "Casting off," said the little gruff voice, and we could just hear a faint "Thanks, skipper, and good luck", as the tug lunged forward, free of the glider's weight. I looked down as we went into a turn to come home. There was nothing but blankness now. But there were a lot of gliders swooshing down in the blankness.'

FLIGHT-LIEUT. JOHN MACADAM, RAF

The gliders, that these planes towed, landed by night in the Orne Valley between Caen and the sea to reinforce the paratroops and to bring heavy weapons to help hold the vital left flank of the beach-head:

8 June 1944

'With grinding brakes and creaking timbers we jolted, lurched, and crashed our way to a landing in northern France early this morning. The glider in which I travelled came off better than most. The bottom of the nose was battered in . . . the wings and tail assembly were slashed here and there, but she came to rest on her three wheels, even though she had mown down five stout posts that came in her path, and virtually crash-landed in a ploughed field. No one was even scratched.

'We shouted with joy . . . and relief . . . and bundled out into the field. All around us we could see silhouettes of other gliders, twisted and wrecked – making grotesque patterns against the sky. Some had buried their noses in the soil; others had lost a wheel or a wing; one had crashed into a house, two had crashed into each other. And yet as we marched off past these twisted wrecks – thanking heaven for our good fortune – troops were clambering out almost as casually as they might leave a bus. Some had to slash away the wooden fuselage before they could get out their jeeps and trailers; but almost without exception they soon had them on the road.

'But as we moved off the landing zone we were promptly reminded that we were still in the middle of enemy territory. We could hear Germans shouting excitedly at a church near by, starting a car and driving furiously off. A quarter of a mile away a German battery was firing out to sea . . . from positions all around us German ack-ack batteries sent up streams of tracer. The airborne forces had gained their first foothold in France by a daring night landing . . . but all of us knew that it'd be harder to hold the ground than it had been to take it.'

CHESTER WILMOT

⁓∾⊙∾

While the airborne troops made good their landing and established themselves during the night, Lancaster bombers pounded the coastal defences. Immediately before dawn the American Air Force completed the preparations for H-hour:

7 June 1944

'We know from reports that in the dawn hours the RAF dropped on each gunsite the same load of bombs that fell on London during its greatest raid, but the air power that we have seen most forcibly was the final attack by the American Eighth Air Force. Immediately before H-hour they dropped a vast weight of bombs on the beaches.

'The beaches shook and seemed to rise into the air, and ships well out at sea quivered with the shock. The captain of our landing-

80

boats, a veteran of Guadalcanal and Italy, put it like this: "By the time they had finished not even a rabbit could have been alive on those beaches." As that weight of bombs fell some of the tenseness of expectation left the faces of the men who were going in to land and was replaced by a smile of the utmost relief.

'As a result of that bombing and the naval bombardment and the work of the paratroops most of the guns were now silenced.'

ROBIN DUFF

At last, as dawn broke, the scene was set for the Navy to move in to the beaches and put the first infantry units ashore:

6 June 1944
'To put a single division ashore with its immediate weapons requires about 500 ships and craft varying from 100 to 15,000 tons. Just imagine the task of the Navy and the RAF in protecting such convoys from air and submarine attack, and from attacks by surface craft which may range from pocket battleships to E-boats.

'The ways of this armada must be swept clear of mines up to the enemy's doorstep. The Germans set great store by mines, and we can depend on them to have used every sort of mine that human – or should I say, and this from personal experience – inhuman ingenuity can think out. Our minesweepers carry great responsibility but they're used to that, and are probably only too glad to be doing a really offensive job, as opposed to the defensive role they have so often had to play.

'The initial assaults could not afford to fail. There is no way round, and only the sea is behind if the soldier fails to get a footing. And this is where ship bombardment comes in. For the Navy's job is to knock out the enemy's guns and defences and plaster the beaches ahead so that the opposition is laid low at the crucial moment when a multitude of ships and craft see the land loom ahead and steer for the touch-down at low tide.'

CAPTAIN G. THISTLETON-SMITH, RN, GM

6 June 1944

This is the day and this is the hour. The sky is lightening – lightening over the coast of Europe as we go in. The sky is lighter and the sea is brighter, but along the shore there is a dense smoke screen as the battleships and the warships, the smaller warships, sweep along there firing all the time against the shore and some of them laying a smoke screen for us. The sun is blazing down brightly now – it's almost like an omen the way it's suddenly come out just as we were going in. The whole sky is bright; the sea is a glittering mass of silver with all these crafts of every kind moving across it and the great battleships in the background blazing away at the shore.

'There go the craft past us, the other landing craft. Some are left behind, the slower ones, each taking their part and going in at the right time for the right job. Destroyers, Corvettes, patrol vessels. I can hear the sound of anti-aircraft fire – I can't see yet see whether it's our people who are being attacked. There's an enormous cloud of smoke along the shore, not only from the smokescreen but also from us. From this terrific bombardment.

'All the ships are blazing away now. All around us an enormous circle – there are ships: ships moving in, ships on patrol, ships circling, ships standing to and firing. We are passing close by a cruiser – a cruiser that has been taking part in the bombardment but is now I imagine a sort of general patrol.

'You can't imagine anything like this march of ships like soldiers marching in line. I've never seen anything so expressive of intent and purpose. It's a purpose shared amongst many ships and among many hundreds of thousands of fighting men who are going in now to the coast of Europe to do the biggest job they've had to do. I can't record any more now because the time has come for me to get my kit on my back and get ready to step off on that shore. And it's a great day.'

COLIN WILLS

The first detailed account of the beach landings came from a correspondent who was twice capsized into the sea and lost all his notes, but managed to get back to a transmitter in England in time to give an exciting eyewitness story on the night of D-Day:

6 June 1944
'I'm sitting in my soaked-through clothes with no notes at all; all my notes are sodden – they're at the bottom of the sea, so as it's only a matter of minutes since I stepped off a craft, I'm just going to try to tell you very briefly the story of what our boys had to do on the beaches today as I saw it myself. I won't go into the build-up, which was taking place as you know for a very long time, but I'll start with first light of this morning. The landing-craft were lowered and, as the light broke and we really could see around us, we began to become aware of the formidable character of this invasion fleet of which we were a part. I was in a barge which was due to pick up the brigadier of an assault group, and we were going in with the first assault wave. So we circled round with the various types of vessels opening fire on the beach, which we could see quite plainly in the dim morning light, opening fire on the beach in their own manner and at the appointed time.

'First of all the cruisers started with rather a loud bang. And soon the air grew heavy with the smell of cordite and loud with the sound of explosions, and looking along the beach we could see the explosions of our artillery creating a great cloud and fog of smoke.

'Well, we in my particular craft picked up our brigadier – not easily because the sea was very rough – and we headed straight for our appointed portion of the beach. We could see as we went in that that particular portion of the beach wasn't altogether healthy, but we drove towards it with our planes overhead giving us the sort of cover we'd been hoping for, and which we'd been expecting.

'As we drove in we could see shell-bursts in the water along the beach, and just behind the beach, and we could see craft in a certain amount of difficulty because the wind was driving the sea in with long rollers and the enemy had prepared anti-invasion, anti-barge

On 6 June 1944 American invasion troops come ashore on a
Normandy beach under heavy machine-gun fire.

obstacles sticking out from the water – formidable prongs, many of them tipped with mines, so that as your landing-barge swung and swayed in the rollers, and they're not particularly manageable craft, it would come in contact with one of these mines and be sunk. That was the prospect which faced us on this very lowering and difficult morning as we drove into the beach.

'And suddenly, as we tried to get between two of these tripart defence systems of the Germans, our craft swung, we touched a mine, there was a very loud explosion, a thundering shudder of the whole craft, and water began pouring in.

'Well, we were some way out from the beach at that point. The ramp was lowered at once, and out of the barge drove the Bren gun carrier into about five feet of water, with the barge settling heavily in the meanwhile. Well, the Bren gun carrier somehow managed to get through it, and we followed wading ashore. That was one quite typical instance of how people got ashore, and when they got ashore seemed to be in perfectly good order, because the troops out of that barge immediately assembled and went to their appointed places, and there was no semblance of any kind of confusion. But the scene on the beach until one had sorted it out was at first rather depressing because we did see a great many barges in difficulties with these anti-tank screens, and we noticed that a number of them had struck mines, as ours had struck mines. But then we began to see that in fact the proportion that had got through was very much greater, and that troops were moving all along the roads, and that tanks were out already and going up the hills, that in fact we dominated the situation; and that our main enemy was the weather and that we were beating the weather; that we had our troops and our tanks ashore, and that the Germans weren't really putting up a great deal of resistance.'

HOWARD MARSHALL

6 June 1944

'The first parties ashore this morning worked at splendid speed. By half-past ten, quite apart from the sappers, the infantry, and the tanks already pushing into France, there were two sizeable bulldozers ashore, working on a stretch of road that may well become the Royal Air Force's first landing-strip in France, and it's going to be ready very soon for the fighters to use.

'Of enemy troop movements there was, until noon today, little or no sign from the air, even close to the immediate battle area. Long stretches of empty roads shining with rain, deserted, dripping woods, and damp fields – static, quiet – perhaps uncannily quiet – and possibly not to remain quiet. But here and there a movement catches the eye, as our aircraft on reconnaissance roar over a large and suspicious wood – three German soldiers running like mad across the main road to fling themselves into cover. And, nearer the battle area, much nearer the battle area than they, a solitary peasant harrowing his field, up and down behind the horses, looking nowhere but before him and at the soil.'

RICHARD DIMBLEBY

7 June 1944

'We came sliding and slowing in on some light breakers and grounded. I stepped ashore on France. Walking up a beach where men were moving casually about, carrying equipment inshore.

'All up and down the broad beach as far as I could see, men, jeeps, bulldozers, and other equipment were moving about like ants. A few columns of black, greasy smoke marked equipment which had been hit by shellfire and set afire.

'The German shelling continued steadily at various points up and down the beach, but so far had not reached the area in which I was walking. It would work over an area, then move on to another. It was accurate, landing for the most part close to the water's edge, and I saw one small landing-craft catch fire after taking a hit. Men came spilling out of it into water waist deep.

'From time to time there were huge concussions as the engineers set off demolitions; the ground would shake, and the troops would throw themselves violently on the ground. I climbed a rock embankment and came to a piece of flat land where hundreds of men were digging slit trenches. When they got down about a foot and a half they struck water. Some of them were lying in water, and I asked if there were much shelling. "There is when there is," one man said; "right now there isn't, but when it comes it sure comes." I asked him what German fortifications he could point out. He showed me some tunnels at the top of the palisade; the palisade rises above the beach along this stretch of coast. A long column of men was winding up the palisade on a narrow path; they weren't moving; at the skyline they seemed to be knotted up; to reach the palisade I joined a column who were wading across a slough; the water came nearly to their armpits, and they had to hold their rifles and equipment over their heads. The water was rather warm at the bottom of the slimy mess. When a man got to the far side of the slough he would always stop in a maddening way holding the rest of us up. We shouted angrily, but when we got there each one of us stopped too. The reeds on the far bank were loaded with mines. One man lay at the top of the bank, dead. The mines had been marked with bits of paper, and soldiers at the top advised just how to climb so as not to venture into dangerous ground.

'There were more dead men along a narrow path which led up the palisade. The column had stopped moving, and I began to step past men following a captain. Suddenly a voice said: "Watch yourself, fellow, that's a mine." A soldier sprawled on the bank was speaking; he had one foot half blown off; he'd stepped on a mine a short time earlier. Now while he waited for litter-bearers he'd been warning other soldiers about other mines in that vicinity. I can stand the dead, but the wounded horrify me, and I only looked at him to thank him. He looked very tired but perfectly collected. "What you need is the 'medics'," I said; "I'll try and get them for you when I go back down." "Yeah," he said, "but how're they goin' to get up here?" He was right; the pathway was so clogged with men and so heavily mined that it was impassable. The engineers would have to get up there first.

'I waited a spell longer and the line didn't move, so I began to make my way down the path again. It was slow work. The soldiers were so alarmed that I would step on a mine right next to them that one man told me to walk on his back rather than step off the path. I promised I would try and get the engineers up to disarm the mines. While I was going down the slope the Germans began shelling our area. It was hard not to throw myself on the ground willy-nilly, but the thought of those mines kept me from it. The shells were still landing at some distance on the flat. I took a last look at the greatest armada in history before going on the flat. It was too immense to describe. There were so many transports on the horizon that in the faint haze they looked like a shoreline. Destroyers were almost on the beach, occasionally jolting out a salvo that was like a punch on the chin.'

THOMAS TREANOR, NBC

Company Sergeant Major Stan Hollis of the Green Howards was the only serviceman to be awarded the Victoria Cross for his actions on D-Day:

21 August 1944
'My company of Green Howards was one of the assault companies on D-Day. We had to take a coastal gun battery at Mont Fleury. I

was in charge of a group of 2-inch mortars laying down smoke, but I noticed that two of our platoons running up to attack the guns had gone past the pillbox. This was only about a foot above the ground but I spotted a Spandau machine-gun in the firing slip. I went along with my company commander, one of the bravest men I know. They fired at us but once we were on top of the box, grenades and Sten guns killed some of them, and when I went down inside with my Sten gun I got half a dozen prisoners. It was a big place – two storeys deep – and we got all the equipment intact so that made things just a little safer for the rest of our company in their attack. The fighting all through D-Day was fairly warm. But one piece of trouble we ran into were on account of some dogs I noticed at the end of a country lane. There was nobody there, but the dogs were wagging their tails. When I went along with the major, we found a German field gun supported by machine-guns in a farmyard. Elements of D Company attacked from some farm buildings but every time our lads got up on the next wall they were knocked out by machine-guns. I tried to get the gun crew with a mortar, but they started blazing away with a gun at a hundred yards. Open sights and big stones were flying all over. The gun concentrated on one of our Bren guns and things looked bad for them – they couldn't get back. So I tried again with the Bren.

'And this time the Boche got so worried they left our lads alone and we all got back safely. The field gun was taken later. Some days later, we had the hardest fighting the battalion had ever seen in the whole war. We had heavy losses. There again, another farmhouse held us up. Again I was lucky with a Sten gun from 15 yards this time – it knocked out all the Boche except one who came out of a trench and I got him too. So we pushed on into France. Now these don't sound like VC affairs and I don't know if they really are. I do know it was the sort of thing that was happening all over in the first five days in

Normandy. And jumping into a pillbox full of Germans wasn't so wonderful when you saw your own lads fighting like heroes on every side of you. And when you saw lads you knew dropping dead you wanted to do something to smash the guns that were doing it.

'Just after we were out of the water on D-Day, I saw one lad go down wounded. Now he saved my life in Sicily. And he comes from Middlesbrough too. That sort of thing makes you forget to be scared. I've always been scared when we've gone into action with the BEF at Dunkirk, Alamein and Sicily. But if your lads see the sergeant major's got his head down well, it's a bad do isn't it? And once, when we were shaving, I heard one of them say "I felt lousy. I was scared stiff in case Hollis saw it". So that's the way it goes. And things like snipers' bullets on your cheek and being blown out of trenches and looking into German gun muzzles, they don't count as much as you think when you've got men like that round you.'

C.S.M. STAN HOLLIS

On this momentous day the last word comes, appropriately, from General Montgomery:

6 June 1944

'We have a great and a righteous cause. Let us pray that the Lord, mighty in battle, will go forth with our armies and that His special providence will aid us in the struggle. I want every soldier to know that I have complete confidence in the successful outcome of the operations that we are now about to begin. With stout hearts and with enthusiasm for the contest, let us go forward to victory; and, as we enter the battle, let us recall the words of a famous soldier spoken many years ago. These are the words he said:

"He either fears his fate too much,
Or his deserts are small,
Who dare not put it to the touch,
To win, or lose it all."

Good luck to each one of you – and good hunting on the mainland of Europe.'

GENERAL SIR BERNARD MONTGOMERY

CHAPTER II
Beach-Head

'The sea is filled with their ships'

The vital beaches had been seized and held. The Atlantic Wall was pierced and, as the Allied troops poured in, France and the people of France began to emerge from the stifling fog of occupation:

9 June 1944
'How they survived the bombardment, how they lived during that bombardment, it's difficult to say, but here they are obviously tired, obviously strained, but relieved, smiling, gathering in groups at street corners. I remember so many little glimpses of them – an old man carrying a couple of gaily-painted buckets; another old man in a bar, whistling; behind, his bar with empty bottles on it, a couple of them broken. A woman carrying a bundle of flowers, children playing with troops, cattle in the fields, orchards in blossom, farmhands in their blue jeans bicycling home; a man right up in the forward line, with the smoke of the guns not far away from him, leading a white horse back to his farm. Then we saw some strange and sometimes rather sad sights. I remember right on the beach, in one of the beach villas, there was a French postman in his blue and red uniform delivering the letters to a lady standing at the gate of her villa, but only the gate was there – there was no villa; that had been blown up. Just the postman and the lady leaning over the gate, and no villa.'

HOWARD MARSHALL

8 June 1944

'The people are pleased to see us. We apologise for the bringing of war to their homes. But in little ways they show they are glad to see us. A dead paratroop is laid out on a bed in the best bedroom covered from head to foot with local flowers. This is the story up to the early hours of the first day. That is typical of the things they do – small gestures – just small gestures.'

GUY BYAM

8 June 1944

'The first evidence of what the French are feeling today came from a woman living in a village. "God has sent the British and Americans," she said in a trembling voice. "The Germans are afraid, I tell you, afraid. They told me as they came through here: 'The Allies have so many men, so much material; the sea is filled with their ships.' "

'Then we entered Bayeux. Men, women and children lining the streets yelled, waved, gesticulated. It was a hysterical welcome. Young and old people stood in the cobbled streets of this town from which Allied troops had just driven the Germans, some with tears streaming down their faces, all shouting "Vive l'Angleterre! Vive l'Amérique! Vive la France!" and raising fingers in the Victory "V" sign. Over their heads the Tricolour fluttered from nearly every balcony. But no people were ever more justified in hysteria than these.'

JOHN HETHERINGTON, COMBINED PRESS

That town was Bayeux, first town in France to be liberated. Farther east, in the Orne Valley, the going was more difficult. The task of holding this exposed flank fell to the British 6th Airborne Division, whose magnificent tenacity stands out even from the crowded and brilliant scene of the first days of the invasion. Before D-Day the

Commander of the 6th Airborne Division told his troops just how important it was for the whole operation that they should hold this flank. It was obvious that the Germans would strike here in the hope of delaying our general advance inland. The 6th Airborne were to prevent any such delay:

13 June 1944

'On rising ground near the coast east of the River Orne there was a strong German battery position. Its guns were sited to fire along the beaches on which the 3rd British Division had to land. It was a prime task of the 6th Airborne Division to capture that battery before dawn. . . . Parachutists were to do the job, but in the darkness and bad weather the paratroops were widely scattered and only 150 men reached the rendezvous for the attack in time. The colonel couldn't afford to wait for the others, so he went in with what he had. The battery position was strongly wired and mined, but they blew the wire with bangalore torpedoes and the first assault wave dashed in over the mines regardless of those that burst . . . and regardless too of the machine-gun posts, they raced for the guns in their concrete emplacements. They got there . . . blew up the guns while the second assault wave fanned out inside the defences to silence the machine-guns. This took all the colonel's men, and just as the second wave went in he was warned that two German platoons were advancing up the road behind him. At that critical moment help came from the skies. The original plan had provided that as the infantry went in, three gliders should swoop down out of the night and land right inside the battery position and take the defenders in the rear. But the night was so dirty that the gliders couldn't find their targets . . . one pilot took a chance and crashed his glider into an orchard right on the edge of the enemy position. As it landed the Germans turned their machine-guns on to it. . . . Some men were wounded, the glider caught on fire . . . but the rest, rallied by a warrant officer, went straight into action to deal with the German reinforcements. For over an hour they held them off, while the main party mopped up the Germans in the battery itself. At 4.45 am, with only a quarter of an hour to spare, the position was ours . . . 150 men had done the job of a battalion. The colonel fired a success signal and dispatched a carrier pigeon off to England with the news. The courage that took that battery is the courage that's held this flank.'

CHESTER WILMOT

After that first desperate struggle to secure a foothold reinforcements came in by glider. The ground was held, and held securely, in spite of the expected counter-attacks that developed in the following days:

12 June 1944

'I was riding in a jeep along a lane in Normandy on my way to visit a front-line battalion of the 6th Airborne Division. A man with a Bren gun was on the bonnet; another with a Sten sat behind the driver, alert for snipers. This was no idle precaution: on the day before, this lane had been the scene of heavy fighting.

'An hour earlier I saw some booty acquired from the Germans – three motor vehicles that had been driven down a road straight into one of our ambushes. One truck had thousands of francs aboard – the pay of a full company. Another was carrying hot soup and coffee and fresh bread for the forward German troops. Other battalions which met this attack told similar stories. In one sector the Germans got through between two of our positions. They reached a reserve battalion position, but they suffered the same fate as their colleagues – they, too, were stopped in their tracks by point-blank fire from hidden positions, and those that survived were cleaned up in the afternoon by infantry and tanks.

'This victory accounted for the broad smiles on the faces of the men who were manning the forward positions yesterday. They're in splendid heart, even though they've been through the great strain of the initial landing and attack, and the further strain of six days' fighting in nerve-racking country. And it *is* nerve-racking. Even when the men aren't involved in repelling attacks, they're out on patrol, stalking through woods and cornfields infested with snipers. And the positions they man are just holes in the drenched ground, and they snatch a few hours' sleep when they can, and it's chilly sleep, for no blankets have got through to them yet. Their meals are just what they can cook for themselves on their little "tommy" cookers.

'But in spite of all this they're full of fight. They're delighted that their Division – the 6th Airborne – has been mentioned on the air. They're hungry for news of the battle at large, and those that can do so gather round signal sets to listen to this War Report each night.

'They'd have learned something of how the battle's going if they'd driven with me back to the coast late last night. The roads were packed with traffic – guns, tanks, trucks, mobile workshops, and so on, coming forward; empty vehicles going back; and along the side of the narrow, muddy roads, lines of marching infantry-fresh troops coming up to give new weight to the assault. And as far as I could see, on either side of the road, the green fields are studded with dark shapes, camouflaged shapes, dumps of ammunition and guns, vehicles, tanks, and all the vast impedimenta of modern war. The expansion even in the two days since my first visit to the beaches was tremendous; and down on the waterfront itself, the activity is even more intense. And in the securing and holding of this vital ground no troops have played a more vital part than the 6th British Airborne Division.'

CHESTER WILMOT

At home we were learning to talk of 'the build-up', the massive accumulation of men and stores and equipment coming on to the beaches and moving up to the depots and forward areas:

11 June 1944

'I saw the shining, blue sea. Not an empty sea, but a sea crowded, infested with craft of every kind: little ships, fast and impatient, scurrying like water-beetles to and fro, and leaving a glistening wake behind them; bigger ships, in stately, slow procession with the sweepers in front and the escort vessels on the flank – it was a brave, oh, an inspiring sight. We are supplying the beaches all right – no doubt of that. We flew on south-west, and I could see France and Britain, and I realised how very near to you all at home in England is this great battle in Normandy. It's a stone's throw across the gleaming water.

Richard Dimbleby was with the RAF on D-Day
and reported from above the invasion beaches.

'I saw it all as a mighty panorama, clear and etched in its detail. There were the supply ships, the destroyers, the torpedo boats, the assault craft, leaving England. Halfway over was another flotilla, and near it a huge, rounded, ugly capital ship, broadside on to France. There in the distance was the Cherbourg peninsula, Cherbourg itself revealed in the sun. And there, right ahead now, as we reset course, were the beaches. Dozens, scores, hundreds of craft lying close inshore, pontoons and jetties being lined up to make a new harbour where, six days ago, there was an empty stretch of shore.'

RICHARD DIMBLEBY

9 and 11 June 1944

'Almost as though on conveyor belts, the regular steady stream of ducks was moving. Hundreds of them, they went out empty from the shore, changed from wheel drive to propeller a few yards out, and made tracks, or rather wakes, for the merchantmen lying out to sea.

'They were coming inshore, reversing the process, and driving their piled cargoes of sugar crates, tyres, petrol shells, up the coast roads to the depots. "They're doing a magnificent job, the ducks," an RASC officer told me – the RASC man these amphibious craft – and he confirmed it with figures. Two thousand tons they brought in on this small sector alone yesterday, and it will be nearer three thousand tons today. That's only the ducks, mind you; there are LCTs, Rhine ferries, and innumerable other craft piling in supplies for our armies ashore. The beaches are alive with vehicles and men. There's a stream of traffic coming off the craft and going away up the roads and into the interior. There's an immense fleet off the beaches; it seems as if all the ships in the world were concentrated there. As you come in towards the beaches, it's rather like driving in on the roads towards an industrial town; it's like a great, enormous industrial area – a remarkable sight.'

MICHAEL STANDING AND HOWARD MARSHALL

12 June 1944

'From the lips of every man comes a smile or a joke. And up the roads they move, the long roads by the beaches, with their heavy loads, their weapons, and their food; they move towards the thunder in the south; towards the gunfire, towards the battle. Sometimes they're not moving towards the front but trudging back, weary men who've seen the German almost face to face; men who have struggled with wire and minefields; men who have fought tanks at closest range with piats and bombs. And the usual word to these men coming back is, "How's it going on at the front?" The answer is generally non-committal, but always the same: "Fine," "All right," "Very well." '

GUY BYAM

Inevitably the first question in everyone's mind was 'How's it going at the front?', but the source and sinew of that front line was primarily the sea. The sea-lanes had to be kept free and busy. Close inshore the minesweepers carried on their monotonous, dangerous, imperative work:

13 June 1944

'Our captain, a Lieutenant-Commander, a DSO, and a DSC, says quietly to his Chief Yeoman of Signals: "Make to Flotilla Leader as follows: 'What action do you take if coastal batteries open fire?' " A mile away a lamp winks back at us the answer: "None." The sweep continues. Suddenly the sea seems to shudder: there's a hollow, echoey boom, and a great tower of water flings up astern of the second line of sweepers. That's one mine less.'

MICHAEL STANDING

99

The way was cleared. The supplies came in – came in in bulk and in comparative safety; but not without danger and not without losses:

15 June 1944

'I hitched a ride on a Liberty ship. On deck the skipper James Hassell told me he was happy to have me and that he thought we'd get back to England all right. "You *think* we'll get back to England?" "Yes," he said, "you see we've been hit. They put a hole in our stern, knocked out most of the bearings in the propeller shaft and bent the shaft itself into an S curve. We are supposed to be on the bottom of the Bay of the Seine, but as you can see for yourself, we are not." "Yes," I said uncertainly and cleared my throat.

'One morning this ship was just making up to its anchorage preparatory to discharging its load of troops. Bam, bam went two separate explosions. Two of the liferafts broke loose and went sailing out into the air. Hatch covers blew straight up. That's all they knew on deck. Down in the engine room Roger Jones was standing on a platform oiling a huge connecting rod. The shock threw him off the platform . . . he caught on to the connecting rod and hung precariously. He started going up and down with the connecting rod, travelling its 48-inch stroke every second for a few terrifying minutes until everything stopped. He was going 480 feet per minute, or faster than the elevators in Radio City, and furthermore he was changing direction every half-second. The first assistant engineering officer was wearing a helmet, and so when the overhead and pieces of valve pipe and machinery started raining down, he grabbed a 5-foot 2-inch fireman and covered his head with his arms. When Leonard Valentine, the chief engineer, got below, he found this situation plus a hole back near the stern with forty-five tons per hour of water coming through it. That is more water than the pumps in the shaft alley could handle. Chief Valentine was the first to dive down eight feet below the level of the water in the stern and attempt to plug the hole. After twenty-four hours they finally got most of the leaking stopped, but when they had a chance to look around they found five of the eight bearings on the propeller shaft a total loss and the 157-foot shaft itself bent all over the place. Valentine carved new bearings out of wood and with the aid of four hydraulic jacks borrowed from the army he connived that huge twisted shaft back to where it should have been. Hoses rigged up to cool at the points of greatest stress. Bracing chopped out of wooden timbers. "How high was the water when all this was going on?" I asked him. "Oh, it was up to your neck," he said. "Did you think about abandoning ship?" I wanted to know. "Yes, I thought about it, but I never abandon a ship until the water gets up to my chin."

'This was the ship which I had chosen to get me back to England. The terrific force of the detonation had blown the whistle so much out of whack that it wouldn't blow. Nevertheless we blew four blasts of steam, no sound, just steam, upon joining up with the rest of the ships in our convoy, England bound. I have come to the conclusion that the Merchant Navies were in there pitching with the rest.'

GEORGE WHEELER, NBC

The Royal Navy was 'in there pitching' too, but in a more active role than that of universal provider:

12 June 1944

'In this wood, just ahead of the British position, which on the map looked to be about half a mile square in area, was a concentration of enemy forces, and into this wood the *Warspite* poured fifteen-inch salvoes. Every shell fired from one of the fifteen-inch guns weighed a ton . . . there was sixty tons of high explosive poured into that little wood fifteen miles away from the ship. When the guns fired at once, the great 35,000-ton battleship gave a tremendous shudder. Everything on board that can fall or break loose has to be fastened or battened down when the ship goes into action. Cabin doors in the bridge have to be removed or the blast that rushes from end to end of the ship when she fires would splinter the panelling. Ears have to be plugged with cotton-wool.

'The naval bombardment razed the wood and blasted the tanks off the face of the earth. Some of the tanks were left burning, and the heat was so intense that from 3000 feet the pilots could see the whole outline of the white-hot tanks through the dense black smoke which came up from the battered wood.'

ANDREW COWAN, CBC, AND BILL HERBERT, CBC

The German West Wall had been decisively breached. The secrets of its construction were open secrets now – ripped and torn open by the storm of bomb and shell, and then cleaned up by engineers and ground forces:

7 June 1944

'Any suggestion that the West Wall was a myth, or that it was largely a bluff, is wrong. It's wrong by our battle reports, and it's wrong by the stories of the wounded who fell in breaching it.

'Imagine the heaviest steel picket fence you ever saw on a country estate. That's what one of the obstacles looks like. The soldier calls it Element C. Units of this fence, which is deeply sunk into the ground, weigh a ton and a half and some have steel rollers attached so that they can be towed round from one place to another. Sections can be linked together to make a continuous fence. They're primarily an anti-tank obstacle. So are the great lengths of steel embedded in concrete and sticking four and a half feet out of the ground. Their purpose is to expose the bellies of tanks to gunfire. There are the usual hedgehogs and vertical steel joists bedded in a six-foot thickness of concrete.

'But the bombed steel mills of Germany couldn't supply enough metal for all these defensive needs so they fell back on wood. They set up tripods of logs under water to trap the "ducks", which would be impaled if they ran on to them. But never did the Germans anticipate a landing at anything but high tide. Gone then were their hopes of landing-craft foundering and blowing up on their cunning obstacles just below high-water mark. Gone their hopes of a shattered armada with ripped entrails strewn along the beaches.'

JOSEPH DRISCOLL AND DAVID MACNICOLL, COMBINED PRESS

9 June 1944

'The part of the French coast on which our troops landed and fought their way inland was a good sample of the West Wall. Prior to operations, it is true to say that you could not have put a pin down on any part of that coast which was not under direct fire from machine-guns and mortars, or under fire from heavy guns. The wall was breached by bombardment by the Allied Navies and Air Forces, and it was cleaned up by the soldiers who went ashore under fire. The Germans knew that no fortification however strong could stop a determined assault concentrated on one sector of the coast. The purpose of the West Wall was to slow down the occupation of the beaches, and therefore to slow down the build-up, so that their own build-up of troops in that area would be faster than ours. Then they could meet us in the field with superior forces and drive our army back into the sea. That, broadly speaking, was the meaning of the repeated boast to drive us into the sea.

'There were, however, surprises for the defenders. One was the tactical surprise achieved at H-hour, another was the width of the beach-head. A third was the strength of the landings. But nothing was left to chance. Along this coast there were concreted defence-posts linked together into strong-points. These in turn linked into strong-point groups, whose crossfire supported each other, and which were equipped with light and heavy anti-tank guns and anti-aircraft guns; one of these strong-point groups held out for a long time on D-Day. Then there were the divisional coast-defence sectors. They are self-contained with underground passages, heavily concreted ammunition chambers, concreted gun emplacements, concrete several feet thick; and all the other defensive tricks of the Todt organisation. And, just last winter, Rommel inspected the defences which we have breached along the Normandy coast, and some of the emplacements on this coastal strip were rebuilt this year. There were minefields round the strong-points, anti-tank pits and anti-personnel areas between the strong-points, and low-lying ground was flooded. Battle reports tell of our soldiers wading waist-deep through flooded fields.'

ROBERT BARR

In spite of every obstacle, we were in. The 'lodgement-area' held. The sea-lanes held. We were back in France. As the reports came through, the detail of the story gradually filled in. It was a story of spirited heroism, of determination, of ingenuity appropriate to its high occasion; and it was a story not without its own particular sort of grim humour:

11 June 1944
'I landed in Normandy with the first glider forces in the invasion, before dawn on D-Day. The aerial procession was a sight I shall never forget. The sky looked like a giant Christmas tree, aglow with heaving clusters of red and green lights.

'Great balls of fire started to stream through our glider as we circled to land. I loosened my safety belt to remove my Mae West and could not get it fastened in the excitement. I was thrown to the floor as our glider smashed and jarred on the earth, slid across the field, and crashed into a ditch. For a moment I lay half stunned, but the red-hot zip of machine-gun bullets an inch or two above my head revived me in a hurry. I took a wild dive out of the emergency door and fell into a ditch, waist-deep in stinking water overlaid with scum. We had landed in a strongly defended zone several miles from our designated point. Lights still glowed in the glider. There was a deafening crash: a mortar shell had split it in half.

'I don't know why, but I looked at my watch. It was 4.15 am. Mortars and machine-guns chattered. I was – and I admit it – in a panic. My one desire was to get back home. I must have got out of the glider on the wrong side because I was all alone. For a moment I thought of all my friends and wondered what the office would think if it failed to get any dispatches from me. I wrote myself off as a dead loss – literally and figuratively. I clung to the mud and prayed. In my crawling I met Lieutenant-Colonel Charles Schellhammer of New York. He had been in my glider and I felt a little better. I had lost my tin hat. Lieutenant-Colonel Schellhammer ordered me to go back for it. I suddenly hated him with a black venom, but I dived back and got it.

'That afternoon the area was cleared of snipers and we reached a little town which had just been captured by Americans. Those khaki uniforms were the loveliest sight I had ever seen. An old Frenchwoman came out with a bottle of cognac which I gulped for medicinal purposes only.

' "The Boche has gone. The war is over," she said. Ten minutes later the Germans counter-attacked and the war started all over again. Eager to keep out of trouble I hiked for the woods and spent a miserable night with an American colonel and a very dolorous sow in a clump of super-sharp raspberry bushes. Then I proceeded to the HQ establishment. It was a hike along the hedges of about three miles, and I know I shall be permanently humpbacked from keeping my head down. A sergeant who watched me from a distance introduced me to his friends as the "best in the hedge-crawling business". It is an honour I am proud to accept. Whatever else, correspondents do make some contribution to the war effort. I calculate the Germans used about 5000 rounds of ammunition on me that first day.'

MARSHALL YARROW, REUTER

CHAPTER III
Moving In

'Welcome to the Continent'

As the first week of the invasion ended it was clear that the German threat to throw back the Allied forces instantly into the sea had passed into history as an unfulfilled promise. A firmly occupied coastal area now stretched continuously for sixty miles, and forward troops were already moving out beyond the protective cover of the Navy's guns. On the right the Americans were beginning their great drive towards Cherbourg. Round Caen and in the Orne Valley British and Canadian troops, in intensely bitter fighting, were drawing in German reserves piecemeal. A quarter of a million of Rommel's men had been swept into the battle without achieving a sustained full-scale counter-attack, and Montgomery still held the initiative. The only role available to the Germans was an obstructive one, for their reinforcements from beyond the Seine – which might have turned the scale – were held up by the systematic bombing of the Seine bridges:

15 June 1944

'Day by day now we're watching the whole course of the river for signs that the enemy is trying to rebuild bridges or to lay pontoons across, and he is doing neither. The bridges are too pulverised to be worth the rebuilding, and he knows that to start laying pontoons is to court another sharp and accurate attack from the air.

'To fly along the course of the Seine is to see a succession of proofs of the power of accurate bombing. There are the two great parallel bridges of Rouen, one cut as though a huge knife has sliced through it, and the other slipping and sagging into the water; and at Oissel, just outside Rouen, where the main line crosses the Seine over an island to enter the city, not only has one-half of the structure disappeared, but the whole length of the track where it traverses the island is lost in a shambles of rubble and craters. Nothing will cross the Seine at Rouen for a long time to come, until someone dares to put down pontoons.

'And so it is, east and west along the river – at Courseulles, where you can't count the bomb craters that lie in a great network round the remaining jagged lengths of the bridge, and at Vernon, where one-half of the road bridge slopes rather apologetically straight down into the river to meet its own shadow in the morning sun. And so it is all the way up the Seine to Pontoise.'

RICHARD DIMBLEBY

This isolation of the Normandy 'box', by bombing communications over first the Seine and then the Loire, threw a decisive emphasis on the fact that, from the German point of view, the Allies had landed too much too quickly. The traditional advantage of the repelling forces, in weight of metal and speed of focus, had been denied by the Allied onslaught from the air and by the ability of the Navy to bring in a great bulk of supplies swiftly and with negligible losses, and incidentally to support the land forces with their guns. The Navy's contribution was personally inspected by Winston Churchill when he crossed to Normandy on 12 June, less than a week after D-Day:

13 June 1944
'I travelled with Mr Churchill on his visit to Normandy yesterday.

'As we neared the French coast we spotted the beach area by the thick clusters of silvery barrage balloons floating high in the sunlight.

'Admiral Sir Philip Vian came aboard, and we went inshore in a motor launch to inspect the hundreds of small craft that were working along the beach. Many of the sailors were stripped to the waist and suntanned; some had a seven days' growth of beard on their chins – beards just as old as the Second Front. About a quarter of a mile from the shore we transferred to a "duck" and drove through the water and up on the beach where General Montgomery was waiting with three jeeps. As Mr Churchill made his appearance – literally right out of the water – soldiers and sailors stared for a few moments before they realised just what had happened. After lunch we inspected the whole British and Canadian sector of the beach-head from the sea, sailing inshore. It seemed half the fleet were lying just offshore shelling the German positions.

'*Nelson* and *Ramillies* were there, and cruisers and monitors and destroyers. The *Kelvin* edged her way past *Nelson* and *Ramillies* and took up a position right on the German flank. Here we slowed down, and the order was given: "Three salvoes into the German lines."

'Mr Churchill, cigar in the corner of his mouth, and his sea cap on the back of his head, smiled and raised his binoculars. And then the guns of HMS *Kelvin* began to pound the German positions.'

ROBERT BARR

Not only the capital ships but small vessels too, the LCGs – landing-craft guns – play an important part in close bombardment. Moving in to about a thousand yards from the shore, the ship takes its instructions by radio from a forward observer ashore:

19 June 1944

' "Enemy troop concentration so-and-so," he says, and gives a map reference. Perhaps our own troops are on three sides of the area, so you put your first round short in a house on the beach which is on the right line. "Up three hundred," says the observer, "otherwise OK." So you creep on to the target while the corrections come in. "Up a hundred, right so many degrees." And while all your interest is on this shoot, the first German shell bursts with a whoomph 200 yards away on the port bow.

' "Both guns load, load, load," says the gunnery officer. More corrections, and two splashes from the German battery. They are much closer. Then the observer tells you that you are on the target. "Bang away for fifteen minutes," he says. "Give 'em hell."

'So you shoot away for all the marine gun-crews are fit, with one eye on the smoke rising above the wood you are shelling and with the other on the enemy bursts.

' "They've got a nice bracket on us there. They'll be too damn close in a minute or two," somebody says.

'You look at your watch. Two minutes to go. "Get ready to make smoke," orders the captain.

'Your eyes are full of spent cordite and you are going deaf. A German shell whistles down beside you and the marine gunnery officer speaks into his telephone. "Check, check, check," he says, and we cease fire.

' "Make smoke number one, starboard thirty, emergency full ahead," and you steam out. The German battery drops a few more shells astern, and then leaves you alone.

'A few minutes later, if you're lucky, you get a signal from the observer. "Thank you very much," he says; "a very nice shoot, our troops are moving in now." And you make back "It was a pleasure" and drop the hook for breakfast.'

LIEUT. MAURICE BROWNE, RNVR

By the second day the West Wall had lost all its effectiveness, but here and there an isolated strong-point held out. One heavily fortified position, at Douvres, was bypassed by the Canadians on the first day, but continued to hold out until 17 June:

17 June 1944

'There is one German strong-point which is still holding out within six miles of the Normandy coast and many miles behind our front line. The Navy have had a try at smashing it. The Air Force had a try. But still the German garrison held out. We've called off all big-scale attempts to clear it up because the commander in the area has ruled that no heavy casualties must be risked in smashing it. But the point is that this strong-point of the West Wall which the Canadians swept past in the first day is still intact. All you can see of it is ordinary fields, with a few grass mounds here and there indicating defence points. You can see a concrete tower hidden amongst the trees, and through binoculars you can see the signs: "Achtung. Minen." Beware of mines.

'This is a sample of what the Germans hoped to prepare for us along this coast. We've surrounded it, we've shelled it, we've bombed it, and it's still unopened.'

ROBERT BARR

It did not, however, remain unopened much longer. On the same night a party of Marine Commandos and assault engineers – with the loss of only one man – forced the Germans to come out and surrender:

18 June 1944

'You have heard of that colossal strong-point just along the coast at Douvres where getting on for 200 Germans held out till last night.

That's a place to see. Somebody this morning called it an inverted skyscraper. That's not an unreasonable description. Fifty feet and more into the ground it goes – four storeys deep. On the surface you barely notice it. The top's almost flush with the ground. But going down those narrow concrete stairways you think of going into the vaults of the Bank of England. And the Germans did themselves well down below there – central heating, electric light, hot water, air conditioning, radios, telephones, comfortable well-furnished rooms and offices, well-equipped workshops and ample supplies of food and ammunition. The Germans who were standing here on this ground fourteen days ago certainly must have thought that they had little to fear, and yet what a change now!

'I'm looking towards the bay now, it is really an almost unbelievable sight. It's stiff with shipping. Warships, landing-craft, merchant vessels – everything right down to motor-launches and small boats. There they are, their signal lights winking in the late evening sun, an occasional siren hooting. Overhead, the sky – there's hardly a cloud to be seen anywhere; but the sky's picked out with silver barrage balloons, as thick as currants in a pre-war Christmas cake. And of course we've got our air cover; they're up there now, as they are every moment of the day. And so, on this ground where a fortnight ago the Germans were masters, tonight the Allies are in complete control. I stood by the roadside yesterday and watched the men and machines and supplies rolling in. And a soldier beside me – I don't know who he was – just turned and said: "Once you've seen all this, you know we just can't help winning this war." That's how we all feel here.'

FRANK GILLARD

The worsening weather over the Channel affected Allied air cover. To offset this the first Allied airfield in France became operational:

14 June 1944

'Earlier this morning, the two emergency landing strips, where allied fighters have been able to touch down to refuel and re-arm over the past two or three days, became fully fledged airfields, and the Allied Expeditionary Airforce now has fighter wings operating from French soil. The airfield I'm on just now is Number One, the first. They've got three wings of Spitfires operating from it, and my first glimpse of it very early this morning was to see a great billowing cloud of pinky-brown dust shoot up over a ridge of green fields. Well, now, out here that might have meant quite a number of things: machine-gun strafing, convoys on the move and so on, but this was a bigger cloud of dust, much bigger than usual. It meant that a Spitfire had touched down and was swinging round to its dispersal, sending the dust of this newly laid landing field flying away behind it.

'It's perhaps just as well that our airfields have started to be operational today. I understand from one of our pilots, who arrived here very early this morning, that the weather is pretty bad over England and that we can't keep up the air umbrella, at least not to the extent to which we've been accustomed. Here's an outfit going off now to patrol, just as I'm speaking, running smoothly along this runway which, just a couple of days ago, was part of the green fields of Normandy. Taking off now, and it's airborne.

'The fact that the weather is bad occasionally and we can't keep up that air umbrella to the full extent doesn't matter so much now that this has happened. The Spitfires are patrolling the beach area and the country inland to Caen, taking off from this field, up here in Normandy, and coming back to it when their patrol is over. Two of them just going off now, going very, very slowly, smoothly along the brown runway.

'When an American patrol fought its way into Cherbourg yesterday, they were shooting their way along an alley, when a Frenchman suddenly ran out from a gate towards them. They nearly shot him because he was wearing a steel helmet that looked German, but he shouted "Friend", and then he said "I have four Americans here". Here they are to tell it to you in person by means of my BBC microphone.

'We'll begin with the first pilot, Lieutenant Harvey Doering, aged 24, of Wakarusa, Indiana. Go ahead, Lieutenant. How did you come to find yourselves in Cherbourg?'

DOERING: Well, we're the crew of a two-carrier aircraft. We were sent over as part of a force to drop paratroops further south in the Cherbourg peninsula. We dropped our stick of troopers all right and then turned for home. That was at 1.30 am on 6 June, D-Day. Shortly after that we ran into heavy flak and were hit. The burst killed the port engine and damaged the port wing. We were too low to maintain altitude or bail out so we just had to crash land. We hit in a field and bounced over a hedgerow. The plane ground-looped in a second field, and I'm afraid that's all I can remember of that. I was knocked out.

MELVILLE: Well, the second pilot can carry on the tale. Here he is, Lieutenant Thomas R. Westrope aged 22, of Harlan, Iowa. Carry on, Lieutenant.

WESTROPE: Well, after the crash, first impulse was to find out if everybody was all right. We were all shocked and cut up a bit but otherwise OK. We took our first-aid kits and rations out of the ship and destroyed all the radio equipment, and set fire to the plane. Then we went to a hedgerow in the next field and laid low in a ditch. We heard the Germans nearby and kept very quiet. We slept in the ditch for the rest of the night, or tried to sleep – it was very cold. The next morning, about ten o'clock, a French lady came and looked at us. We told her we were Americans and managed to indicate to her by gestures what we wanted, and that we wanted to be hidden.

She signed to us to wait and went away. She came back and for the next two days and nights she and her friends hid us in various fields and finally in a haystack. They brought us wine, milk and food. After a day in the haystack a Frenchman in the underground Resistance movement took us to his home. It was pretty good to get into a house again.

MELVILLE: Yes, it must have been pretty good to get into a house again. And how long were you there? Well, I'll let Tech Sergeant Smith carry on. Technical Sergeant Smith, is it?

SMITH: Yes, sir, James E. Smith of Chicago. Well, after we got into the house they gave us food, brought us some mattresses and we went to sleep for quite a long time. It was really good. We stayed there two and a half weeks. The French people treated us with a respect and kindness that were overwhelming. They really made us feel at home.

MELVILLE: Two and a half weeks? What did you do all that time?

SMITH: Well, we played pinochle and took turns doing the dishwashing. Of course, later on our chief entertainment was listening to the American guns getting nearer and nearer.

MELVILLE: Yes, I should think the sound of those American guns was pretty good. Did you know what it meant?

SMITH: Well, yes, the French people brought us news. We knew the Americans were attacking Cherbourg. Those French people were wonderful. They risked their lives to save ours.

MELVILLE: I suppose some of the fortifications that the Americans were bombing and shelling were pretty close to you?

SMITH: They certainly were. It was pretty terrifying at times. We were all hoping they knocked the devil out of the Heinies but still hoped they'd miss us. Every now and then a Frenchman would rush in and say "Many Germans kaput" that means many Germans killed. Well I think I'd better hand over now to the fourth member of our crew.

MELVILLE: OK, what's your name, Sergeant?

DILISTOVIK: Sergeant John A. Dilistovik age 21, of Hoboken, New Jersey.

MELVILLE: Well, Sergeant Dilistovik, will you carry on with the story?

DILISTOVIK: Well, yesterday we were sitting in the kitchen, we heard a machine-gun go off pretty nearby, followed by rifle fire. So we immediately hit the floor and stayed that way for a few hours and all the time there was heavy machine-gun, there was rifle and tank fire in the streets. We had an idea the Americans were there. We were sure of it when we heard a voice holler "There they are over there, let's get them". The rifle fire went on and after a few minutes a Frenchman came in and notified us that the street was in American hands. We went out of the house and ran over to the Americans with our friend in the lead. And boy, were we glad to see those doughboys.

MELVILLE: I'll bet you were. You were on the right side of them again at last.

DILISTOVIK: That's right, I guess we'd been shot at by just about every weapon in the American army. Boy, I'd sure hate to be a Heinie.'

ALAN MELVILLE

The sea and air forces and the special airborne and assault units had done what was required of them to give the Army the conditions of a straight fight on level terms and on a big scale. The task of carrying on what had been successfully begun passed more and more to the ordinary infantryman:

16 June 1944

'I think that one of the things I shall never forget is the sight of the British infantry, plodding steadily up those dusty French roads towards the front, single file, heads bent down against the heavy weight of all the kit piled on their backs, armed to the teeth; they were plodding on, slowly and doggedly towards the front with the sweat running down their faces and their enamel drinking-mugs dangling at their hips; never looking back and hardly ever looking to the side – just straight in front and down a little on to the roughness of the road; while the jeeps and the lorries and the tanks and all the other traffic went crowding by, smothering them in great billows and clouds of dust which they never even deigned to notice. That was a sight that somehow caught at your heart.'

WING COMMANDER L. A. NICKOLLS, RAF

Marching, digging in, fighting, and brewing up indispensable quantities of tea, the British infantryman soon had the measure of life in Normandy as it was lived in June 1944; and the stain of German words began to fade from that war-torn countryside as he got to work on boards and walls with the familiar stubs of chalk and dabs of paint:

14 June 1944

'He's settling down pretty well. He has been living in a slit trench for the past week, and he has taken a good many speedy dives into it by this time. But in the last couple of days, when things have been quieter here, he's found time to make life a little more comfortable. He's winkled the snipers out of the ruined houses, and he's probably now living in the comparative luxury of a cellar or an outhouse. He's found where the nearest water-supply is; he's found that Madame, at the corner of the village street, takes in washing and lets you have it back the following night. One or two eggs have appeared mysteriously on the menu, and someone in our MT Section has just come in from a recce – with a rabbit. The food from the first meal on D-Day has

117

been excellent. The cooks have done wonders with compo rations and with sand getting into everything and shell splinters flying all around the place.

'The flow of men and supplies up through the beaches still goes on day and night; but now there are traffic signs everywhere, military policemen at each crossing, and a one-way traffic system which is alleged to relieve congestion. The placards, marked with the one word "Minen", have been turned round and they now read "Verges clear to twenty feet". A few shops have opened up rather cautiously in the less shattered villages, and the Tommies are getting along fine with the language, the inhabitants, and "la bière" – which, I imagine, consists of 99 per cent water.'

ALAN MELVILLE

19 June 1944

'If you've got a brother or a husband or a sweetheart in Normandy today there's a fair chance you might see your name riding along the dusty roads, your name on a truck, on a lorry, on a bulldozer, on a tank somewhere in France, just a simple name carefully painted on a windscreen, on a tank turret. Generally it's just a simple name – Mary, The Only Helen, Joy, Gladys, and so on.

'But there are other signs up; perhaps the most common is a phrase that always brings a smile to the faces of the troops. It's a phrase that would be quite incomprehensible to anyone but a Britisher. You see it everywhere. "When in doubt, brew up." There are variations on it, of course. I saw one very formidable vehicle the size of a small house with "The Brew-Up Boys from Clapham" written on it. At a crossroads where the shattered houses showed that here was an enemy aiming point, a black notice on a yellow board read: "If you must brew your tea, don't do it here: because you might get hurt." And at that crossroads, as at most crossroads in France, there is the man who only yesterday paced your High Street, the military policeman, doing a grand job controlling what must be some of the busiest roads in the world.'

GUY BYAM

20 June 1944

'It's an ill wind, you know, that blows nobody any good. The whole area round the little town of Tilly is just a nightmare for anybody who's got to move around up there. There are mines and booby-traps everywhere; but this is a story of a stretcher-bearer who turned all this mining and trapping to his own purposes. During the battle he found a nest of twelve eggs. There was no time to take them then, and he knew that other people might stumble on them at any moment; so he found a piece of board and scrawled on it a notice which said "Booby Trap". That notice he left propped against the nest of eggs. Well, when the fighting had died down and he had a moment to spare, he went back to the nest and there were the eggs just ready for the pan.'

FRANK GILLARD

The work of the glider-pilots was finished early in the campaign. They had landed and reinforced the airborne troops on the opening day, and now those troops were securely linked with the beaches and therefore with bulk-transport by sea. Some of the gliders had carried, not men, but loads of ammunition. After the original landings on D-Day a group of American glider-pilots, waiting to cross to England, watched Lieutenant Warren Ward of Minnesota fly in with three tons of high explosives – a cargo which caused some consternation on the beaches as Lieutenant Ward flew over. However, he put his cargo down safely, and was then given the job of assembling and conducting the glider-pilots who were waiting to return by sea:

14 June 1944

'I was told to take all my glider-pilots – I'm a glider operational officer – I was told to take them down to the beach-head. I was also told that there were Germans in between ourselves and the beach-head; so I got them all together and I asked them if they wanted to take a chance on it – and they said they'd be very happy to. A major came along in a jeep; he said: "There's a machine-gun nest right up ahead, and don't you dare go up there." And I turned around and asked my boys what they thought of it. They said: "Let's go up." So we went up. We went up there and the machine-gun nest never did do an awful lot. We finally wiped those out, and we captured a few prisoners – the machine-gunners: that cleared up that particular road. In the meantime there was some P47s dive-bombing right next to us, and orange flames were flashing up in the air and we were very excited about everything, and thought that was a wonderful deal. And we had all these prisoners. And we finally got down there, and then there was some strafing by JU 88s. And it was quite worrisome for a little while, because there wasn't anything much we could do about it, they were just strafing us and going back and forth across the beach; and our P47s came over and they ran those things out. I went up to the Beach Control Officer and I said that I have a hundred and thirteen glider-pilots down here (or think I have a hundred and thirteen); may we have transportation back to England? The Beach Control Officer looked at me and he says: "Are you the one that came over about nine o'clock in the morning?" "Yeah, that's me." He said: "I certainly will see that you get transportation back; I was never so glad to see anyone in all my life." '

LIEUT. WARREN WARD, US FORCES

Inevitably the Germans relied to some extent on the tricks that had been so successful in 1940. The broadcasting in English of orders to withdraw was tried, but now it was too old a ruse. The best reply came from Major-General R. N. Gale of the British 6th Airborne Division who announced that no order to withdraw would be issued by radio, nor – so far as he was concerned – by any other means. The weapon of propaganda was equally unsuccessful; in some cases the speed and vehemence of attack, which had broken the West Wall, overran the psychological defences as well:

15 June 1944

'A German attempt to direct a propaganda offensive in this sector was frustrated by a British patrol the other day, which killed a captain, a sergeant, and captured a corporal of a propaganda unit which had been sent from Lille with loudspeaker equipment for front-line broadcasting.

'The corporal spoke excellent English, but his prepared propaganda material was extremely crude. It followed the usual Nazi line of trying to divide the Allies. He carried a leaflet entitled "Welcome to the Continent", and it contained this very choice passage. And here I quote it:

' "Who on earth," it said, "put into your head the idea that America or Britain are threatened from the Continent? Have we ever attempted to invade your coasts?" '

CHESTER WILMOT

There was no doubt about the warmth of our 'welcome' on the Continent – in both senses of the word – but neither could anyone overlook the terrible paradox that to many French people our first gifts were the ruin and devastation of the battlefield. It was regrettable, it was unavoidable, and there was no lack of official spokesmen to say so; but other armies had had their official spokesmen suitably tear-stained. The true measure of forbearance towards the property of a friend, and of respect for what is sacred, is in the behaviour of the ordinary soldier. No ministerial pledge, however sincere, could have been so reassuring as the awkward, honest decency of individual soldiers like Corporal Tom Galeen of Wigan. Corporal Galeen had to solve the problem of clearing snipers from a church after small-arms fire had failed to do so:

15 June 1944

' "We were told," said Galeen, "to clear the church steeple, but we couldn't get at it, so I took my piat into the upstairs bedroom of the house opposite, stuck it up on the window-sill, and let fly at the tower. The bursts knocked half the top off. And later we found twelve dead Jerries up there; some had been killed by our Stens, and the piat had got the rest."

' "Was the church badly damaged?" asked the colonel. "Not inside it wasn't, sir," said Galeen. "We just knocked the top off; we wouldn't have touched it if the snipers hadn't been there. And when I went in, sir, I did take my hat off." '

CHESTER WILMOT

CHAPTER IV
Coming To Grips

'The guerre – nicht bon'

As German hopes of a swift, annihilating counter-attack faded away, the opposing armies developed the pattern of what was to become the decisive battle west of the Seine. To the east British and Canadian forces were fighting a slogging battle in the wooded Bocage country around Tilly-sur-Seulles for control of the Caen centre of communications. Day by day Montgomery and Rommel raised the stakes for the possession of Caen, until the main tank forces of both sides were drawn into one of the grimmest struggles of the war. To the west, after a fierce struggle for Carentan, the Cherbourg peninsula was cut by the US 9th Division, which fought its way through to the west coast near Barneville on 17 June. While the Allied 'build-up' had suffered by a gale in the Channel, of a violence unprecedented at this season of the year, the German High Command also had its difficulties. It had to provide against the possibility of a second landing, which was anticipated in the Pas de Calais, and this reduced the scale of reinforcements that could be sent to Normandy. Further, the reinforcements that were sent were hampered and delayed by the Maquis and by the relentless and increasing attacks of the Allied Air Forces. In the race for local superiority the Germans were unable to hold the whole line in sufficient strength. At Caen they were most sensitive to a drive aimed towards Paris, so it was here that they spent their armour as fast as it came to hand in a desperate effort to immobilise the main Allied thrust. In theory the Allies – denied the use of a port – should have lost the race for supplies. In fact, due largely to the 'Mulberry' harbours, it became possible for the Americans to exert superior pressure on the western flank, which Rommel had felt he could safely strip of the armour he needed for a more pressing urgency around Caen. A transcript of some telephone conversations, recorded in the secret log of the German Seventh Army, which fell into Allied hands later, throws a revealing light on German difficulties:

22 September 1944

'The first conversation is on the morning of 6 June, two hours after the Allied landings had begun. General Marcks, Commander of 84 Corps on the front south of Cherbourg, is speaking to the Chief of Staff [*Blumentripp*]. He says: "I urgently request mobile reserves for the area west of Caen." A few hours later the Chief of Staff of the Western Command is speaking to General Marcks; he strongly emphasises the desire of the Supreme Command, of Hitler himself, to have the enemy in the bridgehead completely annihilated by the night of 6 June. "This is imperative," he says, "because there is danger of additional sea and airborne landings in other areas; the beach-head must be cleaned up not later than tonight." The reply comes: "I'm afraid that is impossible." Repeatedly on that first day there are frantic demands for air support. On the morning of 7 June Rommel is speaking: "The counter-attack today," he says, "must succeed without fail." This seems to have been the counter-attack against the British and Canadians by the First SS Panzer Corps. The commander replies that he cannot attack because his men are pinned down by the Allied air attacks. Rommel interrupts harshly, and says: "Attack at once, using all three divisions." Rommel himself was deeply anxious because, to use his own words, "he expected larger landings in the Calais–Boulogne area in a few days". He thought our landings in Normandy were perhaps not much more than a feint. Powerful German reserves were held in the Calais area until it was too late. Time after time in these talks, day after day, till they became monotonous, there were demands for air support, and demands for reserves. The commanders in the field call for reserves; the Higher Command saves the reserves in case of new landings, and so the battle is lost. Hitler enters the picture several times a week; he always says the same thing, there must be no retreat, every man must fight and fall where he stands rather than give an inch of ground. Day after day some German general complains that movements of troops are paralysed by Allied fighter-bombers, or Typhoons, and there are signs of rigidity in the German mentality. One general complains in the critical days near Villieux that there are many Navy and Air Force troops in Brittany who are not being used. The reply comes: "They are not under my jurisdiction." As the Americans begin their breakthrough the Commander-in-Chief in the West [*von Runstedt*] telephones to Supreme Headquarters. He describes the seriousness of the situation with impressive eloquence. He says morale is suffering heavily, that French Maquis in the rear are growing bolder every day; that his signals are knocked out, and that orderly command is difficult. But always Hitler replies, angry and stubborn, "Every man must die where he stands." As we know, many Germans did die, rather than retreat.'

MATTHEW HALTON, CBC

In these first anxious weeks everything depended on the speed and volume of supplies coming to the beaches. Could the enormous improvisation of the 'Mulberry' scheme compensate in full for the lack of a major port, particularly as the storm had caused delay and as a full-scale battle was developing only a few miles inland? The results of the first days had been magnificent; now they had to be maintained week after week, in the face of whatever obstruction the enemy could provide. And all the time, as supplies passed through, the unloading and marshalling facilities of this incredible 'dockland' had to be extended and consolidated:

2 July 1944

'These beaches are no longer the ordinary sands like those you knew for peace-time holiday bathing. For the Royal Navy and the Army between them have simply taken hold of a coastal strip, miles long, and with bulldozers, dynamite and steam-rollers reshaped it wholesale to meet the needs of the great build-up. Today it combines the features of a military camp, a vast salvage dump, and the approaches to Wembley on Cup Final Day. Buildings have been demolished, gaps cut in the dunes, German mines, wire and obstacles removed, mounds and hollows levelled on the beaches, marshes drained, roads and tracks laid, bridges built, and here and there landing causeways pushed out into the shallows. Along the length of the beaches above the high-water mark runs a track, overlaid with matting, chestnut fencing, wide-meshed wire, and where there's clay about, with perforated steel planking, just above it rise the grass-tufted dunes. The dunes, beflagged with white ensigns and army colours and festooned with signal wires, are the headquarters of the naval and military beach groups, all of them first-line men, many there since D-Day. That is what I saw myself on the beaches; it's a typical scene.

'It's evening, an hour or more before high water, and for once in a way it's almost glassy calm. Out to sea lie the big ships – a sprawling city of masts and funnels that quite blot out the sea horizon. Transports, freighters, warships – there's a spurt of flame from the *Rodney*'s great sixteen-inch guns bombarding an inland target – yellow smoke drifts away, but we don't hear the explosion for fifteen seconds – another pause and a thump from miles inshore when the salvo lands. And all the time to and fro between ship and shore the amphibious ducks manned by the RASC are plying like so many water-beetles, unloading stores and carrying them up to the inland depots. In the shallows, the tank-landing ships, the big fellows, lie there open-mouthed like stranded whales. They came in on an earlier tide, dried out, and have been lying all day, their bow doors open, their ramps down, disgorging vehicles by the hundred. One by one now they shut their mouths and prepare to pull out as the water deepens round them. But there's a group of blue and white dazzle-painted craft out there waiting to come in – the LCTs, smaller tank and vehicle-landing craft. Aldis lamps wink from their bridges – and are answered from beachmasters on the dunes. Almost in line abreast just a few yards apart they come charging full speed ahead for the beaches. Naval commandos flag them in. The beachmaster gives them instructions through the loudhailer: "Hello, LCT 2012, do not unload until waders have recced the water in front of your door." The bow ramps drop with a splash. A wader – in bathing shorts or battledress, nobody minds which – steps through the few yards of shallow water to make sure that there's no sudden drop. He shouts, "Go ahead." And then the avalanche starts – trucks, jeeps, tanks, Bren-carriers, guns, limbers, trailers – they come streaming out, splash, rev up; through the shallows, on to the beaches, up to the carriage way. Keep on the move. Don't crowd the beaches. A big truck comes off the ramp and stops; water in its engines, steam pouring out. A REME armoured recovery vehicle or a bulldozer, the sort that can push over a house, goes wallowing in. A tow cable's hooked on and in less than a minute the truck's being yanked up the shore.'

MICHAEL STANDING

2 July 1944

'Today there is a fine cement roadway from the beach to the first lateral road; and tanks and mobile guns and lorries and ducks and jeeps are still pouring up it, shaking off the water like a collie dog after a swim. The cement and the concrete-mixing machine and the rails they've laid down – they were all left behind by the Germans, and they've been made good use of. The apparent chaos of the first few days has gone; the business of unloading supplies goes on smoothly and efficiently. But not without interruptions.

'There are two things I'd like to stress: one, that this tremendous influx of men and equipment is still going on, after three weeks, with every tide, day and night. You've only got to drive a few miles across the front with and against a never-ending stream of traffic to realise that we have now turned this part of Normandy into one colossal storehouse. And secondly: this job of getting supplies ashore and inland has been no picnic. On at least one sector of the beaches it has been – and still is being – carried out in the face of everything that the enemy can do to stop it.'

ALAN MELVILLE

The men of the Merchant Navy who brought in the precious cargoes ran great risks, with the stubborn calmness for which they are famous. Typical of many is this story of courage in a ship carrying 700 tons of ammunition within the range of German artillery in the first few days of the invasion:

10 July 1944

'The weather cleared and we were ordered to proceed in closer towards the beach. We were about half a mile off the shore when the first German shells started to fall ahead of the ship.

'The master decided to turn round and come out. A launch off the naval guard ship ordered us to follow him in close to the beach. So we went in with shells falling closer all the time.

'Royal Engineer stevedores started to discharge the ammunition into ducks and motor lorries. Half an hour later the first mortar bombs fell close to the ship, but we kept on discharging. Then a shell hit the stern. Orders were given to abandon ship. All the ship's company got safely ashore, but we had to run 300 yards along the beach through continual shellfire. Every time one came near we threw ourselves on our faces, generally into puddles. Then the shelling stopped; we went back to the ship and got a full sling of cargo out of the holds, then the shelling started again. The first shell missed, but the next five landed clean on the ship and the ammunition started to explode, and we thought it was time to get to hell out of it again.

'This time there was no coming back. We got safely away down rope ladders. One man jumped from the fo'c'sle head into what he thought was deep water and broke his neck The last man off was our Master, Captain James Craigie, who is sixty-three years old. He followed the Chief Engineer, who weighs sixteen stone, but came down a rope like a two-year-old.

'We stayed awhile at a Royal Marine camp which was shelled the whole time we were there. Then we came home, and we're waiting here for another ship.'

CHARLES PROSSER OF THE MERCHANT NAVY

A fortnight after the initial landings, General Bradley's First US Army had secured their cordon across the Cherbourg peninsula and were rapidly advancing on the first big port to come within the Allied grasp. Having failed to break out, the Germans fell back hurriedly to man the imposing fortifications that had been designed to protect Cherbourg against just such an attack as this from the rear. By 19 June the city of Cherbourg was under fire from American field artillery:

20 June 1944

'The American troops are moving so fast up practically the whole width of the Cherbourg peninsula that it's becoming quite a job to keep up with them. Tonight they're ringing the Germans round only a few miles from the city and port of Cherbourg. It's difficult to say at any given time exactly how near any of the advanced elements are to Cherbourg, but the nearest are probably now within four miles. The whole picture of the campaign in the peninsula has changed in the last three days. Then the Germans controlled about three-quarters of the area of the peninsula. Today barely a quarter is left to them. The eastern side of the peninsula and the main national highway up through Montebourg and Valognes bears all the signs of a battlefield – roads cut by bombs, trees and houses splintered by fire, men and cattle dead in the fields. I drove through this skeleton town of Montebourg today, and I couldn't find one whole house. Five miles farther on along a road where, for the first time, I noticed places where the Germans had laid mines, we came to the shattered centre of Valognes. A fortnight ago this had been one of the main German headquarters in the peninsula; now, from the twisted and broken German field gun at the corner as we entered the city to the plaster-covered floor of the Commanding General's office in the main civic building, with a photograph of Hitler crooked on the wall, it was an example of the power of Allied bombing and American shelling. These two towns of Valognes and Montebourg, and the country to the south and east of them, have been the main battlefields. On the western side of the peninsula the picture is different. Here there are more hills, and after the dense growth on the plains it's refreshing to get vistas across the greenery to little villages and church spires. But here the Germans have fought a running action that has been mostly running.'

ROBERT DUNNETT

20 June 1944

'Great credit for our surging advance towards Cherbourg must be given to our traffic control and truck transport. In all my trips to the front I've never seen a single American truck out of action for mechanical reasons. Our military police are all provided with explicit maps of their area, and do wonders rerouting our supply trucks into narrow wooded lanes and avoiding traffic snares. As each American command post moves forward to keep in touch with its advancing troops, our telephone linesmen work incessantly, taking down the wires and stringing them out anew to the most advanced positions. One of the favourite jokes of the American Signal Corps linesman is to call down scornfully from the top of the tallest tree and telegraph posts at our infantry trudging ahead on the dusty road to wisecrack, "Keep your heads down, boys, there are German snipers around." The heavily loaded infantry just look up wearily and sheepishly at the linesmen outlined against the sky and give them an appreciative grin.'

LARRY LESUEUR, CBS

After three days of hard fighting the Americans broke through the crescent of fortifications that shielded the city. This chain of concrete forts and pillboxes had been designed to withstand any assault, but the aggressive spirit of the American attack was too much for them. The secrets of their construction were cracked open, and the lavishly equipped U-boat pens followed a few days later after a period of mopping-up in the city itself:

25 June 1944

'German pillboxes were still burning from the attack of our flame-throwers. It was so hot within the pillboxes that German ammunition was popping right and left from the intense heat. The yellow scar of a

15-foot-deep anti-tank ditch wound its way across the wooded ridges; there were wide vistas of pulverised steel with craters big enough to hold a farmhouse – the result of our air bombardment. The most striking feature of the battlefield, however, was the concrete German fort – the walls six foot thick, they extended thirty feet or more below the earth's surface; apparently the Germans had first dug enormous holes in the ground, built the concrete blockhouses inside, and then they filled in the dirt around the underground fort.

'Covered trenches, now badly dented by our air bombardment, led to other underground pillboxes, of which only the round roofs appeared above ground, with apertures facing in every possible direction. These underground bomb-proof forts contained room after room; the only way the Germans could be driven out was for our men to poke explosives into the apertures on long poles, and this is exactly what they did. From one underground fortress alone 300 prisoners were taken, stunned by the explosion and panicked by our flame-throwers. The whole pattern of the German defences on the rear of Cherbourg appeared to be designed like a miniature Maginot Line, but in much greater depth.

'While I examined the captured German fort, parties of American engineers arrived by jeep, carrying huge charges of explosive. They placed them deep inside the concrete structures and blew them as wide open as an empty sardine can; that was done just in case the Germans might infiltrate back into the captured territory.'

LARRY LESUEUR, CBS

When the famous submarine pens at Cherbourg were inspected they revealed a twenty-foot thickness of reinforced concrete, designed to be absolutely impregnable to air bombardment:

30 June 1944

'In their gloomy depths German submarine men could service their U-boats without fear. There seemed to be nothing that the Germans had not provided for the comfort and well-being of the now defeated defenders of Cherbourg – wine, cognac, champagne, were theirs for the asking. They had good food in plenty, and you can see heavy-calibre shells stacked in rows, capable of sinking the entire Allied Navy. Every German barracks was fitted out with running water and electric heating devices. They had plenty of German propaganda books to read, and the walls were plastered with the German version of the pin-up girl, plump Frauleins in various stages of undress. All that the Germans lacked was the will to win, and from their unmailed letters to Germany you can tell that they were filled with fears of invasion and forebodings of doom, mainly because of the mighty Allied air fleet that thundered overhead incessantly.'

LARRY LESUEUR, CBS

The fall of Cherbourg gave the Allies their first big success on the soil of France. At the other end of the line, in the neighbourhood of Tilly and Hottot, there was very heavy fighting as the British Second Army pushed towards the Villers-Bocage-Caen road and the valley of the Odon. By 20 June, Tilly, which had changed hands several times, was firmly under British control:

20 June 1944

'From end to end we couldn't see a living soul in Tilly. We got out and walked from the crossroads up the street on the far side. It must have been a pleasant avenue a fortnight ago. Now the lime-trees on each side are blasted and twisted and dead. There were German guns overturned by the side of the road. A German half-track armoured car was still burning. A score or more of ploughs and horse-rakes and such had been dragged out of an agricultural implement stores and used to block the road. Now they've been just pushed aside. Our sappers have scrawled notices everywhere: "Keep to the centre of the road." It was death to touch anything there in Tilly this morning. We walked to the top of the street. The way was barred by a strip of white tape stretched right across the roadway. It bore a notice, "Mines". We looked out of Tilly, down the long straight road to the south. It was death-ridden, empty, deserted. Half a mile down there, the Germans were waiting.'

FRANK GILLARD

Frank Gillard takes cover while operating a midget recorder. Gillard became one of War Report's most senior correspondents, forming a successful working relationship with the British commander Field Marshall Montgomery.

From the Tilly sector, on Sunday 25th, a feint attack opened the Odon offensive. On Monday the real attack began, aimed to cross the Odon south-west of Caen, in the direction of Maltot and seize the high ground (Hill 112) between the Odon and the Orne; then, if possible, to go on across the Orne and outflank Caen on the south. The general idea was to pin down German armour which might otherwise have responded to the frantic appeals of the crumbling Cherbourg garrison. While the Americans closed in on the great port, two new British divisions which had been held in England throughout the African and Italian campaigns – the 15th Scottish and the 11th Armoured – went into action for the first time and fought magnificently.

Attacking in the early morning the infantry got through extensive minefields. The following tanks were less successful, but by the next day our forward troops had reached the Odon:

27 June 1944

'Two hours ago before I left the front I listened on the tank's radio to a signal from our forward troops. They'd just reached the River Odon, and they were already established astride the main road from Caen to Villers-Bocage. They'd got through by exploiting a weak spot in the German defence. Yesterday we drove the enemy back from their main positions, and forced a passage through their minefields. Through this the tanks and more infantry moved yesterday evening, and fanned out in the country where the Germans had no minefields or prepared defences. Today was the critical day; the day when we had to expect German counter-attacks. They came, but they were held. On the left, at Tourville, the Germans counter-attacked four times last night, in vain. Then, this morning, the Germans moved up to attack our right flank. At the same time our troops there were also moving up to attack. The two attacks met, and a long battle has been fought all day for command of some high ground south of Cheux. We were checked there, but the general advance wasn't checked. To the east, our infantry and armour found a spot where they could get through. They forced a narrow corridor between the main German forces. The Germans tried to batter in the flanks of this corridor, but our tanks held them off, and the spearhead thrust on southwards to the Odon.

'This exploitation of enemy weakness is the outstanding feature of this attack. You see, the Germans are weak in infantry now that we've broken their main defence line – between Tilly-sur-Seulles and Caen. And they're using armour and their Panzer Grenadiers to try and plug the gaps. But today they couldn't plug all the gaps. Where they're strong – where they're strong in armour – we're content to hold them off with anti-tank guns and tanks hidden in woods and orchards and used in an anti-tank role. Where we find they're weak we're hitting harder and still harder. It's too early to say that we've achieved a real breakthrough, for there's still a lot of German armour about and it's difficult to destroy in wooded country where it can't easily be seen.

'But, in spite of this, today we've not only beaten off the counter-attacks, but we've driven a corridor deeper into enemy territory – and we have the power to widen it and drive it still deeper. Already we're three miles south of Caen on the west side, and the Germans in Caen tonight must be feeling rather uncomfortable.'

CHESTER WILMOT

While the leading infantry established a narrow corridor through to the river, supporting troops waited to follow them:

30 June 1944

'I walked round quietly and talked to some of these troops. One group of them sitting in the back of a truck on upturned petrol tins were playing cards, one or two others were filling in the time shaving. There were several fires going where opportunists were seizing the break as a favourable moment for a brew-up.

'Some troops were writing letters, others were reading papers just received from home, some of them papers a week old or more. They seemed to be more interested in the accounts of the fighting on this front than in anything else. Here and there officers were bending over their maps, maps spread out as often as not on the conveniently flat top of a jeep bonnet, and they were marking in the latest positions.

'You could hear the strange distorted voices calling back over the radio in signals trucks as men up there actually in the battle already passed back the news of their progress.

'Many men were improving their camouflage, putting more green twigs in the netting round their steel helmets, cutting small branches off the trees and fastening them on their trucks and tanks. In one corner of a field quite a crowd of men were squatting round listening to a radio set which was tuned in to one of the BBC programmes. I drink it was a Jack Benny programme; it was a good show anyway and those troops were vastly amused. They were laughing at the wisecracks just as if they were sitting in a London music-hall without a care in the world. Then suddenly there was a crackle and some army loudspeaker came to life. A great bellowing voice shouted down the road over those fields, "All men must stand to now. Prepare to move." '

FRANK GILLARD

By 28 June the success of the first phase of the Odon offensive was assured. In three days of heavy fighting British troops had advanced seven miles:

28 June 1944

'Tonight we hold a thumb-shaped wedge measuring three miles across at its widest, and running nearly five miles deep into the heart of the German defences. The tip of that wedge of ours is only about two and a half miles from the banks of the River Orne. The Germans have lost the Odon River now. We have a massive force of infantry and armour well forward of it, pouring across over bridges near Gavrus and Mondranville.

'And they've lost one more of those vital lateral communication lines. So our men tonight are astride the main Caen–Orne road, only a mile or so from the fair-sized town of Evrécy. The area behind the German lines today must have been in a state of turmoil, for the enemy has been rushing troops up from everywhere – infantry and tanks, throwing them in piecemeal in an effort to stem our thrust. This fact that we've forced the enemy to give battle at our dictation is almost as important as the territorial gains that our men have secured. The Germans have been jabbing fiercely at us all round our salient today, but not one single thrust has had any success. There are still areas where the fighting is fluid; the Germans still hold one or two dominating positions from which their 88s and their mortars are making trouble, but by and large our advance is firm.

'As the battle develops it's becoming more and more an armoured affair, though the country is still not real tank country. So far it's believed we've knocked out sixty German tanks in this last few days. Our losses have been light. The British six-pounder and seventeen-pounder guns have been doing their stuff well.

'So Caen is being outflanked, but the enemy is not withdrawing. He contested every yard of a British advance to the north of the town this morning, but our men went through and seized a château that they'd tried to get three times before and failed. However, the Germans must be very worried tonight. If we reach the Orne they'll find it very difficult with us sitting across their communications to hold the front to the west.'

FRANK GILLARD

∽◌∾

The long narrow corridor, suddenly thrust forward, acted as a magnet to the German armour. Tanks intended to relieve Cherbourg were sucked into the furious fighting which now raged round the British salient:

28 June 1944

'The British corridor through to the River Odon is held even more strongly tonight. This morning the Germans were still holding several strong positions on the flanks, and they refused to withdraw in spite of our deep penetration with armour.

'But we continued to use the corridor, even though our vehicles had had to run the gauntlet of snipers here and there, and even though small groups of tanks have made a series of stabs at our flanks. Occasionally the Germans have mortared the corridor, and several times today I heard the wail of their multiple mortars, which the troops call Wailing Winnie. The troops said they have a very few shells, and today they've put in only one heavy counter-attack against the flank of the corridor. This came from the east about one o'clock, when German infantry and about twenty tanks failed to cut the corridor road near Colleville. The tanks were held off by our seventeen-pounders, but the infantry got close enough to bring the road under machine-gun fire. But by three o'clock they too were beaten back, and when the RAF came over twice and bombed them severely, they showed no signs of returning to the attack.

'The main German weakness in this area, as I suggested before, is his shortage of infantry, and now that we've broken through his main infantry line he's being forced to use his armoured divisions to check our advance. But you can't hold ground indefinitely with tanks. German tanks and anti-tank guns hidden in the woods can hold up our armour for a while, but they can't beat off serious attacks, unless they're protected by infantry, and so far our tanks have seen no sign of German infantry south of the Odon. This policy of using tanks is proving expensive for the enemy, because he's frittering away his strength in ones and twos. We, on the other hand, are holding the walls of the corridor strongly with infantry, armour, and anti-tank guns and self-propelled guns.

'This afternoon I stood on a slight rise looking down into the valley of the Odon. Less than half a mile away to the right and left I could see German territory, but the ground in between was thick with British troops, guns and tanks. Occasionally a German tank would sneak up close enough to fire a few rounds, and three times I saw one of our tanks go up in flames. But through my glasses I could also see the wrecks of four German tanks that had been knocked out in trying to make attacks like these.

'German prisoners have revealed to us something of the German infantry weakness. I have seen a number of them who said they were only eighteen – some seventeen. In one sector the Germans have used engineers in the line as infantry, and several of their battalions began this battle with only seventy per cent of their strength.

'There's no doubt about the superior calibre of the British infantry, and in the end this is going to be decisive. The Germans are now probably trying to form a new line on the east bank of the

River Orne, but if they're hoping to hold this line and to stop us outflanking Caen, they'll need more and better infantry than we've seen so far.'

CHESTER WILMOT

Day after day the 15th Scottish Division hung on grimly to the ground they had won, beating off successive counter-attacks of mounting violence:

30 June 1944

'The Germans attacked twice, first at two o'clock in the afternoon, and for more than an hour there was a tank and infantry mêlée, concentrated mainly around a château, where our troops were established in orchards and gardens. The Germans sent flame-throwers as well as tanks to support their infantry. The infantry were pinned down in long grass, short of one company position. The two flame-throwers under covering fire from heavy German tanks that lay hidden in the hedges moved up. The flame-throwers got close enough to spray the very trenches from which the Scotsmen were fighting. Flames licked the hedges, and burnt up the grass around them, but the men kept their heads down and stuck to their positions. Four days ago these Scotsmen went through their first battle. They've been fighting ever since. But this no doubt was their severest test. They had never even seen a flame-thrower in action before. And while they held their ground, Churchill tanks, hidden in hedges behind them, drove off the flame-throwers and the tanks. The German attack petered out, but it cost them five Panthers which were knocked out by the Churchills and our anti-tank guns.

'The second German attack came in about six o'clock, and it was much heavier, for the enemy used two or three battalions of infantry and about thirty tanks, and they pressed the attack hard. Once again the Scottish infantry held their ground. A number of tanks and a few small parties of infantry infiltrated between our forward positions, but the main force was stopped by our shelling and small-arms fire.

'The Germans who infiltrated got through about half a mile, but then they came under fire from our reserve infantry positions. As they pressed on they were forced by our fire into some low ground between two rises which we held. They were caught in a funnel with our tanks massed on the ridges on either flank, and our field artillery firing at them over open sights. This was too much for them. Twelve of their tanks were knocked out, and by 9 pm the rest were falling back. Then our tanks swept through, clearing up odd snipers and infiltrating parties.

'By ten o'clock the battle was over, but our guns were still pasting the area from which the Germans had mounted the attack. The key to our success was the fact that our forward infantry held their ground, even though the tanks had got through behind them, and had shot up their positions from front and rear.

'And today the Germans sat back licking their wounds. There were no counter-attacks against the corridor, but the Scotsmen didn't rest on the defensive. Today small parties were out looking for German tanks that had been worrying them by sniping from the woods for the last few days. Today men with piats crept out through the cornfields along the hedgerows to hunt for tanks. They got up well within a hundred yards of two of them that they reported were Tigers, and they put them both out of action with bombs from their piats. And by doing this they've shown how vulnerable tanks are in this thick country if they aren't shielded by infantry.

'I saw further evidence of this in a village in the corridor this afternoon. Sappers, who were mending a road, unearthed two German tank men who had been hiding in a house for three days. Fifty yards away their tank, a Panther, was abandoned intact with petrol in the tanks and ammunition in the locker. This is what happened. This Panther and two Mark IVs were fighting from a walled orchard when Scottish infantry broke into the town on Tuesday. When they saw the infantry coming, the tank crews panicked. The Panther tried to break out of the orchard, charged through a wall, and made a nose-dive down a steep slope and got bogged in a ditch beside the road. It blocked the road. The two Mark IVs couldn't get away, and both were knocked out and burnt out by bombs from the infantry's piat.'

CHESTER WILMOT

In country where wide deployment of armour was impossible, infantry and tanks in small battle-groups fought desperately at close range. When German tanks broke through, the infantry stayed put and refused to be disturbed by whatever might be happening in their rear:

1 July 1944
'The senior officer here has told his men: "Don't get bothered if you see German tanks coming towards you. Let 'em go, we'll take care of them. You won't have to look back over your shoulders." And the results of today's fighting bear out his words, for at least twenty-five German tanks have blundered into our positions and been knocked out. Some of them have even got into the little towns of Raurey and Granville and Haut du Bosq, but they've achieved absolutely nothing, and they've been lucky if they have managed to get away again, we're so solid and strong in our positions.

'While he jabs and probes, the enemy continues to reinforce as best and as hastily as he can. He is so badly in need of fresh troops that he's turning them right out of their buses and into the battle the moment they arrive. One eager young German whose map reading wasn't his strongest point was in such a hurry to get into the fight that he drove right up to the front line and through it. He and his transport are now in safe hands.'

FRANK GILLARD

To the calm resolution of the Scottish troops the Germans opposed a mixture of desperation, fanaticism and despair – in addition to the undoubted soldierly qualities of many of their men. The experience of a Canadian pilot as a prisoner, after he had been shot down, showed that some Germans already interpreted the invasion of Normandy as the beginning of the end:

29 June 1944

'Looking back on it now, I can see the Hun knew he'd had it. He was too keen on being pleasant to us. But at the time he had us guessing what it all meant. They brought us some brown bread. Strong-smelling stuff, but there was real butter and it went down pretty well. Then they gave us a bottle of port and a bottle of champagne. They even tipped the can up to show us we'd got the last of their coffee. We wondered what they were up to, and when they invited us to get into a slit trench outside the château we were really worried. It didn't seem a good idea. MacMahon, our rear-gunner who comes from Newcastle, said: "Let's stay in the open where our own fellows'll see us." We didn't fancy being on the wrong end of the bayonet charge.

'But the commandant insisted, and when our own mortars began popping off at the château we agreed, and that was crazier still. When the Huns wanted to pass us in the trench they said: "Excuse, please, British soldier," and gave a little sort of a bend. One or two of them spoke some English and asked us if we got plenty of dancing in England. But they never mentioned the fighting.

'We were glad finally we'd got into the trench when one of our shells hit the stable we'd been in. In the morning we got into the château, and one of the nicest things I've ever seen was that commandant fixing a white flag to the wall. In a little while he came to us and asked us, "Please find British Tommy"; and a couple of us went out and found two fellows from the Signals Corps. We raised a little patrol, and then we lined all the Huns up and handed them over. There were sixty-one of them.

'The big NCO who'd brought us the bread when we arrived had tears in his eyes and shook hands with all of us and told us, "Me sister . . . London." The commandant gave us another bottle of champagne and ticked off about an inch up the side of the bottle. He said, "Too much for one – tronk!" and made a show of being tight. As he went off, he said to me, kind of sadly, "The guerre – nicht bon!" '

FLIGHT-LIEUT. GORDON THRING, RCAF

To combat this air of resignation in some of their troops the enemy command circulated a rumour that the Allies were shooting prisoners. An apparently harmless incident was to show the effect of this rumour on German soldiers who had perhaps themselves enacted or witnessed such scenes on other fronts:

25 June 1944
'Almost the first words a German says when he is brought in to a British or Canadian headquarters on this front are, "Please don't shoot." Thousands have been amazed to find that we've no intention or thought of killing them. The other day, in a forward area, which was being heavily mortared by the enemy, a group of prisoners just

brought in and awaiting transportation to the POW Camp were given spades and told to dig slit trenches for their own protection. Some of them broke down completely on the spot. They thought they were being made to dig their own graves.'

FRANK GILLARD

∽◦⌢

June ended with Cherbourg firmly in our hands and the Navy already working to clear the port. With the main Mulberry port at Arromanches handling bigger loads every day and with the Germans still wasting their armoured strength in vain counter-attacks against the Odon corridor and Hill 112, the Allied build-up was now assured, and the Germans' last hope of wiping out the bridgehead was gone.

CHAPTER V
Behind The German Lines
'Demoralised, decimated, tired, and late'

While the opposing armies struggled for supremacy in a closely matched conflict, the Allies drew added strength from two factors which tipped the balance decisively against the Germans. One was our overwhelming superiority in the air: the other was the Maquis – the French Forces of the Interior. The combination of the two put an intolerable strain on German communications, so that the reinforcements which reached the battle-zone – and many failed to do so – were delayed, harassed, and in no fit shape to go into action. The finest testimonial to the effectiveness of the Allied Air Forces and the Maquis was provided by an order issued by the German High Command:

1 July 1944
'Local German commanders have been warned that if they venture to show themselves by day they will be held responsible for the consequences. Even in darkness main roads have to be avoided and long detours made through leafy byways. Prisoners coming in tell us again and again of the complete havoc behind the German lines here in France caused by Allied bombing, and, getting to be almost equally important now, the sabotage of the Maquis. Bridges are blown up everywhere, they say; roads are blocked and telephone lines are cut, and the poles themselves sawn off so that they can't be used again.

One man, coming in from the Eastern Front, said that it took him only five days to travel from there to the western borders of Germany, but more than a fortnight to get across France to the fighting line in Normandy. There wasn't a railway line that could be used, he said, and the roads were in a terrible state. We know, too, from many sources, that the German losses of transport on these roads, despite all their care, are heavy. It's seldom, for instance, that a new formation arrives in the line intact: out of, say, three battalions which should arrive together, perhaps only two turn up. So many vehicles have been lost on the journey that there are only sufficient left to bring two-thirds of the total force into the fighting area when they finally reach that journey's end.

'Apart from destroying a considerable proportion of the enemy's transport, we're putting a heavy strain on the remainder; wear and tear are bound to take their toll. That must be true of tanks as well. Normally the Germans would like to run their tanks up to a forward railhead by train; we're obliging them to bring the tanks all the way on their tracks, and dozens of them must have to go into forward workshops right away for repairs as soon as they arrive. And lastly, the expenditure of petrol which we're forcing on the enemy by binding him to the roads and compelling him to make long roundabout journeys must be tremendous. A single tank may swallow up three gallons of petrol for each mile it covers – what enormous quantities of this scarce and precious fluid it must take to move one panzer division by devious ways across France.'

FRANK GILLARD

Even at night any considerable movement was difficult for the Germans, for Mosquitoes ranged over the back areas ready to strike at any military vehicle that betrayed itself to the watchful eyes above.

The triumphant days of Germany's dive-bombers were an old memory now; the falcons of 1940 had become the field-mice of 1944:

7 July 1944

'Our job is to hinder and destroy the enemy wherever movement can be found, and we try to ensure that the ground forces get neither sleep nor peace and that the enemy faces his day's battle with tired troops and insufficient equipment. Working on this system we mustn't give him a single night's respite, and it's therefore enormously important that we continue operations in all weathers and under all conditions. When the weather's bad, our job of reconnaissance becomes more difficult as the aircraft must fly very close to the ground in order to see the German transport. Last night my wing was detailed to attack road and rail supply lines leading to the battlefront. We took off as darkness was falling in the middle of a rainstorm. In fact the sorties were carried out under peculiarly difficult conditions, as continuous thunderstorms extended over most of France. As we flew out to sea, the aircraft was continually illuminated by the glare of vivid red lightning, which streaked all around us.

'We always attempt to instil into our pilots a sort of hunter complex, so that they don't go at their targets like a bull at a gate but use their common sense to do the most damage without being shot down themselves. When you see a troop train steaming out of a junction, you needn't attack and bomb it at once, because a mile to the north there's a viaduct over which it must pass, and if it is bombed and cannoned from there it will have left the protection of a flak-defended area. Better still, the troops will find it a bit tricky trying to get away.

'But they are elusive customers, and go to great lengths to escape us. We feel that if these troops pass through our areas on their way to battle, their ride from Germany to the front line is not without interest and excitement. I wouldn't claim that we can entirely prevent them from arriving at their destination. They can creep by without lights, at ten miles an hour, stopping whenever they hear an aeroplane. But when their divisions reach the front line, it's our intention that they shall be demoralised, decimated, tired, and late. This is our ambition, but we shan't know for some months how near we are to achieving it.'

GROUP CAPTAIN PETER WYKEHAM-BARNES, DSO, DFC, RAF

In the immediate battle-areas the Allied Air Forces took on every sort of task. They provided preliminary barrages, supported advancing troops, strafed individual strong-points and concentrations: even the heavy night-bombing Lancasters were called from English bases to deal with local targets in daylight:

1 July 1944

'It was in the afternoon and we were standing by for the normal night attack. Some of our aircraft were flying, while ground crews were working on others. Air crews were either preparing for their night's work or were sleeping. Suddenly the message came that we were to bomb a special tactical target at short notice. Aircraft had to be recalled, crews summoned from all parts of the dispersal camp, bomb and petrol loads had to be changed, cameras and ammunition altered for daylight work. Every man of the squadron was working at full pressure. Minutes sped by, crews assembled for their briefing, without even time to eat their evening meal. The target, so we were told, was a concentration of German tanks, troops and guns which were trying to hide in the area near Villers-Bocage. They were preparing a counter-attack against the Second Army, and they were not going to be allowed to get away with that. After the briefing, the last hurried preparations were completed, and it was a great relief to see the whole squadron airborne on time.

'*En route*, other squadrons joined the stream, and it was a most impressive sight to see hundreds of heavy bombers flying steadily towards the target in daylight.

'The actual target was as small as it was vital. When we got there we saw bombs streaming down ahead and on either side, and all landing smack in the right place. It was twelve minutes of precision bombing, done exactly as it should be done, and what flak there was made not the slightest difference to its accuracy. The weather was good and we were able to make clear bombing-runs. Underneath, dust and smoke and flying debris which had been raised by the first bombers to go in surged up into the air in constantly thickening clouds, blotting out the target indicators. We turned for home, and then I saw something below me which I shall not easily forget. It was, in a way, like some unexpected reward: British tanks were again on the move, nosing forward towards the enemy. Before the last bomber in my squadron had got back to the airfield, the first photographs had been developed, all showing remarkably accurate bombing.'

WING COMMANDER WILLIAM DEVAS, AFC, RAF

The pilot of a Lancaster which was hit by flak after bombing Villers-Bocage made an emergency landing on a fighter strip in France, and was able to go forward and hear for himself the appreciative comments of the infantry:

4 July 1944

'When we got to the front line we discovered that our troops had seen our attack the previous evening – they told us it was a wonderful show. Immediately they heard that we had been one of the attacking force they clustered round to shake hands and slap our backs. Cups of tea appeared as if by magic, from foxholes, slit trenches, and from behind hedges. The spirit of the men was truly amazing, considering the guns were blazing away, and even as we spoke we were sprayed by earth kicked up by shells. We came across a British sergeant-major whose tent resembled a complete arsenal – around it he had arrayed machine-guns, mortars, anti-tank guns and other weapons. Many of them were German, but all were serviceable. That fellow was like a one-man division and certainly wasn't going to be caught napping.

'On our way back we stopped at an estaminet, but the French madame coolly told us she hadn't any wine left. An army officer whispered the words "aviateur anglais", and to my embarrassment the lady threw her arms around me, kissed me, and repeatedly cried, "Bon, bon!" and most important of all, produced bottles of wine. When we finally returned to the landing-strip, the weather had cleared.'

SQUADRON LEADER N. A. WILLIAMSON, DFC, RAF

The provision of these landing-strips in the first weeks of the invasion was one of the outstanding feats of construction in what must be regarded as the classic campaign in military engineering. From the Mulberry harbours to the most advanced fighter-strip, every installation needed by a modern mechanised army had to be created at high speed and sometimes under enemy fire. Behind the successes in battle was the tireless labour of thousands upon thousands of engineers, of technicians, of pioneers, military police, truck-drivers, signalmen. Construction of a single runway meant laying and fastening 800 tons of tracking; and before that could be done, of course, the site had to be cleared and levelled:

7 July 1944
'Some of those airfield sites take a long time to clear. On one field, now in operational use out here, over 3000 trees had to be felled. So

as to be ready in time, sappers and pioneers are moving forward with the leading infantry, making up roads and paths as they go, being useful on the way. Dust is a big problem on these emergency airfields, it comes up in clouds and does great damage to aircraft engines. The sappers are tackling the problem energetically. They're laying hessian under the wire mesh. They're planting grass seeds thickly. They're trying to oil the surface, and they're laying on supplies of water to each strip, so that the ground can be kept sprayed. It's going to take 3½ million gallons of water a day, but they're finding it and pumping it somehow. These airfield construction companies, I found, are amazingly keen on their job. Let me end by telling a story about one pioneer, who was helping to lay a wire-mesh track on a landing-strip when a shot-up aeroplane came in to make an emergency landing on the unfinished airfield.

'The pioneer saw that his strip of steel matting, not yet fully tacked down, was curled up at the end, and he realised that it would wreck the aeroplane if it caught against the undercarriage or the fuselage. Without hesitation, he threw himself bodily on the turned-up strip so that his weight flattened it out. The machine might easily have hit him, and bumped a bit and possibly killed him. As it was, the landing-wheels just skimmed against his shoulder, and one wing passed right over him. And the aeroplane made a safe landing.'

FRANK GILLARD

The most advanced airfields were within sight of enemy observation posts. The commanding officer of one of them – a Canadian wing commander – gave a graphic description of what it was like to work on an aerodrome under enemy shellfire:

4 July 1944

'At the moment we have the doubtful honour of being slightly closer to the fighting line than any other airfield. This enables the Germans to practically lift the flaps of our tents and look inside. Although we're still living in tents, as we did in England, they all have an important addition to them – namely, a slit trench. Some of the more ambitious builders have constructed dugouts which are well underground and ventilated by means of shell-cases.

'During the daytime our aeroplanes flying over the 'drome are fired at by the enemy front-line ack-ack. One German gun-site seems to be manned by personnel who are all anxious to win the Iron Cross, as they fire all the time.

'Last night the Germans threw some high-explosive shells at us, but there were no casualties, other than bruised knees, skinned hands and dirty uniforms, as a result of throwing ourselves into slit trenches. There was little actual damage done to the aerodrome. The daily programme doesn't entirely involve getting in and out of slit trenches. The airfield personnel are all busy about their normal duties: refuelling planes, checking engines, rearming guns, cooking meals, and of course, writing letters home. We are lucky to have a Knights of Columbus supervisor with us, who has shown as many as five motion pictures a day, and last night ran a little bingo game for the boys.'

WING COMMANDER DON MACDONALD, RCAF, OF VANCOUVER

cསྩྩ

While thousands of aircraft worked in the closest liaison with the armies in Normandy, others ranged over the entire continent in a long-distance 'shuttle' service, probing every corner of Germany's European Fortress. Using bases in Russia and Italy, Allied bombers from England could now reach out to Poland and Rumania. Here was the full majesty of that command of the skies for which we had fought so long and so hard. The ring that was closing round Germany gained a more pointed reality when bombers and fighters of the US Eighth Air Force took off for a transcontinental flight that was to occupy a fortnight and include bombing-attacks in four countries before the planes returned to their home bases:

9 July 1944

'We took a northern route to our first target – the Berlin area. The target was an oil refinery south of Berlin; we picked up our fighter escort right over the target area – a force of Mustangs that were to fly with us on the whole trip. We bombed the target with very good results. Now instead of turning back for our home base in England we headed directly through the centre of the Reich for Russia.

'A short time after leaving the target we were attacked by German fighters – about thirty came up – but we just brushed them aside and kept plugging on. When we had been in the air for about ten hours we began to wonder if we could go much further. Four of our Forts were unable to reach our briefed base, but made successful forced landings in Russia. The rest of us made the base we wanted. Our field was an advanced operational base, merely an airstrip in a bombed field. Our ships were met by American trucks driven by Russian soldiers. We were taken into the small town, which was nearly bombed out, and here we ate our first meal for about sixteen hours. This was our first Russian meal, and some of the boys had a job getting used to the food.

'Next evening we moved off to a nearby city, and here everyone turned out to welcome us. We were billeted in a building that just eight months before had been used as a billet for German soldiers, then Russian soldiers, and now American flyers. We were entertained by Russian soldiers – men and women – and from the time we arrived there to the time we left there was a steady playing of an accordion, dancing in the streets, and much throwing of flowers. It seemed hard to believe that some of the women who threw those flowers were snipers.

'Three days later we took off once more and headed for our next target – an oil refinery in Poland, just across the Russian lines. There was some heavy flak over the target and a few fighters, but it was uneventful for the rest of the trip, and having left the target area we headed for our next briefed base in Italy. As we flew along it was good to look up and see the same fighter boys who had been with us since the start of the trip. We landed OK and all in one piece. We stayed here a week, and went swimming in the Adriatic and enjoyed some Italian sun, but we didn't spend all our time sunning, because one day during the week we took a little trip to Rumania and back, and bombed the marshalling yards at Arad. I don't think that they will be running their trains on time there any more for a while. As for us, we got back OK.

'At the end of the week we started out on the last leg of our trip, and set out for our base in England. Once more we were carrying bombs, this time a drop on Beziers in the south of France – another marshalling yard. We left the target burning fiercely behind us, large clouds of smoke coming up thousands of feet. In a few hours we were home, landing at the base we started out from just two weeks before.'

CAPTAIN J. L. ZELLER, 8TH USAF, OF CANTON, OHIO

The bombers and fighters that made these long-distance flights developed a close teamwork. The fighter-pilots guarded their 'big brothers' jealously, keeping them free from distraction over the targets and 'nursing' damaged bombers on the homeward flight. Among stories of the air few are more moving than the account of the last minutes of a crippled Fortress, told by a Mustang pilot who stood by, powerless to help, while his comrades parachuted down to German territory and imprisonment:

25 June 1944

'I was flying alone over Germany, after escorting bombers which had just blasted targets at Berlin, when I noticed a Flying Fort break away from its formation. The two left engines were dead and the props feathered. Then I heard the bomber call me in. "Little friend, little friend, I've got two engines out and am on fire. Can you see me, little friend?" As I was coming down to them I said, "I'm crossing right over you. Let's go home."

'Even though he knew he was badly hit, he didn't seem worried. Seven other P51s came down with me, so I pulled under the big ship, lowered my flaps to slow down to his speed, and then noticed a big hole, about three feet square, on the bottom of the wing where flames were burning inside and eating the skin away.

'I cut in and told him the aluminium was melting away on his wing and flames were beginning to break through the top. I kept alongside and tried to suggest different stunts for putting out the fire. Cut back to the right or the left; dive, pick up speed and have the wind blow out the flame, and so on – but nothing seemed to work.

'Finally he called, "Little friend, I'm afraid I'll have to bale out. Will you stand by and count the chutes as they go out?"

'I told him to go ahead and I'd count. I watched seven of them open out, one by one. Then he called again to check the count. "How does that make us now, little friend?" he said. "That's just seven men out," I told him. A few seconds later another chute opened and then the bomber pilot gave us his parting shot: "Thanks for the escort, fellars: see you after the war."

'That hit us all pretty hard. About all I could say was, "Okay, big friend, lots of luck to you all." Then the pilot's own chute opened out, just before the bomber flipped over on a wing and went streaming down in flames.'

CAPTAIN JAMES CHENEY, USAF, OF OHIO

In addition to bombs, the Air Forces were dropping something else – something with a delayed action. Night after night, all over France, containers of arms and ammunition floated down through the darkness for the waiting Maquis to use at the appropriate time:

7 July 1944
'We flew mostly very close to the ground. Strangely, we didn't see any flak. The only sign of Hun interest was once when we saw a flare go up to help his night-fighters locate us.

'Nobody else seemed to take more than an aesthetic interest in the flares, and I didn't think it my place to put in the vulgar word. "There's the river," said our pilot, Flying Officer Jimmy Stark of Glasgow, and the bomb-aimer agreed and pointed out another feature that confirmed that our navigator had his finger up. We churned steadily on through the murk, and every now and then there was a queer glimpse of a sepia sort of French countryside below. Suddenly Stark said: "This is the place." Those of us who were above-board craned our necks. The bomb-aimer took over for the run up and a moment later we heard his exultant shout: "They're all gone." As we circled low over the tiny clearing, we could see the supply containers nestled there like a cluster of eggs. The Maquis had another lot of material to stack up against the great day.'

FLIGHT-LIEUT. JOHN MACADAM, RAF

The individual valour of the Maquis had never been doubted. Its solid military value was recognised as reports from every region of

France were studied and pieced together. To the destruction wrought by the Air Forces was added an intense and widespread campaign of sabotage and guerrilla warfare, rising in places to the level of pitched battles in which German casualties were by no means inconsiderable:

5 and 14 July 1944

'I have just seen Staff Officers, British and French, poring over a map. A map of France. Of the whole of France. A map of the Maquis. On it are marked whole areas in grey or black with the legend reading: "Area under patriot control", or else "Particularly heavy fighting". Arrows lead from certain towns, certain main railway lines, or from the grid power cables. In the margin of the map at the point of these arrows one can read: "All railways out of Paris cut on such a date", or else "All railways cut in another region, majority of cuts being maintained".

' "Train of thirty tanks derailed." A Panzer division now in the line in Normandy is shown on this map as having been delayed for a whole week between the town of X and the town of Y, by railway cuts. Elsewhere a date with the simple words: "No trains Paris–Bordeaux or Paris–Toulouse." Farther along the line, Paris–Toulouse line cut each night by the Maquis. In the Alps a railway bridge is marked as demolished. "Line blocked indefinitely", one can read. One zone is marked "Two German divisions engaged, 1000 casualties both sides". Another place is marked "Evacuated by Maquis forces after an attack by 10,000 Germans using artillery support and mortars. Patriot losses over a thousand." But elsewhere one reads "2400 Germans defeated, 300 prisoners taken", or "560 Germans killed in this region, own losses less than 300". And better still, just below the most hated place-name of the whole of France – Vichy – the laconic mention "Geissler, Gestapo chief, executed by patriots, 23 June".

'But what does this sabotage mean to our troops in France? Well, at one point where a railway line had been broken a German troop train was stopped. It was stopped on an incline. At the rear of the train were horse-boxes – because German infantry still use horses. Someone uncoupled the horse-boxes and they ran downhill four miles. Someone else let the horses loose and it took all afternoon to round them up. Then the troop train went on its way.

'Accidents like that happened all the way along the line to this train and here is what it meant to us. This was a German division which had been brought from the Russian front. It had taken five days to travel from Russia to the Rhine – but it took fourteen days to get it from the Rhine to Normandy. Another German division had to travel 180 miles to the Normandy front – on foot.'

PIERRE LEFEVRE AND ROBERT BARR

In the liberated area Allied troops grew increasingly accustomed to seeing the Cross of Lorraine on a red, white and blue armband, which distinguished the soldiers of the Resistance. These men patrolled the streets by day and night, rounded up collaborators, and lent a hand against German remnants:

11 July 1944
'Yesterday they were at work routing out the Germans themselves. They were searching a deserted farmhouse, when one of them saw a boot sticking out of a corner of an attic. They fired through the floor and nineteen German soldiers, fully armed, surrendered to four soldiers of the Resistance.

'As you stand in their headquarters and talk to them, to men who have just come back from the Maquis, to boys who are so young that they have only just been allowed to join the movement, you begin to realise something of what this movement really means. You understand why they all ask the same question: "When are we going to be called up for the regular army?" They all say the same thing. They want everyone to know of their gratitude to the armies that have liberated them, but they want still more to show that Frenchmen are ready and able to take their full part in the fight. Their chief summed it up: "Il y a encore des bons français en France." "There are still good Frenchmen in France."

While he was in the courtyard of this headquarters a report came in that a German parachutist had been seen nearby. These parachutists are dropped to carry out sabotage and spying. As soon as the report came in, the chief ordered out three men. They were very young Frenchmen and they wore much-patched suits. On their arms was their uniform – a red, white and blue band with the Cross of Lorraine. Armed with rifles, they started out and two of us went with them. With three combatants and two correspondents, it looked like being the most heavily reported engagement in history.

'As we went along, searching as best we might, three small children joined us. There was a boy of fifteen and his two little sisters. They asked us whether they could help us to look for les Boches. Armed with some chewing-gum, some toffee, and a cigarette, they tagged along. And suddenly, we wanted to laugh.

'It was a serious job, and the three young Frenchmen were going about it in a business-like way. They were thankful to be able to lend a hand to stalk with rifles the men who'd bullied them until a few days before.

'But the picture of this incongruous little band, the little girl stumping seriously along chewing her toffee, was just a bit too much. We left without having captured the German parachutist and without having disgraced ourselves by laughing in the presence of these three enthusiastic, determined young men who might have misunderstood that laughter. Because, it would have been laughter that hid a very real admiration and respect.'

ROBIN DUFF

CHAPTER VI
Caen and St-Lô

'Playing hide-and-seek for their lives'

With the Cotentin peninsula cleared by the Americans, and the British stubbornly enveloping Caen, the German defence was strained to its utmost capacity to contain the Allied forces in the bridgehead, and Rommel now felt obliged to draw even more heavily on his dwindling reserves in order to cope with what he had first suspected to be merely a diversionary landing. On the comparatively short line from Caen to St-Lô and the Atlantic now hung the probable fate of France and the Low Countries west of the Rhine. The next steps for the Allies were to prise the Germans out of Caen, and to flatten the salient south of Carentan across the Vire–Taute canal towards St-Lô and Coutances.

On 8 July, with the Canadians concluding a fierce and protracted battle for Carpiquet aerodrome, British forces moved into the northern outskirts of Caen, after a heavy bombardment by the RAF. The city itself, to which the Germans had clung so tenaciously, was occupied during the next twenty-four hours, though they still held the Colombelles factory and the district immediately south and east of the river:

9 July 1944

'The patrols which we sent forward last night towards Caen have reported that it was almost impossible to find an entry into the city. Every roadway was completely blocked. So, when our infantry and tanks went forward down the slope from Hill 64 just before eleven o'clock this morning, they had bulldozers well up with them. It was close on two o'clock when the commander received a message which made him turn to us and say, "All right; if you want to go in, you can go." Feeling very much like a military target, we shot over the open brow of the hill in our jeep, until we reached a crossroads beyond which there was so much German fire that it was obvious that the only way was to continue on foot, "playing musical chairs from slit trench to slit trench", as one officer on the spot put it. In any case, a vehicle would have been out of the question, for 100 yards or so ahead, just round a bend, we came across the beginnings of the destruction. Rubble and masonry were being shovelled into a great bomb-crater which completely blocked the whole road. Beyond that, the scene was one of absolute and complete devastation. Every building a total wreck, trees and poles and petrol-pumps lying askew across the road, wires trailing everywhere. We picked our way ahead, thankful for the fierce counter-battery fire of our guns which were pouring concentrations into Colombelles factory at that moment, and keeping the enemy up there quiet.

'I made some progress by climbing through into the back gardens and breaking through from one to the other down the hillside. But even then the going was so hard that I had to give it up. I went back to the top of the road and took the right fork. This was the track roughly cleared by bulldozers. But even now it was like a switchback railway. We got down among the ruined houses and met our first two civilians – two men. They told us that there were thousands of refugees taking shelter in the huge buildings of the asylum and in a school. I'd heard of those figures before.

'Away ahead of us we could hear the sharp rattle of machine-gun fire as our forward troops pushed on through the city. There was stiff resistance at points, but the Germans weren't making a house-to-house fight of it. In some more open ground on our left – goodness knows how they ever got into it – a handful of our tanks were taking on enemy targets, perhaps across the river.'

FRANK GILLARD

While the battle raged through the city, the civil population sheltered in churches, in schools, anywhere that offered a chance of survival. The moment it was moderately safe to come into the open, the people of Caen emerged from their shelter to welcome the British troops and to celebrate the liberation of their city:

10 and 11 July 1944

'Caen has suffered terrible things in the last month, yet the reception which its citizens have given to us has been moving in the extreme. Not a word of reproach: not a word of self-pity. This morning the war was still very near at hand. German aircraft kept appearing overhead: German airburst shells were exploding just above the roofs; occasional mortar shells were bursting in the streets. Yet the people of Caen were out, picking their way through the rubble, smiling at us, waving to us, embracing us, giving us flowers, and time and time again I saw it – weeping for sheer joy. There is no hysterical demonstration: the feelings of these people were far too deep for that; but there was a tremendous conviction and sincerity in their welcome.

'As we went down the roads, crowds gathered round us. They spoke of the savagery of the SS troops in the last few days of the German occupation: of their wholesale looting; of the shooting of French civilians who were political prisoners in the jails; of the wanton burning by the Germans of the gendarmerie, of the theatre, and of many private houses and shops into which enemy troops had tossed hand grenades as they left Caen. One man spoke most glowingly of the bravery of a British colonel who led the entry into Caen: bullets were spraying all round him, but still he held himself erect and walked forward – this man said of the colonel: "My wife screamed: she was sure he'd be killed. But not a bullet hit him. Ah, he was a brave man – a hero."

'In a small courtyard outside a church the people were already preparing for a ceremony and the raising of the Tricolour over liberated country. The ridged French Army helmets appeared from nowhere. One man even had on a creased uniform of the regular army. It was rumpled from long hiding in the closet. And every other person wore the Cross of Lorraine. But strangest sight of all was that the men wearing helmets also carried arms. Some had the long rifles of the French Army; some had German rifles; one or two even had some British Sten guns which they had bargained from the liberating troops. They were ready to resume the war where it left off in 1940. Most of them were in tattered civilian clothing, but they weren't waiting to be dressed up to fight the Boche. And this motley group of soldiers representing the resurrection of Fighting France formed a proud colour-guard for the French Flag, virtually under the muzzles of the German guns. British, Canadian and American officials appeared. They were the military and civilian authorities come in to administer the city. A squad of British soldiers snapped to attention. Everyone in the crowd took off their hats; the mayor of the town, wearing a French helmet and a badge bearing the Cross of Lorraine, gave the command and the Tricolour was raised. It was quiet for a moment for there was not even a sound of gunfire; then the people began to applaud and shout again and again: Vive la France!'

FRANK GILLARD AND BILL DOWNS, CBS

Almost simultaneously the Americans launched an attack on St-Lô. Here – as at its eastern counterpart, Caen – the Germans reacted strongly, throwing in more tanks than they had yet used on the American front. Standing at the junction of nine roads, St-Lô was bound to be fiercely contested, and the American attack was preceded by a full-scale bombardment:

11 July 1944

'In the bright sunlight this morning the whole area of St-Lô was mantled in smoke, a great white piling mass of smoke spreading around the town as the artillery battered at the German defence points. An officer said: "We started this morning by giving them a serenade" – a serenade it appears is a certain very heavy type of barrage – "and," he added, "we are stepping it up now." I should say that one-third of that town will be no use to the Germans by this evening.

'At a forward airstrip I watched aircraft take off to give their support to the attack. A signaller who was on duty at the foot of the airstrip said: "You can watch them take off, drop their bombs, turn away and come home and never once are they out of sight of this airfield. It's marvellous."

'All morning this airstrip had been busy. Twice German tanks had been spotted moving up to the line and within a few minutes fighters were out attacking them. Once some tanks did break through our lines. This time the infantry dealt with them, using bazookas and flame-throwers. Four tanks broke through and four were destroyed.

'The drive for St-Lô is on, and everyone in the battle area, ground forces and air forces, are throwing everything into it.'

ROBERT BARR

The town of St-Lô was soon reduced to a waste of rubble and dust, but the Germans were well dug in. The ditches round the fields north of the town had been deepened and linked in a system of trenches, and the Americans were hotly resisted and counter-attacked. When all other opposition had been suppressed, there were still the ever-present snipers to be cleared up:

12 July 1944

'I went up in a jeep along fairly quiet roads, and passed the gun positions which are plastering the enemy the whole of the time. Then we began to run into the tide of war. Newly-battered hamlets and farmhouses, lines of infantrymen plodding along the dusty road. There were linesmen laying signal wires as hard as they could go. There were fire-reddened, burnt-out tanks, both German and American, by the side of the road; one with its turret blown clean off.

'A jeep came swaying down towards us with a stretcher projecting over the side. Away up the road an officer stopped to caution us. "No dust, please, or you'll draw fire – go right ahead." Then the traffic, both human and mechanical, began to thin out significantly. The infantry one saw now were peering over hedges and ducking as they passed field gates. Tanks were rumbling through the cornfields and orchards.

'And all the while, enemy small-arms fire was smashing away over our heads, with the occasional crash of mortar shells in the nearby field, across which our men were edging in the direction of St-Lô. The post commander wouldn't let us go on, so we headed back down the lane, feeling a shade too conspicuous as we sat there perched up on the jeep, with our heads just showing above the hedge, and with all that small-arms fire whanging and whining around the place; I tried to shrink into my tin hat, but not very successfully. We hadn't gone fifty yards down the lane before an officer flagged us. Could we pick up two wounded men and take them down the line to a dressing-station? A mortar burst had just caught them ahead of us. One of them was an officer with a shoulder wound; the other, a youngster from Pittsburgh, had been hit in the leg. They'd caught it trying to establish a forward artillery observation post. The youngster from Pittsburgh, a fine type of lad, was taking it all very calmly. I gave them a cigarette as we jogged down the lane, and he took one

167

deep puff, glanced up at the blue and white fleecy sky, and remarked conversationally, "Odd, no rain today." '

ROBERT REID

14 July 1944

'The trouble with this campaign at the moment is that it's being fought in a sort of gigantic shrubbery. I've just been to the little village of Le Dazère on the western side of the Vire River where the Americans are pushing, field by field, southwards towards the line of the Lessay-St-Lô road. It's about the middle of their offensive line. At the highest points on the straight French road we found ourselves overlooking dense stretches of woodland. We weren't high enough up to see that in between the trees were tiny fields and many slow rivers and drainage ditches. Generally through the gaps in the roadside hedges we could see the fields on either side of us, but not those beyond. Away to the left black smoke was surging out of the dark green trees where a shell had burst and started a fire. But most of the fighting came to us in sound. There were spurts of fire as American infantry poured machine-gun bullets across from a ditch on one side of a field into the German positions behind the hedge on the other side.

'Invisible and embowered American artillery would startle us as, unwittingly, we came abreast of their positions when they decided to open fire. We could hear the shells go over, but only the spotter in the slowly-wheeling aircraft just ahead of us above the enemy lines could see where they landed. We know because we'd seen the dispositions on a map that the countryside was full of men, but they were lying in the ditches or in holes they'd dug, and hidden in hedges and slowly edging their way towards other men in holes and ditches and hedges. In this country where tanks may, and do, come round corners and engage each other at point-blank range with no room to manoeuvre, infantry can never make great sweeping advances. They've got to watch and stalk and crouch and wait, and play hide-and-seek for their lives.'

ROBERT DUNNETT

17 July 1944

'In the corner of any hedge, or in any one of the incredibly leafy trees, there may be a sniper. There they sit, left behind by the main body of their troops. The prisoners say that these snipers are nearly all fanatical Nazis. They chain themselves to the tree, so that they won't fall if they're wounded, and cover themselves with a sort of camouflaged apron, and then wait for men who are alone. When they run out of ammunition they drop down from the trees and surrender. You've heard the word before, "Kamarad". Generally they assure you they've nothing but friendly feelings towards us. And they didn't really want to fight. One other thing: there've been a lot of reports of wooden bullets. Now the Germans are very certainly using them, I've got one of them in my pocket, but I've heard it suggested that this means that they're short of material for bullets. In fact, for the most part, it's the snipers who use them. They use them when firing towards their own lines, and they use them for very good reasons; they only carry a short way, and there's no danger of their killing their own troops if they miss their intended victim.'

ROBIN DUFF

The reduction of Caen and St-Lô necessarily took time. Until this double task was completed there could be no spectacular breakthrough; the Germans therefore staked everything on holding these positions and thus preventing any notable extension of the battle-line. Even when they were driven from St-Lô they clung desperately to the fringes of the position and counter-attacked. It was the same at Caen where the village of Maltot, a few miles south-west of the city, became a hotly disputed battlefield, changing hands several times in a day as tanks and infantry struggled for mastery under heavy barrages from both sides. A most effective element in German resistance was the heavy and accurate fire from 'nebelwerfers' – multiple-barrelled mortars that came over with a high wailing note. At Maltot, within a few hundred yards of the forward infantry, an adventurous correspondent recorded the mortar barrage as the bombs fell round him:

11 July 1944

'When it got too hot, I left the recorder playing and took refuge in the bottom of the ditch – much to my humiliation! Anyhow, this is the only recording I know of that's ever been made of what the troops call "Wailing Winnie" or "The Sobbing Sisters", which is the German multiple mortar. Unfortunately, when they burst they blew me off the air. The sapphire jumped, the cutting-head jumped, and the sapphire dug into the disc and she stopped. But I got to it just at that moment and did succeed in recording, immediately after that, another burst of them coming down.

'The Germans have now begun and they're thumping down . . .'
[*commentary drowned here – sounds of mortar fire and wailing*].

CHESTER WILMOT

༄

After a preliminary feint west of Maltot, the British Second Army swung round secretly on the 'blind' side of Caen and launched an attack towards Troarn, in an effort to gain full control of the right bank of the Orne and thus free Caen completely. The manoeuvre tricked Rommel into sending his armour in the wrong direction, though it must be added that he was quick in recovering from the initial surprise:

19 and 20 July 1944

'The Germans were fooled because we used, as our jumping-off place, ground that had lain fallow from a military point of view since D-Day. On that day the 6th Airborne Division seized the bridges over the Orne between Caen and the sea, and they gained a small bridgehead – about four miles long and two miles deep – on the eastern bank.

'Last Friday I paid a casual visit to the original bridgehead. The front was just as quiet as it had been for weeks, but at once I saw signs that it wouldn't remain quiet – bulldozers were cutting new tracks for tanks – sappers were putting in two new Bailey bridges . . . infantry of a British division were moving in small scattered groups along the lanes and through the cornfields . . . and then I saw several armoured vehicles that had been fighting elsewhere. Those signs were enough – so I stayed in the bridgehead east of the Orne all the weekend.

'By day there was little sign of increased traffic on the roads, but each night the bridges were alive with transport that came across by dark and was hidden before dawn under trees and beside hedges. Several times on Sunday German reconnaissance planes came over; the ack-ack drove them off, but we wondered how much they'd seen, how much their spotters could see from the top of the Colombelles factory chimneys that looked right down upon the river and our bridges.

'Then on Sunday evening one of our photo-recce Spitfires was shot down in German territory. Was the camera intact? Might the Germans get the films and see that it had been photographing the area behind Caen? We must stop them. Orders were flashed to the artillery to shell the area where the "Spit" had crashed. Mustangs came over and poured incendiary bullets into the same area. But we looked in vain for the smoke signal that would mean the plane and its photographs were burning. We wondered how much the enemy knew.

'That night our armoured forces began to cross the bridges – from last light they came rumbling over in a steady stream – armoured command trucks, scout cars, half-tracks, jeeps, supply trucks, self-propelled guns. Twice during the night German planes swept in to take flashlight photographs. We wondered how much they could see. The same thing happened the next night – Monday night – the night before the attack, for then the tanks came over. By dawn they were in position . . . but by dawn it didn't matter whether or not the Germans knew they'd come. By then it was too late – the bombing had begun.

'In the half-light I stood on a hill on the east bank of the Orne, looking down on an open field at the foot of the hill. I could see the camouflaged shapes of tanks, hundreds of them – tanks that hadn't been there the night before, but now they were assembling to attack. And in the distance, there was the sole surviving chimney of the great steel factory at Colombelles and the towers and buildings of the suburbs of Caen that the Germans still held.

'Then I turned and looked out to sea . . . the Lancasters and Halifaxes were beginning to darken the northern sky . . . they came over the horizon in a black swarm. The markers dropped their target indicators and in a few seconds bombs were cascading down on the steel factory and the suburbs of Caen . . . and on the German strong-points on either flank of the line along which our tanks were to advance.

'For a while the flak was thick . . . but every minute it got less as our field-gunners found their targets – the German ack-ack positions – pinpointed for them by spotting planes – little Austers – which seemed to be worming their way in between the very sticks of bombs, searching for the flak positions that dared to fire.

'For forty-five minutes the procession of bombers came on unbroken, and when they'd gone, the thunder of the guns swelled up and filled the air, as the artillery carried on the bombardment.

'In the field below the tanks were moving forward towards their start-line – on the crest of a rise about two miles from me the bombardment drowned the rumble of their tanks, for now the Navy joined in and huge shells were crumping down on German guns, which our field pieces couldn't reach.'

CHESTER WILMOT

At seven o'clock the Marauders came in to scatter fragmentation bombs across the fields that lay in the path of the tanks; and here the pilot of a Marauder takes up the story:

19 July 1944

'As we approached the far side of the Channel I could see great bursts of fire from the heavy guns of the Navy standing offshore. They are great guys, those Navy fellows. They sure know how to sock those shells in. We could see them land dead on the targets as we flew in over the coast towards Caen. Great billows of smoke and dust were rising from behind the city and climbing to a height of many thousands of feet, the result of the terrific blasting in this area by the RAF, the Navy, and the Ninth's [*US-Air Force*] Marauders. I know it sounds crazy, but the sun streaming through the haze and smoke created weird and beautiful effects. It was hard to realise the terrible destruction below. But I soon saw it. Trees and hedgerows had been levelled as if by a giant plough. A great path had been cut by the Allied bombers through the German defences. Allied artillery was doing its bit too. Not even on D-Day did I see anything like this. From our side of Caen the artillery was sending shells over the city in a steady stream, laying them right in on the German concentrations.

'We were already in the flak belt. The Jerries must have pulled themselves together after the other attacks and were now sending

173

up a huge barrage. It's a funny thing about flak. When it bursts it looks like a great gob of liquid black silk, like something you might see in a Walt Disney fantasy. It's only when you hear it go "Umph" that you know it's rugged stuff. That Umph has a sound that seems to say to me – "Go Home!" But you don't, you go on with the bomb run. We were just coming into it when the plane nearest me on my right got a direct hit in the fuel tank. Sheets of flame streamed from it. Then it blew up. The tail gunner said he saw some chutes get away. I was mighty glad because all those guys are close friends of mine. We began to get it then. Six bursts right under us. They bounced us around and tore a few holes in the plane. Then our bombs were away, scattered over the area where Jerry was hanging on by his eye-teeth.'

FIRST LIEUT. JOHN NYDEGGER, 9TH USAF

19 July 1944

'In the meantime our armour gathered in the cornfield just behind the start-line . . . and with them, armoured half-tracks carrying infantry, armoured assault and anti-tank guns . . . armoured scout cars . . . General Montgomery's fist of mail . . . that was soon to begin punching through the German defences.

'Before the Marauders had finished not an ack-ack gun was firing; the only enemy aerial activity was one lone buzz-bomb that shot along the coast and out into the sea.

'Five minutes' silence and then the crackle of machine-guns in the woods on the left of the tanks told me that our infantry were moving . . . And then the guns spoke again, hundreds of them putting down a rolling barrage in front of the infantry on the flanks, and the armour in the centre. As the first shells came down great spouts of dust shot up along the crest of the hill that was the start-line. The barrage lifted, and the tanks began to roll forward.

'The cornfield was alive with them, and then they were swallowed up in the smoke and dust of the barrage, but I followed the leading tanks' progress by listening on my radio, and I heard them say, "Advancing steadily . . . close behind the barrage . . . can't see much . . . but there's no opposition."

'All that came back were a few mortars that landed in the field behind the start-line, which was already filling up with fresh waves of tanks and mechanised infantry . . . and soon they were moving up the hill and into the smoke and their radios were coming into action . . . and their guns too, for they sprayed every hedge.

'Overhead the bombardment was carried on by Fortresses and Liberators. At eleven o'clock I drove back across the Orne . . . the guns were still going as hard as ever, as they had been for five hours. And the tanks were still rolling relentlessly forward . . . What the plan is no one could then say, but at least we knew of the power behind the plan.'

CHESTER WILMOT

⟨≈⟩

What that power achieved was superficially unimpressive – a five-mile advance on a narrow sector. The door to Paris and the Rhine was still shut; but now both lock and hinges were beginning to give under the blows of the Allies, and any further pressure on either side threatened to dislodge the whole. At Caen and St-Lô the Allies were steadily gaining freedom to manoeuvre, as the close protracted grappling in the Bocage country came to an end.

The issue was now clear-cut. Could Rommel hold the British armour on the more open ground beyond the Orne and still preserve the strength to prevent the Americans from exploiting their capture of St-Lô? If not, the German armies in France were in peril. That there were now grave misgivings among German senior officers was dramatically revealed when on 20 July, immediately following the fall of St-Lô and the attack across the Orne, an attempt was made to assassinate Hitler.

The strain was beginning to tell. The period of desperate battles for a single village, for a farmhouse or a hill, of advances measured in hundreds of yards, was nearly over. The Germans still had their heels dug in, but they were 'leaning over backwards'. Everything pointed to some decisive upheaval when the Allies burst out of the bridgehead. The scene was set now for one of the major land-battles of history. All France waited, seething under the surface of apparent submission – all France, that is, except the small strip of Normandy over which the fighting had already passed. Here, close to the beaches, life was returning to something like normal. Here, in a few trivial incidents – touching in their simplicity – was to be seen a token of the liberation that France and Holland and Belgium awaited impatiently after the long years of anxious hope.

18 July 1944

'There is a little girl aged about six who is standing all by herself with a handful of flowers, field flowers, and she is offering them, rather timidly, as the drivers of the transports pass. The drivers take no notice of her, but she doesn't seem to care; she's just playing a game that she saw grown-ups play a few weeks ago. She offers one to you, well, you missed the flower throwing, so you lean over and you accept one. And with it you get a smile, a real smile, a genuine sudden smile, and she gives you all her flowers, all of them. It seems you're the only customer she's had all day. Other children cluster round you; a little boy aged about five is smoking a cigarette; you sign to him to put the darn thing out, but he frowns and blows smoke at you. You follow the stream of traffic through a little village, admiring the freshness of the houses. They must have been repainted this spring, you think; the gardens look tidy too. The people look quite happy; the battle

176

must have bypassed this place, that's what you think, until you reach the foot of the village; there four corner houses have been smashed and burned, their walls raked and pitted by machine-gun bullets and scarred by mortar bombs. This is where the fight for the village took place. It's the same at the farms; you'll pass three farms, quite pleasant and untouched, the farm people going ahead with their work. But the fourth farm is a shambles; the buildings are smashed, the barn is wrecked, and there are black circles in the fields where haystacks were set ablaze and burned to the ground. The trip has been slow and dusty, and you haven't seen as much as you'd like to have seen, and already it's time to turn back to the airstrip; and as you go back, in slow dusty convoy again, one scene sticks in your mind. In the front garden of a house a rug has been stretched on the grass and on it a tiny baby is asleep. As you pass you catch sight of the mother, busy with her housework, glancing from the window to see that baby is still asleep. It's asleep all right in the open air and within half a mile of the front line.'

ROBERT BARR

CHAPTER VII
The Breakthrough

'Hitler, count your men'

In the last days of July a great Russian drive in the East carried Red Army troops into Bialystok, Stanislavov, Dvinsk, Rezhitsa, Siauliai, and Lvov, while the fall of Brest–Litovsk was imminent. Simultaneously the Americans launched a full-scale attack on the west coast towards Coutances and Avranches. The dreaded 'war on two fronts' – or, more strictly, on three fronts [*Italy as well*] – was now an active reality, straining German resources everywhere.

27 July 1944

'The Americans have made a complete breakthrough in the middle of their offensive line west of St-Lô. American armour is within five miles of the important centre of Coutances on the west coast of the Cherbourg peninsula, fifteen miles south of Lessay. American infantry attacking south down the west coast have bypassed both Lessay and Périers, which are in their hands. Considerable numbers of Germans are threatened with encirclement between Coutances and Lessay. Already the Americans have taken over 2400 prisoners. The American attack has in fact disrupted the whole German defensive system between St-Lô and the west coast. But apart from this westward drive towards Coutances, American tanks are moving south down the western side of the Vire River in the centre of their front. On the eastern side of the river, which is to say east of St-Lô, American infantry have gained distances of up to two miles and are pushing on against weakening opposition. The weakening of the enemy's resistance on the western and eastern limits of the present defensive line is a natural consequence of the swift and powerful breakthrough which the armour has achieved in the centre. Enemy resistance has been split up into several compartments. In some of these compartments the Germans are fighting very bitterly until the last moment, but the total effect of the attack as it has developed now must be to make the enemy seek for a new line a considerable distance south of the line he held three days ago.'

ROBERT DUNNETT

29 July 1944

'At this moment Field-Marshal Rommel [*it was not known by the Allies that Rommel was in hospital, having been injured in an air attack on 11 July*] is a victim of the old army game – a game in which the Allied forces in Normandy again have called the tune. The American breakthrough on the western sector of their Normandy front has completed a series of bluffs and counter-bluffs made by the Allied Command, and is now finding its pay-off by the successes of the US Army forces south of the Cherbourg peninsula. The way the Allies have played this game is an interesting study of military strategy. After the fall of Cherbourg the German Command deduced incorrectly that there would be a lot of consolidation and regroupment on the American sector before there could be any further action there. So Rommel concluded that the next move would be an attack on the British sector to the east. He obviously figured that the next Allied move would be a drive for Paris. So he committed some seven divisions around the British and Canadian sector, leaving less concentrated forces more thinly spread along the line of the American sector. When this became clear, the Allies decided that the German Command should go on thinking like this. So the British and Canadians staged a series of sharp, heavy attacks between Caen and Tilly that gained the British bridgehead across the River Odon. This was followed by the attack on Caen itself, which resulted in the capture of the northern half of the town. And then there was the big air blitz down the eastern side of the Orne River, which ended in the complete capture of Caen, and the establishment of a comfortable bridgehead around the city.

'By the time these attacks had finished, more German forces were concentrated on this eastern sector. Then General Bradley made his big move five days ago. And now Rommel is in the position of a poker player who has put so much money into the pot that he cannot afford to drop out of the game. And he has to play it the way the Allied Command wants it to be played.'

BILL DOWNS, CBS

28 July 1944

'It was a true Blitzkrieg – American style – a 1944 repetition of all the stories you've heard about the German armoured breakthrough in Poland, France and Russia. Smashing through a break in the German lines, created by American infantry, came the big American tanks, boiling up the dusty French roads, uncoiling in the German rear and spreading panic in the German supply-lines. On both sides of the tremendous whine of American tanks we could hear the rattle of machine-guns and the bark of mortars, but the tanks ignored them and fought relentlessly behind a fiercely-fighting German rearguard. Creating their own roads through the French apple orchards, bowling over trees, smashing through the six-foot-high Normandy church walls with their newly designed equipment, the American tanks shot up everything in sight. They passed through flaming villages littered with German tanks, self-propelled guns, even wrecked German field-kitchens. There was the greatest toll of destroyed German equipment that I've seen since D-Day. In vain the Germans tried to withdraw their guns to prevent our armour from piercing their tender rear, but so obviously had they been taken by surprise that at one place I saw a burning German tank from which they hadn't even time to remove the camouflage netting. Standing high in the open hatches of their big Sherman tanks rode the American tank men, big husky fellows, looking like professional football players in their tank helmets, a look of exultation on their dusty faces, and their huge goggles giving them a grim, inhuman expression. Standing in the burning town of Canisy, south of St-Lô, I heard their voices coming in from the extreme advanced tip of the tank column. Once I heard them say: "We're up against German anti-tank guns. Meeting intense fire on our flank." But the American general added in an uncompromising tone, "Get along there, tanks, keep pushing, keep pushing"; and the tanks kept pushing.'

LARRY LESUEUR, CBS

While the tanks kept pushing, the control posts were busy with new directions as the General in Command [*Bradley*] telephoned his men forward to exploit the advantage that had been won:

27 July 1944
' "All right, boy," said the general, "all right, boy. I'll tell you – it's your job. You handle it. All right. Oh I think the whole thing's going to loosen up shortly because Schinburger is twenty-five hundred yards south. He's on his objective 'C'. And now, is Bailey's left as far down as this map of mine indicates – is he down as close as two hundred yards from the road?

' "Well, he ought to be able to move in – and cut it then. Yes. But without him you just got to tell – tell Bailey – that he's got to get in there with some grenades and clean that out." '

ROBERT DUNNETT

After the fall of Cherbourg in late June the clearing of the port became a priority. One correspondent joined the diving team clearing mines in the harbour.

19 July 1944

'I've just returned from the bottom of Cherbourg Harbour, where in several fathoms of water I was watching a diver – one of the many working over there. I was walking through a forest of wavy green tentacles and trying to follow that diver.

'The light from the day above us came down in a shaft of green twilight like green moonlight through a hole in the roof of an old cathedral chancel. I could just see him through the six-foot waving weeds laboriously walking in front of me like a slow-motion picture of a Frankenstein fighter. He had his hands spread out from his sides knee-high. He was searching for enemy mines. The enemy had laid quantities of every conceivable type of mine in that harbour. A few block ships were sunk, but not many.

'When I scrambled over the side, and slid down that rope into the water, I'd had a pat on my helmet from the attendant, and then down I went into the green dimness. It seemed as though the going down would never stop. I thought of Alice in Wonderland. A dull flash went by my vision glass – some sort of fish. I'd lost the sense of those dragging weights on my diving gear and now that wavy grass started to weave around me. My feet were going in some slimy stuff and then the grass was suddenly higher than my head. A tremendous weight seemed to be pressing in on my eardrums, they went dead, a sharp stab came in my forehead: it increased, it became intolerable and for a second I think I blacked out. Then my brain cleared and I could see again but only horizontally for a distance of about five feet. That was when through that waving forest the diver I was looking for came into view.

'He was able seaman John Mell from Bedfordshire and he walked ponderously past me while a little dribble of bubbles went up from his helmet. He's an eerie, shadowy shape in a bottle-green world searching for any hidden menace that his 18-pound diving boots might crash into. His life depends on slender air holes and the men up on deck who look after it. If a mine that has been overlooked should go up now anywhere in the harbour, he'd be just a jelly. There are many more like him, searching the basins, working round wrecks and patrolling where the minesweepers cannot reach.

'It was my intention to record what I saw through the microphone in my helmet up to a recorder on deck and I signalled that I was ready to begin. But after about three minutes I was talking as if I'd been running upstairs. When I came to listen to the records that I'd made – here is what they sounded like: [*indistinct watery noises "this is Stanley Maxted talking from the bottom of Cherbourg Harbour with difficulty . . ."*]. The sound that you heard and which was drowning out my voice is the pulsing bubbles of air that are pumped down and are coming into my diving helmet.

'As soon as I was finished talking, the lads on deck hauled away and the waving grass dropped below me and gradually disappeared. I went up hand over hand with no effort of my own and at last my head burst into daylight and as I clung on the iron ladder that hangs over the side of the ship they wrenched my helmet off and I gulped great gusts of lovely cool fresh air and yet I thought that these fellas do it all the time.

'As I looked around me I saw two little mine-sweeping motor launches steaming in from outside. For days now these little ships have been plodding steadily up and down in the harbour clearing such of its mines as could be swept – and not without loss. Coming through the gap in the breakwater behind them was the first of a group of Liberty ships also the first to enter Cherbourg Harbour.

As that leading one steamed gingerly in I saw her name – *Nathaniel Bacon* – the forerunner of many others and of even larger ships. By the time I was undressed and in my right mind again they were unloading on to huge lighters and I saw these chugging through to the hards against the background of gargantuan rubble, battered harbour forts and skeleton buildings.'

STANLEY MAXTED

While American spearheads were breaking through towards Brittany, British forces in the centre of the line pushed southwards from Caumont and seized Le Bény Bocage in a dramatic race against time before Rommel could switch his armour from the neighbourhood of Caen:

1 August 1944

'While our columns of tanks and infantry were fighting southwards towards Bény Bocage, part of a German Panzer division was hurrying westwards from the Caen sector to occupy that village and the high ground on either side of it. We won the race primarily because of a daring sortie by four British armoured cars early yesterday morning.

'While our main forces were still held up at St Martin, five miles north of Bény Bocage, these four armoured cars found a gap in the German line and slipped through before the German anti-tank gunners realised what had happened. Four more armoured cars tried to follow, but they were shot up.

'The first four shot on, southward, through empty villages; by 7 am they'd reached the River Souleuvre, just short of Bény Bocage, at the point where the main road crosses it; they'd got the bridge, the only bridge for six miles, but four armoured cars couldn't hope to hold it. So they radioed back for tanks and infantry, and meantime they hid in the trees, only a few yards away from the bridge, waited and watched the Germans passing back and forth across it.

'And back near St Martin our tanks tried to get through; six of them did so before the German anti-tank gunners woke up. But the seventh was mopped up and it blocked the track. No more could get down until St Martin was taken in the middle of the day.

'By this time the six tanks had joined the four armoured cars at the bridge, but this was a very slender force to hold an objective so vital. Early in the afternoon we sent an armoured column down the road from St Martin; for the sake of speed the infantry rode on the backs of tanks, which roared down the narrow lane the armoured cars had taken, but by this time the Germans had troops astride the track.

'Three times the infantry had to dismount and clean out machine-gun posts before the column could go on, but it got on, and it reached the bridge yesterday evening just as a Grenadier battalion of that Panzer division was moving on to a wooded hill beyond the bridge. Again the infantry dismounted, surged forward into the wood, and caught the Germans just as they were sorting themselves out.

'In a couple of hours the British infantry cleared the wood, took thirty or forty prisoners, and sent the remainder scuttling back into Bény Bocage. During the night Panzer Grenadiers tried to organise the defence of the village, but by dawn this morning we had brought up fresh infantry and tanks. As they pushed on to Bény Bocage French civilians came out to warn them that there was no need to bombard it. The Germans were already pulling out.'

CHESTER WILMOT

Where speed was all-important, the RAF often played a decisive part in interrupting German movement. As the American thrust developed, more and more German armour tried to disengage and hurry westward. The situation was so critical that German tanks were obliged to travel in daylight and risk attack from the air. Very often they paid the price of their recklessness:

3 August 1944

'There was considerable confusion late yesterday afternoon in the town of Condé-sur-Noireau. I am afraid that our Typhoons were again responsible. Condé-sur-Noireau is one of those little towns that is difficult to get through even in a normal traffic jam; but when you come into it from Vire on the west or from Falaise on the east, you've got to negotiate sharp bends in the town itself; and right in the middle a single and not very wide bridge spans the River Noireau. It's not the best spot for two large convoys of vehicles to meet coming in opposite directions and wanting to go places in a hurry, which is just what happened yesterday. By late yesterday afternoon Vire was showing signs of being surrounded, and this morning it's virtually in a state of siege. A large number of German vehicles, with quite a high proportion of staff cars among them, scuttled out of Vire yesterday afternoon and made for Condé-sur-Noireau. Meanwhile, to try to help an increasingly difficult situation on the high ground south of Aunay, German armour was being rushed across from around Falaise. The two convoys met in Condé-sur-Noireau, and even before the RAF took a hand in the proceedings there must have been a good deal of hearty Teutonic swearing going on on that narrow bridge over the river. We sent in everything we'd got to add to the confusion – both bomb-phoons and rock-phoons [*bomb-carrying and rocket-carrying Typhoons*]. Pilots came back clamouring for more ammunition, and with stories of batches of twenty or thirty Germans running in all directions and being shot up as they ran, and a really superb traffic jam asking for our attention. We killed a lot of Germans. We destroyed a large number of enemy transport; but the most important item in our claim is twenty tanks definitely left blazing.'

ALAN MELVILLE

✑∞✒

Around Vire British and American forces worked closely together as they advanced, and it sometimes happened that the two armies overlapped:

5 August 1944

'For example, the other day a British armoured unit was ordered to occupy a wood. It so happened that the Americans also were told to occupy this wood. Over one of the British tanks' radios the headquarters asked the British tank commander what he had found in the wood. "Millions of Americans," the tank commander replied. Headquarters then said, "We have learned that German tanks also have been ordered to occupy that wood." The British commander was silent for a minute, and then said, "Sorry, there won't be any room here for them!"'

BILL DOWNS, CBS

✑∞✒

And indeed, there was increasingly little room in Normandy for the Germans. Every road now seemed to be crowded and choked with all kinds of Allied transport moving steadily southward, south to Avranches, to Rennes, to Brittany. The German defence-line was breached; hour by hour a great procession of vehicles poured through the gap:

6 August 1944

'It was almost dark, and the only light allowed on the jeep were the "cat's eyes" – little tiny thin points of light that show just a few feet off to warn other drivers that you're coming. The glow-worms in the hedges – and there are a lot of them round here – seem to throw out more light than those "cat's eyes". If you put on your dust goggles, you can't see at all; and if you leave them off, well, the dust almost blinds you. And all the time huge dark shapes loom up on either side of you.

'It's not just tanks, tank destroyers, and guns, and armoured cars: you take them for granted. It's the completeness of the material that staggers you. Great bulldozers for cutting new roads; trucks that pack a tank aboard and make it look small; headquarters on wheels, and even special devices for setting up telephone poles along the sides of the road. It's a mechanical army down to the last detail, and it's an army that's moving forward at a tremendous pace.'

ROBIN DUFF

Every tank was needed now, but not less imperative was the call for bulldozers to clear the way:

1 August 1944

'Although we've advanced some twelve miles in three days, several senior officers have told me that our progress would have been even better if we'd had more bulldozers. One commander said, "I'd rather have another fifty bulldozers than fifty extra tanks," and today bulldozers were priority traffic. In one convoy I saw ten of them riding in state, on transporters usually reserved for tanks. Bulldozers were even borrowed from the RAF and they moved up to cut new tracks and to widen the existing ones. And they were badly needed. For almost every road and lane today was jammed with traffic, and the dust was as bad as anything I've struck in the desert.

'On these roads I think the Military Police have about the worst job of all. They must stand at their crossroads all day regardless of dust and shell. The MPs that I saw looked as though they'd been sprayed with grey paint. Many of them had been on duty almost continuously day and night for the past three days getting the traffic forward, and that's no easy job.

'At one crossroads yesterday a convoy of armoured vehicles was streaming forward. A colonel in a jeep wanted to cut across the convoy, and so he shouted to a Military Police officer near by: "I must get back, I have to report to General Montgomery." "That's all right," came the reply, "this traffic must get forward to fight for General Montgomery," and the MP on duty continued to wave the convoy through.'

CHESTER WILMOT

Maintenance of clear traffic-ways was one problem. Maintenance of the vehicles was another:

6 August 1944

'It used to be the custom to deal with broken-down or damaged vehicles at a central depot run by REME. But now, when you drive along the roads in Normandy, you see vehicles that have been hit or have had some serious mechanical trouble – and you see a sign that has cut out a wealth of organisation with the typical cryptic simplicity of a Montgomery army: it says, "Help yourself to spares." If you need a new spark plug, a back tyre, a carburettor, a headlight bulb, well then, if that vehicle can supply you, you can have whatever you want from it. And it's amazing how well this system works; you see a truck that's been by the side of the road for a month or so, and you'll find that it's been stripped right down to its chassis; and most likely some sapper has had a bit of that to use as a light girder. Yes, it's an economical way of doing a job; there are no forms, no indents, and it needs no one to run it.'

DAVID BERNARD

Roads clear of obstructions, vehicles in good running order – and, almost as important, maps. New maps to keep pace with fast-moving armour:

6 August 1944

'On more than one occasion this week when I've set out for the front, the sheaf of maps I've taken with me, the ones I used yesterday, they've turned out to be no good, for the Americans have run right off the map during the night and I've had to get a new set to keep up to date. But maps are always there, thanks to the field topographic units which work close up to the line with their mobile printing-presses, their teams of surveyors and draughtsmen and lithographers, who turn out maps of all sorts by the hundreds of thousands, in eight or nine different colours according to the purpose for which the maps are required.

'I am now standing in a field printing-press – actually it's housed in a four-ton truck. This reminds me very much of my newspaper days: there's a rotary press in front of me with coloured rollers. It's turning out twenty-five thousand copies of a special map. In a few hours' time, this map will be in the hands of all the troops who are helping to push the Germans right back into the heart of France.'

ROBERT REID

In the first days of August, while the Normandy farmers toiled to bring in their harvest wherever it had escaped ruin, the leading American tanks drove into Rennes. In some of the cornfields there was a strange partnership between peace and war as farmers and soldiers tried not to hamper each other's efforts:

3 August 1944

'I watched three fields being cut this morning. In the first we had dumped about thirty neat stacks of ammunition: the peasants were cutting right up to the edges of the ammo boxes, and now the field has the appearance of a neat symmetrical wallpaper – with three stooks of neatly-cut corn, then a stack of ammunition – then three more stooks and another pile of ammunition, and so on. In the next field we had four ack-ack guns: you could just see the noses of the guns pointing out above the ripe corn, and the crews were hidden altogether. They had cut tidy little circles in the corn round their guns, and the narrowest possible track leading out of the field to their tents up on the roadside. But in this field, too, the peasants were hard at work and, by the time they'd finished, the guns and their crews were standing out looking rather naked in the middle of the freshly cut field. And in the third field, they'd cut all round a Dakota which had dumped itself down in their midst, and then they'd got out their scythes and were attacking the last blades of wheat standing right under the belly of the Dakota.'

ALAN MELVILLE

As the Americans began their great wheeling movement towards Le Mans and Falaise, and a second heavy blow threatened the Riviera coast, the Germans struggled frantically to redress what was rapidly passing out of their control. The attempt to confine the Allies in a narrow space as a kind of grandiose landing party had failed. Now it was to be Army against Army in the grand manner, with room to move and half a continent at stake. The appropriate comment came from an artillery battalion:

29 July 1944
'Their accuracy has been notable. One of the battery commanders has a war-cry which inspires his gunners. After each round is fired he shouts toward the enemy lines, "Hitler, count your men." '

CHARLES SHAW, CBS

CHAPTER VIII
Falaise: The End Of An Army

'We moved up, we moved in, we moved back, and here I am'

On 5 August, after a headlong dash through Brittany, an American column reached the outskirts of Brest [*it finally fell on 19 September*]. During the two following days the Germans made a final bid to defeat the threat to their whole Normandy positions, launching a counter-attack towards Mortain and Avranches with the aim of cutting American communications at their narrowest point – the junction of the Brittany and Cotentin peninsulas. It was a gambler's last throw, for it meant staking everything on success: if the American supply-line held, there would be little prospect of withdrawal from the salient into which the Germans were now advancing.

Things went wrong from the start with this counter-attack. It had been expected; the movement of German armour was quickly noticed by a Rhodesian wing commander on reconnaissance, and he at once called up rocket-firing Typhoons to take advantage of the target that presented itself:

8 August 1944
'Suddenly through the mist I saw a large formation of what appeared to be enemy tanks and transport vehicles. I could hardly believe my eyes. I took a good look at them from about 4000 feet. I would have sworn they were enemy tanks. I went down closer and had another look. This time Jerry was a bit touchy and set off some flak. It was a

bit rough but I got by, and there they were, sitting there like ducks on a pond. I still couldn't believe it. So I went down even farther, almost to the deck, and had another look: it was no mirage, there they were, enemy tanks and MT vehicles. I got back to base at twenty-five minutes past one. Twelve minutes later a fully organised attack was under way, and every twenty minutes after that Jerry caught hell in capital letters. I have never seen Germans run so fast as those chaps in the tanks did as we put in our attack. Some ran to both sides of the road, some of them jumped for the hedges, others took off for the ditches; one pilot of my squadron said he watched some of them climbing trees. It was terrific, and for once the weather man had given us the nod. For there was no doubt that, with the mist lifting as fast as it did, it gave us a very good break. It was just the sort of thing we've been waiting for, and this time we really had him flat-footed. When the first attack started I've never seen aircraft come from so many directions in all my life. They poured down on both sides of me just like rain. The Hun is a master of salvage, so to prevent him from tidying up any of his tanks that were hit we kept burning them up all afternoon and evening. He can't salvage tin cans.'

STEWART MACPHERSON, RECORDING STORY OF
ANONYMOUS WING COMMANDER

છે૭

Von Kluge's last attempt faltered and petered out. [*Von Kluge had replaced von Rundstedt as C-in-C West at the beginning of July, and had taken over direct control of Army Group B when Rommel was injured.*] American supplies continued to pour southwards, and nothing now could stop the triumphant doughboys. In eighteen days one US column [*of Patton's Third Army*] travelled 300 miles. A security blackout concealed their progress for some days; but, when the full extent of the German disaster was disclosed, it showed that

Orléans, Chartres, and Châteaudun had fallen in quick succession, and American tanks were still running wild in the German rear:

14 August 1944

'This American armoured column has raced forward several more miles today and liberated twenty French villages in its secret drive against the dazed and broken remnants of several German divisions. Details of this manoeuvre cannot yet be disclosed, but it is one of daring strategy against the breaking German troops in France. Some Germans are still fighting stubbornly, but in the last few days the majority of the Germans in this area have lost all discipline and have fled individually across fields and down bypaths in retreat, looting food and stealing horses, cars and carts as they go. We can hear isolated small-arms fire behind us in the field as Germans left in the rear by our drive attempt to sneak through hidden trails or hide in French farms and barns. The approaches to one important town, which was captured by this column, are still a flaming graveyard of burning tanks, lorries, pleasure cars, and carts loaded with dead Germans, hanging grotesquely out of their vehicles or remaining grimly in their seats. Many of them ran directly into the approaching American tanks.

'On one main highway the American tanks raced through village after village, pausing only to knock out any remaining anti-tank guns or rounding up large groups of resistance. We passed the usual wildly cheering French throngs who awoke this morning to find American tanks rolling through their streets where only yesterday were Germans. In one little village people had remained locked in their homes for ten days before our arrival, so bad had been the German looting and pillaging.

'One large convoy of German Tiger tanks attempted to escape this column, but American dive-bombers got over it and left it a smoking skeleton a mile long.

'A captured German colonel was crying when he was brought into the American camp, dazed and bewildered by the sudden Allied onslaught. A captive lieutenant, who had fought in Russia and Italy, said the attacks in this secret operation were the most terrifying he had ever experienced, chiefly because of the devastating Allied air and artillery blows.'

ROBERT REUBEN, REUTER

Secure along the banks of the Loire the Americans now wheeled to the north, captured Alençon, and pushed ahead to Argentan in a wide encircling movement designed to gather up the remaining German forces in Normandy. Simultaneously the First Canadian Army fought its way down the Falaise road from Caen to narrow the Germans' escape gap. The Canadian assault, made in darkness, was preceded by a heavy bombing attack:

8 August 1944

'I watched the tons of bombs plunge into their targets last night; strange flashes lit the sky, the effect was weird and terrible, with a three-quarter moon rising over the Orne Valley shining blood red through the haze, and the dust, and the smoke. The concussion of the bombs pressed my clothing against my body, even though I was several miles away, and the ground trembled under my feet. It is a difficult operation, this fighting in the dark; units get confused, lost, and mixed up, so there were other special methods devised to guide the infantry and the tanks forward in the dark. The infantry were given heavily armoured carriers which had been specially converted for them so they could ride forward with the first wave of tanks. These carriers gave them maximum protection against light enemy fire, and against shell and mortar bursts. To guide the ground forces forward the Canadians employed the old trick which the British used at the Battle of Alamein: lines of tracer bullets were shot over their heads, stretching out like rows of electric light bulbs sailing slowly in the air. The tanks and the infantry and their armoured carriers moved forward while the bombing was still on, the lines of tracer bullets (there were more than half a dozen columns of them) floated over the battlefield looking like a roman candle display, and all around hundreds of guns seemed to grab the atmosphere and shake it, and bounce it, and tear it to shreds.'

BILL DOWNS, CBS

8 August 1944

'Our aim was to get our infantry through the enemy's forward defences, his close-knit zones of fire. We were relying on our speed of movement to make the penetration before the Germans could recover from the bombardment, and on the strong armour-plating of the carriers which would deflect bullets and splinters if any enemy troops were able to attack us. 'By dawn the enemy was beginning to recover himself, and to realise what had happened. Then the expected furious reaction began. Fighting became very fluid; it was going on all round our forward troops, north of them attacks from the enemy they'd bypassed, as well as south and east and west. A German armoured battle-force struck at Tilly (south-east of Caen, not Tilly-sur-Seulles) from the east, and drove us clean out of it; our men attacked again with tanks actually recalled for the moment from more forward positions to assist, and we retook the place, taking four German officers and forty other ranks prisoner, and destroying two tanks. Enemy 88-mm guns began firing in our rear and across our line of supply. We couldn't call down air support because our own men were so close to them. The gunners were given the job of silencing them. Both Fontenay and Rocquancourt were attacked from the north, but our men stood firm; they refused to be bewildered by the swirling battle round them. They'd got inside the enemy's skin, and there they were staying. With another tremendous air bombardment throwing up a dust cloud which obliterated the sun, our attack was renewed at one o'clock this afternoon. As I left the battlefield some of those armoured troop carriers were coming back filled with enemy prisoners.'

FRANK GILLARD

Hemmed in on three sides, and with the gap between Argentan and Falaise steadily closing, the Germans had no alternative but retreat. In little more than a fortnight their situation had deteriorated so rapidly and completely that all hope of recovery had gone. Their plight was indeed pitiful, for they had neither the transport nor the air cover to support an orderly withdrawal to the Seine; and even there they could hope for little respite, as almost all the bridges were down and Allied planes in their hundreds waited to strike at every barge that tried to cross:

13 August 1944
'To some small extent the Germans are using ferries across the Seine to replace the destroyed bridges. The wooded banks of the river allow barges to lie up without being seen by day – they ply to and fro by night.

'But as an army the Germans are only about fifty per cent mobile, so any idea of pulling out and rushing back is out of the question. They're necessarily committed to a slow move back. It looks as if the present movement of enemy columns may be caused by a redisposition of his armour so as to hold off and press back the American movement on the southern flank. The best enemy divisions are still fighting well, but many of the others are in poor shape. A staff officer quoted one German prisoner who, when he was taken, described his division's battle practically in these words: "We moved up, we moved in, we moved back, and here I am." '

FRANK GILLARD

In two months of hard and fluctuating fighting the Germans had been outmanoeuvred and outfought. The army that had tried to hurl the Allies back into the sea was disintegrating in the confused carnage of the Falaise pocket, and its commander – Rommel – lay gravely wounded. The pick of the German armour might yet escape, however, so on 14 August General Eisenhower issued an order of the day calling on every man in the Allied armies to take full advantage of the fleeting but definite opportunity to achieve a major Allied victory:

14 August 1944

'He sent it to the field commanders to be forwarded and read to the men in the front line – the troops in the field, to pilots on the airstrips, and to naval units on patrol at sea. The commanders themselves were trying to take full advantage of this fleeting opportunity; and they asked that every means should be used to get this message straight to the men. Here at his command post this morning it was decided to flash the order of the day to London, and to have it broadcast immediately and to have it broadcast again and again – there was no time to be lost.'

ROBERT BARR

While American, British and Canadian troops pressed in on three sides, Allied planes added to the confusion and destruction on the escape-routes east of Falaise, which were soon scarred with fires or columns of smoke every quarter of a mile:

13 August 1944

'The pilots told me that there was complete and utter chaos on the roads. The Germans were being forced to use the back lanes and the narrow winding country roads as well as the main highway from Falaise to Lisieux to try to release their transport. It was impossible, the pilots told me, to determine exactly who hit what and how, so great was the concentration of our aircraft in the sector. It seemed to them that the entire fighter strength of the Second Tactical Air Force, plus a few planes from the American sector, were out today, and the pilots were clamouring to their flight commanders for a chance to go out again and again on sorties which, they added, were just picnics. Fires were burning merrily throughout the whole area, woods were pouring up clouds of black smoke, and dust shot up into the air as high as a thousand feet in some cases. These woods were reported to contain concentrations of enemy mortars, guns, and infantry and tanks. In ditches and in small fields alongside the roads, the pilots said that literally hundreds of vehicles, staff cars, armoured cars, motor cycles, small runabouts, half-tracks, and other types of vehicles were blazing or smoking.'

BILL HERBERT, CBC

Powerless to stop or hamper these incessant attacks from the air, the Germans resorted to an old trick – the use of the Red Cross as the only camouflage likely to be effective:

14 August 1944

'I've talked today to the pilots of three different RAF wings over here – all of whom have been hammering away most successfully at the Germans' precarious escape-route east from Falaise. They all report the same things: an excessively large number of ambulances taking to the roads and heading away from the danger gap.

'Now we've seen these large convoys of ambulances with their roofs clearly marked with the Red Cross – we've seen them before now – sneaking out of towns that were due to fall to either the British, Canadian, or American armies. We watched them racing out of Vire, we've watched them in quite a few places. We've watched them and wondered. There's no need to wonder any longer. I spoke tonight to a very angry intelligence officer at one fighter wing. He won't call them "ambulances" in his reports. He uses the phrase "vehicles marked with red crosses". I've met some angry pilots too – the pilots of a Typhoon wing who were shot at from one convoy of ambulances as they raced south-east from Falaise this afternoon. Pilots who saw the ambulances stop abruptly as our aircraft got near them – who watched the doors open and a surprisingly large number of obviously healthy Germans nip out and beat it as fast as they could for the ditches and hedges. Pilots who, having seen this happen and being consequently quite certain that these were no ambulances at all, opened fire and discovered that the Hun is getting petrol as well as men away from the Falaise area under the cover of the Red Cross. The ambulances made an unmistakable and satisfactory conflagration. And pilots who actually saw convoys of vehicles tearing along the roads with one German soldier sitting on the top of each vehicle. He had a very important job; when our aircraft got anywhere near, it was up to him to pull a white sheet with a big red cross on it over the roof of the vehicle.'

ALAN MELVILLE

By fair means or foul, the Germans were trying frantically to pull out before the dwindling gap finally closed. Riding on anything they could find – sometimes three men together on a horse or a bicycle – they turned eastward and fled:

18 August 1944

'We know now that the first series of columns attempting to escape from our grasp a week or so ago were administrative units pulling out. After that, the enemy seemed slow to react to the situation. Possibly he didn't realise how serious it was. There was a steady seep away, but nothing more. But as the day before yesterday and during yesterday the escape gap began to close, there was a sudden convulsive attempt to get away. Masses of transport were seen assembling in fields and side roads; the Seine ferries appeared even in daylight. At first the plan seemed to be that the armour should hold the line while the infantry got out. Then suddenly the SS divisions realised that the Poles were closing their escape gap on one side and the French on the other. At that point they abandoned the infantry and concentrated on getting out themselves. Today the gap has become still narrower, and we've been watching most frantic efforts by the Germans to get through it before it becomes too late. Those who have managed to escape are obliged to go north-east towards the Seine; they can't attempt to get out through the Paris–Orleans gap, because if they go that way they're cutting themselves off from all their supplies. Within a very short time now we should be counting heads and finding who and what we've caught in our trap. It's bound to be a very sizeable force, most likely with elements – in some cases comparatively few in number, perhaps – of a round dozen German infantry divisions and probably of four Panzer divisions.'

FRANK GILLARD

As the Battle of Normandy closed, with the junction of the Allies at Chambois, the Allied Air Forces made a last great attack on the German transport and armour that choked the roads in a last-minute effort to escape:

18 August 1944

'A few moments ago one of the ace Typhoon pilots of the Royal Air Force – a wing commander – set his Typhoon down on a landing-strip here at an advanced airfield in Normandy, jumped out of his aircraft, and walked briskly into the briefing room where several pilots were having a sunbathe, and in a few curt words started the greatest Typhoon attack of the war against enemy transport. Those words were: "Quickly, all of you lads, get around this map. Now here's something you've all been waiting for: it's bigger than Mortain. I've just seen close to five thousand enemy vehicles of all ruddy sorts choking these roads and bridges east and south-east of Les Moutiers. You can't miss; get cracking and fill your hat."

' "How many aircraft, sir?" asked a squadron leader. "Every blank blank thing that can fly, but get going," replied the wing commander, and the attack was on.

'Minutes later, the sky was one long, unbroken string of Typhoons racing for the area where the wing commander had reported a mass withdrawal by the enemy. "They must be desperate," he said to me. "Every sort of transport and armour is to be seen. There are hundreds of Huns just walking along the roads in a daze. I went down almost to the deck to see what was doing and there wasn't a single shot fired." In a few minutes Spitfire cover was laid on to provide the Typhoons with protection, and the attack was now in full swing. The first pilots back from the attack were almost incoherent as they burst into the Intelligence Hut; there was no attempt to keep an up-to-the-minute score of transport destroyed or set on fire. All they wanted to do was to get back on the run.

'I've only just left an airfield, just in time to make this report. The pilots up there are tired, but they're wild with excitement. I've seen them tonight filling their own tanks up with petrol, and helping the ground crews to rearm, saving precious seconds in the turn-round. I've even helped fill tanks myself. Remember those ground crews tonight, as well as the pilots, because they have been magnificent today.'

STEWART MACPHERSON AND ALAN MELVILLE

At last the smoke began to die down. The battle rolled to the eastward, away from the area of Falaise. German remnants were fleeing towards the Seine pursued by fighters and fighter-bombers and armoured pursuit columns. All that remained in Normandy of the German Seventh Army was the thousands of prisoners filtering through our lines – nearly 100,000 taken in one week – and the miles upon miles of burnt-out wreckage littering the roads. Between the Falaise area and the Seine we found wreckage of more than 10,000 vehicles, tanks, and guns of all kinds:

21 August 1944

'The road from Falaise to Argentan runs straight as a line across rolling country; driving down it this morning we came over the brow of a hill and there, stretched out before us, reaching right back out of sight, was an enormous column of prisoners, such a sight as I haven't seen since the last days in North Africa. They were marching, or, I should say, they were trudging three abreast, packed tightly together with a few Bren carriers interspersed down the column carrying the wounded – the weary, tattered, unshaven remnants of the German Seventh Army, tramping back in the pouring rain towards the prisoners' camps, lugging their kit with them, and with their blankets draped over their heads and shoulders trying hard to keep dry.

'Rear of the fighting line we met a rather harassed-looking officer doing his best to cope with battle and prisoners at the same time. "I don't know what to do with them," he said. "They just keep coming in on us." At a Brigade Headquarters we were told: "Our brigade and a Recce regiment took over 1100 yesterday. This morning at nine o'clock the Recce telephoned to say they'd got sixty more; at twenty past nine they said it was 300; by half-past ten it was over 1000 again."

'I saw a list of the divisions from which these prisoners came. There were fifteen divisions named, infantry divisions, para, Panzer, and SS. What a mix-up! And what a revelation of the present disorganised and confused state of the German Seventh Army!

'Five miles from Argentan we turned off the road north-east along a country lane. This had been one of the German escape lines through the gap; now it's just a graveyard of German equipment and troops. Bulldozers had to be used to sweep away the piled-up wreckage along this lane, and open it to our advancing infantry. It's an almost indescribable scene; every conceivable kind of vehicle is there, German guns and tanks and trucks and armoured cars and staff cars and amphibious cars, and wooden carts loaded up with ammunition, with stores and with food, all utterly and completely smashed up. You could see where motor engines had been wrenched from their bearings by the force of the explosions and hurled twenty and thirty yards. Panther tanks had their turrets shorn clean off; the hull of the tank would be one side of the road and the turret on the other. That's what a rocket-firing Typhoon can do.

'You can see how the Germans time and time again had desperately swerved off the road to avoid air attacks, seeking shelter under the trees in an orchard or under the thick hedge of a field. How on earth our pilots found them I don't know. Some had completely smothered themselves in greenery, yet they'd had their dose of trouble just the same.

'Some of the most frightful slaughter of the whole of this war must have taken place up and down this road a few days ago.

'I met some gunners along the lane looking at the results of their work, for they too had a very big share in the destruction of these trapped

German forces. They told me that they'd called this area their killing ground. Scores of enemy vehicles had just been abandoned for lack of petrol; they'd been smashed up in some way and left. And through it all our own troops were going forward on foot to continue the chase. Greatly elated they were at the victory they'd won. Some of those I saw this morning had been fighting with scarcely any break since June. Today, they could see the results of their efforts. Many of them were singing, shouting, whistling, laughing, as they came down the road in the rain.'

FRANK GILLARD

It was victory, such as we had scarcely dared to imagine victory over a mighty German army, fighting on ground of its own choosing and led by a brilliant general. Here was an exact measure of comparative strength: if the Germans were unable to check the Allies on the short line between Caen and Avranches they could hardly hope to make an effective stand west of the Siegfried Line – perhaps not there even. In the intoxication of a great success, it seemed as if the final collapse of Germany might be very near; but, to the men who pursued towards the Seine, war was still just war – war against mines and booby-traps and rearguard actions, war against the elaborate technique of retreat in which the Germans had proved themselves to be adept:

21 August 1944

'You have to move a little faster, the convoys are more crowded, and you spend a lot more time looking at the back end of the truck ahead of you, and you don't spend more than a night or two in the same slit trench – you move forward all the time. You eat a lot of cold rations because you're on the move and when you bump into the enemy rearguard the fighting is just as bitter as it was before. And when you take the Nazi-held position you find that there haven't been many Germans because the enemy has retreated, and there isn't much booty and not many prisoners – yet. But there are mines, hundreds of them. They lie in the roads, and sometimes there is a string of six of them down a road. You set one off and the whole road goes up for ten yards ahead and behind you. And there are plenty of the S mines – the nasty anti-personnel type that jumps into the air before it explodes and then hurls bits of steel and ball bearings to kill or wound anything living within a hundred feet radius. You have to be mighty careful where you step. And then there are the booby-traps. Maybe you see a bottle of wine lying beside a bombed building, but you don't touch it. And maybe there is a tempting apple-tree beside the road – the apples are just getting big enough to eat, but you leave that tree alone too because it might blow up in your face if you pulled a branch down. There are plenty of snipers, but you've learned to pay not much attention to them any more, for if someone gets it from a sniper a detachment is sent out to clean him out and the advance continues.

'This might be the big retreat of the defeated German Seventh Army, but it's still just war to the man with the job of pushing the Nazis back. And the German kills just as effectively when he retreats as when he advances.'

BILL DOWNS, CBS

༄

In the same way there was a price to be paid for the first ecstatic moments of liberation, as it was realised what the years of oppression had irrevocably taken away from the life of France – relatives dead, industries ruined, buildings wrecked, homes destroyed, the priceless commonplaces of existence obliterated and befouled. Behind the resounding words 'Victory' and 'Liberation' there lies always the desolation of the battlefield, the indiscriminate tragedies of individual lives:

12 August 1944

'When I got into Granville, I drove down towards the harbour where an uncle of mine had a ship's chandler's shop. I inquired about it from the people on the corner as I waited in the traffic queue. "You've been away four years, haven't you, my boy?" said a woman, her eyes filling with tears. "Well, your uncle died a year ago; and your cousin – he died in an air raid by the RAF only last week." As I went round the town, gay and happy to be free, the same sad tale of death met me everywhere. My father's cousins – four of them – had all died. They were getting on in years, but privations and worry had hastened their deaths. Many of the young people I'd known were not back from Germany, they were still in the Stalags. Others had been deported to Germany in the past two years, slaves for the German war machine. The leader of the Resistance movement, a quiet, philosophical old professor of English at the local school, had been found cudgelled and full of tommy-gun bullets in a field seven days before the liberation he'd worked so hard to bring about.

'I found an aunt of mine in the street – she wept with joy, took me home, and after all the excitement and kissing was over, she still had to cook on a little fire of charcoal in the backyard – they'd been blitzed out of their house some weeks ago. My uncle still had to count the slices before he cut the bread, still they have no electricity, no gas, no candles either; but they don't worry about these things any longer. They think of the future; the conversation turns continually to the subject of rebuilding, of reorganising. The main topic is the prisoners – do they know their fathers, their mothers, their wives, their children, are safe and free? Each family, remember, has a prisoner or deportee in Germany. They talk also of the people in the large towns – Paris, the industrial cities of the north, who write such pathetic letters asking always for food.

'I asked: "How's my cousin so-and-so?" "Didn't you know?" they say: "he was arrested six months ago – and taken to Paris as a hostage. He's been shot."

'Yes, you see, when the great, deep joy of the first hours of liberation have passed, the hardships of war, both physical and moral, are still there.'

PIERRE LEFEVRE

Free French war correspondent Pierre Lefèvre broadcast to France as well as making memorable dispatches on the effects of four years of occupation on ordinary French families.

CHAPTER IX
The Road To Paris

'They do not have enough flags'

While the closing of the Falaise Gap and the virtual annihilation of the German Seventh Army were on the point of completion a fresh Allied invasion was reported. Landing at points on a 100-mile front between Marseilles and Nice, American, British, and French forces of Mediterranean Command added a new and grave complication to German difficulties in the West. Mr Churchill's presence in Italy had increased German suspicions that a landing in southern France was imminent, but the enemy was quite unable to hold off the Allied forces, which swept through the coastal defences and pushed swiftly inland:

15 August 1944
'I flew in an observation plane alongside a great fleet of troop-carrier planes, each towing a glider. Ahead of us at dawn another fleet of carriers had dropped hundreds of parachute troops, British and American; and dropped them inland of our beach-head, and before the seaborne force landed. Our air armada was a tremendous sight. Tow-planes and gliders, four abreast in one great procession a mile or two long, flying at 2000 feet high in the blue sky, with fighter cover glinting, and whirling overhead and the placid blue sea below. We sighted the coast of France and braced ourselves; but no, we crossed a jagged rocky coast of twisting corniche roads and red-roofed villas and flew on, on and on, over land, over occupied southern France, and there still wasn't any shot fired – no flak, no enemy fighters. Over

the hills we went, and then down into a valley with fertile fields and rolling farmlands. It wasn't merely that there was no shooting. There wasn't a solitary sign of life – not a person, not a vehicle was to be seen down below. And I could see it all very clearly in the hot brilliant sunshine. Moreover our plane went wheeling down provocatively to not much more than 600 feet; and still not a thing happened – not a gun, not a movement. That, at any rate, was our party's experience. It was uncanny. It was fine. Just some smoke coming up from near one village and some more smoke from near what looked like a barracks. And then as we flew we saw where the parachute troops had come. We flew over that spot where they had come and dropped before us. For there were hundreds of bright-coloured discarded parachutes lying on fields and hedges and tree-tops below us; all well together – excellent drops they must have been. Those parachutes, lots and lots of them, made the country look like a giant garden of lovely vivid flowers.

'And then, one after the other, our gliders slipped their tow-ropes and slid and circled down to make excellent landings. I myself saw only one crash. It was most skilful – I saw fourteen gliders land beautifully, close together, in one not too big field, half grass, half ploughed. They raised just a dust cloud, and then they stopped and out came men. And we, we wheeled and back we went, our plane and the tow-planes, and still unopposed, back over the coast, a Riviera coast, that was lovely, beautiful there in the hot sun. Still not a shot, still not a soul to be seen, not a vehicle, not a movement. This is a great day, a new assault on the enemy in great strength. Great things are happening in the area between Nice and Marseilles.'

GODFREY TALBOT

16 August 1944

'The first indications are that the Germans, as well as the local people, were completely surprised. One big gang of Germans were just setting off to work on the railroad when they were caught by our fire. As our jeep rolled ashore we found army and navy engineers rolling vehicles along over wire and steel mats on the soft sand. Piles of life-preservers lay where our assault soldiers had tossed them. White paint and sandbags marked a newly made road. A German cement wall eight feet high, five feet thick, thirty yards from the sea proved no obstacle.

'Our men here are already resting under pine-trees, eating fresh grapes, talking with girls. One ringleted girl was wearing a GI helmet and a broad smile. A jeep is shaded with a great white beach parasol; while a barefoot soldier dozes, in complete peace, despite destroyer shells passing overhead on their way inland.

'There are a few wrecked villas, a few dead horses on the road, but during the entire day the only evidence of resistance which I have seen has been two shells which landed near our LST this morning. The general of the division I am with has just told me the Germans were alerted in this area at midnight last night, with the first word that we were coming. They apparently didn't believe we could land successfully in the small and narrow beaches we chose. And they thought their defences – such as cement walls – would make penetration impossible.'

ERIC SEVEREID, CBS

∽∾

Coastal resistance in the landing area was quickly confined to the two great ports of Marseilles and Toulon. While appropriate units were detached to deal with them, General Patch's main force [*US Seventh Army*] drove swiftly up the Rhone Valley. There was never any question of manoeuvring for a battle in the Normandy style: having failed to stop the landings and conscious of a disastrous defeat in the north, the Germans pulled out at once. [*The German Nineteenth Army on the Riviera coast, together with the First Army on the Biscay coast, formed Army Group G under General Blaskowitz.*]

After four years of occupation, France was on the eve of liberation. The southern naval bases were beleaguered, and the enemy's grasp of Lyons was being challenged. What remained of Army Group B was in flight towards the Seine. The Atlantic U-boat bases were isolated [*Lorient, St-Nazaire and La Rochelle remained in German hands until the end of the war*], and Allied patrols – heading for Paris – had reached Versailles. Spontaneous risings by the Maquis added to the confusion already caused by the collapse of German communications and the 'blackout' on news of General Patton's tanks. In some districts all semblance of a coherent 'front' dissolved in a general mêlée – to the consternation, at times, of both sides. There was one occasion when two petrol supply columns met on a lonely road: one was German, the other American, and no combat troops were attached to either. Both sides, in sudden surprise, stepped on the gas and whizzed past each other at full speed. On another occasion two American war correspondents, Thomas Treanor and Donald Grant, were sleeping in a French village when a German tank column drove in:

16 August 1944

'The column stopped and I heard a boyish voice some distance down the column shout something. I couldn't catch the words, but at first I thought it was a Frenchman. In a moment another voice just a few feet from the window called out roughly, "Ich will schlafen." My knowledge of German is limited, but I understood that. He was saying he wanted to sleep. It occurred to me that he might soon be wanting to sleep in my bed. It was a miserable thought. It was the closest I have ever been to the enemy. Grant says that sometimes these commanders standing in their turrets were so close to the second-storey window that he could have lit their cigarettes for them. We decided that there were two main courses open. We could either lie low or we could go out the back door and cut across the fields. Grant went into the old woman's room and woke her to ask her advice. He probably speaks the most atrocious French in all the world and the woman was so old that she's quite deaf. His whispers sounded like escaping steam, and I could hear the old woman saying in a voice like a bullfrog, "What, what?" Finally she said, "Ah, you want a light." Grant almost screamed in his next whisper, "No, no, no, no want light; it's the Boches, Boches." "Ah, the Boches," she said; "no, they have gone since yesterday." He gave up trying with the old woman and meanwhile outside the Germans were having a quarrel about which way to go. They were yelling at one another in irritated voices. One commander jumped out of his tank and ran a few yards to the corner, where he switched a flashlight on the road sign. Then he ran back. One man roamed around in our garden just below my window where I had planned to jump to escape in case they entered the house. But eventually the column pulled out. A great deal of shooting went on during the rest of the night. In the morning the French were back in the town, and one messenger said that altogether they had knocked out nine of the German tanks. We went down the road and found in one place at least two of the knocked-out tanks, burning and smoking.'

THOMAS TREANOR, NBC

North, south, east, the Germans were on the run – that was the one clear fact that emerged from the rumours and delayed reports. And now all eyes turned to Paris. How near were the Americans? What was happening inside the city?

24 August 1944

'Wherever we drive, in the areas west and south-west of the capital, people shout: "Look, they are going to Paris!" But then we run into pockets of resistance here or there and are forced to turn back. It's clear that we are seeing the disintegration of the German Army – but we never know when we are going to be shot at. There are still some units of the German Army, fanatical men of the SS or armoured divisions, who are willing to fight to the last man. They are moving here and there all over this area, trying to coalesce into strong fighting forces. But most of the Germans are glad to be captured.

'Here in the blue, almost in the outskirts of Paris, no one knows what's happening. The only way we can find out whether Versailles or some other place is captured is to go and see; and that means racing down long empty roads and risking being shot at. Sometimes we reach an American spearhead and find them in hot action against a screen of German tanks – that happened today at Latrappe, east of Rambouillet. At the front yesterday we didn't hear a shot; but back in Chartres last night there was a small fight in the streets just a few hundred yards away from the house where we slept. The people everywhere are tense with emotion. Their love of freedom is so very deep, and now a nightmare is lifting from their lives; and history races down the roads towards Paris.'

MATTHEW HALTON, CBC

On 23 August General Koenig, Commander-in-Chief of the French Forces of the Interior, announced the liberation of Paris as the result of a general uprising. After four days of street-fighting the German garrison had agreed to an armistice which would allow them to withdraw and would prevent further bloodshed and destruction in the city. The first great rejoicings which followed this announcement were cut short, however, when an appeal from the Parisians to General Bradley for reinforcements revealed that the Germans had renewed the fighting. Appropriately, it was the French 2nd Armoured Division, under General Leclerc, which broke through the remaining enemy defences in the western outskirts and helped to complete the task which the Parisians had valiantly begun. The presence in France of Leclerc's division – veterans who had fought on for just this consummation of their hopes – had only just been revealed. They had travelled from Avranches to Alençon in three and a half days. From Le Mans onwards they fought the German 9th Panzer Division: in the first three days of the fighting the French killed 2000 and took well over 4000 prisoners. The 9th Panzer Division, which had already been mauled in previous fighting, was now so battered that it had to be reformed and rebuilt before it could fight again:

18 August 1944

'The nucleus of Leclerc's Division are the men who fought from Chad across the Sahara, and who later fought in Tunisia. There are the men who fought as French units under the command of the Eighth Army, and there are regiments from Giraud's troops. There's a naval regiment, who now fight on land as tank destroyers. There are the Spahis, with their crimson caps, who have given up their horses for motorised cavalry. They've been equipped by the Americans, and now that they fight as a part of the American army they wear ordinary GI uniform. The only difference is in their soft caps, and the small Cross of Lorraine on their steel helmets. It took eighty ships to bring them across from England, and they landed on the beaches. Some of the men jumped overboard and swam ashore when they found there was a delay.

'Alençon was the first town to be liberated by the division, and at 4.30 in the morning the general and a small detachment went in.

They found a body of Germans coming towards them, and neither side knew what was behind the other. The Germans opened fire, without hurting any of the French. The French replied, killed one, and took the rest prisoner.

'As the main body of troops came through the town they sang *Madelon* and the *Marseillaise*, and all day long the main street was filled with the sound of their singing and the cheering of the civilians. German resistance was fairly stiff. The French had to fight hard in the woods and fields, and they suffered losses. But their spirit was and is tremendous. There's an air of festivity in the midst of great efficiency and courage. When a tank stops for a few minutes beside the road you see little groups of civilians clustering round it, talking quietly and excitedly with the soldiers. They've all got news for each other, and the soldiers have come home.'

ROBIN DUFF

In the early morning of 25 August Leclerc's Division, approaching through Meudon, entered Paris by the Porte Châtillon and moved down the Boulevard Brune towards the Porte d'Orléans. From Paris radio, now in the hands of the FFI, came the first description of Leclerc's trimphant entry:

25 August 1944

'All along the French advance route soldiers and people are embracing one another, women and children wave French and Allied flags, shouting "Vive la France! Vive de Gaulle!"

'The crowd was able to read on every tank names dear to us: Franche-Compté, Champagne, Alsace, and so on. Towards nine o'clock a small detachment of Leclerc's Division passed through the Boulevard St Germain escorting about fifty prisoners. They moved to

217

the Place de la Concorde where the Germans are holding a centre of resistance.

'Shooting continues in the streets of Paris, while Allied troops arriving in greater numbers fight side by side with the FFI and the people of Paris. French and Allied flags are appearing at all the windows and everyone is singing the *Marseillaise*.'

25 August 1944

'From the Porte d'Italie to the Ile de la Cité, Leclerc's units have had a delirious welcome. Men, women and children literally rushed the tanks shouting with joy – joy which for four years and two months had been suppressed.

'But it wasn't the triumphal parade of which some of us had dreamt. The first Allied detachment found a Paris in full battle – a Paris which had to carry out a definite mission to occupy the Prefecture of Police and the Hôtel de Ville and to liquidate several German tanks which still move about in the area. This mission they are accomplishing from the Hôtel de Ville. From where I am speaking to you I can hear the explosions of shells and the spatter of machine-guns: Boche machine-guns, machine-guns of the regular army, and the machine-guns of the FFI. Last night a burst of bullets swept the hall of the Hôtel de Ville. Four persons were killed, and since then machine-gunning has never ceased. The Germans set fire to the Navy Ministry and the Hôtel Crillon and the sky is ablaze in the direction of Neuilly and Vincennes. These are the last jerks of the beast receiving the mortal blow.'

AN AMERICAN CORRESPONDENT, NAME UNKNOWN

There were still snipers, suicide squads, rearguard parties to be cleared up, but the liberation of Paris was assured. From Paris radio came news of the pleasantest shortage the people of Paris had faced since 1940 – and a charming suggestion for dealing with it:

25 August 1944
'Parisians! You are asked to put out flags. Many persons are embarrassed because they do not have enough flags. One of our listeners proposes that windows should be decorated with the most beautiful carpets of your apartments. You will thus be able to give an air of holiday and rejoicing to the sombre façades of the houses.'

Throughout France these last days of August were indeed a time of holiday and rejoicing, for the street-fighting in Paris was echoed in another great French city – Marseilles:

24 August 1944
'I've just returned from Marseilles – this morning it was still a city of strange contrasts, a city where people were queuing up for bread in the suburbs, while the big guns of the port fortifications boomed away over the city, but the water and the electric light and the telephone services are still on, saved by the Maquis – and where, according to rumour, you can still be put through to the German command post if you only ring the right number. And there's still a daily paper being published; and where you can still have a drink in a bar in one street, it's death to put your nose around the corner.

'I went down to the centre of the town – almost untouched by fighting and bombing as far as I could see – and there were groups of citizens gathered around French Army trucks, there were families out to watch the traffic roaring past under the plane-trees, and it was the usual excited scene that we now almost expect in all these liberated cities. But once you swung your car down the bend of the road leading to the Cannebière, Marseilles' main street, you found yourself suddenly right back in the middle of the war. The Germans are still in some of the buildings in this famous avenue – shells and small-arms fire echoed along it, and it was quite obvious that the Cannebière is not a healthy spot to stroll in this morning, as you did once in peacetime.

'The Maquis are at work mopping up small points of resistance. I saw a group of them, revolvers in hand, crawling across a machine-gun-swept crossroad, while on the wall beside me was a huge poster of the latest film to be shown in Marseilles. "A Great Police Romance", it announced, *Inspector Grey de Scotland Yard*. But Inspector Grey's powers would have been taxed to the utmost to keep up with the enthusiasm of these men of Marseilles, cleaning up their own town.'

WYNFORD VAUGHAN-THOMAS

From the Channel to the Mediterranean the German occupation of France was rapidly ending. Model [*who had replaced von Kluge as C-in-C West on 17 August*] was unable to hold the line of the Seine, and from the Riviera coast General Patch was racing northwards to join General Patton's forces south-east of Paris. In Paris itself the last German resistance was quickly overpowered after General Leclerc's arrival, and the morning of 26 August found the city streets more or less safe for the exultant crowds that swarmed toward the Arc de Triomphe and the Tomb of the Unknown Warrior:

26 August 1944

'They began flocking in from the suburbs on foot or on bicycles as early as seven o'clock. Great droves of them wheeled through the Place de la Concorde and away up the Champs Elysées – shimmering and beautiful in the autumn sun – and away to the Arc de Triomphe, to the tomb of France's Unknown Warrior. There were so many of those cyclists that it was virtually impossible to cross the Place de la Concorde unless you were particularly nippy.

'Boulevard cafés began to reopen and to do a thriving trade, and on every street corner hawkers were peddling red, white and blue favours. But even they'd got the Bank Holiday feeling. If you didn't buy a favour they just thrust one in your jacket and wrung your hand if you happened to be British or American. In fact anybody in khaki walking through the streets of Paris today moved in a state of perpetual but rather pleasant embarrassment. You were liable any moment to be pounced on, pressed to some matronly bosom, and then passed round the whole family from papa to little Réne – and even if you escaped those heartfelt embraces you stood a jolly good chance of suffering from a sprained wrist before you'd gone far from the doors of the hotel.'

ROBERT REID

26 August 1944

'Paris is still Paris. Her heart is still warm and young and gay. Nothing the Nazis have done has penetrated into the spirit of this city. There are bicycles in the streets instead of taxis, but they only add to the charm of the picture, because many of them are ridden by girls in summer dresses – nothing saucy about the dresses, you see very few women who are chic in the Rue du Louvre tradition, but every one of them there is smart and every one of them has that old "je-ne-sais-quoi", that certain something that sets them aside. Their menfolk were, and are, cheering us; at least, part of them are. The rest – the streets are full of them – are a grim and determined lot – the French Forces of the Interior. Last night the battle of the rooftops was still going on, one of the oddest and bloodiest engagements of this campaign, fought out between snipers on the roofs and the FFI marksmen who went up to the roofs to get them. Civilians and members of the FFI group died in that fighting. The French paid a heavy price to help throw off the Nazi yoke, but it's worth it. Everyone you meet – every Frenchman, that is – tells you that he's waited four long and bitter years for this moment, and that last week, during which Paris was almost free but not quite, was the longest of all. But at last you're here, he will say, and then he will thank you, and you can't possibly mumble "You're welcome" to that. You can only feel sorry and have a sense of shame, which doesn't feel quite right but which is nevertheless present, that you weren't here earlier and sooner. Another couple of youngsters on bikes come riding by and wave and suddenly burst out all by themselves and sing the *Marseillaise*. Or you'll lunch as I did today with a group of Resistance fighters – Jacques, Marcel and Louis, and Henri and Jean. And you'll slip a morsel from your skimpy plate for a gorgeous little setter pup named Cherbourg, because he was born the day Cherbourg was liberated – born of a mother called Tobruk because she in turn was born the day the Allies broke through to liberate the Tobruk garrison. And you know that no people who can face the grim days with that impudent humour can fail to be reborn. Indeed it seems a bit silly to think that Paris or France needs a rebirth – when these things can happen. Or when a little old man can suddenly set down a big box in the centre of the Place de l'Opéra and take out a French horn and suddenly start a solo rendering – not too good, but magnificently carefree – of the 'Stars and Stripes Forever' march, and when he's finished solemnly bow and pack his horn and stroll on off. That's Paris today. I can't stay at my typewriter, I can't stay off my balcony away from the spectacle of all the delight that's outside. Words can't describe Paris today. You need music for it. Some tune that is a cross between the spine-tingling *Marseillaise* and the rollicking roll of "Turkey in the Straw", and the rhythm of the Brazilian samba. The whole set in a jam-session – I can't write it for you – I can only suggest it as the best image of Paris today.'

HERBERT CLARKE, BLUE NETWORK

A huge crowd gathers to greet General de Gaulle at the Place de la Concorde on 26 August 1944 after the liberation of Paris. The General and senior figures from the Free French Army and the Resistance then made their way to Notre Dame for a service of thanksgiving. De Gaulle's sangfroid inside the cathedral as he ignored gunfire from enemy snipers added considerably to the General's legend.

28 August 1944

'Now that the first excitement of the entry into Paris has died down, it's possible to step back for a moment and look at this amazing city – certainly the strangest city in the world today. It's a city of violent contrasts – a city celebrating the entry of the Allies with wild enthusiasm and gaiety – and yet a city still at war, with all its gaiety broken by gun flashes and the rattle of machine-guns at street corners. You can walk down the boulevards in the sunshine and imagine for a moment that you are in a peaceful pre-war Paris – when suddenly from the rooftops comes the crack of a rifle, and you see a Maquis lad answering back from the cover of a doorway. There are Germans in civilian clothes – Germans hidden in the Metro, who come out at night to shoot up the streets. I've lost count now of the times I've had to watch these street battles; there's the crack of rifle fire going on sporadically at this moment.

'The hatred of the Germans is profound: in a little bar in Montparnasse where we took shelter during a burst of street fighting, I asked what they thought of the Germans – it was a poor, almost unfurnished room, lit by a swinging lamp – with a piano in a corner and half a dozen couples dancing on bare boards – and only very thin wine to drink – vinegar and water it was. When I asked about the Germans a Frenchman picked up his glass and threw it on the floor and ground the pieces with his heel and said: "There – that is what we must do to them – the Boches are animals – animals of the worst kind," and he paused and added: "And what is more – they never smile. Imagine that – they never smile." And all round the room they nodded and said: "Yes, that is true – they steal everything from us – and they never smile." And then an old man sat down at the piano and picked out "Tipperary" with one finger – and the barman put on my tin hat, and everyone cheered and laughed so loud that the firing outside couldn't be heard.

'I spent some hours on the night of the Allied entry going round with a French radio car with lights blazing and radio blaring and rifles poking from the windows, and whenever we came to a sniper's nest the car would stop, defiantly playing the *Marseillaise*, and figures would come out of the darkness to wish us luck, and the rifles would crack back at the snipers.'

HOWARD MARSHALL

The sudden dramatic contrasts between the cheering crowds and the sporadic outbreaks of shooting reached an amazing climax during

26 August when General de Gaulle narrowly escaped being shot. The first incident occurred in the Place de la Concorde, shortly after General de Gaulle had left: a BBC correspondent who was in the Place recorded a commentary mixed with the sound of the shooting:

27 August 1944
'I've been trying to get to the microphone, but it's been very difficult because there's been some shooting broken out from the – one of the buildings – I think it's in the neighbourhood of the Hôtel Crillon, just following the passage through the streets of General de Gaulle, and there's smoke now rising from the building there, and the people – there's a great crowd – has broken out [*confusion of voices – French and English*]. The policeman has just come up to explain to me – I couldn't see in the confusion – that somebody had fired out on the crowd from the Hôtel Crillon and the tanks are firing back – the tanks massed in the square are firing back at the hotel, and I'm standing looking just straight across at it – smoke – smoke rising, and whoever opened up on the crowd from the hotel is [*several voices speaking in French*]. We're looking – [*more remarks in French*] – the tanks were all lined up facing the hotel, and they gave it a terrific salvo. There's still one firing now, straight into the hotel, and whoever shot out from there is going to be a pretty unfortunate person. But the crowds are keeping remarkably calm really. They've been able to get behind the tanks and they're just pushing their way back. There's no disorder, no rioting – pushing their way back as the tanks open up again, and blast a hole in the building. I can see the smoke coming out. The tanks have shot at the left-hand corner of the building and just under where the flag of France is flying – it's a remarkable thing, because a lot of people were standing on the – on the roof of the building looking at the procession, and somebody must have been underneath them – some sniper or other must have been underneath and opened

up' on the crowd. Now the tanks are blasting away at it and raking the building, which has already been considerably damaged, with fire. [*Sound of gunfire*] That was a salvo which hit on the roof and it's smoking still, and I can see the tracer bullets going right up there over the roof. Now a tank behind me has opened up, and the crowds ducking down come running back – come running back towards our car here. I haven't seen anybody hurt yet, but I'm afraid probably up at the front some people were.

'It appears that there are very big cellars in the Hôtel Crillon and some of the Germans may have succeeded in hiding in there, just waiting for this moment to come up and work their way through the building while everybody was watching the procession. There's a moment's pause – a moment's pause while the crowd gets away. There are two big buildings at the top of the square here, equally dividing the top side of the square, and it may be from either of these buildings that the fire came – we just couldn't work our way any further forward as the tanks are all there blocking the way – and also from the Hôtel Crillon and from the building on the other side of the road leading into the Concorde at the top. I see in order to keep the crowd calm a Red Cross man has stood right up on top of a balustrade in the centre of the square here; in this sort of confusion it's a pretty brave thing to do – standing up there, right opposite where the shooting's coming from – and he's waving his flag and telling the people to be calm, and he's having a magnificent effect on them. A policeman just beside me has got a bit of shrapnel, I think – it hit him on the nose; it may have been a ricochet. It's nothing serious, just took a little chip out of his nose. Now I've retired to a rather safer position behind the recording car. There are people hiding under the tanks which are firing. I think there's some shelling, isn't there? It's rather difficult to place where all the fire is coming from. I certainly can hear bullets going past at the moment – that peculiar whistling noise they make – and still these men with the Red Cross flags stand up on this balustrade, right out in the open here, holding up their flags and waving, smiling – "People, just take it quite easy, it's all going to be all right".'

ROBERT DUNNETT

This was, however, only a prelude to the sensational scenes at Notre Dame, where 40,000 people had gathered to cheer General de Gaulle as he entered the cathedral. Here another BBC correspondent was stationed, unsuspecting that he was about to make probably the most remarkable running commentary ever broadcast:

27 August 1944

'Immediately behind me through the great doors of this thirteenth-century cathedral I can see, in this dim half-light, a mass of faces turned towards the door, waiting for the arrival of General de Gaulle, and when the general arrives, this huge concourse of people both inside and outside the cathedral, they'll be joining in a celebration of the solemn *Te Deum* in the mother church of France.

'You may be able to hear that I'm talking amid the noise of tanks; now those are the tanks from General Leclerc's Division, the boys who were instrumental in punching a hole right through the German defences outside Paris and into the heart of the capital. I believe the original intention was that these tanks were going to be used as a guard of honour, but thousands of Parisians have now climbed on to the top of those tanks and I believe I can only see one track of the end tank. The police are having rather a bad time trying to keep the crowds back – they're all trying to press right through to the cathedral.

'Immediately in front of me are lined up the men and women of the French Resistance Movement; they're a variegated set of boys and girls – some of the men are dressed in dungarees, overalls, some look rather smart, the bank-clerk type, some are in very shabby suits but they've all got their red, white and blue armlets with the blue Cross of Lorraine, and they're all armed, they've got their rifles slung over their shoulders and their bandoliers strapped round their waist. And now here comes General de Gaulle. The general's now turned to face the square, and this huge crowd of Parisians [*machine-gun fire*]. He's being presented to people [*machine-gun fire*]. He's being received [*shouts of crowd-shots*] even while the general is marching [*sudden sharp outburst of continued fire*] – even while the general is marching into the cathedral. . . . . . . [*Break on record*].

'Well, that was one of the most dramatic scenes I've ever seen. Just as General de Gaulle was about to enter the Cathedral of Notre Dame, firing started all over the place. I'm afraid we couldn't get you the noise of that firing because I was overwhelmed by a rush of people who were trying to seek shelter, and my cable parted from my microphone. But I fell just near General de Gaulle and I managed to pick myself up. General de Gaulle was trying to control the crowds rushing into the cathedral. He walked straight ahead in what appeared to me to be a hail of fire from somewhere inside the cathedral – somewhere from the galleries up near the vaulted roof. But he went straight ahead without hesitation, his shoulders flung back, and walked right down the central aisle, even while the bullets were pouring around him. It was the most extraordinary example of courage that I've ever seen. But what was to follow was horrible, because it happened inside Notre Dame Cathedral. While the congregation were trying to take shelter lying flat on the ground under the chairs and behind the pillars, the firing continued at intervals; the police, the military, and the Resistance Movement – all these people, they came in and were trying to pick off the snipers. Some of the snipers had actually got on to the roof of the cathedral.

'There was an awful din going on the whole time. Just by me one man was hit in the neck, but I will say this for this Parisian crowd, there was no real panic inside the cathedral at all; they simply took reasonable precautions. Round every pillar you'd see people sheltering, women with little children cuddled in their arms. I saw one child being carried to safety in the arms of a young priest who sheltered the youngster to his breast and carried it to the shelter of one of the pillars.

'It was – as I say – it was a most extraordinary scene, as the snipers were spotted around the gallery by the police and by the soldiers, and there was a smell of cordite right throughout the cathedral. But Paris had come to celebrate the solemn *Te Deum* and it did; even while the firing was going on the people rose to their feet and stood there and sang the *Te Deum* with General de Gaulle at the head of them. And then, when it was all over, the general marched right down the aisle; heaven knows how they missed him, for they were firing the whole time; there were blinding flashes inside the cathedral, there were pieces of stone ricocheting around the place.

'I saw him marching down the aisle, this very tall upright figure, with his chin well in the air, his shoulders flung right back; and his exit was the scene for another attempt. There were battles – there were bangs, flashes all around him, and yet he seemed to have an absolutely charmed life as he walked down the aisle towards the door, because nothing touched him, and he never hesitated for one moment. And when he got to the door it was a signal for another burst of firing outside. But I don't know how many people have been hit; I doubt possibly whether very many have. As I say, I only saw one casualty myself.

'But even now the firing's going on there are people still about the square, so I think the firing which is apparently coming from surrounding roofs must be rather erratic, because I can't see anybody being carted away. But a lot of people are taking shelter, and I don't mind saying that at the moment I'm just squatting cross-legged on the floor by the side of the cathedral making this recording; I thought it was rather a wise precaution to take. I didn't want to be too conspicuous standing up with the microphone in my hand.

'That shouting and cheering you can hear is four prisoners just being taken away. These are four of the snipers who've been caught inside the church. They were all in civilian clothing – grey flannel trousers, and simply white singlets; they've got their hands above their heads, and they look very obvious Germans. They're being brought out by the gendarmes, and are now being taken through the square with crowds running around them hooting them. And even now firing is still going on here. (*Shot.*) That was one that just came over us.'

ROBERT REID

CHAPTER X
And Then Brussels

'They took out their guide-books and motored north'

It is one of the ironies of the war that, while Paris was celebrating its liberation, London was suffering gravely from flying-bombs launched along the Channel coast. While the Americans swept on to Paris and beyond, over the upper Seine the British and Canadians were engaged in the final destruction of the German Fifth Panzer Army and the Seventh Army. The bloody work of Falaise had to be completed first; and then the British troops in turn headed east, with three objects in view – to complete the rout of Model's forces, to continue the pursuit into Belgium at a speed rivalling Patton's tanks, and to smother the flying-bomb sites.

The first effective barrier appeared to be the Seine, already littered with smashed bridges and ferries as the Allied Air Forces harried the fleeing enemy; but, with over a third of a million casualties in the north since D-Day, the Germans were in no condition to contain the bridgeheads we had secured at Vernon and Louviers. On the final day of August Canadians entered Rouen and the Germans lost their last stronghold on the Seine:

31 August 1944
'Outside in the square, our jeep was being used as a grandstand. Twenty-six people had somehow managed to climb up on to it to see what was going on. Standing by there was a young man wearing the FFI armlet. He told me how, yesterday morning, the officers commanding this secret army, which numbered over 11,000 in

Rouen, decided that the time had come to take action. The Canadians were at the approaches to the city. So orders went out, and suddenly the Germans, making frantic last-minute preparations to leave, found themselves set upon by armed Frenchmen. There was fierce fighting in the streets. Many Germans were killed; many more were taken prisoner. The rest fled as the Canadians came in. Meanwhile, the City Police were rounding up the worst of the French traitors: the Gestapo. Fourteen members of the Gestapo were killed in the skirmishes which followed, and all the rest were put safely behind bars. This man, who had a close-up view of the whole thing, was enthusiastic about our air attacks on the Germans in the last few days just south of Rouen in the loop of the river.

'He said that thousands of Germans had been killed in these bombardments.

'They'd only managed to get the remnants out by running rafts to and fro and laying temporary pontoon bridges – all in the darkness.

'Rouen is not extensively damaged. The waterfront is pretty much in ruins; the cathedral, unfortunately, has lost one of its towers and it's in a pretty bad state, and the eastern end of the city has suffered a little, but it's certainly the least damaged town of any size yet entered by the Allies on this part of the front. The people of Rouen were aching for every crumb of news they could get. Since the electricity failed, many of them, so they told me, had made crystal sets, so that they could listen to the BBC. They were almost overwhelmed at the flood of good news that we were able to bring them.'

FRANK GILLARD

Not only on land were the Germans retreating. The failure to hold the Seine made the harbours at Le Havre untenable, and the E-boats which had been based there now fled up Channel. They sailed by night to avoid our aircraft, but their old opponents, the British MTBs, were waiting for them, and there was savage fighting at close range in the darkness:

3 September 1944

'For four fierce nights battles raged off Cap d'Antifer as the enemy ships – coasters, escort vessels, E-boats, and R-boats – crept close under the shore, eastward bound up the Channel. They kept very close in to their cliffs so that the heavy guns of their coastal batteries could give them cover, but our forces were not prepared to be kept away. The other night a unit of MTBs fought a gun battle with a party of R-boats at fifteen yards' range. Of course, that's unusually close, but quite normally the range is only a few hundred yards, with the bright coloured tracers, blinding streaks, criss-crossing between the opposing forces and the roll and thunder of automatic guns.

'Through smoke screens, and the tall pillars of shell splashes and under the glare of bright white starshells, our MTBs have had to carry out their torpedo and gun attacks against a wide-awake and desperate enemy who was less than half a mile from his own cliffs, so close that our own starshells often burst in the fields on the cliff top. Still they were sometimes able to get in unobserved. It's a lot easier to take careful aim along a torpedo sight *before* the tracer bullets start to fly, but often it had to be done afterwards when the air was already alive with the nasty things, singing overhead and popping and crumping all around. That needs a lot of concentration. And then at last the levers are pulled, the torpedoes leap out with a "whoosh" and a splash and speed off towards the enemy. Less than a minute later if the aim was true comes the red glow, the column of water, and the thud of the explosion. These were the sort of battles being fought last week. These battles are still going on as the remnant of the enemy shipping streams eastward.'

LIEUT.-COMMANDER PETER SCOTT, MBE, DSC AND BAR, RNVR

The next port up the coast from Le Havre is Dieppe – Dieppe, where the Canadians had made their gallant raid in 1942. Now they were in Rouen, forty miles away. From Rouen it took the Canadians just about twenty-four hours to avenge the memory of their losses at Dieppe two years earlier:

1 September 1944

'One of the most important entries in any Canadian war diary is Dieppe. At twenty-five minutes past twelve this afternoon, Canadians made another entry in the Dieppe account. This one was 1 September 1944, and completely wiped out the entry of 19 August 1942. They say they never come back. That's a saying long associated with champions, but today from a scout aircraft I watched the 2nd Canadian Division – champions, if I've ever seen any – come back to Dieppe, this time to stay. Flying straight down the main axis of advance, I could see them on the main road from Rouen, through Tôtes, speeding on their way to Dieppe. Even in the air you could almost sense their desire to get as much out of their machines as possible – anything to get them into Dieppe in a hurry. I suppose I noticed that because I was a Canadian. They were all there. The first troops into the town were the Essex Scottish, the Royal Hamilton Light Infantry, and the Royal Regiment of Canada, and speeding up behind them were the Camerons of Winnipeg, the South Saskatchewan Light Infantry, the Fusiliers of Montreal, the Toronto Scottish, the Black Watch – they were all there – all the regiments that were there on that fateful day of 19 August 1942. But today it was their turn.'

STEWART MACPHERSON

1 September 1944

'Many of these troops were the same men who'd made that gallant attack just over two years ago. What a memorable return this was. At one point in the town the people had crowded out into the road, leaving only a very narrow lane for traffic to pass through. We wondered why until we reached the spot, and then we saw. A Nazi flag was spread out on the ground, and you were simply obliged to drive right over the swastika and trample it into the dust.

'The people of Dieppe told us that the Germans started to get away yesterday. They blew up their great ammunition dump in the vaults of the castle, in fact explosions were still going on there this morning every few minutes as more and more magazines went off. The Germans fired their oil supplies. Down on the waterfront immense columns of black smoke were coming from the storage tanks, and they demolished and smashed up everything in the harbour area. All the dock installations were blown up, and ships sunk everywhere to block the harbour. They blew the great bridge over the river and then, as a last act before leaving, they destroyed the power station and the town water-tower. But Dieppe itself is not greatly damaged. Its streets are just as attractive as ever they were. Today they were bright with flags and bunting and streamers – for it was a real carnival day.

'It was about the flying-bombs that the people wanted to talk to British people like myself. They reeled off a great list of bomb sites just around Dieppe which are now lost to the enemy. Most of them, they told us, had been blown up by the Germans a few days ago. They described how these robots used to come over the town just after they'd been launched – how any amount of them had crashed into the sea – how some had exploded within a few seconds of being sent off. They were anxious to know how the people of Britain are standing up to these attacks, and how much damage is being done. These people of Dieppe were delighted to feel that the liberation of their town by this amazingly rapid forty-mile advance of the Canadian troops had also brought at least some slight measure of relief, if only comparatively light, to southern England.'

FRANK GILLARD

The 'bomb-coast' and the road to Belgium were wide open. Famous battlefields of the last war, which had then been contested yard by yard, now passed at bewildering speed as British armoured columns brushed aside enemy resistance and drove all out towards Brussels:

1 September 1944

'The British Second Army is going hell for leather to the buzz-bomb bases. Our troops know that the task is to get the flying-bomb sites and there's no holding them. Already British columns have overrun five sites which the Germans had prepared for the launching of flying-bombs and one that was to be used for V2. And this afternoon I was with one of our armoured columns which crossed the southern border of the Pas de Calais and, as they advanced, men of the FFI came in every few hours with the news of the location of another launching site and of the dumps of flying-bombs themselves.

'For twenty-four hours the survivors of the German Seventh Army and the Fifth Panzer Army have been virtually without orders. Their Commander – General der Panzer Truppen Heinrich Hans Eberbach – was captured early yesterday morning. He was taken by surprise at his tactical headquarters in the woods just south of Amiens. As the British tanks came in one side of the wood about half-past six, the general and two officers of his personal staff jumped for their cars and tried to race out the other side, past the English tanks which were fast outflanking them. Machine-gun bullets riddled the cars. The occupants dived to a ditch and the tank crews raced in to grab their prisoners.

'Today I drove twenty-five miles north of Amiens in a column that raced through the countryside as fast as the roads could carry it. Our armour began its advance from the Amiens bridgehead in three columns about seven o'clock this morning. In the first villages they met a couple of dozen Germans with machine-guns. But they had neither tanks nor anti-tank guns to support them. After that our troops virtually put away their military maps, took out their guide-books, and motored north. At the time I had to turn back to make this broadcast the leading tanks had bypassed Arras to the west and were north of it.'

CHESTER WILMOT

In the words of one American broadcaster: 'The British Army has kept going like a cat on its way to heaven. Already it's so far from this transmitter that we almost have to cover its movements by crystal ball.' This was sweet amends for the days before Dunkirk. We had promised the people of Brussels we would come back: now, on 2 September, our leading armoured columns had come within seventy-five miles of the Belgian capital and were still continuing their headlong advance at a speed unsurpassed at any time during the war:

2 September 1944

'Troops of the British Second Army entered Douai yesterday evening, and they took both the French and the Germans by surprise. As our tanks halted in the main square, the mayor came out and apologised profusely because the town wasn't organised to receive us. "We didn't think you'd come until tomorrow," he said; "and I have not any reception prepared. We have not begun to round up the Germans for you." But the tanks were barely in the town when the FFI appeared from nowhere with their rifles, and flags sprang up at every window. And soon the French were bringing in the Germans.

'Meantime, in the Town Hall, a British officer asked the mayor what the situation was in other towns near by that the Germans still held – the mayor picked up his telephone, spoke to the prefects of police in the surrounding towns and got very useful replies. From one of them came the answer: "There are hundreds of Germans here – but they're getting out as fast as they can – a few are manning defences on the outskirts of the town but they're merely covering the retreat of the others."

'Within half an hour by telephone we had a complete picture of the German situation in the country round about, but the Germans had no idea that we were in Douai at all – and during the night several parties of SS troops duly tried to drive through. They were soon stopped.'

CHESTER WILMOT

On the fifth anniversary of the war British troops crossed the Belgian frontier. The same evening they were in Brussels. In a whirlwind drive to the capital the Guards Armoured Division had covered the last seventy-five miles in thirteen hours, as the climax of an advance of 430 miles made in nine days:

5 September 1944

'Their main trouble was not dealing with the scattered German resistance but getting through the crowds who thronged the road-sides every mile from the frontier to Brussels . . . cheering, laughing, shouting people with wild delight in their voices and tears of joy in their eyes. They didn't wait for the Germans to go. As the news of our coming spread like wildfire from village to village, along the main roads from Tournai to Brussels, Belgian men grabbed their hidden arms and went hunting for the Germans, Belgian women and children went down into cellars and cupboards to produce the mass of flags, streamers, rosettes, banners, placards, and dresses that they'd been getting ready for months for this very day.

'On the outskirts of Brussels we were halted again by a traffic block and suddenly machine-guns opened fire from the wood beside the road. Tanks swung their guns round and fired. Civilians threw themselves upon the ground, troops jumped from lorries and raced into the woods from one side while armed civilians went in from the other. They collected twenty-five Germans from what had been a headquarters, and as the Germans left, Belgian civilians – men and women – swarmed in and came running out from the German headquarters with bottles of wine and beer, boxes of cigars and cigarettes, chocolates and sweets that had belonged to the Germans, and they pressed them into the hands of the British troops.

'And so it went on until we came to Brussels itself, and there our welcome was wildest of all. There had been Germans in the streets only an hour before, and not a flag had been in sight; but by the time we arrived every building was plastered with flags and streamers. The streets were decked with banners – "Welcome to our liberators", "Welcome to our Allies", "Through Brussels to Berlin", they said, "through Belgium to victory". These were mostly huge signs which had been printed or painted weeks ago in anticipation, but how the Belgians got them up in time I don't know.

'For months the people have been secretly buying red, yellow, and black material to make their own flags. The demand had been so great that people have had to register weeks in advance for the material. Banned Belgian flags were secretly manufactured and secretly sold. Printers ran off thousands of paper flags and distributed them through the underground movement. Thousands of women and children have made themselves special dresses in the Belgian colours – such as red skirts, yellow blouses, and black scarves or bandannas. And these all appeared as if by magic just as the Germans left.'

CHESTER WILMOT

5 September 1944

'I'm speaking to you from the Place de Brouckère – it's right in the centre of the capital and, as far as the eye can see, there's just no pavement at all, it's just one black carpet of humanity; all the office buildings around are covered in the yellow, red and black of the Belgian flag, ribbons – all the young ladies have rosettes or hair ribbons of the national colours, and to get protection we just had to go up on the roof of the van because there's no holding a microphone anywhere near these people – they just nab you. Well, that's the scenery in Brussels, it's just joy unrestrained. All the way up through the highways, which were lined with people, we were covered with fruit and cookies and home-made cakes and it was something that just defies description.

'The trams are running – they're covered in bunting and flags, and all around, everywhere you look, no matter where you look, in the shop windows it's just like a human pincushion – flags of Old Glory, Union Jack, Belgian flag, the Red Flag of Russia. It's an absolute maze of colour.'

STEWART MACPHERSON

To have liberated Brussels was a proud achievement, but the British Second Army had its eyes on a further objective – the great port of Antwerp. Striking ahead from Brussels while chaos still reigned in the German Army, our armoured spearheads were in Antwerp within twenty-four hours. The speed of the attack caught the enemy unprepared: the docks and port installations were intact.

This outstanding success was due partly to the speed of the British 11th Armoured Division, and partly to the conduct of a man on a bicycle who met our tanks in the town of Boom, a few miles short of Antwerp. His help had such important results that the story of it was withheld for two months:

6 November 1944

'The leading tank was stopped by a civilian cyclist. He said he was a Belgian engineer, and told the commanding officer that not only did he know the enemy dispositions in Boom and Antwerp, but also he knew all the bridges and the docks. The bridges and the docks, he said, were prepared for demolition, and to save his beloved Antwerp he was prepared to guide the tanks in by the safest route. Could they use him? The commanding officer contacted his brigadier and permission was given. The Belgian engineer discarded his bicycle and climbed aboard the leading tank. He led the Shermans through a narrow side street and round tortuous byways and over bridges which were so flimsy that they caused the tank commander some concern. But this wasn't the time to hesitate. First one and then another of the tanks pushed over these flimsy bridges, which mercifully held. The bridges were across the River Rupel about ten miles from Antwerp and, as the armour reached the other side, two tanks disengaged themselves from the main body and raced round the main bridge. The effort proved only to show how valuable the Belgian engineer's guidance was, for as the tanks reached the main bridge the German demolition party set the charges and the bridge just disintegrated. Still clinging to his unaccustomed position in the leading tank, the Belgian patriot guided the Shermans to a narrow path through the minefields and fortifications which surrounded the city. In single file the tanks pressed through. As they entered the city the people of Antwerp came in their thousands to greet them.

'The city had by no means been liberated, and our principal goal was the dock area. The Belgian engineer was anxious for the safety of some vital installations and in particular the main sluice-gates. If they went it would take months for Antwerp to be operative as a port. The sluice-gates and the quays had been prepared for demolition. That same night a party of our infantry set off under cover of darkness and seized the sluice-gates before they could be blown. The quays too were captured intact. It must have been with considerable chagrin that the Germans had to retreat and leave us not only with the port, but with wharves laden with *their* accumulated booty.'

LIEUT. RONALD HOWSE, BRITISH 11TH ARMOURED DIVISION

Our long lines of communication were now promised relief by the possession of this great port; and, as a more immediate advantage, the German forces strewn along the Channel coast were virtually cut off. The estuary of the Scheldt and the open sea were their last unattractive hopes of escape. Large forces in the Pas de Calais and the remaining Channel ports now found themselves trapped and prevented from taking any part in the defence of the Reich itself. Between them and the Siegfried Line, where they were sorely needed, were the British; and driving up from the south, from Rouen and Dieppe, came the Canadians. The fall of Brussels and Antwerp was accompanied by the clearance of the flying-bomb coastline from Dieppe to Boulogne – a welcome opening to the sixth year of war. The people of southern England were particularly pleased to hear a correspondent's account of his visit to this newly liberated coastal region:

5 September 1944
'At first, particularly around Abbeville, you could see where the Germans had held out stubbornly – bridges were blown, roads partly

blocked, buildings smashed up, and then came mile after mile of open road, across country from which the Germans had fled so hurriedly that they'd had no time to destroy anything, but destruction had been done to them all right. I remember hearing a couple of days ago about a strike by some Typhoons on an enemy horse-drawn column heading out towards Germany. I'd been told at the time that the column had been turned inside out and upside down – today I saw the remains of it, and I assure you that description was, if anything, an understatement.

'Just a couple of miles from Boulogne, we found the Germans making a stand – obviously they were not intending to give up the port very easily. They'd guns on each side of the road – firing on everything that came in sight, and a fierce encounter was going on between them and the advancing Canadians. Our jeep was ordered back. Half a mile away we pulled in under an embankment to eat our sandwiches – there was a house by the roadside, and to my surprise the housewife came out and asked if she could do anything for us: "Had we food?" "Had we drink?" "Well, at least we must allow her to make us a cup of coffee – she'd been saving coffee since 1939 for this moment." Well, think of that – a battle going on half a mile off and this Frenchwoman, not sheltering in her cellar or in some ditch, but insisting on giving us coffee. We went into her house, and there in the living-room, in his shirt sleeves, was the local Resistance leader with a pair of headphones clamped over his head, listening on a crystal set to the BBC's French Service in London, giving the one o'clock news. He told me that the Germans had planned to build 600 bomb sites in his area – many had already been in use. Work started on them almost exactly a year ago – the Germans went to a lot of trouble, he said, to make them non-magnetic, so they should be difficult to locate by instruments. But the French people who were compelled to work on them filled their pockets each morning with any scraps of iron they could lay hands on, nails, bits of wire, even took the hinges off their doors in some cases, and they worked all this metal into the concrete when the German bosses had their backs turned. This Frenchman said that, as the Germans rushed away – going like a lot of tramps, he said – some on stolen bicycles, but most of them on foot, pushing their belongings in perambulators and wheelbarrows, he and his friends rejoiced not only in their own liberty but because the enemy's departure meant there were 600 bomb ramps or potential bomb ramps the less to trouble their friends and Allies in England.'

FRANK GILLARD

CHAPTER XI
Over The Threshold

'Every house flew a white flag'

The first great phase of the liberation of Western Europe had ended in an overwhelming and unqualified victory for the Allies. Paris and Brussels were free. The Belgian and French nations had largely regained their liberty. The people of Britain realised that the grand assault of Hitler's V-weapons had been throttled and smothered, even if the last kicks could still be vicious. And the men who had accomplished all this – the armies in the field – knew now with absolute confidence that the conquest of Germany was assured. Within a hundred days after the Normandy landings the Allies had crossed the German frontier and were preparing to break through the Siegfried Line. The disaster of 1940 had been avenged, and in addition the Siegfried Line was no longer the obstacle it had been: its fortifications had become to some extent out of date, and Germany no longer had the resources to man it adequately. The fate of her commanders in the West emphasised the general plight of the Wehrmacht: von Rundstedt dismissed, Eberbach captured, Rommel and von Kluge dead – each by his own hand. The reinstatement of von Rundstedt as Commander-in-Chief on 4 September suggested a mood of desperation (Model took over Army Group B).

One of the British heroes of the Blitzkrieg of 1944 was Lieutenant-General B. G. (later Sir Brian) Horrocks, CB, DSO, MC, who on D-Day was in a convalescent home recovering slowly from a wound received at Bizerta in May 1943. Going to Normandy early in August, as Commander of XXX Corps, he took a prominent part in the advance across the Seine to Brussels. At Brussels he discussed the campaign with a Canadian correspondent and described some of the experiences of the corps he commanded:

9 September 1944

'I first saw General Horrocks on Bare Ridge at Alamein. I saw a group of soldiers sitting in the sand and walked over to ask a direction. I saw that one of the soldiers was a general. "Sit down," he said. "I'm just telling these lads how we are going to smash Rommel's last attack in two or three days." And now he was in Brussels describing the defeat of Germany. First, he took us back to Mont Pinçon in Normandy. That high ground south of Villers–Bocage was to the British what the road from Caen to Falaise was to the Canadians. That is, it was a bloody hell-hole where men gasped and fought day after day, day after day for every foot of ground – but a hell-hole where the guts were torn out of the German Army.

'The General told us how one British division – the 43rd (Wessex) – took Mont Pinçon in twenty-four hours. He said: "It was a brilliant attack by exhausted men. There was the bitterest fighting I've ever seen. And what really made it possible was the work of six tanks. Six tanks, no more, made a wild dash into the enemy and got up on top of the hill, and stayed there fighting in the middle of the Germans. They sent a message back: 'We are lonely but we're all right.'"

'That was the climax of the Battle of Normandy. But there was still hard fighting all the way from Mont Pinçon to the Seine. "It was still very difficult," said the general. "It was quite plain that the Boche was beginning to crack – there were the same signs we had seen when he began to crack in Tunisia. But when an enemy begins to crack you have to attack all the harder. You have to accelerate the defeat before he can rally. And we were very tired. We had to take the divisions out of the line one after another for a short four days' rest. We had to. Once we had nothing but a reconnaissance unit covering our left flank. What the men had to have was victory. They had to see German prisoners coming with their hands up. They were nearly at the end of their endurance.

' "So we had to blast our way forward with artillery and tanks. I had 350 guns on the end of my wireless mast; and whenever we met the slightest opposition I called on them. Guns and tanks. And that did the trick. The enemy broke and ran. Morale went up. And so we came to the Seine.

' "The crossing of the Seine was a classic. The divisional commanders got to the river and saw that in order to cross we had to have surprise. We had to get every man and every duck and every pontoon down to the river without the Germans knowing it – though they were standing on the other side watching us. Yet we did it.

' "Then, at 6.30 on the evening of 26 August we brought every gun we had down on the enemy for twenty minutes. Then the men went across in ducks and assault boats.

' "There were fierce moments. Many boats got stuck on submerged islands, and we had heavy losses. But they got across. I was terrified lest we should be hemmed in on a bridgehead. So I gave the division a brigade of tanks and told them to get out of the bridgehead. And they did the job.

' "Then I ordered the armour to go like mad for Brussels. It wasn't a tidy party, because one of the armoured divisions was behind the other, and it wasn't easy, it wasn't a triumphal procession. There was considerable opposition all the way. In every village there were German 88-mm guns. But it was good tank country, and I had the pick of the British Army, and nothing could stop them.

' "On the 29th they went sixteen miles through hard fighting. The other armoured division came up and then we were sitting pretty. The Germans intended to hold their strong line on the Somme. Our problem was to get there before they could blow the bridges. So at four o'clock that day, forty-five miles from Amiens, I went to see the commander of one of the armoured divisions. I said to him exactly what I'd said to him one day in Tunisia. I said: 'There's moonlight tonight.'

' "You know, it's very tricky to move an armoured division at night. But I could smell that it was all right. Sometimes you sniff the air and it doesn't smell right. But this time it smelled right.

' "That night the armoured division moved forty-three miles. The Germans were flabbergasted. We captured their general. By first light we were in Amiens and had the bridges intact. So we had moved sixty miles in twenty-four hours, despite pouring rain. All this time the other division was steaming along behind. We spent the 31st getting across the Somme. On 1 September we went to Arras and Douai; that division did forty miles that day against real opposition. On 2 September we did only fifteen miles. The next day we got to Brussels. As you know, you travelled seventy-five miles in one day with that division against opposition, to get to Brussels."

'That's part of the general's story.

'We are in Brussels. Behind us, the Germans are trying to get out. The Canadians are driving them along from the other end, along the coast, and the Germans are trying to break through us.

'And strange things are happening round about. The general said that the other day a Panther tank got loose in our rear and decided to shoot up one of our camps or laagers. The laager it chose to attack was an anti-tank regiment full of seventeen-pounder anti-tank guns. In less than a minute that tank was shot through by sixteen anti-tank shells. Sometimes we find German trucks driving along the road in one of our own convoys. And the general said: "My rear headquarters keep complaining that I have left them in the middle of a big German Army."

'That's what the war is like.'

MATTHEW HALTON, CBC

The confusion into which the German Army had been thrown began to clear up as groups of stragglers and encircled units surrendered or fought it out; and something approaching a formal battle-line reappeared as the Canadians mopped up the coastal area towards Zeebrugge while the British Second Army massed to cross the Albert Canal.

Meanwhile, in the south, General Patch's forces were pursuing the Germans towards the Belfort Gap and trying strenuously to compete with the good news from the north. The liberation of Marseilles had coincided with that of Paris: now, with Brussels, Lyons fell. In nineteen days the Seventh US Army had made its initial landings and advanced 275 miles:

4 September 1944

'None of us will forget the tumultuous, heartfelt welcome we've been receiving from the people of the Rhône Valley – but in Lyons that welcome reached its climax. Even today you daren't stop your jeep in a main street without it getting almost buried with people who just want to see you or pat you or just be near an Allied soldier. Our jeep was almost festooned with humanity – with FFI fighters, and small boys, businessmen, everybody who could hang on. And all madly eager to show us the city. In Lyons there still is a city to show. There's no damage in the main town – only, of course, the broken bridges and a litter of smashed glass along the quays. But these broken bridges are a spectacular sight – the Germans blew all the Rhône bridges, and nearly all the ones across the Saône.

'In this city of many bridges the sagging spans and trailing wires now form the main vista along the waterfront. This morning we did get across over the rickety structure laid between one of the arches – Wilson Bridge. Half Lyons was trying to do the same thing – there seems to be a delightful but good-tempered scrum suspended above the swift racing waters of the Rhône. There are bicycles and the FFI and most of the population coming one way and our jeeps coming the other, with four policemen blowing variations of the *Marseillaise* on their whistles, and nobody paying the slightest attention, but getting right ahead with the celebrations and the back-slapping and the general jollifications. Across the river we were taken on a sort of planned tour. We looked at the barbed-wire defences of the Gestapo headquarters, then we raced to the great squares, past the many churches of the city – under the avenues of flags that covered every possible place that a flag can be put; and I got the impression of a great city rapidly wiping out all traces of hated German occupation – tidying up the minor damage and getting ready for normal life as soon as possible.'

WYNFORD VAUGHAN-THOMAS

South of the Loire, a correspondent saw a large German force surrender after a failed attempt to reach the Siegfried Line.

17 September 1944

'This morning I watched a long winding column of German troops march out of the Maquis country to the south of the Loire River, discard their weapons and equipment, and surrender unconditionally to a small force of American soldiers. In all there were about 18,000 German troops, but even their Commanding General didn't know quite how many. All he knew was that he had started off twenty-two days ago with 20,000 men, hoping to lead them back to Germany.

'I had spent five days in this Maquis country with a young American lieutenant, Lieutenant Samuel McGill who had literally talked this force into surrendering without a fight. As I watched the surrender scenes this morning, McGill was standing with me, completely at ease for the first time in eight days. It was an amazing sight that we watched. No one who hasn't seen a German infantry column on the move can understand how unlike a modern army it is. There were soldiers on bicycles: all kinds of bicycles, ladies' bicycles, men's bicycles, racing bicycles, tall upright bicycles. There were soldiers on foot loaded down with equipment like soldiers of the last war, and there were hundreds of horse-drawn limbers, and farm carts and high-wheeled wagons, full of hay and straw, with soldiers sleeping on top. There were horses and mules and donkeys. I'm sure there was even a bullock cart somewhere but I didn't see it.

'This was a German force that had set out to fight its way to the Siegfried Line. At first sight it looked more like a colony of tinkers – you'll see it on the newsreels – with high-wheeled carts piled with bedding and hung around with pots and pans and pails, and festooned with steel helmets and metal gasmask cases, which looked like more pots and pans. And with every Company there was a cooking wagon, with a tall thin chimney. It looked just like a tar-boiler. And this tar-boiler was shackled to a cart and the cooks walked slowly behind it stirring the soup and throwing more wood into the fire. I've never seen anything quite like it. The one phrase which occurred to everyone was: "Napoleon's retreat from Moscow".

'Three columns just like this marched to the south bank of the Loire River this morning. One was headed for the bridge at Orléans, one was headed for the bridge at Mer, and the third was this column headed for the newly repaired bridge at Beaugency. Two thousand yards short of the bridge, there was a loudspeaker van and in it a German-speaking American officer, who kept telling the various units just what to do. Cyclists were to go into the field on the left and leave their cycles; wagon-drivers into the field on the right and leave their wagons. All were to go to the area marked with white tape and drop their hand grenades. Then to the next area and deposit their rifles and revolvers, then their steel helmets, then their cameras and finally, with only their personal equipment left, they were to cross the bridge and file into the prison cages.

'For hours they filed through until the field on the left was filled with bicycles, and the field on the right was like a scene from a Wild West film of the days of the covered wagons: hundreds of wooden wagons and hundreds of horses roaming free amongst them, cropping at the grass. And to add to the Wild West scene, an American soldier had found a saddled pony and he was riding herd on the grazing horses. And still the column came on – more cycles and more horses, and more hand grenades and rifles and machine-guns for the dumps. And down the road the officers were saying goodbye to their men and, with each goodbye, there was a great deal of *Sieg Heil*-ing. And then the men filed over the bridge to the prison cage.

'It was a motley army: some 7,000 or 8,000 marines, some 6,000 Luftwaffe personnel, and some 6,000 of the Wehrmacht – about 18,000 to 20,000 well-armed men of March Group South who had set out on 26 August from south-western France to march to Germany and man the Siegfried Line.'

ROBERT BARR

The first entry into Germany was made on 11 September by the US First Army, and from a border town east of Eupen came this account of the historic occasion when German civilians in the west for the first time saw Allied tanks in their streets:

14 September 1944

'I never expected to set foot on German soil so quietly. The first Germans we saw were an elderly couple standing on the roadside in front of the first house in the town. They looked at us without either a smile or a frown, and they made no movement at all. Farther into the town, people were at their garden gates. Every house flew a white flag. Everybody carried something white – even if it was only a handkerchief in their hand. Some of them waved and smiled. A girl came running out of one house with a basin full of plums, reaching up to the Americans in the turrets of their tanks. There were children dressed in their best clothes, waving handkerchiefs in one hand and clutching their toys in the other. The people looked well dressed, well fed, and certainly not either angry or afraid.

'I went into one house, where the woman of the house spoke French. She and her sister sat in their living-room, with the big photograph of their brother in German uniform on the wall above my head; and they had a wireless set in the corner. And they told me they had constantly listened to the BBC news in German. They giggled when we asked them what they thought of the war now. One said that they had been waiting a long time for the Americans to come; that every hour had been too long to wait. They said that all the Nazi leaders in the town had fled with the army, and that seventy-five per cent of the people were really against the Nazi regime. Their brother was somewhere or other – they didn't know where – fighting in the German Army, and they had a cousin who had been killed in Russia. They had two Russian servants in the house, a man and a woman who were Ukrainians from the Dnieper area, brought to Germany for forced labour and assigned to these people. As we were leaving the house the Russian man came running after us to ask if we couldn't help him to get a permit to go back to his camp, where he thought he might have a chance to get back to Russia. The two German women, between gales of giggles which seemed to be occasioned by the fact that the correspondent who was with me was talking in Russian to the Russian, told us that Germany would never be right again till we went right to Berlin and changed it all. We said that we were sure that was the plan.'

ROBERT DUNNETT

From Belgium, as from France, came many stories of the gallant work of partisans in sabotage and guerrilla fighting. In addition, many Allied airmen shot down over occupied territory owed their escapes from captivity to the heroic people of the 'Underground' who constantly risked their lives to cheat the Germans of a prisoner. Behind a strange dinner-party in newly-liberated Brussels lay one such story – the story of a Lancaster bomber, D for Dog, and its crew:

14 September 1944

'Once upon a time D for Dog was taking part in a night-raid over Germany. Badly shot up by night-fighters and flak, the aircraft became unmanageable and the crew were forced to bale out. When the crew of D for Dog jumped into the night, somewhere over Belgium, they never dreamt that it would be seven months till they would meet again, if they were to meet again. They never dreamt that when they did meet it would be in the heart of Brussels, wildly cheering the entry of Allied troops. They never had any idea what adventures lay ahead. That is why I start this story "once upon a time", for it really is like a fairy tale.

'The rear gunner, Jimmy, and the wireless operator, Tommy, landed together near each other near a stream, where they were unlucky, for within a hundred yards was a German ration dump and they were immediately captured. Jimmy and Tommy were soon on a train that was to carry them to a prison camp. A short time after the train suddenly stopped; the guards in the carriage looked anxiously out of the window along the track, and then sat back. Soon the boys

254

saw the driver walking along the track, tapping the wheels with a hammer. As he passed the open window he whispered, "Have no fear, you will be safe soon"; and hardly had he spoken when shots rang out from behind the stone fence at the side of the track. The train was ambushed by patriots and over twenty Allied airmen were set free. For the next six months Jimmy and Tommy were fed and clothed by patriots as well as hidden from the Hun.

'Gordon, the bomb-aimer, and Pete, the mid-upper gunner, were very unlucky, for they landed right bang in the centre of a prison-yard and for the next six months they were held captive there. The guards at this prison were Belgian traitors, and one of their chief pastimes was to smoke cigarettes in front of the cells, and never once would they offer any of the prisoners a solitary smoke.

'Hank, the pilot of the aircraft, was rather badly burned and after wandering about the country all night he was sheltered by an old Belgian farmer and his wife. For six months Hank helped out the farmer with his chores during the day and each night he would lower himself to his bed, which was at the bottom of an old well. That was just in case the Gestapo should drop in.

'Clem, the navigator, ended up all alone. He was hanging in a tree where his parachute harness trapped him. A German staff car whirled along the roadside the next morning and there was no escape for Clem. He was placed in a train carriage where he was forced to stand with nine other Allied airmen who were being taken to a camp in Germany. Standing at the door of the carriage the German guard engaged Clem and some of the others in conversation; he'd spent some time himself in England as a member of a German swimming team, and they talked about sport in general and the possible length and outcome of the war. He was very pleasant, Clem said. "We asked him if we could have the window open, for it was very stuffy in the car. He said no, not until we got on a bridge, in a few minutes. Soon we were on the bridge; a huge steel-spanned affair, and the Huns apparently thought no one would dare jump from the train going over that bridge. Imagine my surprise when, just as we were in the middle of the bridge, my German guard nudged me and whispered, 'My orders are to shoot anyone who tries to go through this door.' My mind was made up. An American and I just looked at each other and we jumped. We were lucky, for we managed to miss the spans and, although getting good and wet, we were away at last."

'From then on, Clem and his American pal sneaked their way through the countryside until they located a member of the Belgian Underground with whom they stayed until the day Allied troops came to Brussels. When our BBC recording van arrived here in Brussels, we were pounced on by six English-speaking lads, dressed in all sorts of odd clothing. They were the surviving members of the crew of D for Dog. They were all together again.

'Jimmy, Hank and Tommy invited the patriots who had sheltered them for six months to dinner at one of the top-line restaurants here in Brussels, and believe me, it was quite a dinner: the boys were still in their tattered clothes; the patriots came in their Sunday best. Gordon and Pete went back to prison – but this time of their own accord. There they walked down the cell block to their old cell where one of their former guards was now a prisoner. Standing in front of the cell they passed in packets of cigarettes, with the comment, "See what we mean?" '

STEWART MACPHERSON

About the same time there was another reunion in Brussels – in the Chamber of Deputies, where the Belgian Parliament assembled for the first time in four years:

21 September 1944

'Formal orations were made by Monsieur Van Cauwelaert, the President of the Chamber of Deputies, and Monsieur Robert Gillon, the President of the Senate. Both paid homage to all the Allies. But at the name of England the whole assembly rose to its feet in a tide of applause. It was the same at every mention of the name of Winston Churchill, whom Monsieur Gillon called "the voice and inspiration of the nation that saved the world".

'There were specially loud cheers for Canada. "Twice in a lifetime," said the President of the Chamber, "Canada has spilled her young blood in the service of Belgium." But first and foremost, the tribute was to Great Britain and her leader. The deputies rose, clapped and cheered, and the President turned towards the British flag and bowed, and as he did so the cheering and applause grew in volume. Most of the deputies have been in Belgium throughout the occupation. Nearly all of them were in hiding or virtually so. The few who were not in hiding, and who collaborated, are not here today. Among those who are here are several in British uniform. There are many deputies who haven't met for four years, and just before the President came in there were many scenes of reunion. One deputy who was most warmly welcomed back was Monsieur Frere, the deputy for Eupen, the Belgian town near Aachen that was incorporated in Germany by Hitler in 1940. This is significant. For the first time territory seized by Hitler and incorporated in his Greater Reich is again able to send its deputy to a democratic assembly.'

MATTHEW HALTON AND CHESTER WILMOT

CHAPTER XII
Arnhem
'The Picnic is Over'

By the middle of September the great pursuit was slowing down everywhere. In Belgium mixed German groups, organised in a piecemeal fashion from the remnants of regular formations, were able by desperate resistance to hold the canals and waterways while the defence of Holland was prepared. The US armies had the slow and arduous task of fighting through the Siegfried Line; and farther south the Mediterranean forces came to the end of their great hue and cry when they reached the Belfort Gap:

19 September 1944

'There is a steady drenching rain falling, and in the farmyard the sentries are trying to get some shelter under the dripping trees. The dispatch riders have been churning up to the entrance in a thick mud as they come in with their reports, and on a large map, pinned against the florid wallpaper of the farmer's best bedroom, I've been watching these reports being plotted on this huge big-scale map.

'As each strong-point was carefully marked in on that map we began to get a picture of the German defences in the small portion of the Belfort Gap immediately before us. It is pretty obvious that the enemy is now on the ground in strength. The colonel looked at the map and stroked his chin thoughtfully, then turned to me and said: "Well, it certainly looks as if the picnic is over." The picnic, that wild fantastic chase halfway up France after a beaten army, is obviously over. We're still advancing, of course; at the moment we're getting ready to put in an attack on that strong-point, but now that attack has to be in some strength if we're to push the enemy out of it. There's going to be an artillery preparation and the enemy guns will have to be neutralised before the troops go forward.'

WYNFORD VAUGHAN-THOMAS

The German High Command, grievously as its armies had suffered, had the advantage of stronger defensive positions than at any time since D-Day. The Siegfried and Maginot fortifications in the south and the delta-like terrain of the Low Countries provided a formidable barrier, behind which the most battered and shaken army could hope for some respite.

The decision that the Allies had to make was a difficult one. They could rest satisfied with the great things they had achieved and delay a further offensive until the spring, when the opening of the Channel ports and Antwerp would give them short communications: they would then, however, meet an enemy refreshed, recuperated, and well prepared. Alternatively, in the desire to strike again while the enemy was still reeling from earlier blows, they might shrug aside their own difficulties, the hazardous length of communications, the outpacing of heavy installations and particularly of airfield equipment, the need to rest and repair.

Courageously the second decision was taken. An immediate frontal assault was out of the question, but an airborne landing might seize the vital Dutch bridges over the mouths of the Rhine and open the way to an armoured dash into north-west Germany. If it succeeded the powerful western defences of the Reich would be outflanked; but its success depended on the ability of the airborne troops to seize the bridges before they could be demolished, and to hold them until the armour came through from the south. A gamble, with a high dividend and a narrow margin.

On 17 September passengers on a train in England saw the First Allied Airborne Army passing overhead on the way to Holland:

17 September 1944

'The sky was dotted as far as one could see with tugs and gliders; hundreds and hundreds of them; right away towards the clouds in the east.

'Looking away south towards the engine, there they were, pouring eastwards across the track. Looking back to the guard's van, more hundreds of them, still flying over the station we'd passed through a few minutes back. And, overhead, a constant roar of two- and four-engined tugs with there silent gliders; the slender cables between them sometimes flashing in the sun.

'Sometimes dozens of Dakotas – twin engines and uptilted wings – and then a group of Halifaxes. Then more Dakotas and more Halifaxes; endless it seemed, passing low over the train and away to the east. A seasoned aircraftman, with four service chevrons, standing next to me in the corridor struggled hard to look blasé; but he gave it up in the end, put his paper away and stared, as excited as the rest of us, at this simply tremendous display of airborne strength.'

ANONYMOUS

From Belgium a correspondent took off in a scout plane to meet the Airborne Army as it came in:

17 September 1944

'As we drew near the area where we expected to sight the air armada, swarms of fighter aircraft swooped and dived from all directions, but we could not see any sign of the transport aircraft. For a few minutes we dodged in and out of the fighters, which were everywhere, then my pilot suddenly shouted, "Look, straight ahead!" I looked, and if there ever was a sight that defied description, there it was. The sky was black with transport aircraft flying in perfect formation. They were completely surrounded by Typhoons, Spitfires, Mustangs, Thunderbolts, and Lightning fighters. It was an aerial layer cake. The transport planes were in the middle with their fighter cover flying at three different heights. From the ground below coloured smoke suddenly belched up, and the whole armada banked to the left. Not one single aircraft one inch out of position. My pilot signalled to me that he was going to try and get up higher, and for the next five minutes or so we tried to squirm our way through hundreds of fighters that continually whistled by on both sides of us. They raced overhead and roared up from under us, it was like the Glass House in the Fun Fair – there just seemed to be no way out. One fighter immediately above us whined its way down and flew straight at us, he came so close I could see the pilot grin as he waved and rushed by, followed by the rest of the squadron. The armada flew on, and everywhere you looked were aircraft – Allied aircraft. As my pilot shouted to me, "No room up here for Jerry!" '

STEWART MACPHERSON

As they approached their destination the paratroopers got ready to jump:

17 September 1944
'By now we were getting towards the dropping area and I sat looking down the length of the fuselage.

261

'The crew chief is on his knees back in the very rear talking into his intercom, talking with the pilots. The rest of the men have folded up their yellow Mae Wests, as there is certainly no possibility of our ditching in the water on this trip. They're looking out of the window rather curiously, almost as though they were passengers on a peacetime air liner. You occasionally see a man rub the palm of his hand against his trouser leg. There seems to be just that – oh – sort of a film over some of their faces, as though they were just on the verge of perspiring but they aren't. Every man the whole length of the ship is now looking down at this Dutch countryside. We see a few stacks down there that seem to be wheat. There's a small factory off to the right, about half of it demolished. The country is perfectly flat of course; a little while ago we saw some of those big thirty-passenger British Horsa gliders being towed in, and it looks much better glider country than it did in Normandy.

'Suddenly the pilot called our attention to the parapacks coming out from the aircraft in front of us.

'There go the parapacks from the formation ahead of us – yellow, brown, red, drifting down gently, dropping their containers. I can't see, we're a little too far away – I can't see the bodies of the men – yes, I can, just like little brown dolls hanging under a green lampshade they look. . . .

'Just before our men dropped we saw the first flak.

'I think it's coming from that little village just beside the canal. More tracer coming up now, just cutting across in front of our nose.

'They're just queued up on the door now, waiting to jump. Walking out of this aircraft with no flak suits, no armour plating on the ship, we're down just about to the drop altitude now – there are more tracers coming up – nine ships ahead of us have just dropped – you can see the men swinging down – in just about thirty seconds now our ship will drop and those fighting men will walk out on to

Dutch soil – you can probably hear the snap as they check the lashing on the static line – there goes, d'you hear them shout 3–4–5–6–7–8–9–10–11–12–13–14–15–16–17–18 – there they go – every man out – I can see their 'chutes going down now – every man clear – they're dropping just beside a little windmill near a church – hanging there very gracefully – they're all going down so slowly it seems as though they should get to the ground much faster – we're now swinging about making a right-hand turn.

'As we came out there was the blue-grey haze of battle smoke. The parachutes dappled the green fields. And more planes and more gliders were going in. Only a few minutes after the drop we looked down and saw parachutists moving along the road towards a village. They had formed up, were properly spaced, and were moving on their first objective.'

EDWARD R. MURROW, CBS

Meanwhile, British armoured columns moved forward from the Escaut Canal and crossed into Holland, and General Eisenhower broadcast a call to action to the Dutch Forces of the Interior. Breaking through intense opposition, General Dempsey's spearheads raced towards Eindhoven and Nijmegen:

18 September 1944
'We attacked yesterday on a narrow front. Our tanks just had to batter their way down the main road, for the surrounding country was too sandy and swampy for the tanks to move over it. The tanks went forward behind an intense barrage from massed guns, which concentrated their fire down the sides of the road, over an area only five miles deep, and one and a half miles wide. Thousands of rounds came down along the side of the roads, but the gunners had orders to

avoid the road itself, so that craters wouldn't impede our advance. I saw only five places today where shells had hit the road.

'This barrage silenced the Germans at first: our leading squadron of tanks shot its way through the German roadblock, slipped through a minefield that lined the road, and drove on with machine-guns and cannons firing into the trees on either side. But when the next squadron came up, with infantry riding on the backs of the tanks, it came under a hail of fire as it reached the middle of a small clearing. There the Germans had laid an ambush with anti-tank guns and bazookas hidden only a hundred yards off the road. Within a couple of minutes, nine of our tanks were on fire. Fortunately nearly all the crews got out, and the infantry riding on top dived into roadside ditches and opened fire. By this time, other tanks farther back had spotted one German gun; they shot it up, and the crew surrendered. But the tanks had no means of sending the prisoners back, so they were ordered to ride on the backs of the tanks. The Germans were so scared that they immediately told our troops exactly where the other German guns were. The tanks called in the Typhoons, and they did the rest.

'With the help of the Typhoons, and of another barrage by the medium guns, our tanks finally fought their way out of the wood in the late afternoon, and they advanced into Valkenswaard just after nightfall. As they entered, their path was lit by two huge fires started by the Typhoons earlier; there were a few short skirmishes in the streets, but most of the Germans had gone.'

CHESTER WILMOT

This daring attack by tanks closely supported by Typhoons met with remarkable success, and on 19 September at six o'clock Belgian wireless listeners heard their Home programme interrupted by a speaker in English:

19 September 1944

'Hello Brussels, and Hello the BBC in London. This is Frank Gillard on the Second Army Front.

'This is Frank Gillard, War Correspondent of the BBC, speaking from Brussels with a special dispatch bringing good news of today's fighting in Holland. I want to thank listeners in Brussels, and I want to thank the radio authorities at this station for allowing me to break into your programme in this way, and to bring this dispatch to you, because I'm sure you'll be interested in the news – it's good news – and also for letting me in this way bring the news to listeners in Great Britain and throughout the world.

'The British Second Army is off again. It has joined up with the airborne army near Eindhoven, and struck out for the Dutch Rhine. Yesterday afternoon just south of Eindhoven at the little village of Aalst there was some fierce fighting. The enemy made, or tried to make, one more stand. Our infantry stormed the German positions and turned the enemy out of concrete fortifications guarding the road, and then our tanks broke through. By seven o'clock our men were in Eindhoven from the south, and there they linked up with parachutists who fought their way in from the north round about midday. Earlier in the afternoon the Second Army forces bypassing Eindhoven to the west had made an earlier junction with the airborne troops. Now the Second Army's armour pushed on to add its tremendous weight to the airborne strength already landed farther north. On the Wilhelmina Canal they were held up by a demolished bridge, but sappers worked right through the night, last night, and by 5.30 this morning a new bridge was open. The Second Army streamed over and a most amazing advance began. It was an express drive right across Holland, linking up all the way with parachutists and airborne forces who prepared the ground and made the advance possible by seizing the bridges and the road junctions. In five hours, five hours only – an advance of almost thirty miles had been made, and our armoured columns had reached a point only three miles from Nijmegen on the banks of the Waal River, one of the lower stretches of the Rhine, and they were only seven miles from Germany itself.

'It's an incredible achievement; certainly one of the outstanding operations of the whole war. And now what is the result? The result is that the airborne and the Second Army troops between them have almost cut the whole of Holland south of the Rhine clean in two. Once we reach Nijmegen every German west of our new position will have to fight his way through our lines to get back to Germany, or somehow get across the river to the north. That's the immediate result of this amazing thirty-mile dash. More may follow, for the momentum of General Dempsey's troops, both the old-stagers of the Second Army and the airborne newcomers, is by no means expended yet.'

FRANK GILLARD

Gillard had himself been in Eindhoven earlier that day:

19 September 1944

'On Sunday afternoon the people of Eindhoven cheered as they watched from their windows and their rooftops the parachutes descending from the sky a few miles to the north of the city. The Germans heard the cheering too, but they felt very differently about it, they were terribly scared. One man told me in Eindhoven this morning they thought they were cut off, they dashed round the streets questioning everybody, trying to find out what the position was. Knowing that the moment of liberation was near, the people of the city got their flags and their banners ready; they began rounding up the collaborators, they set out to defend key points. The Germans had already destroyed some installations, but one little Dutchman, single-handed, saved the telephone building. Eight Germans had been sent to blow it up; he met them in a narrow corridor, his rifle was up first, and they gave in. He made them file past him, throwing down their arms as they did so, and then he marched them off.

'The Germans had looted all the most valuable equipment from the great Philips radio works, and there were four trainloads waiting to be taken off to Germany; only two of those trains got away. Incidentally, what has infuriated the radio engineers of Eindhoven more than anything else is that the Germans were not content with looting the factory's plant, but they also seized all the notebooks in the laboratory recording the results of years of painstaking research work, and they carted them off too.

'Eindhoven is a pretty big city with a population getting on for 120,000. Factories there turn out textiles, tobacco, matches, but the main industry, of course, is radio. Twenty-four thousand people are employed in the great radio works. Twice those works were bombed by the RAF. Beautiful bombing, they said it was. The entire office block, the nerve centre of the whole concern, was burnt right out. "The RAF did just enough damage to enable us not to have to work too hard for the Germans," one of the workers said to me this morning with a wink, "but not quite enough for the Germans to have to deport us into Germany."

'The Germans long ago confiscated all the wireless sets belonging to the people of Eindhoven, but it was a futile thing to do in a city where almost every other man is a radio engineer. The Philips workers turned out thousands of clandestine sets – in fact they practically mass-produced them, made in tiny biscuit boxes out of parts which they took from the works when the Germans were not looking. In the great factories they used to test out the finished receivers by tuning them in to London. You just can't stop these people from listening to

London. One man told me this morning that when the power supply failed he brought his bicycle into his house, he connected his radio set to the little dynamo which generated electricity for his bicycle lamp, and then he and his wife took it in turn to listen while the other kept the wheel of the bicycle spinning round.

'Our welcome at Eindhoven was just as wildly enthusiastic as it has been in the Belgian and French cities. I drove in at first light this morning just as the mist was lifting. People came running out of their houses, some still in pyjamas and nightgowns, to wave us by. By eight o'clock in the morning the streets were packed; the flags and flowers and bunting and streamers were out, and huge banners of orange-coloured cloth hung everywhere. Everyone wore an orange-coloured favour. Many people were dressed in orange carnival costumes from head to foot. There was tremendous rejoicing.

'A man took me aside to tell me that his wife had just had a son this morning, the first baby of the new generation of Free Netherlanders, he said, and they're going to call him "Tommy".'

FRANK GILLARD

The first of the major river crossings was the great bridge over the Maas at Grave:

19 September 1944

'The commanders of the two leading battalions of the British armoured column at the head of the advancing Second Army met General Browning, commander of the airborne operation, at about 9.30 this morning. This means that the British tanks are over the Maas, having crossed it earlier this morning by a bridge [*at Grave*] taken by American airborne troops on Sunday night [*17 September*]. They've reached this point from Eindhoven over canal bridges also taken and held by American parachutists and glider-borne infantry, but had been delayed a little at the one crossing where the Germans had managed to forestall it and destroy the bridge [*at Zon*]. The first tanks crossed there over a Bailey bridge, which the engineers were still finishing.

'There had been some sharp fighting, the British told us, in the Eindhoven area both before and after they'd joined forces with the American airborne troops. But here the bridge had been taken pretty easily and the cost was only two men killed. Grave, a clean cosy little market town in the middle of dairy-farming and orchard country, was almost untouched by battle. The German parachute troops quartered there, 600 of them, had packed up and cleared off incontinently as soon as they saw us dropping in the fields around the town on Sunday afternoon. I saw their barracks, still littered with all kinds of arms and gear together with the photographs and letters that the soldier will usually stick to until the last.

'I slept in a bed which had held a German junior officer the night before. His bedside books were still on the little table, almost too typical to be true. And his slippers and an empty brandy bottle were on the bedside rug.

'I spent yesterday in Grave waiting with the Americans for the British to arrive. It was festooned with Dutch flags and the schoolchildren, orange ribbons in their hair, or in gigantic bow-ties round their necks, were dancing round the town in procession, singing. Half the boys were in boy-scout or wolf-cub uniforms – much too small for them because the organisations had been banned throughout the German occupation – shouting out tremendous salutes and grinning with self-importance. I got more salutes than anybody. My red beret marked me out as the one Tommy among the tin-hatted Americans, and Tommies are in great favour. It was all very bright and cheery in the mild September sunshine, a town full of excited happiness. Not the

269

wild abandon we've met in Italy and France, but heartening all the same, and all the more homely to an Englishman.

'This morning the Mayor announced from his town hall that the British troops were only five miles away, and off the town went to meet them – every man, woman and child, it seemed – headed by a shrill boy-scout band. Everything was sunny again, and the jollity and excitement were greater even than yesterday.

'It was during the night, appropriately in the dark, that there had been the ugly post-liberation business of unofficial summary courts and head shaving. But head shaving has been the severest punishment meted out, I think.

'Since the armour was met, first by the boy scouts, then by General Browning and a young American Brigadier-General, it's been massing to continue its drive. The Germans have pulled in a little to our right and brought 88-mm guns up that were not, happily, available when we first landed. So there's a certain amount of shelling going on and a lot of small arms fire from our outposts keeping the roads clear, but I doubt whether there's much to stop, or even delay, the continuation of our armoured thrust. The Germans are pretty thin on the ground here and haven't been strong enough to interfere unduly in the course of forty-eight hours, even with the lightly supported airborne troops.'

CYRIL RAY

The airborne landings at Nijmegen had been heavily opposed, and General Dempsey's tanks were having a hard time of it through marshy country which kept our columns from deploying off the road to outflank German strong-points. Nevertheless the airborne men were fighting on grimly, and on 19 September the British Second Army reached Nijmegen:

20 September 1944

'A fierce battle is still being waged around the Dutch town of Nijmegen on the river Waal, one of the main outlets of the Rhine. It's a battle for bridges, for at Nijmegen the Waal is 500 yards wide, and for twenty-five miles on either side of Nijmegen there are no other bridges over the Waal or the Rhine, which it joins ten miles to the east. Last Sunday American airborne troops were landed south of Nijmegen; one of their main tasks was to seize the Nijmegen bridge intact, but they encountered stiff resistance and even though armoured columns from the Second Army thrust through from Eindhoven yesterday and linked up with them, these troops couldn't drive the Germans back from the strong positions they had taken up around the approaches to the main road bridge. The chief strength of these German positions is the ack-ack guns; this bridge has always been very heavily protected by 88s and lighter flak guns. But now the Germans have moved their ack-ack weapons into key positions for ground defence. These guns are difficult to deal with, because the southern approaches to the bridge are covered by a maze of streets and the ground to the east is laced with canals. Already there has been a good deal of street fighting and that's slow and costly. But our patrols have reached the river north-east of Nijmegen. Meantime the Germans are striving to cut off the armoured spearhead which thrust through from Eindhoven to Nijmegen yesterday.'

CHESTER WILMOT

❧

So far the Allied plan had succeeded, in spite of heavier fighting than had been hoped for and the inability of the airborne troops to seize the bridge before the British tanks arrived. And the bridge at Nijmegen was still intact:

24 September 1944

'American airborne patrols reached the area at the southern end of the bridge on Sunday night, 17 September, shortly after they landed, but at that time they were not in enough strength to do anything about it. On Monday the paratroops and glider forces were too busy beating off German counter-attacks to co-ordinate an assault on the bridge. By this time the armour of the British Second Army was on its way northwards from the Escaut Canal. Then on Tuesday British tanks arrived on the outskirts of Nijmegen and an attack was commenced, but still the Germans held on strongly in the fortification and houses on the south end of the bridge. American airborne infantry and British tanks were only 300 yards from the bridge in the streets of Nijmegen, but they couldn't get over it.

'Tuesday night was the strangest. The American troops took machine-guns to the top of the houses and sprayed the approaches and the entrance to the bridge with bullets. All night they shot at anything that moved. Perhaps it was this constant fire that kept the Germans from blowing the bridge then. But still the shuddering blast that would signal the end of the bridge did not come. And when morning arrived a new plan was devised. It was dangerous and daring and risky. The commanders who laid it out knew this; and the men who were to carry it out knew it too. Thinking a frontal assault on the bridge from the south was impossible, American infantry were to fight their way westwards down the west bank of the Waal River and cross in broad daylight to fight their way back up the river bank, and attack the bridge from the north. On Wednesday morning the infantry made their way westward through the town and got to the industrial outskirts along the river bank near the mouth of a big canal. Some British tanks went with them to give them protection in the street fighting and to act as artillery when the crossings were to be made. Accompanying this task force were trucks carrying twenty-six assault boats brought along by the British armoured units in case of such an emergency. Most of the men who were to make the crossing had never handled an assault boat before. There was a lot of argument as to who would handle the paddles and preference was given to the men who had at least rowed a boat. Everything was going well. The Germans were supposed to be completely surprised by the audacity of the move.

'But late in the morning – the impossible happened. Two men showed themselves on the river bank and were fired at by the enemy. No Americans were supposed to be in that part of the town. The 88-mm shells began plastering the area. The gaff was blown. Reconnaissance spotted batches of German troops being transferred to the opposite bank. A few hours later, machine-guns were dug into the marshes on the far side – the plan had been discovered. The task force was under shellfire, and several hundred Germans with machine-guns were sitting on the opposite bank waiting for the crossing. This was about noon. There was a quick conference. It was decided that the original plan would proceed, but this time the men crossing the river would have the help of heavy bombers – Lancasters and Stirlings flying in daylight to drop their bombs on the opposite bank in tactical support of the men from the assault boats.

'Working under enemy shellfire, the assault boats were assembled. When they were put into the water, another difficulty arose. The tide was moving, but with a downstream current of eight miles an hour. Some of the boats drifted 300 yards down river before they were retrieved and brought back. Meanwhile machine-guns spluttered on the opposite bank and German artillery kept smashing the embarkation area regularly.

'At last everything was ready. The bombers went in, but didn't drop their bombs close enough to knock out the machine-guns. Twenty-six assault boats were in the water. They would carry ten men each. Two hundred and sixty men would make the first assault. Waiting for them on the other bank were some 400 to 600 Germans. The shelling continued. Every man took a deep breath and climbed in. Someone made a wisecrack about the airborne navy and someone else said they preferred airborne submarines to this job. And off across the river they started. At the same time, behind them, the British tanks fired their heavy guns, and our own heavy machine-guns fired into the opposite bank giving the little fleet as much cover as possible. A smoke-screen was laid, but it wasn't very effective because of the wind.

'And over on the other side of the river the enemy tracers shrieked at the boats. The fire at first was erratic, but as the boats approached the northern bank the tracers began to spread on to the boats. Men slumped in their seats – other men could be seen shifting a body to take over the paddling. One man rose up in his seat and fell overboard. There was no thought of turning back. The paddling continued clumsily and erratically, but it continued. One of the boats had so many holes in it that the men were baling out with their tin helmets – it was almost splintered when it reached the other side.

'The fighting, though, had only just begun. The hundred or so men who had arrived on the opposite side fought their way forward with bayonet and grenade, going from one machine-gun nest to the other until they had established a bridgehead only a few yards deep and several hundred feet wide. The thirteen boats had hardly left for the return trip for the reinforcements, when the men on the north bank saw specks in the water. The men on the opposite bank, seeing the casualties suffered in the landing under fire, were not waiting for the boats. Some of them had stripped off their equipment and, taking a bandolier of ammunition, were swimming the river with their rifles on their backs. And thus it went – the thirteen little boats going time after time across the river under fire, the men on the bridgehead digging in and firing as rapidly as possible, routing out German machine-gun nests by hand, while British tanks fired for all they were worth. After an hour and a half of concentrated hell, the infantry were over. They held a bridgehead several hundred yards wide and 100 yards deep. At that time, one officer counted 138 Germans dead in a space of sixty yards of that bloody beach-head.

'There was a welcome pause as the men consolidated and rested in their foxholes. Some had thrown the German bodies out of the Nazi machine-gun nests and were using these to stiffen their defences. The plan was to turn eastwards and assault the northern end of the bridge. But on the left flank of that minute bridgehead was another menace – for there on the high ground overlooking the bridge and firing at us with some 88 guns was an ancient fort. It is called Hatz van Holland and was supposed to have been used centuries ago by Charlemagne as a fortress. The Germans had been using the fort as an anti-aircraft gun-position to defend Nijmegen, and now they turned the ack-ack guns downward to bear on the bridge and the airborne bridgehead. While these guns were firing at the back, the troops could not fight their way to the northern end of the bridge. A detail was formed to attack the Hatz van Holland and put its guns out of action. That, as warriors centuries ago found out, was extremely difficult because the Hatz van Holland was completely surrounded by a moat.

'This moat had a few feet of water in it – black dirty water, covered with a layer of bright green slime. Also, the attacking party would have to advance under point-blank 88-mm fire. But anyhow the party set out. They crawled towards the high ground and the 88s banged away at them. And then they came to a zone where there were no 88 shells. It was found out that the other 88 guns were so installed that the guns could not reach downward that far. The German gun-crews discovered this too late and rushed to put up a rifle and machine-gun defence along the moat. But the Americans by this time had faced so much that a few machine-guns were nothing. They made a stand-up attack, shouting like Indians, and, with tommy-guns blazing, knocked out the historic Hatz van Holland. A few Americans with blood in their eyes left seventy-five Germans dead in that moat. The remaining troops fought their way up river all right. They captured the northern end of the railroad bridge and worked their way to the junction of the railroad highway from the main bridge. The entire German position on the northern side of the river was cut off.'

BILL DOWNS, CBS

The American paratroopers pushed on from the rail bridge towards the northern end of the 600-yard road bridge, which was the real prize of the battle. At the southern end of this bridge, where there had been fierce fighting the day before, other American paratroops with tanks and infantry of the Grenadier Guards had already put in another assault. The Germans had exceptionally strong defences here, in a park with surrounding buildings which had been turned into blockhouses. The park was honeycombed with trenches, and near the south-west corner of the bridge there was a wooded knoll with pillboxes built into it:

25 September 1944
'The American paratroops cleared the southern part of the park and the British went for the blockhouses and the fortified knoll right near the bridge itself. The tanks smashed open a way through the blockhouses. They put armour-piercing shells through the concrete and sandbags and then fired high explosive inside. They carved large gaps in the walls so that infantry could move from house to house under cover. In some houses the Germans held out until the Tommies were near enough to blind them with smoke grenades and blast the

pillboxes with piat bombs. Then at last they were through to the edge of the park and only the fortified knoll lay between them and the bridge. In small groups of half a dozen or so they formed up in the wrecked houses; fixed bayonets, drew safety-pins from grenades, and then burst out into the open, with Vickers guns mounted on the roofs firing over their heads. The Germans below ground had every protection. But they couldn't stand this sudden onslaught. The leading British company commander was killed by a German only twenty yards away. But his men raced past him and into the German trenches. Then the hunt began. As one of the platoon commanders said to me later, "It was like flushing bolting foxes." The Germans turned and ran along their trenches with our men after them. The trenches were deep and one of them ran for 150 yards. But we fired down the straight stretches and threw grenades round the corners; and then when the Germans reached the end they had to come out. They bolted for the bridge, but we had machine-guns waiting for them, and not many got away. The day after the battle you could still see them lying where they'd fallen; and on that knoll there were dozens; I've never seen anything like the destruction there. It had been mortared and shelled and finally overrun by infantry, and there were dead Germans in every trench.

'Our troops picked up fifty wounded prisoners and another thirty who weren't hurt. But twice as many must have been killed in the last desperate battle to keep us off the bridge. Once the blockhouses and the knoll were captured, and as soon as the Americans had silenced the last anti-tank gun farther down the park, the way was clear for the tanks to rush the bridge. At seven o'clock, just as it was getting dark, five British tanks made their run. As they got near the bridge they were fired on from the other side of the river, but they were ordered to keep going regardless of the fire, to push on across the bridge. As the two leading tanks roared down the long straight 600-yard stretch of bridge, guns on the far side kept firing. Germans in the girders let loose with machine-guns and bazookas. But the tanks went on. They shot straight through a gap in the concrete roadblock at the northern end of the bridge and went on up the road. They got through. But beyond the bridge the next two tanks were shot up; and when the fifth one reached the northern end its commander realised there was no one else there. And so he stayed there. And for half an hour his tank held the northern end of the bridge alone until American paratroops got through to support him. Meantime, the leading tanks had pushed on and linked up with other Americans who'd crossed the river and cut the main road north of the bridge. And they had managed to silence most of the 88s that were meant to cover the bridge with fire. By capturing these the Americans had ensured the success of that dramatic dash across the bridge by the British tanks.'

CHESTER WILMOT

In the fighting round Nijmegen the American airborne units were able to draw some advantage from the character of the land they were contesting:

24 September 1944
'The American paratroops fighting south and east of Nijmegen have done an excellent job in extremely difficult country. The terrain in this particular area is thick with forests and brush. The ground is hilly. But all in all it is perfect country for self-contained units such as the airborne forces operate. Here the American soldier can use the elementary woodcraft that he learned as a boy, and in this type of country the independent task force, even though it is only a couple of dozen men, proves its value. The German soldier is inferior in this type of fighting.

'One American unit captured a German train shortly after it landed on Sunday. The train was headed for the Reich loaded with soldiers being taken back to form new units. Since it was Sunday there were numerous German Customs officials on board after a weekend in Holland, and various other people on board who suddenly found themselves prisoners of war. Included was the German Consul for Nijmegen. He called himself the "Honourable Consul", the soldiers said, and that's how we listed him, the Honourable Consul. But now he's the Honourable Prisoner.

'One group of American paratroops captured a number of German 88-mm guns near one of their dropping areas, and set about destroying them. An HQ was set up in a nearby building where the staff was settling down to work. However, the demolition squads did not notice that the Germans had abandoned one gun leaving it fully loaded. The 88 went off and the shell went directly through the HQ building – no one was hurt, but a lot of people were frightened. Such incidents are common along the Dutch corridor that now stretches two-thirds of the way across eastern Holland. But it's not all comedy and this fighting is not done by a bunch of boys out on a walk. Here's what happened to one unit fighting south-east of Nijmegen in German territory.

'There had been a stiff battle between patrols in a forest just over the German frontier. A number of American and German soldiers were killed but the Nazi patrol was wiped out and the Americans re-formed to press on. Six men went one at a time down a trail in the area and not one of the six came back. And then a unit went down and found nothing but a group of dead Germans lying among the trees. Beyond this area were the bodies of the six Americans. Examining the bodies of the supposedly dead Germans, they found one 15-year-old Hitler youth – a paratrooper kicked him and he groaned – underneath him he hid an automatic rifle. He was the sniper who had picked off the patrol. His face and his hands had been coloured a deathly yellow. His uniform had been purposely splashed thickly with blood. The sniper was shot.'

BILL DOWNS, CBS

Meanwhile, what of the men further north at Arnhem? Not only was it ten miles further on, but two SS Panzer divisions were regrouping in the area. Model's headquarters were also nearby and he took personal charge:

22 September 1944

'Between the two outlets of the Rhine, the Waal at Nijmegen and the Neder Rhine at Arnhem, some very severe fighting is going on. The Germans are putting up a furious battle to prevent a link-up between the Second Army and the group of our airborne forces around Arnhem, and not only to prevent that junction, but also to bring this whole advance to a standstill. The armoured columns of the Second Army which crossed the bridge at Nijmegen, the bridge which they and the airborne troops had successfully seized intact, these columns met intense German opposition just two miles to the north of Nijmegen town. The Germans, it seems, had brought round very considerable forces from the wooded country away to the east, where we always knew they were holding strong reinforcements. These enemy troops in many cases had been ferried in from across the River Waal which makes a wide loop in this neighbourhood.

'The German intention, without doubt, was to drive our spearhead back over the Waal at Nijmegen and, if possible, to hold us; but, at the very least, to delay any further Allied advance by carrying out this time the plan which we frustrated two days ago of blowing the Nijmegen bridge. But they were too late. Our forces were over the river in too much strength; and though our advance was brought for the moment almost to a standstill, we were able to stand firm against all the furious efforts of the enemy to repulse us. Again and again the Germans attacked, but without success, and this morning, having built up our strength across the river in spite of the enemy's efforts, we resumed our pressure.

'Meanwhile, just to the north around Arnhem, our airborne forces are facing very strong German formations. The enemy troops here seem to be well equipped with automatics, and with SP guns and other supporting weapons. Their mortar fire too is intensive, and it's accurate. We're close enough now to these airborne units to have good communication with them, and though there's still little detailed news of the fighting, we know that it's hard and it's bitter. The Germans are out to destroy this still isolated force if they can, but so far, and considering the circumstances, it's believed that the position around Arnhem is reasonably satisfactory.

'There's no news yet about the bridge at Arnhem, the bridge across the other Rhine outlet, the Neder Rhine.'

FRANK GILLARD

The British Second Army fought valiantly to push on from Nijmegen and bring relief to the British 1st Airborne Division, but now their own rearward communications were cut. Supplies and reinforcements coming up through Eindhoven were halted, and the Allied Air Forces had to replenish the relief column by parachute and glider in addition to supplying the beleaguered force at Arnhem. Only the most urgent necessity could justify the continuing of the advance north of Nijmegen – but that necessity existed, in the plight of the men who, by holding the bridge at Arnhem for nearly three days, had prevented the Germans from rushing help through to their troops in Nijmegen.

The British Second Army recognised its debt to those men and was resolved to reach them – even if it could do no more than evacuate the survivors:

27 September 1944

'On Sunday 17 September as our airborne troops were landing in Holland, the Second Army began that great drive from the Meuse–Escaut Line. Ahead of our ground troops lay a series of water barriers, a succession of immense obstacles, each of them likely to involve us in a full-scale and prolonged battle, unless it could be seized and held by swift attack. It was the British and American airborne troops who provided most of the surprise. They landed behind the enemy lines with the task of taking the key points and, above all, the river crossings, all along the line of the intended advance.

'It was a hazardous task as all airborne operations are bound to be. But it was vital to the whole plan. By the evening of the 17th the Second Army had driven two miles into Holland. By the evening of the 18th they were in Eindhoven and had linked up with the first group of airborne troops. The Germans had just succeeded in blowing the bridge over the Wilhelmina Canal at Zon, but our sappers worked all through the night to repair it and on the next morning, the 19th, the Second Army thrust swept across Holland.

'The airborne troops along the route had the great satisfaction of seeing their hopes completely fulfilled, as our armoured columns reached them, one formation after another, and swept on over the crossings which they'd seized and defended so gallantly.

'It was at the very approaches to Nijmegen that the advance was halted. Here the Germans had concentrated in great strength south of the bridge over the Dutch Rhine [*the Waal*] – a tremendous bridge spanning the greatest waterway of them all. Our spearheads launched a blitz attack against the Germans in Nijmegen there and then on the

Paratroops of the 1st British Airborne Division in their aircraft
during the flight to Arnhem on 17 September 1944. They had the
toughest objective of the whole operation, to capture the bridge
over the Neder Rhine at Arnhem. War Report correspondents
Stanley Maxted and Guy Byam jumped with the airborne troops
and stayed with them until the withdrawal.

evening of the 19th. But it was not successful. During the next few
hours an assault crossing was made over the Rhine, the northern end
of the bridge was seized, and finally by this joint action of American
parachutists and British armoured forces Nijmegen bridge was in our
hands intact by seven o'clock on the evening of the 20th. That was
Wednesday.

'This was a tremendous achievement, and it was made possible
only by the gallantry of British airborne troops still further north
at the next water barrier, the Neder Rhine at Arnhem. These men
fought with a gallantry which has never been surpassed in any war.

From the start they knew that theirs was the most dangerous task of all. For they were furthest from the relieving armies. They were nearest to German reinforcements. They had to take the brunt of overwhelming German attacks while their comrades further south were being relieved by the advancing Second Army. Those who were with these men at Arnhem will tell the story of how they lived and fought through those critical days, how they denied the bridge over the Neder Rhine to the enemy right up to midday on Wednesday, so that he couldn't send reinforcements south to Nijmegen by the quick route, but instead he had to move all his troops around through Emmerich in Germany, with the result that they arrived too late.

'It was the battle fought by our airborne troops at the Arnhem bridge which enabled the Second Army and the other airborne troops to seize the crossing at Nijmegen and sweep across the great river. Now the fighting became even more bitter. The position of our airborne troops beyond the Neder Rhine around Arnhem was becoming critical. On 21 September, Thursday, the Second Army battled on towards Arnhem. The enemy resisted fiercely. He fought his way back hedge to hedge and cottage to cottage. Our armour was moving in country where deployment was impossible. Each road ran along a high embankment. It was difficult to get off it and every vehicle moving along it made a perfect target silhouetted against the sky. Rain poured down interminably. The low-lying fields became swamps.

'The orders were that all risks were to be taken. The advance must go on. All risks were taken, but it was physically impossible to use our tanks under such conditions. The command was given for the infantry to go forward. Somehow the traffic problems on the narrow roads were overcome. The infantry leap-frogged over the armour and took the lead. By nightfall we'd advanced a further three miles.

'By the evening of the 22nd, after a hard day's fighting, infantry and armoured cars had reached the south bank of the Neder Rhine some distance west of Arnhem. Without pause, a plan was prepared for an assault-crossing of the river under cover of darkness. Assault boats and ducks were sent forth, preparations were made for rafting. It was an incredibly difficult task. The Germans on the far bank were constantly on guard, their machine-guns were ready, and from the first moment they kept up continuous cross-fire on fixed lines. The current was too swift for the rafts, they were swept away. The heavy rain had so softened the marshy river banks that the wheels of the ducks couldn't get enough grip to approach the water. Only a handful of troops had succeeded in making the crossing when daylight put an end to all operations. Meanwhile the enemy had scored a temporary success in his attacks against the flanks of our advance further south, and he had for the moment cut the line of supply so that no more convoys could come forward.

'The next day, the 23rd, was a day of heavy shelling and mortaring along the banks of the Neder Rhine. Any daylight operations were out of the question. That night a much larger infantry force was carried across the river, but attempts to get much-needed food and ammunition over to the very hard-pressed airborne troops failed. The enemy fire was fiercer than ever. Only as long as our barrage lasted did the Germans keep their heads down. As soon as it ceased they were firing again, but, unfortunately, interruptions to our line of supply limited the amount of fire support we were able to give.

'On the 24th a decision was made. We must get across the river in strength within the next twenty-four hours to relieve the airborne troops, or we must withdraw from the far bank of the river. On the night of the 24th we did get many many more troops across than before, and a few tons of supplies, but still not enough men or supplies to tip the scales in our favour, not enough to secure a bridgehead deep enough for further exploitation. So, during Monday the 25th it was decided to abandon our position on the north bank of the Neder Rhine, and on Monday night under cover of a tremendous bombardment our men withdrew, a depleted, a gallant and undaunted force.

'It was not a defeat. This operation must be viewed as a whole, though naturally we all of us became preoccupied with the fighting of our beleaguered troops in and around Arnhem. In those few days from 17 September onwards, the Second Army swept forward over no less than five major obstacles, the Wilhelmina Canal, the Dommel River at St Oedenrode, the Zuid Willemsvaart Canal at Veghel, the great bridge over the Maas at Grave, and the Dutch Rhine itself, the Waal, at Nijmegen. The tremendous effort of the airborne troops at Arnhem aided this great advance beyond all measure. We've failed, so far, to hold a crossing over the last big waterway, the Neder Rhine, at Arnhem. Arnhem town itself is dominated by high ground to the north. A frontal attack could only succeed if the troops making it could sweep right through and on to that high ground. It would be impossible to consolidate in a small bridgehead under observed enemy fire from such dominating positions, so our withdrawal, under the circumstances, was a wise move.

'The Germans may try to crow, but looking at the picture as a whole the battle for Holland has so far gone very decidedly in our favour, and the glory of the men who fought this first battle of Arnhem against such odds will last for ever.'

FRANK GILLARD

The disappointment of that withdrawal was keenly felt. What it meant to individual soldiers engaged in the action, and what it had been like there, became movingly clear when two reporters – Stanley Maxted and Guy Byam – emerged from the carnage to give their vivid first-hand accounts of valiant men pushed, day by day, to the limits of human endurance:

27 September 1944

'The time is 0900 hours on 18 September. On landing there was no chance, no time to record. After casting off from the tug-planes our pilots, Staff Sgt Miller and Sgt Hollingworth, sat easily at the glider controls. It gave some sickening bumps on landing, then braked quickly to a stop. At the same moment a yell came from the cockpit: "Out, out, everybody out." The side-door slid up and I jumped, blindly, landing in soft ground among young turnips. I started to run; looking up, I saw another fleet of planes without gliders. Wisps of something started to stream from them; then suddenly the sky blossomed into many-coloured flowers that floated down with tiny dolls of men jerking and swinging below them. Four times this happened. Our team was back unloading the vehicles from the glider; I ran back to help. Everyone knew what they were doing but me, but I waded in anyway. Meantime machine-gun and rifle fire seemed to be all round. I didn't know where from or who was being fired on, and there was no time to find out. Airborne troops don't fool – they don't wait – they're trouble-hunters. Someone yelled "Get on", and I climbed on the trailer of one jeep. We careered away through the turnip field out on to a road; there was a tidy red house with a smiling, staid Dutch family outside, smiling and waving, in their Sunday clothes – I'd forgotten it was Sunday; the Dutch are so friendly, and scrubbed-looking. They're not so demonstrative, but you feel there's a lot back of their gestures.

'We pulled up in a wood and started to dig; you find you can dig in a kind of concentrated frenzy when you have to. Prisoners started to come in, some wounded, some not; when mortar shells landed near, they started to run; they came back when a burly paratrooper pointed his Sten gun and shouted at them. Darkness came, no word yet of the situation elsewhere, our wounded are coming in, only those badly wounded, the others keep fighting. Golly, it makes you proud to be with guys like these. Unless the army follows through, they'll stay surrounded and fighting until – well, until.

'We bumped over into a potato field in the dark and started to dig again – that's how I knew it was a potato field. Fires made a glow just over the crest to the east. I was hungry, I chewed a block of oatmeal and ate chocolate from my 24-hour ration. Before daylight we were up and away again and now we're in another wood. Hot tea has miraculously appeared and the sun's up and warming us. Getting here we passed guns in position and firing; they've been there since yesterday afternoon. We passed men who were dirty and weary but right on top of the world. We passed more German prisoners – there was a girl among them, in Nazi WAAF uniform, she had been taken armed. There was one officer with his arm in a sling, scowling and trying to look tough; I guess he was too, and there are more men streaming by now; they're pretty dirty, but they're so darned cocky in their bearing. They know they're good, and so do I.'

STANLEY MAXTED

27 September 1944 (recorded 20 September)

'Just a few minutes ago the fighter cover showed up and right behind them came those lovely supply planes which you can hear up above us now. Yesterday and this morning our supplies came and were dropped in the wrong place. The enemy got them, but now these planes have come over and they've dropped them right dead over us.

'Everybody is cheering and clapping and they just can't give vent to their feelings about what a wonderful sight this is. All those bundles and parachuted packages and ammunition are coming down here all around us, through the trees, bouncing on the ground, the men are running out to get them, and you have no idea what this means to us to see this ammunition and this food coming down where the men can get it. They're such fighters, if they can only get the stuff to fight with. But it's a wonderful sight – it's a shame when they can't get the stuff to fight with. You can hear the kind of flak that those planes are flying through, it's absolutely like . . . [*noise of flak*] . . . hail, up there. These enemy guns all around us are just simply hammering at those planes, but so far I haven't seen anything, I haven't seen any of them hit, but the bundles are coming down, the parachutes are coming down . . . [*noise of planes and flak*].

STANLEY MAXTED

27 September 1944

'About five kilometres to the west of Arnhem, in a space 1500 yards by 900, on the last day, I saw the dead and the living – those who fought a good fight and kept the faith with you at home, and those who still fought magnificently on. They were the last of the few.

'I last saw them yesterday morning as they dribbled into Nijmegen. They had staggered and walked and waded all night from Arnhem about ten miles north, and we were busy asking each other if this or that one had been seen. Everyone wondered what the final check-up would amount to. I walked up to one young lieutenant to ask him about his sergeant – a stout lad if there ever was one – and he started to explain what had happened and then turned away. Remember, all of these men have been practically ten days and ten nights under the most murderous concentrated fire I have seen in two wars. Then he turned again and said: "It's hell to be pulled out when you haven't finished your job, isn't it?" That's the way they all felt. It doesn't occur to them that if they hadn't held the horde of enemy force at Arnhem, that force would have been down at Nijmegen upsetting the whole apple-cart.

'Late on the afternoon before, we were told that the remnants of the 1st Airborne Division were going to pull out that night. The enemy was making it impossible for the elements of the Second Army to relieve us. BBC's Guy Byam, Alan Woods of the *Daily Express*, and I were told by Major Roy Oliver of the Public Relations Division – who, incidentally, proved himself a great soldier as well – we were told to destroy all our equipment with the exception of what would go into one haversack. We were told to muffle our boots with bits of blanket and be ready to move off at a certain time. When the various officers were told to transmit this news to that thin straggle of hard-pressed men around the pitifully small perimeter, a great silence seemed to come upon them even in the middle of the shelling – you see, day or night the shelling and mortaring never stopped. The ones I saw just drew a deep breath and said; "Very good, sir." Then these staring eyes in the middle of black muddy masks saluted as they always would and faded away to crawl out on their stomachs and tell their men.

'Perhaps I should remind you here that these were men of no ordinary calibre. They had been nine days in that little space I mentioned being mortared and shelled, machine-gunned, and sniped from all around. When a tank or a self-propelled 88 gun broke through, two or three of them detached themselves and somehow or another had put it out of business. For the last three days they had had no water, very little but small-arms ammunition, and rations cut to one-sixth. Luckily, or unluckily, it rained and they caught the water in their capes and drank that. These last items were never mentioned – they were airborne, weren't they? They were tough and knew it. All right, water and rations didn't matter – give them some Germans to kill and even one chance in ten and they'd get along somehow.

'Well, at two minutes past ten we clambered out of our slit trenches in an absolute din of bombardment – a great deal of it our own – and formed up in a single line. Our boots were wrapped in blanket so that no noise would be made. We held the tail of the coat of the man in front. We set off like a file of nebulous ghosts from our pock-marked and tree-strewn piece of ground. Obviously, since the enemy was all round us we had to go through him to get to the River Rhine.

'After about 200 yards of silent trekking we knew we were among the enemy. It was difficult not to throw yourself flat when machine-gun tracers skinned your head or the scream of a shell or mortar-bomb sounded very close – but the orders were to "keep going". Anybody hit was to be picked up by the man behind him. Major Oliver had reconnoitred the route earlier on with a headquarters' officer and had it memorised. The back of my neck was prickling for that whole interminable march. I couldn't see the man ahead of me – all I knew was that I had hold of a coat-tail and for the first time in my life was grateful for the downpour of rain that made a patter on the leaves of the trees and covered up any little noises we were making. At every turn of the way there was posted a sergeant glider-pilot who stepped out like a shadow and then stepped back into a deeper shadow again. Several times we halted – which meant you bumped into the man ahead of you – then when the head of our party was satisfied the turning was clear, we went on again. Once we halted because of a boy sitting on the ground with a bullet through his leg. We wanted to pick him up, but he whispered: "Nark it – gimme another field dressing and I'll be all right, I can walk." As we came out of the trees – we had been following carefully-thought-out footpaths so far – I felt as naked as if I were in Piccadilly Circus in my pyjamas, because of the glow from fires across the river. The machine-gun and general bombardment had never let up.

'We lay down flat in the mud and rain and stayed that way for two hours till the sentry beyond the hedge on the bank of the river told us to move up over the dike and be taken across. Mortaring started now and I was fearful for those that were already over on the bank.

I guessed it was pretty bad for them. After what seemed a nightmare of an age we got our turn and slithered up and over on to some mud flats. There was the shadow of a little assault craft with an outboard motor on it. Several of these had been rushed up by a field company of Engineers. One or two of them were out of action already. We waded out into the Rhine, up to my hips – it didn't matter. I was soaked through long ago – had been for days. And a voice that was sheer music spoke from the stern of the boat saying: "Ye'll have to step lively, boys, t'aint healthy here." It was a Canadian voice, and the Engineers were Canadian Engineers. We helped push the boat off into the swift Rhine current and with our heads down between our knees waited for the bump on the far side – or for what might come before. It didn't come. We clambered out and followed what had been a white tape up over a dike. We slid down the other side on our backsides, and we sloshed through mud for four miles and a half – me thinking, "Gosh! I'm alive, how did it happen?" In a barn there was a blessed hot mug of tea with rum in it and a blanket over our shoulders – then we walked again – all night. After daylight we got to a dressing-station near Nijmegen and then we were put in trucks and that's how we reached Nijmegen. That's how the last of the few got out to go and fight in some future battle.'

STANLEY MAXTED

27 September 1944

'They came out because they had got nothing left to fight with except their bare hands, maybe. All day, as for six days before that, the tanks and the mortars and the flame-throwers had smashed at the positions. For some time the men had been fighting without food, and practically with no water, fighting an enemy whose growing strength was almost in our midst, fighting with small arms against armour. Every brick, every wall, every house was a part of the battle that ebbed to and fro, a yard here and a yard there. And those men who climbed out of their foxholes and slit trenches weren't beaten, mind you; no, they had to get out because of events the other side of the river. No, the German soldier never really beat them; their tanks could come in and they could shell us from a distance, hour after hour of it, but when the SS troops were sent in against our men they got murdered, and they hated every minute of it.

'In the morning of the day that we came out I was asked as a non-combatant to go through the lines to contact the enemy, to enable us to evacuate our wounded. As I was making my way back to the area where we were dug in, after having seen a German medical officer, I was stopped by an SS lieutenant who said I was his prisoner, this despite the fact that I carried a Red Cross flag. I managed to get away, however, and soon got back to our own lines in a jeep going to fetch some more wounded. I must admit it was with dread that, in the morning sun, I came back to my lines.

'And all through the afternoon it went on, the afternoon of that last day, more and more of it, shells and shells, mortar and sniping and machine-gunning, and one found oneself almost wanting to stand up and scream, "Come and show yourselves. Let's get to grips with you." But they just sat away, two or three miles away in the woods, somewhere in a world outside that didn't seem to matter any more, and shelled us.

'And yet the men found time to laugh. Oh yes, they didn't look like men much by now; many were wounded, and many were so tired that when they smiled, they smiled as if it hurt them to move their mouths. And the afternoon wore on, and attack after attack came in. The log sheet at Divisional Headquarters, fifty yards away from where the nearest front line was, by the way, went something like this: "3.35. Enemy forming up such and such a position. About one company strength and two mobile guns," and we would wireless our own artillery over the river to give us support. "3.45. Glider pilots are hard-pressed in their sector." That was about a hundred yards away from Div. HQ. "The enemy is blowing the houses away from over their heads with mobile guns. 4 o'clock. Attack has died down. Glider pilots have restored position."

'It was like this every day. We'd lived this far, but tomorrow, well? And then the division heard that they were to be evacuated over the Rhine. They hated to go, because they were not beaten, but they got ready, smashed their equipment, their meagre equipment they had left. They put sacking over their shoes, and prepared for this last ordeal. At Div. HQ the padre said a prayer.

'At about ten o'clock we slowly groped our way through the woods, while the artillery on the other bank poured fire into the surrounding countryside to make the Hun believe we were attacking farther along the river. And in the drizzle and the wet the men felt their way through the dense trees where the foliage was split and where one could hear the Germans talking as they sat somewhere in the darkness crouching in their slit trenches, and we groped our way on and the whole wood smelt of the dead, and the farms and little houses were on fire. And then we came out of the woods into a field and crept in long lines down to the Rhine. The mortars were bursting in what seemed like a spray of sparks, almost amongst us now, and we lay on the ground, pressing our faces into the wet grass. It was then that I decided to have a go at swimming the river. The men themselves patiently waited their turn to get in a boat, and if a man floundering in the dark got ahead of somebody else, there would be a quiet "Come on, chum, take your turn". And the boat-loads got over the Rhine, and swept down by the current I at last managed to reach the other bank. The hell was behind us. But not all of them got across, for as it got light the last ones were still left patiently waiting their turn. Not all of them could swim. And the Germans, seeing them, poured machine-gun fire into the men who huddled against the hedges and lay on the causeway.

'The weeks to come will tell how valuable has been the stand of these men, not only in the pocket out of which we got, but the 1st Brigade, the one that fought in the school in Arnhem itself; men who put out nineteen fires in the building they were fighting in, men who fought when tanks cruised up and down the streets thirty yards away, blasting the walls that were their protection into rubble, and other men, men who fought on silently in groups in the woods, men who died round their gliders, who died in the skies; and amongst these the 1st Division, I am sure, would include the men of the RAF who so gallantly took them there and who so gallantly tried to resupply them. No, the stand of that Division made certain the securing and capturing of the Nijmegen bridge. It prevented large enemy reinforcements from blocking the Second Army; and those reinforcements the Airborne Division largely took it upon itself to fight – and how they fought! Their courage and their devotion are surely amongst the finest in the annals of the British race.'

GUY BYAM

The indomitable spirit of the British First Airborne Division at Arnhem adds an epic story to the records of warfare. The details of that fighting stand were heard by all British people with pride; by the Dutch, with gratitude. From a distinguished Dutchman, Johann Fabricius, came this moving tribute:

27 September 1944

'For ten cruel days and nights the thoughts of the whole of Holland have been with your men west of Arnhem. And it was not only because of the military advantages a quick crossing of the Rhine would involve for all of us – no, it was because of the men themselves, who were fighting in the heart of our little country for an ideal which is ours as well. We knew what they must have been going through; we know what we owe them; we think of them as if they were our own boys.

'This is what I want to say to you. Your men are no foreigners to us. Maybe they never saw Holland before they floated down over it, on a sunny afternoon to liberate her people and the world; maybe they do not speak our language, not one of them, and find it difficult even to pronounce the names of the places where they are fighting, suffering, dying. But they are no foreigners in Holland, and we hope they realise that.

'Some of these brave young men will stay behind in our country for ever. They shall not rest in cold foreign soil. The soil of Holland, which, in the course of our long and glorious history, received so many heroes for their eternal sleep, will proudly guard your dead as if they were the deeply mourned sons of our own people.

'The word "heroes" has been heard so often during this long and grim war that it is in danger of growing trite. But here it takes tangible shape, before the eyes of our people who stand in awe and bare their heads.'

JOHANN FABRICIUS

CHAPTER XIII

The Battle Of Aachen
'We Are A Doomed Nation'

The withdrawal from Arnhem put an end to Allied hopes of turning the Rhine before Germany's western defences could be stabilised. Hopes of victory by Christmas began to fade in face of the necessity to make a frontal attack on the Siegfried Line, with the prospect of deteriorating weather conditions, and in the knowledge that our long lines of communication could not be shortened for some time.

The enemy had thus escaped a swift decisive battle, but he had no cause to welcome the war of attrition which was the alternative. Germany lay exposed to terrible punishment from the air, and steady pressure all along the Western Front put a great strain on the defenders. The Arnhem action was scarcely over before the US First Army launched a heavy attack on Aachen, the first great German city to come under the fire of the Allied Armies in the West:

12 October 1944
'An American outpost waiting on the outskirts of Aachen this morning watched a deserted road leading out of the town. At 10.50 an officer looked at his watch, scribbled a note, and sent a runner back to the rear. An hour later the first wave of American fighter-bombers came roaring over the command post where I was standing, a mile outside the town, and began the bombardment of Aachen.

'Earlier on, the sky had been misty and generally overcast, but a few minutes before noon a big patch of blue sky opened and spread right over the doomed city, just at the very moment when we heard the first of the American planes come riding in from their western airfields – silver shapes gleaming and wheeling overhead before one after the other peeled off and dived steeply on to the town. Red stabs of tracer bullets spurted from their wings, and the staccato rattle of machine-gun fire preceded the heavy rumble of bombs blasting their targets. Mushroom clouds of smoke and flames rose from the shattered buildings of the town.

'American guns were thundering away at Aachen over the tree-tops, while a group of silent spectators watched the attack. Near me in a field were German soldiers who had not waited for their commander to make up his mind. They'd made up their own minds and had slipped out of the town during the night, either singly or in groups of seven or eight, and made their way through the lines. One of them was a lower-grade NCO who was one of the Germans who conducted the three Americans into Aachen when they delivered the ultimatum yesterday. Aged twenty-four, and with a red and black ribbon of the Russian campaign on his tunic, he had been most severely ticked off last night by a German officer because he shook hands with one of the American officers. That proved to be the last straw. He crossed over bringing nine men with him into our lines.

'Ten prisoners who were either in their early twenties or middle-aged, all looking grey and haggard, said that the conditions in Aachen had been very bad. American artillery fire had smashed all communal services and there'd been no water supplies for the last three days. Both troops and civilians had been subsisting on rain-water and pond-water. Food supplies were also running short and almost every house or building in the town had been damaged by shellfire.'

ROBERT REID

With the Americans went a Czech correspondent, accompanying the combat troops as they fought their way grimly, street by street, through the devastated city:

17 October 1944

'On both sides of the deserted streets stood empty carcasses of burnt-out houses. Glass, wreckage and tree branches were strewn on the pavements, and in almost every street a building was burning.

'Occasionally we were stopped by the rattle of a sniper's automatic pistol. To get him out the Americans threw a few incendiaries into the building. The flames did the rest. We came to a huge concrete shelter. These shelters are ugly, gloomy constructions with many floors above and below the ground, and in them hundreds of Aachen civilians have been hiding for the last five weeks. In this shelter there were German soldiers also, and they refused to open the doors. For several hours the shelter was besieged by the Americans. Then a German officer said he would surrender . . . if he were allowed to take away all his things and his batman as well.

'Lieutenant Walker, a young company commander, made no effort to accept such a ridiculous offer, and threatened to use flame-throwers. That helped. The doors opened . . . and out came the drabbest filthiest inhabitants of the underworld I have ever seen. They came stumbling into the light, dazed. Then, catching a breath of fresh air, they started to jabber, push, scream, and curse. Some rushed up to me brandishing their fists. "Where have you been so long?" they shouted. "Why don't you deliver us sooner from these devils?"

'It was a sight to stun you. *There* were the people of a German town occupied by the Allies . . . and they were weeping with hysterical joy amid the smouldering ruins of their homes. "We have been praying every day for you to come," said a woman with a pale, thin face. "You can't imagine what we have had to suffer from *them*."

'And then came the insults. "Bloodhounds", "Bandits", "Gangsters". All this against the beloved Führer. There is no one who can hate and curse so thoroughly as the German, and these people were all green with hate for the Nazis. It was no trick. *I*, certainly, would not be cheated. It was the breakdown of a nation after having played the wrong cards for five years. It was a hatred you find only in civil wars.

'You may ask: "How is it that the German soldier still resists under these conditions?" Well, quite a lot of them don't. They keep coming out and giving themselves up. They bring us news of mass prayers organised inside the town – organised by the population – prayers for our victory, and they tell how the commander of the German garrison had twenty civilians shot when they came asking him to surrender. I spoke to a woman who had lost everything, and had a husband in the army somewhere on the Eastern Front. I asked her, "Will Aachen be a warning to other German towns?" She shook her head. "*They* don't care," she answered, "Hitler wants to destroy Germany. He wants to have us all squeezed by the Allies in a corner where your bombers could finish us off. We are a doomed nation." Others kept saying: "We hate Germany. We want to go away and we shall *have* to stay. Nobody wants us. We are the most hated people in the whole world."

'A dreadful darkness had descended on these guilty people living in stinking dark cellars and having nothing but hope to sustain them. The suffering people of Europe had their faith to help them through their trials; they knew their cause was right. These Germans have nothing. Meanwhile the Americans were advancing methodically from street to street. I went forward with them. Ahead of us, a few yards ahead, a Sherman tank sprayed the buildings with machine-gun fire.

'Suddenly it stopped. There was a German machine-gun nest. We squeezed against the wall until the tank had dealt with this by firing its gun at point-blank range into the house. The street was shaking with the thunder of reports. Above our heads mortar bombs were whining through the air. It was raining. A dead German soldier lay on the pavement in front of me with water streaming down his sallow face. We advanced again. Every ten yards a new house had to be searched from top to bottom for snipers; doors broken in, grenades thrown into suspect rooms. We were making our way towards the heart of the city where the dark dome of the cathedral still stands over the grave of Charlemagne.'

GEORGE MUCHA, A CZECH CORRESPONDENT

By 20 October Aachen – or what remained of Aachen – was firmly occupied by American troops, after days of mopping up by groups of infantry detailed to tackle snipers and small German patrols:

20 October 1944

'Theirs is a tough job rooting out snipers from pillboxes, foxholes, cellars, attics, and piles of rubble. I stayed at a company command post well inside the town, in the undamaged two-thirds of a comfortable German house – and I slept soundly despite the constant roar of the guns and occasional visits from the Luftwaffe – in a comfortable German bed; but there was not much sleep for the troops. German patrols sneaked about at night, and a house cleared one day might be a snipers' hide-out the next. I saw many German soldiers being killed and many taken prisoner.

'Most of the prisoners – and they were on the whole a sorry-looking lot – said they were glad to be out of it and would have given themselves up earlier but they were scared of their officers. Two prisoners were Aachen policemen – elderly men who had been given rifles and told to go out and defend the Fatherland.

'The fighting methods of these Germans is extraordinary. They lurk in their foxholes and take sniping pot-shots at any unaccompanied

American soldier they see; and when they are discovered they quickly throw down their rifles and give themselves up. An expert at rooting Jerries from their hiding-places is Technical Sergeant Wilson Costello of Homer City, Pennsylvania. When I was with his company he brought in half a dozen prisoners from a machine-gun nest. They had all been asleep in the cellar of a ruined house. Costello wakened the guard by poking a tommy-gun muzzle into his ribs, then he made him lead the way to the others. When they had been immobilised, Sergeant Costello discovered that their officer was asleep upstairs, so he went up and captured him too. And it was a very angry Nazi he brought into the command post, very angry indeed when told that his men had been caught asleep.

'Costello loves trouble and doesn't think much of the Aachen Germans. He had just left school and was on the way to become a boxer when the war intervened. So far he hasn't had to KO any Germans, but he's quite capable of doing so. When I last saw him he was riding into Aachen on a German motor-cycle looking for trouble.

'Another outstanding character in this infantry company is tall, bearded Sergeant Hugh Coltron of Roseburg, Oregon. He came in to report his platoon's position at nightfall. "Where are the Jerries from you?" asked the company commander. "Hell, they're next-door. I can hear them talking," replied the sergeant.

'That's how it is inside Aachen. The front line is very often only the wall that separates two houses. Two other correspondents and I found this out for ourselves two days ago when watching the battle from a street we had seen cleared the previous evening. A patrol of five Germans sneaking through the American lines tiptoed down the side of the street and went into the next house, and we had to lie very low indeed for a long time before we got out of that awkward situation.'

IAN WILSON

The ruins of many a city lay behind the retreating Germans, but this time the ruins were German. The civilian refugees who now abandoned their personal belongings in the shelters and fled from the fighting were the kindred of the men who had failed to withstand the Allied onslaught:

21 October 1944

'I went down into one of the deep shelters and lit a candle, threading my way down narrow passageways littered with suitcases, baskets of food, jars of preserves, fruit bottles, wine, fur coats, clothing, candles, novels – all abandoned by their owners when this particular shelter

A group of German civilians, who had been in air-raid shelters for weeks, evacuate Aachen to seek safety behind the Allied lines as British and American forces advance into Germany.

was cleared by the American troops late yesterday. Abandoned also by their own countrymen and women was an old couple, a man of seventy-eight and his wife seventy-five, sitting huddled together by the light of a guttering candle at one end of the passage with tears streaming down their faces. We met some civilians outside trekking through the streets, but I told them to go and see to the old man and woman. I was sure from the look on their faces that they would not do so once my back was turned, so a colleague went off in search of the nearest American Field Ambulance Station on our way to have a look at Charlemagne's Cathedral. That too was an eerie experience, wandering through this historic old place which was comparatively little damaged by last week's bombardment. I walked through the cloisters. Three chickens fluttered in through the shattered windows and began pecking the dirt in search of food. Two American doughboys who'd just finished a meal of bread and cheese threw them some crumbs which they gobbled up.

'In the choir, damaged during an air raid last April, a fragment of stained glass occasionally tinkled to the stone floor, torn from the almost blind fluted windows by a miniature October gale which sprang up. In the Octagon chapel, which is untouched, Charlemagne's throne is still there in its gallery encased in concrete. Many other religious and historical relics had been removed from Aachen before it became a battlefield. Nearby is the Town Hall, now a shattered mass of broken masonry and drunken roofs, with the metal girder-work of its towers fantastically twisted by the fire which raged there last week. In the streets themselves I had a difficult task climbing over mounds of rubble, skirting deep bomb craters, and dodging fathoms of trailing electric cables which tangle the wreckage. I have seen many towns like this before. Mostly they were in Britain and in Normandy. But this is Germany. Late this afternoon I watched a group of German prisoners being led out through the wreckage. They were silent, bent, and sick-looking. Maybe they saw more in that terrible scene than the wreckage of Aachen. They were taking with them into captivity a preview of the wreckage of Hitler's Deutschland.'

ROBERT REID

The Normandy battle had mainly been fought around farms, hedges and woods. Aachen was a foretaste of the kind of fighting to be expected in the largely urbanised Rhineland. 'Street-fighting' is the classic name for it but, as one correspondent pointed out, in modern street-fighting an experienced soldier fights anywhere except in the street:

30 November 1944

'It's a bad misnomer, because the last place you see any sane man is in a street where every yard is usually covered by a well-sited machine-gun. It should be called house-to-house fighting, which it literally is. The old hands at the game go through a town keeping inside the houses and using bazookas to knock holes in the dividing walls as they go, and when they come to the end of the block and have to cross the street to the next block they throw out smoke first and cross over under cover of that. They say it's usually better to clean out a house from the top downwards if you can. Break a hole in the roof and get in by an upper floor if possible. A German in a cellar is considerably less dangerous than a German upstairs. But of course a lot depends on the type of defence that's being met with; if it mainly consists of sniping it's best to go slowly and very deliberately, and in small groups. Snipers very often won't fire at a group, when they'll shoot at a single man; they're afraid of giving away their position to the men whom they can't hit with their first shots. But if the defence is heavy you've got to keep dispersed, move fast, and keep on moving whatever happens. Many a man has been hit through freezing and bunching when trouble starts. You feel inclined to drop down and bury your head, and the next shot gets you; you want to cluster together for mutual company, and in this way you give them a real target, but all the old hands will tell you to keep your head up and your eyes open and your legs moving, and at all costs to keep apart. And then, like as not, you'll be all right.

'This is some of the battle lore that's been learnt from bitter experience in this sort of fighting, the kind of day-to-day wisdom that makes all the difference between the veteran and a replacement, and the chances of survival of each of them.'

DENIS JOHNSTON

⟨◦⟩

While the American armies came to grips with the Siegfried Line defences, Canadian and British troops engaged in bitter and difficult fighting in Holland. Their primary object was to clear the shores on either side of the Scheldt Estuary so that shipping could pass unmolested in and out of Antwerp. The bombing of the dikes on Walcheren Island, the hard fighting for the Breskens pocket, and the Commando landings on Walcheren and Beveland were actions which tore away the German grip on the vital entrance to Antwerp.

It was to be a hard winter all along the line, but in Holland there was the added discomfort of widespread flooding. Water – rain and flood water – became in itself a powerful adversary. For the defender it was uncomfortable, for the attacker it was at times almost insurmountable:

25 November 1944

'One effect of this flooding has been to maroon some of our gun positions. I saw several guns of an ack-ack battery out there in the fields, almost completely surrounded by water. The possibility of

306

trouble of this kind had obviously been foreseen, for the guns had been sited on mounds of higher ground, which are still well above water. They're still ready to open fire, even though the only approach to them is by boat.

'The roads fortunately are mainly built up on embankments, but even so, long stretches of them are under water. Before the flooding began, our sappers had driven white posts into the ground at intervals along the roadsides, and now those posts, the tops of them sticking up above water, mark out the road for you and save you from floundering hopelessly into the ditch.

'In many places the water across the roads is axle-deep on a jeep, but in the whole day I've not come across a single road which was closed to traffic from flooding. Trucks and cars move along slowly, not splashing more than they can. Periodically, a vehicle gets water into its ignition system or into its petrol, and it peters out, and then the truck next behind it closes slowly up to it and pushes it forward until at last the column gets on to higher, drier ground, where the broken-down one can be left by the roadside for repair.

'At one point this morning a Military Policeman was directing the traffic along a badly flooded stretch, standing just off the road on a rough-and-ready rostrum made from a pile of cable-drums. I wondered how he got there, for his gaiters were still smartly blancoed, and his trousers were dry. As we passed, I called out to ask him, and he shouted back, "They brought me here in a boat." A few hours later, as we passed that way again, the water was over the top of the rostrum, for the floods were still rising, and the policeman was gone.'

FRANK GILLARD

Such conditions made it impossible to get round an obstacle or an enemy hedgehog. The sole way of advance would be along a causeway or on rising ground – narrow routes known to the enemy and covered by his guns. And for respite there was only the slit trench, hastily dug in what seemed to be dry land – but, even so, liable always to fill with water seeping through the damp soil:

23 November 1944

'Do *you* know what it's like? Of course you don't. You have never slept in a hole in the ground which you have dug while someone tried to kill you . . . a hole dug as deep as you can as quick as you can . . . the site given you by an officer who isn't as much interested in your comfort as in putting you where you can kill Germans. It is an open grave, and yet graves don't fill up with water. They don't harbour wasps or mosquitoes, and you don't feel the cold, clammy wet that goes into your marrow.

'At night the infantryman gets some boards, or tin, or an old door and puts it over one end of his slit trench; then he shovels on top of it as much dirt as he can scrape up near by. He sleeps with his head under this, not to keep out the rain, but to protect his head and chest from airbursts. Did I say sleeps? Let us say, collapses. You see, the infantryman must be awake for one-half the night. The reason is that one-half of the troops are on watch and the other half are resting, washing, shaving, writing letters, eating, or cleaning weapons; that is if he is not being shot at, shelled, mortared or counter-attacked, or if he is not too much exhausted to do it.

'When he is mortared or shelled he is deathly afraid and in the daytime he chain-smokes, curses, or prays, all of this lying on his belly with his hands under his chest to lessen the pain from the blast. If it is at night, smoking is taboo. If there are two in the trench they sit one at each end with their heads between their knees and make inane remarks . . . such as, "Guess that one landed in 12 Platoon," or they argue as to the calibre of the shell. If the enemy are coming the soldier has to stay above ground and does not notice the shelling much. He is too busy trying to keep the enemy away. A trench is dug just wide enough for the shoulders, as long as the body and as deep as there is time. It may be occupied for two hours or two weeks. The next time you are near some muddy fields after a rain take a look in a ditch. That is where your man lives.'

CAPTAIN ATHOL STEWART, CANADIAN INFANTRY

The slow rate of advance, the rain and the mud were met with the same sardonic good humour which had conquered similar conditions in the last war. The spirit which can make a comedy of misfortune found its expression in such stories as this tale of what was called 'The German Indestructible Horse':

16 December 1944

'The roads around this part of the front, in the Nijmegen salient, being as close to hostile fire as they are, it's hardly the place for using motor vehicles, and the Germans use a horse and wagon to send supplies to forward positions – at night. The company outposts used to listen to the horse clumping around, and hear the driver talking to it in German. One night the driver was coughing, and one of our patrols was so close that a young Indian lad swore to his platoon commander the next morning that he'd caught the German's cold. The platoon commanders and the company commander held a conference and decided to cut the enemy's supply line by eliminating the horse and cart.

'They called in the mortar officer – and they thought they had it in the bag, for this mortar officer is famous far beyond his own unit. People say he can put a three-inch mortar bomb down on a dime. Once, after artillery and guns had spent days trying to blow up a

German ammunition dump stored in a concrete fortress, he came along and blew the whole works up in a jiffy by putting a mortar bomb down the ventilator shaft. But that was in the happy days, before he met this horse.

'For nine nights he's fired his mortars at it, and for nine nights the men in the outposts have heard the horse go clumping serenely away after the fireworks. One night it looked like a dead certainty. It was a very still night, and the driver was in a conversational mood, and talking to the horse as they went their rounds. The men in the outpost could plot its course yard by yard; the platoon commanders reported to company by telephone, and company called on the mortars.

'A lot of men solemnly declared to me today that as the mortars whistled, they heard the driver say "Whoa" and the horse stopped. The mortars kept on firing for five minutes. They stopped, and there was silence, and men strained their ears and felt a reluctant sorrow. And then – there was the clump, clump of hooves, and the driver was whistling "The Blue Danube" as he and the horse went home.'

A. E. POWLEY, CBC

CHAPTER XIV

The Battle Of Supply

'Great, great heroes – all of them'

While the opposing armies fought over the defences west of the Rhine, a second battle was in progress – the battle to prevent supplies and reinforcements from reaching the front. With heavily industrialised areas close behind them, the Germans had short and good communications, but this advantage was greatly neutralised by the failure of the Luftwaffe to keep the Allied bombers away. During the autumn and winter the RAF and USAF threw in vast airfleets to wreck and disrupt the whole German supply system, from the armament factories to the forward marshalling areas.

German strategy was necessarily different. The enemy had no great bomber fleets, and there was the further difference that Allied supplies did not enjoy an unbroken overland route. The German plan, from D-Day onwards, had been to deny us the Channel ports, firstly by turning them into self-contained defensive pockets, and secondly by demolitions and obstructions. The prefabricated 'Mulberry' harbour had, as it were, overtrumped the German plan in the first phase: the rapid capture of Cherbourg had been the next step. 'Mulberry' had of course been a closely guarded secret, and not until the middle of October were correspondents permitted to describe the sensational arrival of these ready-made harbours off the Normandy beaches:

16 October 1944

'It was on the afternoon of D-Day plus one that I saw from the deck of my ship lying off the Normandy beaches a huge grey block come looming over the sea horizon. It was literally like a block of flats floating on the water, with a metal mushroom perched on top. A fantastic sight it made, as it came in from the Channel towards the dense crowd of craft and warships gathered in the anchorage. At first I thought it must be a floating dock but, as it approached, I saw that it was boxed in on four sides and the mushroom was a gun platform. It was being towed by a powerful ocean-going tug that looked no more than a midget compared with the monster astern of it. "That's the first one of the big breakwater sections to arrive," said the naval officer next to me. "We're towing over a prefabricated port, you know." He said it as though that sort of thing was an everyday job for the Royal Navy, and he went on to explain: "It's hollow and made of concrete, and there's a good deal more of it that you can't see, below the waterline. When they get it into position farther down the coast they'll sink it. There'll be a good many more arriving within the next week or so, and together they'll make the harbour wall."

'I went down the Normandy coast to see this prefabricated harbour in the making. It was a breathtaking spectacle. A huge concrete wall was taking form two miles out and parallel with the shore. More of these great structures had been towed across from England and sunk with uncanny precision end to end to form the beginnings of a continuous straight line – like a great street of large mansions rising out of the sea.'

MICHAEL STANDING

On D plus three the Navy began to arrive with the bridge spans, towed across by ocean-going tugs, and work commenced on the piers – flexible-steel, floating roadways with anchored pier-heads at the end:

16 October 1944

'Inside the harbour wall, small craft were already clustering gratefully in the sheltered water. Inside it, too, was another almost incredible spectacle. Span upon span of metal-girdered bridges floating on blunt, cigar-shaped pontoons, with little tugs nosing busily around. And there, too, floating a mile perhaps from the shore was a huge steel platform, with four tall columns rising like factory chimneys from its corners. Khaki figures were swarming everywhere over this astonishing array of equipment – astride girders, on the pontoons, clambering up the sides of the columns, busy here with mooring cables, fussing around there in quaint, flat-bottomed little craft. And then out of the apparent confusion of it all began to emerge what was really happening. The Royal Engineers were assembling that bridging into long floating roads; the big platform was to be one of the pier-heads – or landing-stages; and its columns, four legs that would eventually be lowered right through it to stand firmly on the sea-bed. They were getting on with the job, too. As I watched, a long section of bridging was successfully hitched, with the help of half a dozen little American motor towing-launches, on to the very considerable length of roadway that already jutted out from the shore. Other spans were being shifted across the water, and on the shore itself bulldozers were carving out an inland roadway up into the little town.'

MICHAEL STANDING

But ten days later came the worst June gale for forty years. The outer breakwater was not yet completed when the storm broke:

16 October 1944

'Heavy seas swept down on the steel bridge, and continued to do so for four days, but somehow my chaps held it together. They had no sleep at all during the period, except for an odd hour or two snatched on the job. Working on the pier was no easy task, the bridge was rising and falling on the waves and twisting at the same time. Nearly every nut and bolt worked loose at one time or another. Damaged ships and craft smashed into and carried away our moorings. Some of these craft we jumped aboard and sank to avoid further damage to our bridge. In the end we took stock; the stores pier was operating, and had been operating throughout the entire storm. A tremendous tribute, I think, to the men who designed the equipment.

The LST pier had craft piled up against it, and many of the spans were twisted and smashed. But our job was to get stores to the Army at any cost, therefore we had to modify our original plan and to improvise with the equipment we had. Within forty-eight hours of receiving our fresh orders we had two piers completed, thus giving a circular traffic route to the pier-heads.'

COLONEL A. R. MAIS, OBE, RE

A few weeks later the difficulties of construction were over, and the world's most remarkable port was in full operation. The Allies had achieved what the Germans regarded as impossible – the supplying of a great army without possession of any of the Channel ports:

16 October 1944

'It was no longer a confused assortment of bits and pieces. The jigsaw had come together, and now it was a harbour in operation.

'The outer breakwater was almost complete. Nearly a mile out to sea coasters were tied up alongside landing-stages now fixed firmly in position – landing-stages that could be lifted and lowered with the tide. Within the sheltered water ducks were plying to and from the Liberty ships. Harbour-craft were busy everywhere. There were

American soldiers and supplies continue to come ashore
on Omaha beach following violent storms which severely
damaged the concrete and steel 'Mulberry' harbours brought
over to Normandy after D-Day.

all the masts, the funnels, the cranes, the derricks, the smoke, the
din, the traffic, and the shouts of the Merseyside, of Glasgow, of
Southampton – where a month before there had been nothing but a
deserted expanse of sea. And for three-quarters of a mile across that
sea, connecting the landing-stages with the new inland roadways, two
floating-bridges ran right into the shore, clanking and undulating a
little under a two-way stream of heavy trucks. An all-weather harbour
was in being and supplies to the fighting armies were assured. Britain's
most momentous secret weapon was in use.'

MICHAEL STANDING

The victory in Normandy was made possible by 'Mulberry'; but a heavy frontal assault on the Rhine defences called for the opening of Antwerp and the up-Channel ports. The stubborn German resistance along the Scheldt and the siege-actions in the main shipping-centres along the English Channel were designed to throttle and slow down Allied supplies while the Germans gained time to strengthen their defences before the Rhine. And so, while the armies grappled with each other, this second grim struggle was being waged behind them – Allied bombers battering the roads and railways and arsenals of Germany, Allied troops and technicians racing to free the vital ports and restore them to use.

After the prominent role of the Royal Navy in the first landings on the Normandy beaches, the continuing efforts of our ships in the Channel had tended to be overlooked as attention focused inevitably on the army's drive inland. When the tide of war began to flow away from the original supply-points, it was the Navy's task to provide new ones closer to the action. A naval spokesman recaptured public attention for the senior service with a detailed account of what this entailed:

27 October 1944
'On 8 August Field-Marshal von Kluge sent the following message to the German High Command:

' "A breakthrough has occurred at Caen, the like of which we have never seen." [*Von Kluge actually said this to General Hausser, Commander of the German Seventh Army.*]

'Now those were the actual words – "the like of which we have never seen" – very strong words for an experienced general. But quite clear in their meaning. In spite of foul weather conditions the Mulberries, coupled with heroic efforts across open beaches, had done the trick. The first phase in the battle of the ports – for it is on that battle that the whole of our operations on the Continent depend – had proved a clear victory for the Allies.

'There was only one hope for the Germans. With each mile of the Allied advance, lines of communication were becoming more and more stretched to the limit, and the original ports were soon hundreds of miles from the front line. In order to keep up their pressure, the Allied armies must employ the closer Channel ports such as Dieppe, Boulogne, Calais, Ostend and Zeebrugge.

'Orders went out from the Führer that those ports were to be held to the last man, and, if captured, to be so demolished as to be unusable.

'That demolition wasn't a very difficult job. They were all similar in character. Small ports; approaches ideal for mining; narrow entrances perfect for blockships; quays – mostly constructed on wooden piles – easy to destroy. Observers on the south coast of England saw enormous flashes and a few moments later felt their windows shake with the concussion. Those explosions were our urgently needed quays and harbour installations going west! There was only one answer: superhuman efforts of clearance and reconstruction the moment these ports had fallen into our hands.

'On this side of the Channel minesweepers were waiting to clear the approaches – wreck-raising ships and salvage vessels were standing by to get busy the moment the word came. But obviously there was nothing much they could do until effective measures had been taken by men working inside the ports themselves.

'There were two main organisations for this. The Army Port Construction parties of sappers and pioneers under the command of the Port Commandant, whose job it is to clear and repair the quays, get the cranes working, get electric light and power going, repair the bridges, clear the roads, and the thousand and one other jobs ashore; and the Naval Port parties under the NOIC – the Naval Officer-in-Charge – whose job it is to clear the entrances, force a passage through the blockships, sweep all the mines, raise or remove the wrecks alongside the quays so that ships can enter the harbour, berth alongside, and unload in safety.

'Watch them now as they wait behind the artillery carrying out the final bombardment. There are two little groups of jeeps – the NOIC and his reconnaissance party in one; the Army Port Commandant and his reconnaissance party in the other.

'The main units of men will follow in later – but an early reconnaissance by both the Naval and Military Port parties is vital to the whole future of the campaign.

'At last as the tanks and infantry go forward for the final assault, they find themselves well up in the queue of ingoing vehicles. But soon, as the piles of rubble grow higher and higher, they have to desert their jeeps and do the rest of the journey on foot. As they scramble across the ruined lock gates a sudden whine of bullets sends them sprawling to the ground. But there is no time to waste. They work their way on towards a good vantage point.

'At last they reach the top of a wrecked E-boat pen. Yes, they've chosen well. It's a perfect spot. Out come notebooks and they start to make diagrams and notes of what they observe. Their heads turn automatically towards the narrow entrance between the breakwaters, and those of you who crossed the Channel before the war will remember them well. The rows of blue-smocked fishermen, the children waving handkerchiefs. You sniffed the first smells of THE CONTINENT; you had arrived.

'But what a difference now! Those breakwaters are no longer nice and solid and friendly. Splintered wood lies everywhere and large gaps have been torn in them. And in the narrow waters between, a jumble of masts and funnels clearly indicates the large number of tugs, freighters, dredgers, and other ships which have been sunk to block the entrance.

'A few jottings in their notebooks, and they turn their attention to the quays. The cranes lie drunkenly sprawling into the water. Between them barges and lighters have been sunk to stop ships berthing alongside, and the quays themselves have been blown to smithereens... .

'Everywhere they look it's the same – chaos, rubble, and destruction.

'An occasional side of a building with BYRRH or DUBONNET in those enormous letters may just remind them of the good old days. But only just. All they are interested in is that this is a port.

'A mouth of a river fitted out to receive men and supplies from across the water, but now . . . they glance at their notebooks. . . . "At least fifteen blockships in main channel . . . all principal quays blown . . . cranes demolished . . . lock gates. . . ."

'Well, the Naval Officer-in-Charge of this caricature of a harbour closes his notebook and puts it in his pocket.

' "That's about all we can do for the moment. Let's go and chat it over with the Army."

'And so starts the first Port Conference. There will be one every day until the port is in full running order. Later they will be held around a table in comparative comfort and with detailed charts and plans. But this evening it's a case of a few figures clustered at some prearranged corner and swapping pages out of dirty notebooks.

'That night some very weary men swallow their iron rations and curl up to sleep wherever they can find cover. Tomorrow their job starts in earnest.

'Now how that job is done I defy anyone to describe. There are certain landmarks, yes. The enormous explosions as blockships are removed, others as the remains of a lock gate are destroyed; the significant moment when the first minesweepers arrive and clear the approaches, when a repaired bridge is opened to traffic, when the electric light supply is suddenly restored, when the first motor minesweeper creeps in through the narrow entrance in the blockships and starts to sweep inside; and of course the greatest moment of all when the first supply ship is berthed alongside and her precious cargo is hoisted inshore.

'But taking it by and large, it isn't so much a series of marked events, but each day – almost imperceptibly – the whole thing grows and then suddenly . . . the port is working.

'But of all those little groups – the minesweepers, the pioneers, the salvage parties, the sappers, the wreck raisers, the signalmen, and the many others who are setting about their jobs under dangerous and incredibly difficult conditions, there's one little group which I must single out.

'You'll see them on a quay with a couple of lorries close by, from one of which blares out dance music. At first sight they look as idle as a bunch of W. W. Jacobs' longshoremen, sitting there on bollards staring down into the water below. They appear to be looking at nothing – which in a way is true – because their interest is concentrated in their mates who are groping about in the darkness some thirty feet below the surface.

'Now obviously I mustn't go into any details of how they work, but let me assure you that of all the acts of bravery that I have seen in this war, theirs, for sheer cold-blooded guts, is one of the greatest.

'To put it in a nutshell, their job is to go down below in diving-suits, grope about in the darkness amongst twisted girders, dead horses and corpses, and search for any wrecks which might prevent ships coming alongside – and don't forget that some of those wrecks may contain thousands of pounds of explosive itching to go off at a false touch. In pitch darkness, mind you, and in all the difficulties of slithering about in black oozy mud against the pressure of thirty feet of water.

'There are two of them to each team. A youngster – specially chosen for his physical fitness and usually under twenty-one – who actually does the job, and his dresser or link with the surface – chosen for reliability and usually well over forty – who watches every move.

'Now those are the men – the dressers – whom you saw staring into the water from the quayside. They weren't idle . . . far from it. On their attendance depended the life of the kid down below and they were feeling the strain far more than he was.

'Suddenly there's a rustle of excitement, a hauling in of ropes, and a kid comes to the surface. His "Pop" – that's really the only word for him – is immediately down at the water's edge finding out what he has got to report. Obviously the kid can't talk, but those two have a sign language between them which puts all normal efforts at dumb crambo or other similar games to shame. In a moment the news is being passed on to the Officer-in-Charge and the kid disappears back into the depths.

'Meanwhile, other teams are waiting up top for their turn. There's the same, you know, rather hilarious, vaguely unreal, slightly high-pitched conversation going on which one has heard so often before – pilots before a raid, soldiers before an assault, submariners before an attack – whenever the future is in the balance. Great, great heroes – all of them.

'So give a thought – not just sometimes, but very often – not only to the diving lads but to the thousands of others – both Army and Navy – who make up the Port Clearance Parties.

'The headlines are very naturally and properly about the advance of our soldiers at the front. But they cannot advance without supplies. Those supplies must come through the ports.

'It's on the Battle of the Ports that everything depends.'

CAPTAIN ANTHONY KIMMINS, RN

❧

By their tenacity and thoroughness in this battle for the ports, the Germans were gaining time. But time must have begun to seem a doubtful asset when, on 14 October, 4500 tons of bombs fell on Duisburg in twenty-five minutes:

14 October 1944

'I think that not only in the smoke and rubble of Duisburg, but deeper in the heart of Germany, there must be men charged with the defence of the Reich whose hearts tonight are filled with dread and despair. For the unbelievable thing has come to pass – the RAF has delivered its greatest single attack against a German industrial target since the start of the war – more than a thousand heavy bombers, more than 4500 tons of bombs – and it did it, this morning, in broad daylight.

'At a quarter to nine this morning I was over the Rhine and Duisburg in a Lancaster, one of the thousand and more four-engined machines that filled the sunny sky to the north and south and east. A year ago it would have been near suicide to appear over the Ruhr in daylight – a trip by night was something to remember uncomfortably for a long time. Today, as the great broad stream of Lancasters and Halifaxes crossed the frontier of Germany, there was not an aircraft of the Luftwaffe to be seen in the sky, only the twisting and criss-crossing vapour trails of our own Spitfires and Mustangs protecting us far above and on the flanks.

'The briefing officer had described Duisburg as the largest inland port in the world and an arsenal of the Reich when he addressed the aircrews. I saw Duisburg the arsenal, just for a moment, in a hole in the patchy white clouds that lay over the Rhine and the Ruhr. I saw the grey patchwork of houses and factories, roads, railways, and the dirty dark waters of the great river curving its way through the inland port. Then target indicators and bombs, HE and incendiary, nearly 5000 tons of them, went shooting down; and the German flak, and a good deal of it, came shooting up. Duisburg the arsenal disappeared under a filthy billowing brown bulge of smoke. I saw no fires from our Lancaster – there was too much cloud for that – and I had one nervous eye on the chessboard of black bursting shells that had been superimposed on our fine clear piece of sky. But I *did* see heavy bombs, cookies, going down into the brown smoke, and more clouds of it pushing their sullen way up from the ground. Duisburg lay underneath the shroud; and shroud, I think, is the right word.

'In case it sounds rather easy, this smashing of German targets by day, let me say at once that the pilots who are going to do it from now on are taking very great risks each time they set out on such an operation. The best they can hope for is a thick curtain of bursting shells through which to fly, and the sight – the sight that we had this morning – of one or two of their companions twisting down to the ground in flames and smoke. But such hazards do not affect the plans of Bomber Command, that astonishingly versatile organisation that began the war with so little and by courage and perseverance has built up today's striking force. As we flew home this morning and saw a tight orderly patch of Flying Fortresses engaged on their Cologne operation passing us above the clouds, I could not help but realise that, together, Britain and America can now put into the morning or afternoon sky a mighty force of bombers that spells destruction and ruin for our enemies.'

RICHARD DIMBLEBY

A fortnight later Cologne, forty miles ahead of the US First Army, went down in smoke and ruins after a series of prodigious bombing attacks:

1 November 1944

'In the killing of Cologne the city has been shattered and set on fire not only by British heavy bombers, but by American Flying Fortresses and by our own little Mosquitoes carrying big bombs. Today, after last night's attack, the city is a shambles. This week I've been seeing large-scale photographs of Cologne. There is acre upon acre of complete devastation, street after street where life has died and the powdered rubble that was a house has been swept aside and banked up to leave a passage clear. From one end of the city to the other, you can count the buildings that have not been shattered on your fingers. Whole blocks have vanished; whole suburbs lie tumbled to the ground. There is nowhere to live and hardly anywhere to work in Cologne, any more.

'Last night I flew for the first time with the Pathfinders, the force whose job it is to ensure the accuracy and concentration of the attack by marking the exact aiming point with coloured indicators, red, green, and yellow flares. The main force of bombers aims at the centre of the cluster of flares and thus gets its whole load of bombs into the exact ground area chosen as the target. This job of pathfinding, which is done by picked crews, demands a particular skill in navigation and, perhaps, a very high degree of determination, for the Pathfinder cannot let himself be deflected from this precise course as he approaches the target. Last night our job was to replenish the flares already dropped by the Pathfinders ahead. The first cluster went down as we were approaching, red and green lights hanging from their parachutes, just on top of the great white cloudbank that hid Cologne. This was "skymarking": the bombs of the main force, now streaming in above and below us, jet black in the brilliant light of the full moon, had to pass down by the flares. They vanished into the cloud, and soon the underside of it was lit by a suffused white glow, the light of incendiaries burning on the ground and the baffled searchlights. The flares seemed to be motionless, but round them and just under us as we drove steadily over in a dead-level straight line, the German flak was winking and flashing. Once a great gush of flame and smoke showed the bursting of a "scarecrow", the oddity designed by the Germans to simulate a heavy bomber being shot down, and so put any of our less experienced pilots off their stroke. There were fighters around, too. A minute or two before, we had seen the yellow glow of one of the new jet-propelled variety climbing at a great speed above us and to starboard.

'We circled round the flares, watching the light under the cloud going pink with the reflection of fire and, silhouetted against it, the Lancasters and Halifaxes making off in the all-revealing light of the moon. Then we, too, turned for home.

'Once before, this same fate befell a German city, when Bomber Command laid Hamburg waste in a series of concentrated attacks. And now Cologne has gone, and with it a most important forward base and collecting point for the German army in the field. The enemy did not choose to learn the lesson of Hamburg, but he must now realise that any city that lies just behind the battlefront and serves the German Army may have to be destroyed. He knows, too, that we can do it, for with last night's culminating attack on Cologne, Bomber Command has shown that, led by its Pathfinders, it can go on its tremendous errands by night, by day, in darkness, or in the light of the full moon.'

RICHARD DIMBLEBY

While the great cities of western Germany were being subjected to bombing on an unprecedented scale, the enemy railways were harassed day and night by what was known as 'interdiction' – or, in other words, rail-cutting by air attack:

7 November 1944

'If you look at the map, you'll see what this constant cutting of rail-communications means to the Hun; he's now pushed back north of the Maas and he's done a little interdiction on his own by blowing up the Moerdijk bridges. Whether he plans to get out of northern Holland and back to his native land or bring reinforcements and supplies out of his native land to fight on for a while in northern Holland, he needs every metre of railway and every locomotive and truck he can lay hands on. His alternative is to take to the roads, and there are two things that make that a little awkward: shortage of motor transport and the fact that Tactical Air Force gets even more enjoyment out of shooting up things on the road than on rail. So the Hun must use his railway system and, because of this unwieldy and un-English word "interdiction", the German railway system is now not so much a system as a nightmare.

'The best that the Hun can do to combat interdiction is to resort to dodges. We know that railwaymen have orders to stop their trains as soon as an Allied aircraft is spotted, to keep them at a standstill and not to leave them. This is in the hope that our pilots will assume that the train is empty and won't waste ammunition on it. It's a pretty forlorn hope, but even if it does succeed a train at a standstill isn't much use to the men at the front. We know that some German trains carry smoke canisters, which are let off as soon as the train is attacked, to make us think that the damage is more serious than it really is. That doesn't really work either because we have an irritating habit of going back half an hour later to check up and attack again if necessary.

Dummy trains and locomotives are now almost a standing joke with the interdictors. Experience and good intelligence have taught the pilots all they need to know, to be on the lookout for the harmless-looking truck that is really a flak wagon.

'There are now almost as many repair trains alongside the spots where we have made interdiction visits as there are genuine transport trains, and they come in for just as much attention as the others. And, of course, if we can interdict and at the same time destroy a bridge, well that's generally regarded as a good thing. There was one case the other day when we dropped a couple of 500-pound bombs on a rail bridge and scored only near misses. But the whole bridge blew up, not directly through our bombing but because the concussion had set off the charges which the conscientious Boche had placed under the bridge just in case he had to make yet another strategic withdrawal. That, of course, was the unkindest cut of all!'

ALAN MELVILLE

While each side strove to mass troops and equipment at the front, and at the same time to prevent its opponents from doing the same, the early onset of winter threatened to halt any major operations by either side; but General Eisenhower was determined to make as heavy an assault as possible on the Siegfried Line and on the German defences in eastern France (from Metz to the Belfort Gap) so that the Germans could not spend the winter months in making these defences even stronger. Having failed to turn the West Wall at Arnhem, he now set six Allied Armies to batter their way through it. Among these six – between the British Second and the US Third – he brought in the 'secret' US Ninth Army, after a great deal of German speculation as to its whereabouts. In the shattered village of Beggendorf a correspondent watched units of the Ninth going into action on the opening day of what became known as 'The November Offensive':

17 November 1944

'From one of the few houses in Beggendorf that still had a chimney, smoke curled up from an improvised fire that was heating some chow for one tank crew. Around the corner of what used to be the local hotel came the familiar excited plea, "Be good, dice! A nice little seven before the shooting starts. Once dice, seven!" Yes, sir, there was one crew playing dice. Another of the crews were huddled together round their tank working feverishly over a month-old crossword puzzle in a sadly worn-looking magazine. I walked up the street to an old orchard where some of the infantry were standing around scanning the sky for the dive-bombers, for they were due in a few minutes. I got my recorder set up in the attic of 62 Hindenburgstrasse, just as the first wave of dive-bombers streaked across the sky, quickly into position, and then the atmosphere was torn to shreds as they dived down on to their targets, firing their guns full out all the way down. They were followed by a tremendous but short burst of artillery fire from our big guns, which were away to the rear. Soldiers seemed to have appeared from nowhere. They came out of barns, houses, from behind tanks – everyone with their eyes to the sky. Even the crap game broke up as the boys shouted excitedly to each other, "Power to them. Man, look at them go! Ain't they pretty!" and so on. Time was getting short. There was fifteen minutes to go before H-hour.

'Behind the shattered buildings, tough-looking tank men were all in position, waiting. An eerie quiet seemed to grip the ghost-like town of Beggendorf. It was a quiet broken only by the odd angry bark of some of our guns, and you could hear the nervous finger of the wind strumming away on some of the shattered window-panes.

We shouted "Good luck!" to some of the lads, and jumped in our jeep and made our way back to the high ground to watch the start of the attack. Promptly at 12.45 there was a thunderous roar. Our artillery was opening up. Shells screamed overhead, whistling and whining on their way across the open ground beyond Beggendorf towards the German positions. Through my glasses I watched the tanks move out from their hiding-places, and start to zigzag their way towards their first objective. The roar of the artillery was augmented as more and more dive-bombers came in to lend support. The infantry was on the move too, moving ahead quickly to the right and then to the left, like a lot of dogs with their noses to the ground. The attack of the American Ninth Army was on.'

STEWART MACPHERSON

On the flank of the US Ninth Army the British and American forces captured Geilenkirchen and overran the outer defences of the Siegfried Line without great difficulty, but when they assaulted the main defences they encountered a well-prepared network of pillboxes and trenches and minefields which had to be cleared step by step:

21 November 1944

'I saw five or six of the score or so of pillboxes which our troops have overrun. They weren't particularly large, but they were very solidly built of steel and concrete several inches thick. Each casemate was partly sunk into the ground and thoroughly camouflaged. They were well sited at points where their machine-guns could cover several tracks and approaches at once. I think those pillboxes could well withstand ordinary shellfire, but from the great holes torn in them it was clear that they were nothing like tough enough to stand up to our latest assault weapons.

'Then the trenches. The Germans had dug mile after mile of trenches across this countryside. They zigzag along at the edges of the roads and behind the embankments, and I saw one particularly well-prepared system alongside a sunken railway track. Most of these trench systems had culs-de-sac branching out at right angles, leading across fields, up to little bumps of rising ground or out towards other tracks. Obviously, at the ends of these limbs the Germans had listening posts and observation points and machine-gun positions. The main trenches were intercommunicating so that you could pass from one system to another and cover wide stretches of the front without once coming above ground.

'Besides the pillboxes and the trenches there were, of course, the mines. Mines much more thickly sown than I've ever seen them before in Europe. Not without difficulty and loss, we'd cleared breaches in these minefields. Our flails and other instruments were still discharging mines all over the place as we watched. Sappers were sweeping for them and lifting them by hand, working under constant sniper fire, for the Germans had left many a rifleman behind in hidden positions as they retreated. The sniper is quite definitely one of the German Siegfried weapons.'

FRANK GILLARD

Even when the Allied troops had broken down the actual Siegfried defences they found their progress was still delayed by German defences in fortified villages:

3 December 1944
'The Germans have been ordered to defend every town and village west of the Rhine; every house, every cellar, and every garden wall must be reinforced and become part of the defence line.

'The roads that lead to Düren and to Cologne are dotted with scores of small towns and villages. The north and south lines have been linked by anti-tank ditches and communicating trenches; cellars in the villages have been reinforced and fitted with steel doors and fire-points; the villages have artillery support from behind, and their defences are mutually supporting. That is, the defenders of one village can fire on troops approaching the villages on either side. So a complete defence system of villages and townships must be taken in one movement and completely occupied before a move is made to the next defence-line. That is why from this front you hear of the storming of, or the entry into, half a dozen towns at once, and hear nothing more than the names of these six or seven places for perhaps a week. You see, it's not a matter of taking a township or a village, and then pushing on; it's a question of taking a village and digging in under fire until the villages on either side of you have been taken – or until the whole line has been taken, and then getting up from your waterlogged foxhole or from your cellar, and crouching forward to the next line of villages with new names and with more cellars and more machine-guns, and more snipers who are prepared to stay and die for the Fatherland.'

ROBERT BARR

With the Allies attacking on a 400-mile front the Germans could not hope to hold us all along the line. They preferred to use their available reserves to contest every yard of our advance into Germany beyond Aachen, and to yield French territory. At Metz and in the Vosges they defended strongly, but they could not stop the US Third and Seventh and French First Armies carrying the Allied line up to the Saar Basin, Strasbourg, and the Swiss frontier. Much of this advance was made with every condition of weather against us, as the French First Army found:

19 November 1944

'In the icy dawn, over the flat lands of the river areas, which thick white frost has turned into the semblance of a great salt-lake, dense, drab columns of transport roll towards the front by every road. They roll between the bare trees of the avenues, beside the withered edges fringing the lakes and swamps, they ramble over the ugly military bridges that span the swollen streams and then they climb into the hills and cold squalls of rain sweep down on them and drench them, and then the rain suddenly gives place to snow – blanketing, blinding snow, or a cruel, driving sleet that cuts the soldiers' faces and freezes in solid sheets on the windscreens of the trucks. The drivers drive with bare, red hands – the gloves can't grip the slippery wheel that swirls this way and that with every bump and pot-hole, and every slithering skid on the icy road. On they go, these endless, urgent columns, crowding on every highway, debouching into the rough country tracks that are churned into seething glaciers of mud – mud surges up in an oily flood to the footboard, mud flies in a dense spray from the whirling wheels, coating men and machines as completely as paint sprayed from an air gun. Here and there, where a patch of flat land flanks the road, the columns double and redouble until as many as ten lines of trucks and tanks and jeeps hurtle and heave their way on like boats on a rough sea.

'In a field by the road, one comes suddenly on a scene as wildly improbable as the things that happen in a dream. There is a frosty slush, a great herd of baggage mules is being loaded up by figures in long brown robes and loosely swathed turbans – brown men with sultry eyes, with little black beards at their chin tips – Goums from the Atlas Mountains. That brown tide sweeping up through the hills to the front is only the beginning. Armed with these vast supplies, the Army is rolling on into enemy territory.'

COLIN WILLS

In spite of every difficulty the French pressed on, with the added elation of being again able to fight the invader in open battle and with a well-equipped army:

1 December 1944

'Speed is the first impression you get when you are out with the French. No one seems to travel at less than sixty miles per hour, and my memory of a French convoy is of a mile-long pandemonium – lorries coming bumper to bumper one way, lorries meeting them head on coming from the other, jeeps weaving in and out. And everyone hand-waving, tying themselves into knots and backing into each other's vehicles with the greatest goodwill in the world. A famous cartoon in the American Service paper, *Stars and Stripes*, sums it up. It shows a line of disconsolate American lorry drivers being addressed by their lieutenant before departure. "Men," says the lieutenant, "some of you may never come back. There's a French convoy on the road."

'But somehow or other the French convoys do get down the roads, and the French Front advances with a dash and an *élan* that's got impressive results during the last few days. I sometimes think that the reason it goes ahead is that I've never heard any French officer issue any other order except *En Avant*, "Forward". No French command post seems to be anywhere except slightly ahead of the front line. When a French colonel invites you to visit the front – he means the Front. And the first thing you know is a sudden shower of shells as the gallant officer points to the farmhouse a hundred yards away – "Les Boches?" you ask nervously. "Ah! There they are, les Salauds," he says. And you prepare immediately to take off rapidly to the rear. For you know exactly what the next order will be: "Forward – *en avant*." And forward they do go against the toughest resistance.

This new army of France has got something to avenge – something which makes it dare the impossible. It's got nothing in common with the disillusioned armies that went down to defeat in 1940. It's got, as its basis, the armies of Africa with the Colonial troops and a Corps of Officers who have the traditional skill of the French in the business of war. But it's now got armoured divisions of Frenchmen from France – shock battalions of patriot volunteers – and the French Forces of the Interior, fighting side by side with the veterans of North Africa and Italy. And above all, it's thrown up new generals – new leaders! These new generals are exciting, vivid personalities. English generals – and today there are none better – sometimes give the impression that they are a bit apologetic about making war. American generals feel that they are expected to be tough "he-men". But the French generals – "Ah! they are generals in the grand manner." Until you've see General de Montsabert decorating an officer with a double-barrelled embrace on both cheeks or General de Lattre de Tassigny explaining his plans at a press conference, you haven't seen a general. Such clarity – such eloquence – such Napoleonic orders of the day, and out of it all such a resounding, invigorating success as the forcing of the Belfort Gap.'

WYNFORD VAUGHAN-THOMAS

In Strasbourg – at last – troops were fighting for the main road-bridge over the Rhine when a correspondent entered the city under shellfire from across the river:

25 November 1944

'Strasbourg today is a strange, tense city – a city holding its breath, as it were, and waiting. Only a few miles away from the centre of Strasbourg flows the Rhine, and behind the Rhine is Germany. As we drove into the city today, with the great spire of the cathedral soaring up over the medieval house-tops before us, we could see against the rain-dark sky to the east a looming outline of distant hills – the Black Forest, the western barrier of Hitler's Reich, Germany. We felt as if we'd come to the end of a long journey. The people in the streets felt it too. In the suburbs we'd had a wild welcome, with flags waving and crowds at every corner. In the city it was different. The people crowded around us there too, they shook us by the hand, they talked to us with deep emotion. But no cheering, the enemy was too near for celebration. We'd got to the Rhine at last, but we still had to cross it before Strasbourg could breathe freely again.

'We drove over the River Ill into the heart of Old Strasbourg. We found damage in the twisting streets, a hole had been torn in the roof of the north aisle of the cathedral and the glass was out from every one of the tall windows. But the glorious spire of rose-red stone is still there, and the Tricolour on its very top gave a note of defiant colour to this damp November day of liberation. From the Rhine bank we could hear the rattle of small-arms fire, and in the streets everyone we met was emphatic. Yes, they told us, the French have got the great road bridge over the Rhine.

'Now Strasbourg is a city of bridges, bridges first over the River Ill, then over the canal and over a branch of the river known as the Little Rhine, and finally over the main stream to the town of Kehl on the German bank. Not one of these bridges, including the Kehl bridge, has been blown. We rushed the city so quickly that although we know that the Germans have placed charges under the pillars of the Kehl bridge, they had no time to set them off. The bridge then was intact. But we just couldn't discover if we or the Germans held it. You get to the bridge through an industrial suburb, past canals and warehouses and a station, but it's as much as your life was worth today to put your head out of a doorway and try and see the other bank. The Germans are there all right on their side. They shoot at everything that moves. They have the bridge approaches swept with small-arms fire, and when we left our guns were racing towards the Rhine bank to deal with them. Tomorrow will decide if the French or the Germans are going to win the battle for the bridge.'

WYNFORD VAUGHAN-THOMAS

The Germans won this battle – or at least they denied victory to the French – by destroying the bridge; and by the end of November the Allied offensive had been checked. Along most of the front the Germans sat behind flooded rivers or concrete defences. The only real gap in the West Wall was between Aachen and Geilenkirchen. To prevent a clear breakthrough here the Germans had concentrated the bulk of their reserves, and had based a new defence line on the swampy valley of the River Roer and the trackless maze of the Hürtgen Forest.

CHAPTER XV
The Ardennes Offensive
'To the German Commander: NUTS'

By the end of November the Allied offensive had almost petered out. Before the US Ninth Army could tackle the River Roer the US First Army had to seize the huge reservoirs at the head of the river, lest they should be turned loose as floods. The way to the Roer dams lay through the Hürtgen Forest, which became the scene of bitter fighting in bitter weather. By the last day of the month American troops had reached Grosshau, five miles from Düren on the upper Roer:

5 December 1944

'I went into Grosshau down a squelching, muddy road that shelves steeply out of the forest. An infantry platoon was approaching the village . . . crouching watchfully in the ditches, then moving forward to the next turn in the road and crouching again. Three riflemen lay flat in the thick mud on the road itself, rifles to their shoulders, watching the wrecked village for snipers. In stops and starts the platoon edged its way in and fanned out right and left to search the cellars for anything the forward platoon might have missed. A German with his leg swathed in bandages came limping out with his hands well up. Three of his comrades lay dead and mud-splashed beside a garden wall.

'Behind the garden wall the debris had been pushed aside to clear a coal chute which led down to a cellar. One of the soldiers pulled back from his peep-hole and pointing his thumb at the coal chute said: "Go down there and mind your feet."

'The cellar was dark and filled with dust and broken masonry from the grenades that had blasted the Germans out. In the thin shaft of light that slanted down from the coal chute an officer was crouched, marking his map. A soldier with a walkie-talkie lay beside him speaking quietly into a microphone. In the darkness behind, some forty soldiers were lying in groups of three and four around fires made from the grease-soaked cardboard of their ration boxes. Over the flames they were heating water to make coffee. One Joe began to fidget with an overheated can of pork loaf which he was trying to open – and which was burning his fingers. This firelight pantomime inspired a few unhelpful remarks. But most of the men sat around with eyes half-closed getting a bit of rest. In the next cellar an officer was crouched over a small table talking on a field telephone. He was covered in mud, his cheeks were grey and hollowed and his eyes were sunken and red-rimmed from lack of sleep, and from peering at his maps in this dark cellar. He was reading off map references into the telephone. How he could see the small figures in the dark, I don't know. While he talked a dull boomp . . . boomp . . . could be felt in the cellar. Somebody said: "They're mortaring the road again."

'The signaller, lying curled in the shaft of light, went on muttering his code-words and jargon into the microphone, the infantrymen had let the fires the down and were drinking hot coffee from their canteen cups; the officer laid the field telephone down and called: "Who's here from ——?" and he mentioned the name of an infantry company that was flanking him. A soldier rose from the darkness and came over to the table. Quietly the officer outlined his plans for the evening advance, and indicated where his patrols would operate during the night. The soldier repeated the message slowly, saluted, and scrambled up the coal chute into the daylight.

'The officer looked round. "Who's here from ——?" and another soldier stepped forward in the dark. Up above, the smoking wreckage of Grosshau was still being searched for snipers and enemy wounded. But down in the cellar the next advance was being planned.'

ROBERT BARR

⊂◯◯◯

While the Americans were thinking perforce of yard-by-yard advances by platoons and companies, the German High Command was planning an advance of a very different kind. Early in December reports had come through from Germany that the High Command's strategic reserve – the Sixth SS Panzer Army – had completed its re-equipping in the Ruhr and had moved west across the Rhine. Where and how it would be employed, nobody knew – but some indication might have been gained from the fact that von Rundstedt had planned and directed the German breakthrough in the Ardennes in 1940. [*In fact it was Hitler's plan this time; von Rundstedt disapproved of it and left the execution to Model.*]

Nine days before Christmas he launched in the Ardennes the first real counter-offensive since D-Day. For this task he had been given more than twenty divisions, including almost every armoured division available in the West – plus more than a thousand aircraft.

Hitler's plan was to strike through the Ardennes, reckoning that – as in 1940 – the Allies would be relying for defence there more upon the difficulties of the country than on military strength. Having struck, however, this time he was to exploit – not south-west into France – but north-west across the Meuse, to Liège, and if possible to Antwerp. This was obviously a last desperate bid to keep the Allies from the Rhine; everything depended upon a swift success. The attack, cloaked under misty skies, was a savage all-out assault launched with desperate determination.

Advancing between Monschau and Trier the Fifth Panzer Army [*Manteuffel*] and the Sixth SS Panzer Army [*Dietrich*] succeeded in penetrating the US First Army front in several places, and forward units pressed on to within four miles of the Meuse. It was a perilous moment for the Allies, and the first German prisoners who came in were obviously elated by this sudden turn of the tide:

20 December 1944

'They told of the feverishness of the night before the jump-off. They told of American soldiers standing by their guns until they were literally overrun by tanks. They described how they had captured American supply dumps, and fought for the food and cigarettes and gasolene we left. Some German prisoners described how their officers gave them strong propaganda to emphasise the importance of the operation. They were told that the recapture of Aachen would be a Christmas present for Adolf Hitler.

'Every one of these prisoners says that this is the big effort. If this succeeds, things will go well. If it fails, there'll be no chance of launching another drive. They said that their intention was to cut lines, capture so many of our supplies, and inflict so much damage that our own offensive to the Rhine will have to come to a stop. This is the enemy's strategic objective. But he's got another one. He's out to make as much propaganda out of it as he can, to bolster the spirit of his people at home. He has an entire regiment – literally a regiment – of reporters and photographers travelling with the spearhead, sending words back – lurid words – that the German Army is attacking and conquering again. The German reconnaissance columns must have thought it was 1940 again too, because they arrogantly kept sending messages back in open language. But we know our own power, and we know that we can beat the enemy down.'

RICHARD HOTTELET, CBS

For the Americans there was the heart-aching business of withdrawing from villages and towns they had liberated, abandoning perforce the civilians who had welcomed them so eagerly a few months before:

20 December 1944

'During the night the town had been bombed a little, strafed a little, and the siren had wakened us to give warning of paratroop activity. In the morning there was a rumour that German tanks were just over the hill. Armed patrols went out on the roads. Trees were felled as roadblocks, and Thunderbolts and Lightnings came low over the town and began zooming and searching in the woods just east of us. Then the order that everyone hoped would never come came. We had to move out quickly. Somehow the news spread round the little Belgian border town and the people came out to see the leave-taking. Some of the troops had been there for three months, and they had made friends. There was handshaking and many questions. How near were the Germans? Did we think they'd come to their town again? Was it true that German tanks were just over the hill? There were awkward silences. The GIs couldn't answer that question. A truck driver tying a tarpaulin over his loaded truck swore quietly and said, "I never thought this would happen to us." We had been planning a Christmas party for the local children; a GI took the notice down, looked at it, and tore it up. A placard telling of a Friday night dance was taken down. The Belgian people watched it all. Whatever you did, wherever you went, their eyes followed you. A girl asked me if she should leave the town. She had been in the Resistance movement. Were the Germans really near? she asked. It was an awkward question, but the Germans answered it for me by sending a shell over the hill and into the town. The convoy began to move out, past rows of solemn-faced civilians. One or two were crying; others ran over to the jeeps to wish us luck, and to hope that we'd be back soon.'

ROBERT BARR

20 December 1944

'In the past two days I have ranged hundreds of miles in my jeep from the front lines to the rear areas and back again. Although some people in areas not affected by the attack do display nervousness, the majority are calm. It is chiefly among those who are less well informed of Allied strength on the Western Front that whatever panic there has been is shown. Numerous front-line towns in eastern Belgium have been evacuated. I was in one town, and there was an experience I will never forget – the experience of conquest in reverse. The wild cheers of welcome accorded the American liberators three months ago had turned to ashes. Most civilians stood around in silent groups in the streets watching the mud-spattered army trucks moving. American flags were removed from some of the shop windows, and so were forbidden Belgian banners. As I left I wondered how long it would be until Nazi banners would once again adorn those windows which for three months have displayed the Stars and Stripes.'

JAMES CASSIDY, NBC

While disorganised and isolated units fought heroically to slow down the German advance, countermeasures were swiftly prepared:

22 December 1944

'All day and all night staffs have been feverishly active; calls have gone out to battalions, regiments, divisions, to get up and move. The next day's threat had to be anticipated because the roads that were clear for a convoy that night might be cut the next morning. German tanks and armoured cars were fanning out in all directions. And the positions to be taken had to be far enough back so that they could be consolidated, the men and guns dug in, the vehicles dispersed, before they would have to fight. Still, they couldn't be so far back as to give the Germans any ground. Supplies and ammunition, gasolene and food had to be channelled through to outfits that had suddenly moved a hundred miles. It was against a background of threat and confusion that this organisation took place. An officer, wearily putting down one receiver and lifting another, mumbled to me: "It sounds like the Stock Market crash in 1929." But the higher officers and staff kept their heads in work and slowly shaped some sort of order out of confusion.

'I can tell you how much it means to have seen this strength of ours poured down into threatened areas. There have been several misty, cold mornings this past week when I have come back along an empty road from sectors of the front that I knew were held only by patrols and cavalry screens, and I've wondered what would happen if the Germans attacked there. And then, following a couple of jeeps, would come a looming convoy of trucks and tank-destroyers and half-tracks and tanks, and I'd lean out of my jeep and squint to get a look at the unit identification. Sometimes it was an outfit I knew well; sometimes it was a strange bunch, from pretty far away, but I always felt better on the way home because I had seen our strength.

'And it's the same with the infantry. You know the Army is big and powerful, but you're out by yourself in the dark or under a miserable grey sky and you want to see some tangible proof. Well, you'll see it here now. Again this morning I saw still another bunch thundering down to the front and everyone – soldiers, civilians, and war correspondents – looked at it and smiled.

'But all this couldn't have happened if it hadn't been for the work and courage of the average GI. All day and all night they've driven scores of miles over roads jammed thick with convoys moving, moving, moving. Vehicles in ditches were pulled out, lost vehicles and convoys were put right, and in between MPs fished out Germans in jeeps who were riding behind our lines to get information and do damage. With units pouring in from everywhere it's been hard to see how they could all be managed, but they were.'

RICHARD HOTTELET, CBS

ᴄᴏᴇᴏ

One of many gallant stands was made by an American infantry regiment near Stavelot, where on 20 December they succeeded in stopping a crack SS armoured column:

22 December 1944

'When night came, the wreckage of seventeen German half-tracks lay crumpled along the village road and through the fields, and each half-track had its quota of SS dead. But in the night the Panzer Division sent out its pincers to outflank the infantry and by morning they were almost encircled. Only one free road was open to enter or leave their line and that was a narrow winding road and it was under machine-gun fire. In the morning I was guided down that narrow road to see this SS spearhead being blunted. There was a heavy mist lying on the moors, and for a time it was impossible to see more than ten yards ahead or ten yards on either side of the road. Hidden somewhere in the mist, tanks and anti-tank guns were barking at each other. If it was visual firing it must have been very close. We pulled up at a small farmhouse about half a mile from the fighting. A sentry stepped up and his eyes roved over our uniforms bit by bit – battle jacket, trousers, boots, badges, then there was a slow thorough inspection of our papers. We went into the farmhouse where the colonel was sitting by a red-hot stove. "Sorry about the hold-up," he said, "but there are so many Germans around in American uniforms – four of them came past the command post just ten minutes ago and got away in the mist. By the way, which road did you come?" I told him. "Um," he said, "so it's still open."

'We went over to a map standing on an old-fashioned sideboard and he lit a candle so I could see it. "Here we are," he said, "and here are the Germans so far as we know – here and here and at the bridge down here, and two of his tanks were seen over there, and a machine-gun post fired on one of our jeeps just here." He smiled – "Looks like they're trying to get all round us, but getting round us won't get rid of us, and maybe that's something they haven't figured on." '

ROBERT BARR

Christmas brought no unqualified rejoicing to either side. The Germans had undoubtedly gained tactical surprise, and days of misty weather had been worth many squadrons of fighters to them. The American First Army had taken a lot of punishment, the advance to the Rhine had been halted, and a threatening salient was established. On the other hand, the line of the Meuse was intact, Allied resistance in the north was growing, and the magnificent stand of the US 101st Airborne in Bastogne limited Model to a narrow front which he was unable to expand so long as the airborne men held on. When contact was re-established [*by units of Patton's Third Army from the south*], on 27 December, after eight days and nine nights of siege, the men in Bastogne were found to be in high spirits and still full of fight:

29 December 1944

'Meeting the men who'd been cut off in Bastogne for so long was almost an anticlimax. They couldn't make out why people outside the pocket had made so much fuss about them. They said they could have held out for weeks more. From Wednesday 20 December for seven or eight nights, the Germans attacked, at one point or another, in numbers up to a division at a time. The perimeter was held by regular riflemen, by engineers, and by stragglers who had infiltrated into the

345

town from the battles outside. One battalion of riflemen was cut off at the north of the town, and lost for a day before being relieved. One batch of stragglers from various formations was forged into a "task force" which in one week has acquired a regimental tradition of its own and founded a local legend.

'The Americans had tanks and tank-destroyers in the pocket. If they hadn't had them this would have been like an airborne operation with first-class infantrymen encircled by armoured forces with guns. Bastogne might have been another Arnhem. But the men in Bastogne were luckier than the men of Arnhem. They were luckier with weather. Supply-dropping on an enormous scale began on Saturday the 23rd and has gone on every day but one since then. Only one drop, consisting of food, went astray. One man told me that they went into cellars and air-raid shelters as supply-planes came over. If you were out in the street, in the middle of the town, a bag might easily hit you on the head.

'They missed only one meal all the time they were there. That was on Saturday before dropping began. They had eaten all their food and were down to eleven rounds of ammunition per gun. Since then they have been almost over-supplied. All that has worried them has been their wounded. Their field hospital and medical detachment had been captured on Tuesday the 19th – a day before complete encirclement. They had had medical supplies dropped to them, but they couldn't look after casualties properly. They're being looked after now, however.

'American tanks and tank-destroyers were so disposed on each of the seven roads out of the town – and the hill between them – that German attacks were beaten off. And attacks were made from every direction. On one occasion the Germans attacked from the north and the south simultaneously. But they never tried to attack from every side at once. They hadn't perhaps enough forces or had too many commitments elsewhere.

'They got tanks into the outskirts on Wednesday, the first day of complete encirclement. That was the foundation for the official statement of a week ago last Friday, that German tanks were in Bastogne. It was quite true, but what none of us dared to expect was that those German tanks would all be destroyed or driven off. From that day to this – eight days and seven nights – in Bastogne, 148 German tanks and twenty-five armoured vehicles were destroyed or driven off. The Americans did this with eleven or ten per cent casualties. We asked: "What sort of Christmas did you have?" It was rather a feeble joke, but it was replied to very promptly – "Splendid," they said, "splendid – that was the day we got twenty-eight German tanks." '

CYRIL RAY

29 December 1944

'A trip over the road into Bastogne would convince anyone of the determination and fury with which the Third Army soldiers are fighting. Across France you became accustomed to seeing the debris of last stands or particularly bitter fighting, but such piles of rubble were usually scattered at intervals. Not so on the road to Bastogne. The narrow dirt-track is pockmarked yard by yard with shell-holes, and the ditches and fields are littered with personal equipment and with battered and burned-out vehicles, both German and American. Belgian civilians wander about their shattered farm-buildings, dazed and made uncertain by the speed and fury of the fighting. Dead animals cover the ground, and you are almost surprised to see a live and healthy pig trotting up the road.'

CAPTAIN DON WITTY

The story of what happened inside Bastogne during its encirclement was told by the commander of the town, Brigadier-General A. C. McAuliffe:

3 January 1945

'It didn't occur to us, until it was all over, that the eyes of the world were on the 101st Airborne Division and the attached armour during the defence of Bastogne. The first thing we heard was that we'd been "rescued" by the 4th Armoured Division. Now I, and everyone else in the 101st, resent the implication that we were rescued or that we needed to be rescued. When General Taylor arrived on the 27th the first thing he asked me was what kind of shape were we in. I told him, "Why, we're in fine shape: we're ready to take the offensive." General Taylor said: "I should have known it, but all that stuff I read in the newspapers was beginning to worry me just a little." The fact is we were thinking about what a tough time the Kraut was having. We weren't alarmed about our own position at all. After all, we'd deliberately jumped into that kind of position in Normandy and Holland.

'The worst part of it for me was the loss of the hospital and the division's surgeon and the surgical teams. On the first day the Germans captured the divisional hospital and took prisoner every divisional surgeon. After that we couldn't give the wounded the care they deserve, but the wounded were magnificent – not a word of complaint from them. We commandeered some cognac and gave them about three ounces every night – that helped. I went up to one lad lying there with a compound fracture of the femur. I said to him, "How're you doing?" He looked up at me and said: "I'm doing fine, General." You know we've got a new name for ourselves. We call ourselves the Battered – well, let's call it "buddies" – we call ourselves "The Battered Buddies of the Bastion of Bastogne".

'For the first three days of the battle of Bastogne there was fog: on the fourth day it cleared. After that, "terrific" was the only word that described the air support we got from those Thunderbolts. Those are the "gutsiest" fellows I ever saw. The Air Support Officer we had was a captain named Parker. He really knew his stuff and ran a great circus. He called himself Maestro. He has a fine gift for salty language, and when he was telling those airplanes what to do there was always a big crowd of soldiers standing around just listening to him talk. Finally it got so bad we had to rope him off. But Maestro Parker and those Thunderbolts really did a job for us.

'For the first three days we gave the Germans the licking of their lives. On the third day, the German commander had the effrontery to send us a surrender demand. When we got it we thought it was the funniest thing we ever heard. I just laughed and said "Nuts", but the German major who brought it wanted a formal answer; so I decided – well, I'd just say "Nuts", so I had it written out: "To the German Commander: NUTS. Signed, The American Commander."

'The Troop Carrier Command did a great job on the supply end too. They brought us all the ammunition, rations, and other equipment that we needed. Our morale was always tops. Good morale is just as contagious as panic can be. We had several thousand reinforcements – attached troops – and they caught the infectious courage of the old men of the 101st right away. Airborne Divisions always have good morale. We were fortunate enough to have been associated with the First and Sixth British Airborne Divisions, and we saw something of the First British Airborne Division up around Arnhem. They don't come any better. No one should be surprised at what the 101st Airborne Division did at Bastogne. That is what should be expected any time of airborne troops. With that kind of troops I as a commander can do anything.'

BRIGADIER-GENERAL A. C. MCAULIFFE

The holding of Bastogne robbed the Germans of a vital traffic route. As pressure on the northern flank increased, under the direction of

Field-Marshal Montgomery – now commanding the US First and Ninth Armies as well as the British Second – Model was increasingly forced to concentrate his traffic along the St Vith–Houffalize road. The change of weather that came with Christmas Day gave the Allied Air Forces a great opportunity to strike at the main forces before they could get back to comparative security beyond the Rhine. In four consecutive days 500 enemy vehicles were destroyed from the air:

29 December 1944

'We can see now the effect of these air attacks in what has happened and is happening beyond Rochefort. The reinforcements haven't arrived, and those reconnaissance tendrils which were pushed out towards the Meuse have withered for lack of nourishment and are now being looped off and destroyed. Here, our people are on the offensive and the enemy is being driven back from the Meuse towards Rochefort. And so we now have this position along the front. At the western end of the salient the Germans are being forced back. On the southern flank we have a solid wedge driven in as far as Bastogne, so that at its waist their salient is now only eighteen miles wide.

'On the northern flank, where they've put in the main weight of their best Panzer divisions, one strong attack north-west of Lierneux in the middle of the line was repulsed on Tuesday. North-west of Grandmenil, where they've been trying to batter their way up the road to Liège, their attacks have been held, and here the enemy now shows signs of weakening under our counter-attack.

'The relief of Bastogne combined with the holding of our positions near Grandmenil has so pinched in the German salient that von Rundstedt's troops west of this narrow waist must be feeling very uncomfortable; and this is specially so because of our air attacks on their supply lines.'

CHESTER WILMOT

In the closing week of 1944 Germany's final bid for victory [*the battle of the Bulge as it came to be called*] began to peter out. The Panzers, which had once been the terror of Europe, had made their last onrush and been decisively halted. After a tantalising glimpse of the Meuse they turned back, and by 29 December the Americans were in the outskirts of Rochefort:

30 December 1944

'Rochefort is now the most westerly point of von Rundstedt's salient and for three days I've been watching the ragged spearhead of his offensive being blunted and bent. Three days ago the Germans had reached Celles, which is nine miles west of here. Some of them managed to get beyond Celles, and perhaps they caught a fleeting glance of the Meuse River as it sweeps past Dinant. Perhaps they even got a glance at the Promised Land beyond the Meuse, for when I saw them they were near enough. But just then a screening force of our armour slipped between them and the river, wheeled, and – I'll quote the words of the men themselves – they said "we ripped into them and we tore them apart". That was no boasting, no exaggeration, because the tussle that began almost on the banks of the Meuse developed with a ferocity that equalled anything in this war.

'The spearhead of this drive was an *élite* Panzer Division. [*2nd*] They were stopped within sight of their objective, hammered by artillery, tank-guns, and mortar fire. Fighter-bombers were called in to strafe them; flame-throwers were ordered up, but before the flame-throwers arrived the chosen spearhead of von Rundstedt's drive had called "Enough!" [*They had also run out of fuel*] Those who were left were ordered to burn their equipment, take only what they could carry, and get out on foot. They were told to keep away from the roads and get out through the mist over open country, but a swift encircling drive swept one thousand of the retreating division into our prison cages; and what with the dead and the wounded and the wrecked equipment, there was nothing they could do but fall back to the shelter of their defences at Rochefort. I've followed them eastwards for nine miles along roads and through villages which their drive had overrun just a few days ago, and here, outside Rochefort, the battle is on again.'

ROBERT BARR

In the breaking-up of this Panzer thrust, at Ciney and at Celles, British forces fought alongside the Americans. Montgomery had reacted swiftly to the threat, covering the line of the Meuse in case the Germans succeeded in forcing the river and thus menacing the communications of the British Second Army:

5 January 1945

'British troops are fighting alongside the American First Army in our counter-offensive against the western end and the northern flank of the German salient in the Ardennes. It was British armour and infantry which captured the two villages south of Rochefort on Wednesday, and yesterday another British force joined in the attack on the Americans' right. East of Marche they pushed the Germans back nearly a mile, with a series of thrusts into the hills along a five- to six-mile front.

'British troops have actually been fighting in the Rochefort sector since Christmas Day, but they were holding defensive positions in the Meuse valley behind the American First Army several days before that.

'When the Germans broke through in the first weekend of their offensive, Field-Marshal Montgomery at once brought British divisions south in case the Americans needed them and, as the German threat developed, the roads leading back into Belgium were packed with British convoys day and night. It was remarkable how quickly and efficiently we moved thousands of troops with all their guns, tanks, ammunition, and engineering supplies. The Belgians lined the roads and cheered the Tommies, as the convoys moved towards the new front.

'The troops forgot about their Christmas plans, and in rain and sleet they dug defensive positions in the valley of the Meuse. The men who had helped to liberate Belgium were determined that they would not let the Germans come back. But, as it turned out, the main German assault towards Liège was held by American troops alone, and until Christmas Day the British forces had only the role of a long-stop. By then the Germans had captured Rochefort, and had sent a series of armoured columns probing towards the Dinant sector of the Meuse. British tanks, self-propelled guns, and motorised infantry were sent to support an American division in dealing with these. The combined Allied attack brought disaster to the Germans. They had sent the best part of a Panzer division thrusting west from Rochefort. Its leading elements were within sight of the Meuse, but at Ciney and Celles the British and Americans caught them. The Germans were stopped, and most of them were surrounded. We're counting the wreckage in this area west of Rochefort now, and we've already counted lying there, derelict and abandoned, eighty-one German tanks, seven assault guns, seventy-four other guns, and 405 vehicles. In this action the Germans lost the bulk of one Panzer division, and the westwards thrust towards the Meuse was finally stopped.

'Since then the Germans in this sector have been driven back twelve miles. Since then we have held the initiative, and now the Germans' northern flank is being heavily attacked. With the British on the offensive as well, the attack now extends along a 25-mile front, from Marche almost up to Stavelot.'

CHESTER WILMOT

By 3 January the US First Army under General Hodges had so far recovered from the terrific onslaught directed against it initially that it was able to go over to the offensive:

6 January 1945

'The Fifth and Sixth Panzer Armies chose the US First as their attacking point and hammered a fifty-mile salient in its line. Technically they tore the army's front line apart, they hit its communications, overran its weak divisions, threw overwhelming weight against its best divisions, threw paratroops and spies behind its lines, and set its operations chiefs and its divisional commanders a most serious situation to face.

'Every man and every officer stood the test – some by quick thinking, some by swift improvisation, some by good planning, some just by sheer bravery, and some by guess and by God; but they all came through. I know. I saw it.

'For eighteen days they took the most savage pounding that SS divisions and Panzer corps could inflict, and then they returned to the attack.

'It went in at 8.30 in the morning under a heavy snow-cloud that deprived the men of air support or even air observation for the guns that began to fire on them. It went in through snowdrifts and up hillsides and through forests. It went in down ice-bound roads on which tanks slithered and slipped; it went in against an icy wind that froze your fingers and made chilblains on your face. Infantrymen, their wet clothes freezing on their bodies, slogged their way through the snow, and uphill – always uphill – to drive the Germans from their observation posts; while the tanks slithered and skidded down the roads to drive the Germans from the villages.

'The tanks would fight their way in and flush the Germans out of the villages and the barns, and force them out on the snow-covered fields so the infantry could get at them. Then the Germans' artillery somewhere back in the hills would open fire on the village and we had no air observation to spot the guns. When the fire got too heavy, the tanks would be forced to withdraw. When the gunfire stopped, the tanks would race in again to get there before the German infantry could get back into the cottages. The artillery fire would begin again and force the tanks out. And it would go on like this until forward observers could spot the German guns, and call for counter-battery fire. Then the tanks would slip in again, and the village would be ours.

'We took ten villages like that, and by midnight that first day we had also taken 290 prisoners and gained two miles. But by midnight too the snow began again, covering the battlefield with heavy swirling flakes. The day brought the depressing news that there would be another day of hard slogging without air support, and without air observation. By dawn the snow was freezing on the periscopes of the tanks, blinding the gunners and the drivers. It made the advancing infantry white and invisible. It covered the minefields and the enemy pillboxes. By afternoon it became apparent that these American soldiers who had just faced the heaviest eighteen-day battle that two Panzer armies could provide must also face the heaviest slogging-match that winter could force on them.'

ROBERT BARR

As the Germans withdrew, Allied troops were sometimes able to pause for a rest – the first for many weary days. Crouching in the snow, the men cooked a hot meal after a long spell on dry rations:

13 January 1945
'A Tank Destroyer Company had pulled itself off the ridge and was preparing to swing east to a busier part of the line. The snow along the

ridge was churned by the tracks of the great tank-destroyers and by the wheels of the ammunition carriers and the trucks. And some thin scraggy trees on the edge of the wood were splintered and smashed where they had barged their way under the trees for the night. Deep inside the wood there were fires alight.

'It was just coming on dark, and I could smell cooking, so I called in. In the half-light a single file of men, ankle deep in snow, their mess kits ready, were waiting patiently for chow. There were four fires in a row; on the first three great metal trays were sizzling with hot food; the men began to trudge forward holding out their mess kits. From the first tray came a steaming ladle of macaroni and tomato sauce, from the second a ladle of mashed potatoes, with the cook saying: "Is that enough?" And from the third came a chunk of steak and a ladle full of gravy.

'Beside the third fire a captain stood against a tree, watching rather anxiously, watching the sizzling trays and watching the faces of his men as they came into the firelight. The captain was young, about twenty-eight, and there seemed to be something special about the stew; he kept watching his men as he talked to me. "For five days," he was saying, "my men have been fighting on cold rations, mostly crackers and cheese. I've been saving this stuff till we could get somewhere we could cook it. Why don't you have some? It smells good." I said I was pushing on, but could I have some coffee? "Sure," he said, "sure, plenty of coffee."

'It was getting darker and the ghost queue kept filing past, each face lighting for a moment in the glow of the fires. It was a strange pageant of tough, rough, bearded faces. They were all young lads, and the captain apologised for the beards. "We couldn't shave in the front line," he said; "it was too cold. Now we've got hot water, we'll be shaving them off after chow. Do you want to stay and see it?" I said I'd like to, but I'd just crept in for a cup of coffee. "Oh, yes, coffee," he said; "follow me." We wound in and around a few trees to the prize tableau of this forest pantomime. In the darkness under a great fir-tree there was a huge log fire. On the log fire there was a great cauldron, and on the cauldron a great iron lid. It didn't fit too well and steam hissed out all around the edges, and the firelight made the steam turn scarlet. And, in the midst of it all, was a strange hunched figure with a long woollen cap and a long brown beard; he sat with one hand poised over the great iron lid, in the other he held a ladle.

'He sat perfectly still. At his feet were the adjuncts of his profession, a bowl of sugar and a tin of cream. He said nothing. I took some sugar and I held my canteen forward. He lifted the iron lid, scooped a ladle of coffee, and banged the lid down quickly. "He does that to keep the cold air out," the captain explained. "Is that enough?" I said it was; my canteen was brimming over and scalding my fingers. "Are you sure you won't have any chow?" asked the captain for about the fourth time, and when he saw that I was staring at the coffee-man's beard he laughed. "That old man," he said, "is just twenty-six years old. Why don't you wait and see him shave his beard off?"

'I sipped my coffee and I said that I had to go, but I'd come back again tomorrow. "We won't be here tomorrow," said the captain; "we've a date with some Panzers two miles east. Why don't you have some chow, and see the beards come off. Let the war look after itself for one night like we're doing." It was such an unusual pantomime, the dark forest, the snow, the firelight, the long queue of little bearded men, the smell of good food and good coffee, I felt I had to see the whole show. "All right," I said, "if you're letting the war look after itself tonight, I'll join you."'

ROBERT BARR

By the middle of January the situation in the Ardennes was well under control, and towards the end of the month American armour was storming towards St Vith:

25 January 1945

'The great white-painted Shermans with their rubber snow-tracks swished through the snow and cut across the open country under heavy gunfire from German 88-millimetres . . . and on through the gunfire and into a belt of woods. As we entered the woods the tank radios began to chatter . . . to chatter about the position of enemy infantry – enemy "doughs" they called them – who were dug in in foxholes – to chatter about enemy tanks they were knocking out. There was a short silence on the tank radios while German 88s shelled the woods . . . and then the German gunfire stopped and an elated tank commander came on to talk about some "big boys" he had captured. What kind of "big boys", he was asked. He snapped back about a piano . . . about octaves, and in the small front-line Command Post where his backchat was heard there was a chorus of "octaves . . . 8 . . . 8 . . . 8 . . . Oh, 88s". He had captured the 88s . . . how many? Seven of them, he said, seven of them intact and complete with ammunition. Could he have engineers along to demolish them? Well, what he said was . . . could he have some doughnuts. But the doughnuts couldn't get down in time. The roads were busy and snowbound. So . . . instructions on how to demolish them with his own tank resources were sent.

'Then the excitement of the battle increased as a new piece of chatter was radioed from tank to tank . . . in front of the leading tanks German infantry were running in disorder . . . without helmets, some without rifles . . . and there was the battle-wise request: Who should fire on them . . . whose pigeons were they?

'Then came the news from observer planes that a great column of German tanks and vehicles retreating eastwards from St Vith had been caught by our aircraft . . . and were being bombed and strafed.'

ROBERT BARR

The bombing and strafing which now harried the withdrawing Germans exacted a heavy price for their earlier success. Much of the enemy's armour was required for transfer to the Eastern Front to repel the growing Russian threat to Berlin, but a substantial part of it never got away from its adventure in the Ardennes. Allied airmen took full advantage of the large-scale enemy movement along the roads, and this story of twelve Thunderbolts – told by their squadron commander – is typical of many:

25 January 1945
'We'd come in on the road that leads north-east out of Prüm. To our surprise, this road, and others we could see, were jammed with German vehicles of all kinds. Double columns bumper-to-bumper. The concentrations were all retreating toward Prüm – stretched ahead as far as the eye could see (in my 118 missions I've never seen so much enemy equipment).

'As I led the squadron down I found myself headed straight for a flak-gun. I gave it a burst – and knocked it out. Then I took a quick look at the situation and decided to bomb first on a curve in the road. I dropped my two wing bombs on the curve, tore big holes in the road, and knocked out six trucks. This stopped the whole column deader than a duck. Then we really went to work: bombed and strafed the column of tanks, half-tracks, cargo-trucks, and horse-drawn vehicles over an area of about five miles – knocking out flak at the same time.

'Hundreds of the Jerries jumped from their vehicles and ran for cover; others started pulling their vehicles off the road in an attempt to hide them in the trees. But the ground was all snow-covered so it didn't do them any good. We followed the tracks and bombed and strafed them in their hide-outs. After our bombs were all gone, we worked back and forth on the column – and all hell began to break loose as we'd knocked out all the flak in the area and they were helpless. I've never seen so much confusion. The Jerries would run into the woods and then out again. They were like chickens with their heads cut off.

'When most all of our ammunition was gone we took stock of the situation. By a careful count we could see from eighty-five to ninety vehicles of all kinds either completely destroyed or burning and shattered.'

CAPTAIN WILFRED B. CRUTCHFIELD, USAF

And so, after about six weeks of desperate fighting and swaying fortunes, the Ardennes offensive came to an end. In effect, it had been the last savage sortie of a wounded beast, aware that it was nearly cornered. Now both sides rested and regrouped, while heavy snow ended all likelihood of a sudden new development:

29 January 1945

'On the Western Front this morning the biggest thing is the infantry attack in the First Army sector in which about one division is involved. This gives you a good idea how this Western Front has calmed down. Only two weeks ago this kind of an attack, in which we advance a few thousand yards and take a few small villages, would have been only a tiny part of the day's operations. One reason for this is the snow – inches of snow that have fallen on top of the already deep drifts. Quite apart from the bitter cold, the snow wears men out when they have to move; loaded down with their heavy winter clothing, their weapons, and their ammunition, it's a great physical strain to mount an attack. Men who lead a column and break a path through fresh snow have to be relieved every hundred yards or so. That's one reason for the lull. The other, and probably main one, is that the divisions that fought so hard and so well during the German counter-offensives can use a rest. They're drawing extra winter equipment and brushing up on new tactics: the higher staffs are making strategic dispositions, preparing to resume our own winter offensive. Until that comes, it's probable that the Western Front will remain much the same as it is today from the Rhine to the North Sea: constant patrols; short, sharp fire-fights, and here and there a larger attack to get more favourable positions.'

RICHARD HOTTELET, CBS

In spite of some vigorous thrusting in Alsace, the Germans were in no condition to offer more than a stubborn rearguard action when the Allies renewed their general pressure towards the Rhine. No second counter-offensive was attempted.

The flow of supplies through the Channel ports and the inexorable bombing of Germany gave the Allies a mounting superiority in the New Year. The decisive victory, which had been warded off before Christmas, looked to be inevitable in the spring. Just as further withdrawals would be fatal for the enemy, so equally it was certain that he was incapable of holding his Rhineland defences.

PART THREE
Beyond The Rhine

'Twenty-first Army Group will now cross the Rhine.'

FIELD-MARSHAL MONTGOMERY

CHAPTER XVI
One More River

'In thirty seconds from now'

The Ardennes offensive had achieved little more than the gaining of time – time to develop the rocket attacks on London and to scrape up what manpower remained for a last-ditch stand. But mere time was by now a doubtful asset, for it also meant a winter of day-and-night bombing which shattered the cities of Germany and laid waste her industries. The annihilation of Dresden by air attack in mid-February carried its own terrible message.

During February the Allies had regrouped their forces and resumed their pressure across the Roer and through the Reichswald. By March the tempo on the Western Front began to quicken. Mönchen-Gladbach fell on the 1st. Krefeld followed next day. On the 4th the US First Army reached the Rhine. Cologne was entered on the 5th, and two days later the US Third Army was on the Rhine. That same day – 7 March – a surprise dash by the US First Army seized intact the Ludendorff Bridge at Remagen.

That almost accidental success at Remagen was one of the turning-points of the Battle of the Rhine. General Hodges' troops had seized a bridgehead on the east bank of the river. In the whole length of the Middle Rhine no crossing-place less suitable for military exploitation could have been found, for on the far side the Americans were faced with precipitous cliffs as their immediate objective, and beyond them a deep belt of rugged upland country, which constantly renewed the enemy's observation as he fell back step by step. Remagen was a shock to the Germans. The officers who permitted this Allied crossing of the great river were sentenced to death [*and von Rundstedt was once again replaced as C-in-C, this time by Field-Marshal Kesselring*]. Troops were rushed up to seal off the bridgehead. Unprecedented masses of artillery were assembled, and innumerable fighter-bomber sorties were flown in attempts to knock out both the Ludendorff Bridge and the pontoon and trestle bridges which the Americans were now using. But the Americans were in a position to maintain, supply and expand the bridgehead, no matter what the Germans might do. As the enemy forces on the west bank of the Rhine above Remagen were steadily wiped out, General Hodges transferred his army, division by division, across the river into the bridgehead.

As the threat at Remagen mounted, the Germans, having practically no troops in reserve, were forced to bring more and more men and tanks away from the sector opposite Montgomery in the north, and elsewhere they held the river line so thinly that General Patton's Third Army – after a most remarkable advance through the Siegfried Line to the Moselle, and then without pause from the Moselle to the Rhine – was able to establish a second Allied bridgehead in the Koblenz sector on 22 March, making what was virtually an unopposed crossing without artillery bombardment or air support.

By that time Montgomery had already begun to put down an immense smoke-screen, which was to obscure nearly seventy miles of the Rhine. Under cover of this the attack was prepared and on the night of 23–24 March the Twenty-first Army Group, including the Ninth US Army, crossed the Rhine in the areas of Wesel, Xanten and Rees, and established four bridgeheads. Full-scale invasion of Germany from the West had begun. The 51st Highland Division led the assault, crossing north of Rees at 9 pm:

American soldiers train with a Sherman M4 amphibious tank,
fitted with air-inflated sides and twin propellers. These tanks
were successfully used in the crossing of the Rhine.

24 March 1945

'In thirty seconds from now Buffaloes carrying the assaulting troops will begin to cross the Rhine. The Rhine is now dark: the Bofors guns and machine-guns which were firing tracer bullets over its surface have stopped, except for four or five Bofors guns which here are firing single shots to guide the Buffaloes up to the water's edge.

'Yes, there now I can see the Buffaloes moving through the trees on the water's edge – I don't know how many have gone down into the water, but I can see perhaps four or five lined up – moving past the trees – one of them going past the end of a column of trees apparently at the end of a lane – goes down – down the bank and disappears out of sight: apparently it's under the lee of the bank now and it will be nosing into the water. But the remarkable thing is that, although I've got a very wide strip of the river under view with my glasses at the moment, I haven't yet seen any sign of enemy fire coming back; no doubt some is coming back at the Buffaloes, but I've seen no tracers from enemy machine-guns – and they always use tracers – and I've seen no signs of enemy mortars bursting in the water or on the bank between my observation post and the edge of the river. The enemy seems to have been completely stopped in this area by the intense barrage from all kinds of weapons which has been coming down on him for so many hours now. The Buffaloes, at least here, seem to be moving in a steady stream up to the river bank, down into the river and across.'

CHESTER WILMOT

An hour later the 1st British Commando Brigade crossed the river west of Wesel:

24 March 1945

'I watched the Commandos take off for Wesel, long a thorn in our side, and their attitude simply defied description. You would have thought that they were embarking on a Union picnic; they just couldn't care less. A few minutes after they were due to arrive on the far side, Bomber Command were to deliver a crushing blow on the enemy in Wesel, while the Commandos lay doggo over there, a bare thousand yards from Bomber Command's target, and waited. Smack on time, Arthur Harris & Company, House Removers, as they were called by the Commandos [*Air Chief Marshal Sir Arthur Harris was C-in-C of Bomber Command*], arrived and delivered a nerve-shaking blow on the former Wesel stronghold. Back at Headquarters, minutes ticked by. Officers waited anxiously for word from the Commandos

367

across the river. Suddenly there was a signal, and a voice literally purred over the wireless: "Noisy blighters, aren't they? We have taken position so-and-so, and have met no trouble." '

STEWART MACPHERSON

The crossing at Xanten was made by the 15th Scottish Division, also in Buffaloes:

24 March 1945

'The Buffalo – the driver in charge – a man of the Royal Tank Regiment is receiving the signal – the captain's waving to him, and *this is where we move.*

'He feels for the edge of the water – we're guided up right to the very edge by a long line of small green lights that have been laid to take us to the jumping-off ground: we've reached the water's edge and we see the Rhine – not running, as we thought it would, bright under the moon, but running red; because right on the opposite side of the village every single house and haystack you can see is burning, beaten down by the fury of our barrage. We can't tell whether there's anything coming at our boys: we hope all the stuff that we hear is going into Germany, the German positions; but in this thunder of the guns and the tracers that beat all around us, it's impossible to tell which way things are coming. We know which way we are going: we are going now to the German shore. It will take us about three minutes, and believe me every minute's going to seem a year.

'We're in – the Buffalo tips its nose down the bank and now it's opening up full power. Three minutes to go and we're racing across, and side by side with us go racing the other Buffaloes: racing for that hell on the other side. The searchlights cast a white beam, they go right across the river on one side of us, but ahead of us is only red water. The current's carrying us down and we're putting up our nose against it, going clean across it all the time, and the tracer is making a path on either side of us, beating down the opposition. Now we're utterly alone it seems right out in the midst of this whirling stream. You get a complete feeling of detachment, waiting all the time for the enemy to open up: waiting all the time for them to spot us as we lie helpless, as it seems, out here in this wide stream. The Buffalo springs and points its nose upstream now – we're tussling – fighting the current to get over. We're over midstream now. The driver's still fighting the current. It's running at mill-race speed, it seems to us, carrying us down all the time off our landing-point on the other bank. Now the tracer is quiet, drowned by the revving of our engines; but all the time that bank which we've been thinking about so much during the last few weeks is coming nearer and nearer. A signal flashes from the shore – the first Buffaloes are off. We've reached the other side, climbing up into the skirl of the pipes – the men of Scotland who've piped their men into battle across the Rhine.

'We were across, untouched. Well, there was an immense feeling of relief and excitement throughout our little party. The Commanding Officer gave the signal, the piper lifted his pipes to his lips, and he blew, and only an agonised wailing came from his instrument. Again he tried, and again the wail. If ever a man was near to tears, it was our piper. His great moment, and now, as he cried in despair: "Ma pipes, man, they'll no' play." That was all right with us because the Germans were not playing either. They may have been dazed by the weight of our barrage, they may have been preparing their resistance farther back; we couldn't tell in the tiny section of the fighting that surrounded us. All we knew, as we lowered the ramp and jumped out on the firelit river meadow, was that we were on the German side of the river at last; and that, for the enemy, is the fatal thing.'

WYNFORD VAUGHAN-THOMAS

In the morning airborne troops of the 6th British and the 17th US Airborne Divisions followed, jumping ahead of the troops which had crossed the Rhine during the night:

24 March 1945

'The Rhine lies left and right across our path below us, shining in the sunlight – wide and with sweeping curves; and the whole of this mighty airborne army is now crossing and filling the whole sky. We haven't come as far as this without some loss; on our right-hand side a Dakota has just gone down in flames. We watched it go to the ground, and I've just seen the parachutes of it blossoming and floating down towards the river. Above us and below us, collecting close round us now, are the tugs as they take their gliders in. Down there is the smoke of battle. There is the smoke-screen laid by the army lying right across the far bank of the river; dense clouds of brown and grey smoke coming up. And now our skipper's talking to the glider pilot and warning him that we're nearly there, preparing to cast him off. Ahead of us, another pillar of black smoke marks the spot where an aircraft has gone down, and – yet another one; it's a Stirling – a British Stirling; it's going down with flames coming out from under its belly – four parachutes are coming out – one, two, three, four – four parachutes have come out of the Stirling; it goes on its way to the ground. We haven't got time to watch it further because we're coming up now to the exact chosen landing-ground where our airborne forces have to be put down; and no matter what the opposition may be, we have got to keep straight on, dead on the exact position. There's only a minute or two to go, we cross the Rhine – we're on the east bank of the river. We're passing now over the army smoke-cloud.

' "Stand by and I'll tell you when to jump off." The pilot is calling up the – warning us – in just one moment we shall have let go. All over the sky ahead of us – here comes the voice – *Now!* – The glider has gone: we've cast off our glider. We've let her go. There she goes down behind us. We've turned hard away, hard away in a tight circle to port to get out of this area. I'm sorry if I'm shouting – this is a very tremendous sight.'

RICHARD DIMBLEBY

In that glider there was another BBC correspondent, who takes up the story as his machine comes down to land:

25 March 1945

'There was just a minute or two of quiet as the great Hamilcar ran in with the sound of the rushing wind in her wings. Then, when just a few feet off the ground, pandemonium broke loose – the wicked snap of Spandau machine-guns, mixed with the slower bong of 20-mm incendiaries for just a fraction of a second before they started pricking out their trademark in the thin skin of the glider. Things seemed to happen too quickly for me to take them all in at once. There was an explosion that appeared to be inside my head, the smell of burnt cordite. I went down on one knee. Something hot and sickly was dripping over my right eye and off my chin and all over my clothes. There was a doom-like lurch and a great rending as smoke, dust and daylight came from nowhere. I saw the Bren carrier go inexorably out of the nose of the glider, carrying the whole works ahead of it, and wiping two signallers off the top of it like flies. Even then the bullets kept crashing through the wreckage. It didn't seem fair; but then there is no "fair" or "unfair" in airborne fighting. At the moment of impact a jeep trailer that was chained just behind me came forward about six inches and caught me in the small of the back. Mercifully the chains held on. Somehow Captain Peter Cattle and

371

I hurled ourselves out of the mess into a shallow ditch by a hedge. Looking up, and clearing my eyes with the back of my hand, I saw a man pinned across the chest by wreckage. One of the glider pilots was getting him out. How those glider pilots and the two signallers on top of the carrier escaped the mass of that hurtling iron carrier I'll never know, but they did.

'A doctor came along and dressed Peter and me, and helped us to a dressing station. On the way I saw burning gliders, crashed gliders, and the great courage of men going in to fight almost before they had finished touching down. It was the old story of the men with the maroon berets who never worry about odds.

'The ground was covered with a mist of smoke from our artillery bombardment, and that was what had made it nearly impossible for the men to find their landing zones and spots. We spent the next four hours with that regiment; we had to. When contact was made with the men on our left, we made our painful way through them to Divisional HQ. Here, that remarkable young firebrand, their general, told us that all objectives had been reached, and that when the Second Army linked up he would hand them over in good shape and his job would be done. That has now taken place.'

STANLEY MAXTED

One of the first actions of the airborne troops was to seize Hamminkeln Station, and Maxted, though wounded in the glider landing, was happily able to cover the action:

26 March 1945

'The clock in the station was still going, the ticket racks were full of tickets, and the booking-clerk's peaked cap was lying just inside the wicket on a table. Out beyond the platform was a line of box-cars. Men were standing between the box-cars and firing. Others were lying at the bases of some of the trees beyond with Bren guns and automatic rifles. Smack in the middle of the booking-hall on the floor was a wireless set with its fishing-rod aerial. A signaller sitting beside it was listening. Coming through those headphones just then were sounds of some of Germany's best remaining troops in a terrible state of nerves calling through to their command posts that they were surrounded – or under fire – or being attacked, and please send up guns or tanks – send up anything.

'This struck me as being the shape of things to come. A major with a lisp who had discarded his helmet and put his red beret back on was kneeling by a window looking through binoculars at some farm-buildings behind us. Out by the box-cars a man was setting up a mortar. There was a crack from the buildings the major was looking at and he yelled, "I've got the so-and-so! Mortar, left one degree – Three rounds gunfire." I watched while the loading number put out three, dropped three fan-tailed demons in the muzzle of the mortar. They banged out high into the air, and the second one obliterated a sort of dovecot in the end of a low barn among the buildings. The major called, "That's it – that's got him – give him three more." There was no more from those farm-buildings.

'Down toward the river beyond the trees a company of men were deployed. The glider-borne troops involved in this part of the action wear the badges of three very famous old county regiments – the Royal Ulster Rifles, the Oxfordshire and Buckinghamshire Light Infantry, and the Devons. In some other setting their actions might have reminded you of some nursery game. One section would rise up and go forward like Indian bush fighters. They'd be covered by fire from the rest. Then another section went forward in the same way until all the platoons had worked their way in a converging movement on to the bridge that was one of their objectives.

'It really is an occasion, to watch these airborne troops fight. When they first come out of their gliders, with magazines blazing, to fight for their landing zone it's more or less of a scramble, but from then on their operations are cold – deadly methodical.'

STANLEY MAXTED

Some German pockets near the river continued to resist, but they were unable to prevent a firm link-up between the airborne and ground troops on the first day. The first stage of the crossing had been an unqualified success; and for this much credit was due to the ferry services carrying reinforcements of men and material in the wake of the first assault landings. In some American sectors the US Navy ran a cross-river service: behind the US Third Army, which had crossed the Rhine farther south, a correspondent watched US Navy officers piloting their special craft along the roads:

25 March 1945

'This was the first time the American Navy had gone into action 200 miles from the nearest ocean, and the job of these small power craft – all manned by men who've had experience of every amphibious landing from North Africa to Normandy – was to make a quick build-up of men, weapons, ammunition and supplies across the Rhine, in support of the first assault troops to get over. As I motored up to the jump-off point I almost rubbed my eyes, and wondered whether or not I was beginning to see things when we suddenly came up to the tail end of a convoy of landing-craft with USN painted on their bulwarks, and with their crews leaning over the side waving down at us as we passed. It was one of the strangest sights imaginable: these grey-painted craft looking like leviathans cradled on huge trailers. And a ticklish job it was getting them through some of those old German towns and villages with their narrow winding streets. Roadblocks had to be demolished by bulldozers working ahead of them, and in one town, where there was a particularly awkward corner to navigate, the corner house had to be blown down with a charge of explosive. Some idea of the size of this job can be appreciated when I tell you that an LCM – Landing Craft Mechanised – on its carrier is seventy-seven feet long, fourteen feet wide, and nearly twenty feet high. Yet these mammoth convoys had been brought for hundreds of miles over shell-pitted roads and makeshift bridges without the Germans knowing a thing about it.'

ROBERT REID

As the tide of battle passed swiftly beyond the east bank, engineers got to work building bridges to augment the flow of supplies which were already streaming across in 'Buffaloes' and 'Ducks', on rafts and on barges:

25 March 1945

'The Rhine this morning was a very different river from the sinister, mortar-splashed flood over which I had made the assault crossing only a day ago. I went over today at a point where we've got the enemy cleared well back from the bank; the stream ran sparkling under the warm spring sunshine, and the ferries were plying briskly to and fro, Buffaloes were ploughing across against the current, and downstream the Engineers had already got a long bridge in position. Bulldozers were making new approach ways to the bank, and all along the river meadows great assembly areas were marked out with white tape for the lines of guns and lorries and troop carriers making their way down to the crossing. The crossing is a going concern all right, and there was any amount of stuff going over. And once on the other bank you

375

do get a feeling of being well over this last barrier before the heart of Germany. For this bridgehead isn't a mere toe-hold on the other bank; you can now drive well inland, past the riverside farms, most of them pretty smashed up by our artillery fire and all with white flags hanging out of the few remaining windows. And then up into the belt of woodland, where we first contacted the parachute division. The wood was full of our parachutists, digging in, and beyond the wood that fantastic coloured landscape you always get after a big airborne landing, with parachutes dangling from the trees, green parachutes, yellow parachutes, and containers scattered over the fields, gliders flung broadcast over the ploughed land. It looked as if a gigantic litter basket had been emptied over the whole countryside. And, in the middle of the litter, small groups of cowed and completely bewildered civilians were gathered at nearly every farmhouse. They were listening patiently while they were lectured by a paratrooper on how they were to behave in future. They were giving no trouble, there were no desperate guerrilla fighters in this lot, they were only too eager to obey. And they didn't even look up as the long lines of tanks and guns came through the woods to join the paratroops. For in this section our link-up with the airborne landing is no narrow corridor, it's complete and the front is united. And all the way in from the river bank the roads are full of new troops coming up, and infantry marching through the dust, and the farmhouses being taken over as headquarters, ration dumps being set up in the fields. All the signs of the army moving in, in a big way.'

WYNFORD VAUGHAN-THOMAS

A satisfied spectator of this scene was the Prime Minister, who visited the bridgehead within forty-eight hours of the first assault:

25 March 1945

'In warm, brilliant sunshine this afternoon the Prime Minister, Mr Churchill, basked on his balcony overlooking the Rhine and discussed casually with General Eisenhower and Field-Marshal Montgomery just how the Ninth Army bridgehead had been established. Downstream he could see the town of Wesel which the British Commandos had just completely cleared. Through his binoculars the Prime Minister was inspecting the bridgehead just across the slow-flowing Rhine, when quite suddenly he decided to cross. Our planes were still pounding the German positions across the river when Mr Churchill walked down to the river's edge and got into a landing-craft. With him went Sir Alan Brooke, Chief of the Imperial General Staff, Field-Marshal Montgomery, General Omar Bradley, and General Simpson, Commander of the Ninth Army which had forced the river at this point. We cruised across the Rhine in the tracks of the infantry, and the Prime Minister scrambled up the gravel bank on the other side along the same narrow wired path that the infantry had used, and scaled a high earth dike to get a good view. He studied the bridgehead and discussed the morning's battle with the American generals and then he decided to have a short cruise on the Rhine. It was his first cruise on the Rhine since he sailed it in a motor torpedo boat at the end of the last war. After the short cruise, the landing-craft turned back to shore. The Prime Minister went to Wesel along the river road. At the approach to the great steel and concrete Wesel bridge (the one the Germans destroyed when they retreated across the river) the cavalcade of staff cars halted and the Prime Minister got out. Leaving the party, he found a path through the debris, and climbed up on to the first span of the wrecked bridge. The ruins of Wesel were just across the water, and the sound of machine-gun and rifle fire was still coming up spasmodically from the town. Through binoculars the Prime Minister watched the crouching infantry moving through the streets, while

Field-Marshal Montgomery explained how the British assault had been made.'

ROBERT BARR

∽∞∼

The vast conglomeration of men, of weapons, of every sort of equipment – with the British Prime Minister added as a *bonne bouche* – must have been one of the most tempting targets ever offered to any air force. The complete impotence of the Luftwaffe was signally demonstrated by the failure to respond to this opportunity: they had been well 'taken care of beforehand:

26 March 1945

'The bombers of the United States Eighth Air Force began it four days before the battle with attacks so heavy that the Germans didn't try to repair the runways, but started making new ones on adjacent ground. Next day the American bombers gave their attention to the group of bases near Frankfurt, just to make sure. Then on the day the battle opened the heavies poured in again: fifteen hundred of them were allotted to the task. The request from the tactical side was that they should attack seven specified air bases, and that they duly did, but they added eleven more to their list of targets. Once again – just to make sure. Those eighteen aerodromes included every base within 150 miles of the battle from which jet aircraft were known to operate. Meanwhile two other measures for barring the German Air Force were being applied. From dawn onwards British fighters mounted guard over the nearer German aerodromes. American fighters of the Eighth Air Force swept outwards beyond that to a depth of more than a hundred miles. These two banks of fighters had orders to attack anything that tried to get into the air and anything they met in the air. The Americans in the outfield sighted about a hundred in two parties and shot down fifty-two. The British sighted none until evening, and then chased five jet aircraft away. The British fighters on duty over the battlefield never caught sight of an enemy aeroplane all day. The Luftwaffe was held at arm's length. And even now when the big bombers are back at their normal duties the German aircraft find themselves almost as firmly held.'

COLSTON SHEPHERD

CHAPTER XVII
The Great Offensive

'Man, we really have some stuff'

As in Normandy, the next step after the establishing of a bridgehead was to build up sufficient strength to deal with an enemy counter-attack. Constant air patrols and the fire of artillery secretly dug in beforehand close to the river curtailed German counter-attacks. The airborne landings gave the bridgehead depth, and within eighty-four hours the engineers had eight bridges carrying traffic across the Rhine:

29 March 1945

'Masses of material have been flooding across the Rhine for days now – streams of armoured vehicles, fantastic piles of ammunition, hundreds upon hundreds of guns – there goes a truck now with a blood-bank; it's followed by a Red Cross ambulance, then a jeep, then two DRs, now a bulldozer making its way across – every conceivable kind of supply that is necessary to put the finishing touches to what is left of Germany. At this particular point we're in the midst of a traffic-cop's dream – it's one of those traffic jams, however, that does not annoy you one little bit. Tanks, leaving their steel autographs in the mud on our side of the river just before they slide across the bridge, are literally nosing each other to the other side of the Rhine. Most of the vehicles still have their names scrawled on their armour plate and on the fenders, but the fashion's changed somewhat – gone are the favourite French names of Annette, Charmaine, Mariette, and others; there's even a dearth of English names. One going by now has scrawled across the front "And you'd never have thought it would happen!" There's an armoured car – it's got "Rhine Ferry – No Charge, No Sandwiches and No Risk!" Another, more to the point – "Montgomery Express, London to Berlin". And these names certainly appear to indicate the spirit of the tank crews and everyone crossing the river.

'I had hardly put the nose of the car down towards the start of the bridge when an English policeman bellowed: "Come on, mate! Flat out across that bridge!" Halfway across the river another Red Cap shouted even louder, "Come on, mate. You're holding traffic up. Show a pace, show a pace!" By the time we reached the far side of the river we seemed to be flying. And what was so strange – particularly for British policemen – was that the Military Policeman on the far side just smiled and waved us on, up on to the far bank. Standing on the bank of the Rhine, one can look down on one of the great sights of the war. Stretched across the bridge, and as far as the eye could see, were hundreds of tanks, lorries, carriers, bulldozers, ammo wagons, vehicles of every conceivable type, flooding across the river. Overhead, squadrons of Spitfires, Typhoons, Tempests and Mustangs took their turn in patrolling – giving constant protection to our ground forces, just in case the Luftwaffe should dare interfere.'

STEWART MACPHERSON

30 March 1945

'During the last two days I have seen for myself one of the most astonishing sights of the war – I watched an indescribable flood of vital material being rushed along every single road and lane that leads to the forward areas. The Royal Army Service Corps and other units have done a magnificent job in feeding the troops and the armour with the necessities of an all-out gigantic attack. Yesterday afternoon I watched fearsome-looking twelve-wheeled lorries – they just looked like Canadian railway freight cars – thundering their way along the road bringing up petrol. Reaching their destination these lorries are unloaded at a blistering pace, quickly turned round, and back they go for more. They make long hauls, but as soon as they are back at base, fresh drivers are ready to wheel them back again as soon as they are reloaded.

'I watched countless tank conveyers – those rumbling, clattering machines whose very presence makes you think there is a great fleet of heavy bombers rushing at you, they make such a noise – pounding their way along the road bringing up tanks by the score. Twenty minutes later, going back from the front on another road, I saw just as many conveyers on the return trip for many more tanks. We are using every available road and lane to carry our supplies forward. Some of them are not a motorist's dream – but we have that in hand too. All along the main roads are hundreds of men whose only combat weapon is a shovel or a pick – but they are just as important as a tank, machine-gun or mortar, for it is these men who are keeping the road passable.

'On the eve of the Rhine crossing we had tremendous stores of ammunition and supplies right up to the river front. These great reloading points and supply dumps have now moved forward and in most cases are just as close to the fighting troops as they ever were.

'We have a constant watch on all our bridges to make certain they are standing up to the terrific strain being imposed on them by the never-ending stream of supplies that is flooding across the Rhine. It is a common sight to see a sapper – some of them sporting a new spring fashion, a brilliant yellow life-jacket wrapped around the khaki uniform – walking up and down the length of a bridge with a spanner and hammer, keeping an eagle eye open for any signs of wear or tear on the many bridges.

'No. I don't think that those responsible for keeping our supplies up to scratch have missed one solitary trick. As one soldier said as he

watched the endless convoys rushing up to the east side of the river:
"Man, we really have some stuff." '

STEWART MACPHERSON

At the end of a week Montgomery had 2000 tanks and self-propelled
guns across the Rhine – equivalent to half a dozen armoured divisions,
more than he had ever before employed simultaneously, in one battle.
In spite of tough fighting north of the bridgehead, our armoured
columns went through a thirty-mile gap and advanced sixty-five miles
in a week:

29 March 1945

'Away to the north we can still hear our guns hammering at the
enemy because here he is resisting strongly with tough troops and
trying desperately to hang on to some sort of defence line. But on
our road we have had little facing us; in fact, the resistance has been
so light that we've been able to push tanks and guns right ahead. I
tried to get up to them but once tanks are on the move it's the most
difficult job in the world to keep pace.

'One of the liaison officers, coming up from the rear to find
Brigade, went gaily driving down the road until he arrived at a small
village. He could see no one about, and so he decided that Brigade
must be still farther up the road. So he called up on his radio and gave
his position. "I'm at 'Pineapple'" – "Pineapple" being one of those
delightfully incongruous names that the Army tends to use to denote
its objective. "Pineapple," came the reply, "that's not yet taken." The
officer radioed back, "Well, it's taken now, so come on in and get it."
That's the sort of thing that's going on now all the way ahead of us, and
the tanks are driving through a countryside of big red-bricked farms,
and all with white flags hanging out of the windows, and scattered

woodlands in which the farmers and their families have hidden in rough dugouts. Dugouts to which they fled when they heard the fury of our barrage forcing the passage of the Rhine. Now they're drifting back to their farms, looking on in open-eyed wonder at the immense stream of tanks and guns that are this morning plunging deeper and deeper into the heart of Germany. The brigadier had his map set out in the open, with his armoured cars grouped around it. His officers were marking up the lines of our future advance. I said, "Well, we'll be up to see you again tomorrow. Where will you be?" "Where will we be?" he said. "Well, you just keep following up this road, we'll be a long way up it by the time you come back." '

WYNFORD VAUGHAN-THOMAS

Along with the armour, somehow keeping pace with it and at times outstripping it, went the British 6th Airborne Division – 'organising' their own transport on the way:

29 March 1945
'They're trained for this kind of footloose fighting on a fluid front, and they thrive on it. At one point yesterday afternoon they struck quite a strong German position blocking the road, and three tanks of the Airborne Reconnaissance Regiment were soon knocked out. Undismayed, the paratroops worked round through the woods, waited for dusk, and then stormed the guns that had held them up. They captured two 75s and four light ack-ack guns and their crews.

'Yesterday and last night, as they beat through the woods, they came upon half a dozen self-propelled guns. They ambushed two of them and knocked them out with anti-tank bombs. They captured four others intact, two of these with the crews still sleeping inside.

'I saw some of their captured armour on the road today. They had pressed it into service and had found scratch crews from among their own paratroops. The SP guns had joined the strange convoy of airborne forces on the road eastwards today. The airborne troops are always short of transport. They can't bring much with them, and they rely on capturing vehicles from the enemy. And now the 6th Airborne has a fine assortment. As I drove along, I passed men on German bicycles, in Volkswagens, in farm-carts drawn by draught horses. One man had a smart jinker, and another was driving a German bulldozer towing a German trailer. Some of the troops were carrying their ammunition and packs in little handcarts they had found on farms, and some were even pushing their equipment in perambulators.'

CHESTER WILMOT

As our foremost spearheads pressed into the Westphalian Plain they passed through undamaged villages where the inhabitants stood watching in astonishment and apparently in relief at their easy exit from the war. Now, too, began the heartening spectacle of Allied prisoners and enslaved workers cheering our troops and moving westwards to freedom:

30 March 1945
'Today I've been with our armour east of the Rhine; roaming over the rolling farmlands of Germany's great north-western plain. The leading armour is now far beyond the area which was slashed and torn by our shellfire. We've left behind that belt of Germany where every village was in ruins, every house had its scars of shell or bullet, every field was pitted with craters or scored with tank tracks. Today we drove for mile after mile, past farms where the peasants were still working in the fields, through villages where women were doing their

washing or tending their gardens; they hadn't felt the shock of battle. And the almost peaceful way our tanks had arrived was a surprise relief.

'When they heard our tanks approaching most of them had gone to their shelters and left their white flags fluttering outside. But when they heard little or no firing, they soon came out to watch. We saw them standing by the roadside, with their white flags in their hands, and soon, as the traffic streamed by, the Germans began waving and smiling. They didn't get any encouragement from the passing troops, but they continued to stand there and wave . . . not really in welcome but as an expression of their relief that the war for them was over and that the battle had swept past them so quickly and so painlessly. But even so, it was strange to drive past and see the Germans waving.

'In some of the villages and along most of the roads there were other people who were waving in real welcome. They were foreign workers and prisoners-of-war who had been liberated at last. Today we passed hundreds of them: Frenchmen, Belgians, Poles, Czechs, and Russians. You could pick the prisoners out because most of them still wore tattered uniforms of their own armies. They said they'd been working on the nearby farms for years. Yesterday they'd still been working there, but this morning when they saw the British tanks go by they had packed up their belongings, and now they were heading westwards. For the Frenchmen and Belgians this was homewards as well.

'To speed their movement many of them had borrowed German bicycles or handcarts, and so they made their way in little groups, waving to the passing convoys. For the first time in years they were walking as free men.'

CHESTER WILMOT

386

Farther south, it was the same story. Crossing near Koblenz, Patton's famous 4th Armoured Division was off again hot-foot. In four days they had reached Frankfurt and swept on beyond it:

26 March 1945

'This promises to be the biggest rat race in history. The 4th Armoured Division simply cannot be held back. They race on in a drive which has already outstripped all previous achievements. They are just riding down everything in their path, and haring on so quickly that urgent messages have had to go back by radio from the leading tanks, asking for somebody else to take care of the mounting army of German prisoners who are left sitting by the roadside. The 4th is too busy with other things. Today they captured fifty locomotives and 700 railcars loaded with brand-new gear: half-track vehicles, ordnance, equipment, clothing, weapons, and bombs.

'Single German tanks occasionally put their noses out of the woods, but they soon get knocked off either by our tanks or by supporting aircraft. And this afternoon a laconic message was flashed back to the rear from the spearhead of a column saying, "Backbone of resistance shattered."

'All told, the 4th Armoured Division has covered forty road miles in eighteen hours. Opposition has been mostly light. The 90th Infantry Division reported that some civilians had attacked them at one spot, and orders have been issued to the troops that all German civilians found firing at our forces are to be shot on the spot. In the early stages of the crossing the Germans made one big effort to stem the tide of our advance by throwing in 900 students from an officer cadet school in a counter-attack. This force was cut up. Five hundred of the students were taken prisoner, and 200 were killed. At one point the Frankfurt police were also thrown in as infantry.

'Everything points to hopeless confusion ahead. The roads in front of us are jammed with German Army traffic attempting to escape eastwards. It is being attacked all the time by our fighter-bombers. Indeed a mass withdrawal is indicated by the fact that on the railway between Frankfurt and Giessen three eastbound trains were attacked within five miles of each other. They were all on the same track, pelting east as hard as they could go.'

ROBERT REID

30 March 1945

'The most significant thing about the operations of the last three great days on this part of the Western Front has been, not the vast areas captured or the amazing depth of our penetration beyond the Rhine, but the complete failure of the Germans to raise any organised opposition. General Hodges and General Patton have been able to send out their armoured columns swarming all over the map, almost on motor drives. There's been literally nothing worth talking about to stop them. A few roadblocks have been lightly defended, many not held at all. Again and again important bridges have been allowed to fall into our hands; very few mines have been laid in our path – the German troops have had no time and perhaps no heart to plant them. The occasional sniper along the way has soon been taught that that sort of thing doesn't pay. German supply dumps, ordnance stores, field hospitals, workshops and rear installations have fallen into our hands, just there for the taking. The feeble forces sent to meet our columns have arrived without their artillery, without their tanks and SP guns which have run out of petrol far back along the road, without their motor transport which has been shot up from the air and shelled from the ground; they've arrived just with their small arms, and realising that to put up any fight would simply invite a massacre, they've surrendered. Prisoners counted so far in this one week total over 70,000. Many thousands remain to be passed through the prisoner camps. During this period the First Army alone has liberated 4360 Allied soldiers. It will take months to count the booty which has fallen into our hands; two complete motor-vehicle plants have been captured; six solid miles of railway trucks have been seized, large numbers of them loaded with truck and tank engines.

'Five loading docks were taken on the Rhine; bituminous coal mines were captured in the northern sector and a total of 82,000 tons of coal. And among industrial plants we've taken a chemical-manufacturing centre, textile mills, leather works, an ordnance plant, a tyre-recovering plant, and a projectile plant. Thirty-eight railcars full of machine tools were captured; huge quantities of ammunition and signalling equipment, and medical stores, also came into our hands. All this was achieved at amazingly little cost. The greatest number of American troops killed in the entire Army Group in a single day numbered 141. On one day, we lost only fifty-five men from the whole of the First and Third Armies. Nothing could show more clearly than these figures the extent of the German collapse on this sector of the Western Front.'

FRANK GILLARD

South of the Ruhr, Patton's tanks were running wild. The Ruhr itself was rapidly being encircled in a great enveloping movement by the US First and Ninth Armies. To the north British armour of the 11th Armoured Division succeeded in smashing the potentially formidable defence position of the Dortmund-Ems Canal and the Teutoburger Wald:

2 April 1945

'Last Saturday evening, just at dusk, tanks of the 3rd Royal Tank Regiment reached the Dortmund-Ems Canal, the line on which the

Germans were expected to make their next stand. Our tanks had orders to seize a bridge, but as they got within striking range of the canal half a dozen white Very lights shot up into the sky. On this signal German engineers somewhere on the far bank pressed the switches that led to the high-explosive charges in half a dozen bridges; and up the bridges went. But our orders were that if the tanks couldn't get a bridge, the infantry of the KSLI, the King's Shropshire Light Infantry, who were following close behind, were to get across the canal as best they could and hold a bridgehead on the far side.

'They had no storm boats and the canal at high water is forty yards wide. But when they reached it well after dark they found that the RAF had prepared the way for them; because our bombing had breached the banks farther up, the water-level was only three feet instead of the twenty they'd expected. At one point they found a huge barge was aground, and what's more had swung round so that it lay across the canal forming almost a ready-made footbridge.

'Along this barge the KSLI scrambled across. But they hadn't gone far beyond the bank when they ran into some difficult customers – some young Germans who'd just been sent up from an NCOs' training school in Hanover, where they'd been training to become sergeant-majors and warrant officers. Our troops soon found that these young Germans were as tough as sergeant-majors in any army are usually reputed to be.

'The Germans moreover had an ideal defensive position. The canal here runs under the lee of a thickly wooded ridge that rises sharply and dominates the whole area. This ridge is part of the famous Teutoburger Wald where the Germans in the past have stopped so many invaders, including Charlemagne. Our infantry soon found they couldn't get on and might even be in danger of being forced back if they couldn't get some heavy weapons across the bridgeless canal that night. The Engineers came to the rescue. Near the barge, where the water was shallow, the canal runs between two high embankments. With an armoured bulldozer, the Engineers pushed these embankments into the bed of the canal, and within a few hours that night they had the tanks across.

'The tanks also towed over some guns, and with this double support the KSLI were able to hold the enemy off all yesterday, while Engineers built a bridge over the canal behind them. This was no easy task for the bridgehead was under fire and it even drew on itself an attack from the Luftwaffe. The bridge was nearly finished when some German fighter-bombers came over, and they put one bomb less than twenty yards from the bridge where the Engineers were still working; but the bomb stuck in the mud.

'With this bridge in action we soon had more troops and tanks across, but the German NCOs on the timbered ridge couldn't be shifted easily. Last night and today infantry of the 11th Armoured Division have been beating through these woods, having almost to drive the Germans from tree to tree; and while the NCOs held out here, some of our reconnaissance tanks got through along the main road. There they forced a passage up a narrow defile that was defended by a second-rate reinforcement battalion. By getting round this way, they reached the top of the ridge, swung round behind the German NCO battalion, and when I left the front this afternoon its defence was cracking under this sandwich attack.

'Meantime, having opened up the road up the escarpment, the 11th Armoured Division was pushing on, rolling up the defence of the bridge by attacks on the flank. At one town they reported they were having some trouble with civilians. Presumably the SS police had been sent into this town also to make the people fight. But now, having broken out on to the plateau behind the Teutoburger Wald, the 11th Armoured is barely twelve miles from Osnabrück. Today's battle yielded them even more than that. Hidden on that wooded ridge they found one of Germany's great secret oil refineries. The loss of this refinery at this stage of the war is probably almost as serious for the Germans as the loss of the Dortmund-Ems Canal.'

CHESTER WILMOT

An American correspondent, pursuing the British spearheads, caught up with them as the attack on Osnabrück was being launched:

5 April 1945

'You jeep and jeep until you feel your kidneys are jarred loose from their brackets and you pass through one undamaged village after another, punctuated occasionally by a complete mess of a town that happened to be a railroad junction, or which was unfortunate enough to offer resistance to our advance. Then, as you get closer to the front, you notice the soldiers sitting cheerfully in convoys, or a lot of horseplay in the fields, for everyone is in high spirits these days, and you keep a weather eye out for headquarters. But somehow you miss it; but you keep on driving anyway. Occasionally in the distance your own artillery may let loose a barrage to remind you that there still is fighting ahead. But no one pays any attention, including the civilians of this particularly unspoilt bit of Germany. The people smile, and sometimes wave, and the girls mostly just smile. It's hard not to pay any attention to that – ask any soldier.

'You drive on, stopped occasionally by a road jam. It's April, and the spring showers seem to dampen no one's spirits. Then you drive over a hill a mile or so from Osnabrück. More serious-looking soldiers are sitting on tanks, with bayoneted rifles. The sun happens to be shining, and you see one of them asleep. Suddenly, from beyond an ineffective German roadblock not fifty feet away, an unholy splutter of machine-gun fire gushes out towards a factory building sitting in

392

the valley. Then a tank's heavy gun barks with a ferocity that echoes through the forest. Then it's quiet, and you wait for the enemy's return fire. But there is none.

'A British paratrooper lieutenant walks up to the tank with the men sitting atop it. He yawns, and stretches. "You chaps get ready," he says, "we'll be moving up pretty soon." But he says it with the air of a man with spring fever, who didn't care when, if ever. As I left, the column started rolling into the town.

'Apparently the British do this sort of thing with that careless unconcerned air all the time.'

BILL DOWNS, CBS

CHAPTER XVIII
Swanning
'Vee hev had it'

The technique of swift motorised advance, first exploited by the Germans in 1940, reached its apotheosis in the closing weeks of the war. Individual German units fought back stubbornly in some places, and occasionally civilians – including women – fired from their houses at passing tanks; but over the whole front the German Army had deteriorated beyond the point where it could cope with our armoured columns, which either shot up or bypassed the sort of opposition that was offered:

7 April 1945
'Our armour is now "swanning" as they say in the British Army, or, in American parlance, "the rat race is on". "Swanning" means that our tanks are having an almost free run, and it's the strangest possible experience to follow in their wake. To begin with, an armoured drive doesn't fan out over the countryside, it goes straight on down one or two parallel roads and it can bypass a town like Osnabrück, leaving other units to mop it up, and the leading tanks can push on perhaps fifteen or twenty miles beyond. And in between the armoured thrusts, you can have whole tracts of the countryside to the north and the south of the roads on which you're moving completely unvisited by even our reconnaissance elements. Of course, you can only "swan" when the enemy's front has been utterly broken, and when he has no reserves left to push in on your flank and nip off the heads of your armoured columns. That's just the situation now, between Osnabrück and the Weser.'

WYNFORD VAUGHAN-THOMAS

9 April 1945

'Out on the flanks of our advance go our recce cars. Their job is not so much to fight as to find out where the enemy is, and they keep watching the side roads while the regimental group is pushing up the main axis, the road we've chosen for our advance. This group has in the lead perhaps a squadron, perhaps two, of tanks; and with a squadron, sometimes actually riding on the tanks or else carried in their own carriers, are the infantrymen of the armoured division, specially trained to work with the tanks. The tanks of the regimental group headquarters follow close behind, and not so very far behind them come the guns of the group, mobile 25-pounders. There's a gunnery officer up with the forward elements ready to call up his guns by radio the moment they are needed. So the forward tanks start up the road. When you watch them as I did from a hill overlooking the whole seemingly deserted countryside, they seem to probe and stop and hesitate around corners, moving by little fits and starts, for being in the lead tank is one of this war's most uncomfortable jobs. The officer in that lead tank has got to make absolutely certain, before he moves, that the house up the road, say, is not hiding an anti-tank gun, or that the woods on either side do not contain foxholes with the Germans manning bazookas. If all is clear, then he radioes down the line, and the column moves on to its next bound. But if the enemy opens up, then the flexible structure of the regimental group allows the commander to decide exactly how he should deal with the opposition. It may be that it's only a small and extremely frightened flak unit firing one round for form's sake before surrendering. The tanks can deal with that roadblock by blasting away at it. But the defenders may be made of sterner stuff. Then the infantry may have to dismount and work around the roadblock to outflank it, while tanks and the 25-pounders give them fire support. The regimental group can in some cases call up our fighter-bombers to hit the strong-point before they move to the attack. And it may take an hour or so. Small-scale fighting, but nevertheless, to the men who take part in it, hard fighting, before the roadblock is smashed and the spearhead probes forward again. So when you watch it on the ground, our advance seems no wild race, but rather a series of little actions fought along the road, as I said, almost in fits and starts.'

WYNFORD VAUGHAN-THOMAS

7 April 1945

'Our 11th Armoured Division, with the 6th Airborne on its southern flank, has raced down the main roads from Osnabrück towards the River Weser. As they went they threw out little parties to form roadblocks on the side roads to the north and south of them, just in case any stray Germans should come in on the flank. And the airborne boys travel in the most varied collection of transport I've yet seen, in fact they can't call themselves airborne any longer, they're either lorry-borne or tank-borne, motor-bike-borne, even cart-borne infantry.

'The Germans have little before us now to stop our racing columns. They rushed some units up, but their trouble is that they're at least twenty-four hours behind in their information. One of our columns bumped into a regiment that had come down from Denmark. Apparently these Germans were on their way to defend Osnabrück, oblivious of the fact that it had already fallen days before. We caught one battalion of it just as it was moving into billets in a small village. Well, those Germans are now billeted in our prison cages.

'But speed brings with it its own problems. Apart from that ever-present nightmare of supply, how to get the petrol and the food up to our leading tanks, there are one or two other headaches for our Army. There's the problem of the prisoners, for example. What on earth are you to do with these thousands upon thousands of shabbily uniformed, middle-aged, and undersized warriors that are all the

High Command has got left with which to try and stop our armies. For now we really are coming to the bottom of the bag. The German manpower is exhausted. One officer told me yesterday that he went into a house to requisition billets and he found it occupied by five families. Out of those five families, twenty men – sons and husbands – had been killed. But here are the survivors of warfare, cluttering up the roads and offering to give themselves up to the first person who will have them. It's difficult for an armoured division to begin to cope with them. Our tanks have got to get on and our lorries are wanted to bring up supplies. The only thing to do with the prisoners is to disarm them and send them off to the rear. And with an advance as fast as ours the rear may be sixty miles away. These are just the ordinary spectacles – miles behind the line, long columns of prisoners, sometimes led by their officers, quietly tramping along in the middle of our back areas. And with nobody paying the slightest attention to them. And with none of them making the slightest effort to escape.

'I'll say this for them. They're the most polite and the most helpful lot of prisoners I've ever seen. One gentleman who spoke reasonable English stopped me on the road and inquired, "Please. Where is your prison?" I told him it was about twenty miles to the rear. And then he said, "Oh but please! That is too far. You have not got one a little nearer?" I told him that if he waited a few days we'd have one right on his doorstep. But the irony was lost on him. All he said was: "Good. Now I will tell my friends. They're all so tired too." And off he went into a wood to fetch out twenty more extremely shabby supermen who meekly lined up and awaited orders.

'But if the prisoners are a nuisance, the civilians are also in the way. By mistake we got off the road and entered a little town called Iburg; it's miles to the rear of our forward tanks. And we found that we were the first car that had bothered to stop there. Well, all we wanted to do was to ask the way. But the town wanted to surrender and was almost indignant when we wouldn't accept it. A citizen came out and explained that he'd seen to it personally that every house had had its clean white flag. We saw a young girl carrying two rifles and a bayonet. For a moment, we thought we'd at last met that rare phenomenon – the genuine German guerrilla fighter. And we prepared to sell our lives dearly. But there was no need; the Hitler maiden stopped and explained that she was taking the guns immediately to the burgomaster. No one in that town was going to fire them. We had the greatest difficulty in escaping from the burgomaster himself. He, it appears, was waiting patiently in his office to obey our orders. What are you to think of these fantastic people?'

WYNFORD VAUGHAN-THOMAS

Behind the armoured columns came the supply and communications services, working at high pressure to ensure that the advance was not slowed down by any defect of organisation. Ahead went a complex fighting machine that had to be maintained in all its elaborate detail; up the roads in the rear travelled a great procession of every sort of vehicle:

5 April 1945

'This is the road into the Reich – the most exciting and impressive sight you could hope to see east of the Rhine. We pulled our recording truck off the road for a moment because without pause, almost bumper to bumper, our immense supply columns have gone racing past. Tank conveyers; petrol lorries; jeeps and trailers. Bulldozers carrying great trucks. Everything is moving at speed. For although here we are over fifty miles beyond the Rhine, this is now a back area. And we're way behind our forward tanks. With these supply columns, to catch up with them means that they drive day and night. Headlights full on.

And all along the road the Military Police have posted up notices on the trees: "Hurry with the Supplies", and: "You Will Drive with your Headlights On". So now rolling past us goes this astonishing spectacle of the power and weight of the Second British Army. And it's only when you stop for a moment and look at it going by from the sideline, as we're doing now, that you realise exactly how much power we've got. It's overwhelming.'

WYNFORD VAUGHAN-THOMAS

5 April 1945

'The corridors opened up during these advances are often no wider than the roads along which our columns move; often enough the German defending forces close in again behind our troops and cut them off in the rear. To attempt to chase in a jeep after such a column is to invite disaster, for somewhere or other along the road down which our tanks have passed you're certain to run into a group of Germans hurriedly rushed up to seal off our armoured spearhead. Every day we lose men and vehicles; sometimes quite a few vehicles at a time, in ambushes of this kind. The total number of vehicles lost in this fashion over the last few weeks must be considerable. We have to pay for the chances we take, but the results we gain make the price a cheap one.

'If supplies have to go up to these armoured spearheads we follow naval practice and send escorted convoys through with them. Instead of the merchantmen of the sea we have here three-ton trucks; and instead of the protective screen of destroyers and frigates we have fast-moving armoured cars and light tanks. Every third or fourth vehicle in the convoy has a bite to it – something which can take good care of enemy guns and snipers now closing in along the roads. And, of course, the fighter-bombers cover the convoy overhead, seeking out and dealing with enemy opposition before it can become really serious. Quite often we lose a truck or two in such a convoy, but the great bulk of the supplies get through.

'Meanwhile, while their supplies are coming up and while their motorised infantry are mopping up behind them, the spearheads up ahead are fanning out from their original objectives deep in the enemy's rear, generally playing havoc with the German communication and supply system and rapidly loosening the enemy's grip on the entire territory. They create such chaos that the German troops through whom they've just driven a corridor are thrown into utter confusion; the Germans just don't know what's going on; they can get no orders, no information, no supplies; they are, in fact, ripe for mopping up.'

FRANK GILLARD

Considerable risks and long hours were the lot of the transport men. The signalmen too worked until they were exhausted, to keep pace with the advance:

5 April 1945

'I've just returned from an unsuccessful attempt to try and catch up with some of General Patton's tanks now thrusting deep into the heart of Germany, but after jeeping for five hours without catching even a glimpse of them I gave up the chase. Jeeps cannot compete with Third Army tank columns on the loose.

'This is surely the fastest advance in the history of war – an advance where divisional command posts make big jumps forward two or three times a day, which is some indication of the way things are going out here. And if the burden of the fighting is thrown on the shoulders of the tank men and the doughboys who are racing behind them in trucks to take over the towns they've overrun, the bigger burden of keeping the army commanders behind in touch with every move in this swift game is falling on the shoulders of the tireless signal corps men – the wire-stringers who are performing incredible feats of sheer endurance in keeping open the lines of communication. All day long, out on those roads on the east bank of the Rhine, I've watched fleets of small trucks spewing out cable behind them – cable which runs through the leather-gloved hands of the wire-stringers, mile after mile of wire which in a short time will be carrying vital orders. Signal corps sections are working in leap-frogging movements along these roads, dozens of teams wiring up long stretches of road all at the same time, then quickly linking up each section: German facilities are commandeered and used wherever possible. These wire-stringers are giving everything they've got to get the job done. An eighteen-hour day is commonplace. Some of them have worked right round the clock, spurred on by the excitement and the knowledge that theirs is a vital job. And here and there along those roads I came across wire-stringers who'd just finished, dead to the world, sprawling fast asleep, undisturbed by the thunder of passing trucks and clouds of dust.'

ROBERT REID

And the correspondents, trying to catch up with where the news was, nearly wore out their jeeps in driving through endless miles of the German countryside:

12 April 1945

'We live in the jeep, we drive as much as 200 miles forward to get a story, and after an hour up there we have to come back 200 miles to get the story out. And the jeep is a tough, rough little mustang; but fortunately, after years of this, we're getting calloused in the right places. These long rides are always exciting, exhilarating.

'You start out for the front. On a fixed battlefront you can drive from Army Headquarters to the front line in an hour. But now you leave Army and pass the Corps Headquarters and the traffic thins out. And then you're driving through miles and miles of villages and forest and farmland, where there's not an army vehicle to be seen. You race along a lonely forest road, alert, uncomfortable. The fighting units have gone through, but you may be ambushed by paratroopers or sniped at. You round a corner and see two or three German soldiers, your heart stops, and you see they have their hands in the air. They're asking to surrender, but you can't be bothered with prisoners and on you go. I've never been sniped at yet, I've never met a hobgoblin or a werewolf, but I always sigh with relief when I see some of our own vehicles and find myself among soldiers again – our soldiers, and I wish somebody would give me an armoured car. But the great sensation these days is exhilaration. How often we've dreamed of this. In the long dark nights of the London Blitz, in the shelling on the road to Damascus, in the jungles of Burma, in the dreary sandstorms or blinding heat of the Libyan Desert – in the white dust of Sicily, and in the cold bloody winter on the Moro River in Italy. And then in Normandy when it seemed that the SS divisions would never crack, I've looked forward to this day, and now here we go through the ruins of Germany.

'The rich farmlands and pleasant villages of Germany have escaped destruction. Germany's a beautiful country, spacious and massive. You can drive for a hundred miles through open country and forests. You see no obvious need for more *Lebensraum*. It's a clean well-ordered country, the buildings are solid and strong. And you think what a great people the Germans could have been if they hadn't had a demon in them. And to see them now you wouldn't think they had a demon in them. Some of them are grim, but thousands of them want to be friendly. They're obviously glad it's over, and they show no rancour, that's the simple fact of the case. Often we go to a farmhouse and ask for eggs, offering cigarettes or chocolate in exchange, and generally they press us to take more eggs than we ask for. They often offer us cakes and meat. Sometimes, far from home, we have to find a billet for the night. We knock at the door of a German house, they give us rooms and huge beds, with those thick German feather beds. And we sleep in the same house with them, never even thinking of werewolves or knives in the dark. These people want us to like them, but nobody will play ball. What a strange thing this is!

'Your hate rises of course against everything German when you see, as I saw the other day, Dutchmen who had been tortured to death. And it rises again when you see the streams of freed slaves thronging down the roads. This astonishing sight is one we see every day. In the areas we've already overrun in Germany we've liberated over two million of these slaves, chiefly Russian and Polish but also French, Czechs, Yugoslavs, and others. We've seen them in bands of several hundred at a time. They're not always emaciated, starving, ragged. Sometimes you wouldn't know they were slaves, except for their language, and the fact that they're laughing and chattering away, and waving and singing. But I've seen others, hungry, and even barefooted, mad with hate of the Germans, looting shops for food and clothes. What an extraordinary thing this is, in the twentieth century! You see these things and wonder if you're not back in the pages of an historical novel, back in the Thirty Years War. Freed bondsmen – ten or twelve million men and women of Europe have been uprooted by the Germans and enslaved. It makes you hate all right when you question some of them, and women tell you how they were brought from Russia, put up on auction blocks, pawed and mauled by lecherous fat Germans, and sold into slavery. I've seen women on their knees, tears running down their cheeks as British tanks rolled past and they knew they were free. What a story that told, millions of Ruths sick for home, who stood in tears amid the alien corn, and even now many of them will go back and find their homes destroyed and their families dead or gone. Is there any measure for the rivers and tides of sorrows and tears that the Nazis have set flowing in Europe?'

MATTHEW HALTON, CBC

While the massive processions of Allied power moved continuously towards the East, a strange and poignant cavalcade came down the roads in the opposite direction – a ragged motley army, the human loot that Hitler had stolen from the nations he struck down, a wealth of manhood now seeping away and impoverishing the hated land they had been forced to enrich:

22 April 1945
'The basis of German agricultural prosperity was slave labour, and as soon as the Allied armies swept by these prosperous farms, the slaves, very naturally, stopped working. We've opened the floodgates of a dam, and every single person who can get away is off. The roads of Germany today are one of the unforgettable sights of the war. You can walk a few hundred yards from the transmitter from which I'm speaking and you'll see for yourself the wealth of the German farmlands flowing away to the west. There go the farm tractors, towing the German farmers' carts, filled with jubilant Poles or Yugoslavs; there go his farm-horses ridden by Russian prisoners of war, there go his bicycles and his lorries, and his eggs and his chickens and his pigs. This great flood goes steadily on day after day, and now in the semi-deserted fields the German farmer has got to work himself; you see him with his wife and his daughter and the young children, for his sons have long since left for the Army, maybe they'll never be coming back to this farm. You see him working to salvage something

out of the wreck. It's impossible he can salvage enough to feed the townsfolk of Germany, for the labour with which he cultivated these rich fields is gone or is living on his farm as self-invited guests. Yes, the Germans are in for a grim winter. But then, they might have thought of that before they based their agriculture on slave labour.'

WYNFORD VAUGHAN-THOMAS

Between the armoured spearheads and the occupying forces there was often a nebulous military situation in which anything might happen. There were groups of Germans making suicidal ambushes, and others only too anxious to surrender: there were liberated slave-workers intent on loot or revenge, or hurrying westward on the journey home: there were German civilians seeking to have their towns and villages occupied quickly while they were still intact. To drive unarmed through this country was an experience by turns eerie and comic:

20 April 1945

'We drove down an empty road, uncomfortably empty, with no sign of anyone on it. We reached the crossroads, when suddenly out of the woods appeared eight Germans; it was a frightening sight, particularly when I remembered that the only gun we had was the driver's Sten gun, and it was buried under our raincoats, and the bullet clip was somewhere in a corner of the jeep. However, these were very tame Germans, they all had their hands up. We stopped, searched them, and rigged up a white flag for them and told them to march on down the road and somebody would pick them up. That took care of the first eight.

'Sergeant Arthur joined our party. We drove on down a side road, and there we ran on to five more German soldiers, who were waving a white flag. Again we told them which way to go, but this group were more frightened and one of them asked, "What do we say when we want to surrender later?" Sergeant Arthur had the answer; he wrote the words down on a piece of paper. As the prisoners walked off they were practising the phrase "We have had it". It's a British expression used to denote the completion of about anything. As the prisoners walked off, the five of them were muttering "Vee hev had it".

'About that time, another young American flyer rode by on a motor-cycle. He also was an ex-prisoner getting himself some food and fresh air for the first time in months. "There's a town down the road that's just begging to be taken, why don't you go and have a look?" Then about that time he spotted a chicken running across the road and that was the last we saw of him.

'We took the two British boys back to the camp; there I told the story to two BBC engineers who had been with me making recordings at the camps. They were all for taking the town. Again there was kilometre after kilometre of distressingly empty road, but it seemed like a good day for conquering and no one worried particularly. Finally we reached the crossroads village of Hohne just west of the town of Burgen. I knew the traditional way to capture a place and maybe stick a sword in the ground, and proclaim the place was ours, but I had no sword, and besides, it was a beautifully hard road, and no sword would stick in it anyway. But Sergeant Tinker knew what to do – he went in search of eggs – fresh eggs, and meanwhile Sergeant Arthur got interested in the farm across the road. There was a big German Army car – with a white flag flying from it. We went into this farmyard to find out what it was all about and to our surprise up stepped one of the most magnificent German officers I've ever seen, complete with Iron Cross and a number of other decorations. My first-year college German was still intact enough to understand that he wanted to surrender – he had his belongings all packed including a pair of ski shoes – what he wanted with ski shoes I was never able to find out. He turned over his pistol and said that we could drive him back to captivity in his own car. Then the German colonel said that he'd like very much if we would take his entire battery prisoner. He was the commander of a battery of 88-mm combination anti-tank and anti-aircraft guns. We decided against capturing the gun battery for we were not sure that a battery of 88s would appreciate being captured by just one Sten gun, no matter what the colonel said, but we took the colonel up on his offer to use his car. Sergeant Arthur drove the car – Sergeant Tinker reappeared with a cap full of eggs. The colonel climbed in and we made up a convoy – my jeep in front, the colonel's car in the middle with two sergeants, and the BBC truck with the two unarmed engineers bringing up the rear.'

BILL DOWNS, CBS

CHAPTER XIX
Out Of Bondage

'Is Shirley Temple still alive?'

When they advanced up the Channel coast and into Holland our troops had had the satisfaction of knowing that they were freeing, in many cases, their own homes and relatives from the bombardment of flying-bombs and rockets. Now, as they broke into Germany, they began to liberate their brothers-in-arms who had been captured in earlier campaigns. The Stalags and Oflags were broken open, and men who had been in captivity for years came out to freedom again. One of the first to be liberated was a BBC correspondent who had been captured in North Africa:

31 March 1945
'Rumours had been flying around for days about where the American troops were. German trucks returning from the front were continually claiming to have missed capture by minutes. But early on Wednesday afternoon it became plain that the Americans were very close. Our temporary camp was a group of huts out in an open field, with a slag-heap and an arms factory which had long since ceased active production behind it. About three o'clock in the afternoon things began to warm up; shells began to fall ahead of us in the field, and machine-gun fire began to get more and more intense. Soon we could see figures appearing on the horizon. It was decided to evacuate the camp to the German air-raid shelters which were dug deep under the slag-heap. Our German guards no sooner entered the shelters than they unbuckled their arms and threw them in heaps in corners of the

shelter. They'd been a little bit embarrassed about their arms for some time; they thought they wouldn't get a very good reception from the Americans if they were armed. I dumped my belongings in the shelter and went outside. The noise of the battle increased; and then suddenly out of a wood came the American tanks and tracked troop-carriers. Everyone became delirious with excitement.

'"Come on and see the American tanks," I shouted to some Russian girls who'd been working in the station restaurant. "American tanks? Nie vozmozhno!" they cried. "Pas possible," cried the French – but it was possible, it was true. One of the troop-carriers stopped, two men jumped out and came down to the far bank of the Lahn River, which separated us from them. I ran down the steep bank on my side. By the greatest piece of luck there was an old barge tied up there. "How's things over there with you?" the Americans asked. "Fine," I said, "do you want to come across?" "Yeah, can you get that boat over?" "You bet your life I can." And with three others, including the only American POW in the camp, I poled the rickety old craft across. "How are your guards?" the Americans asked when we were about in midstream. "Like lambs," I said, "you needn't worry about them." "Oh, we're not worrying," said one of the Americans, fingering his gun. We nearly upset the boat on the return trip, but we got our deliverers safely and dryly across. They forced their way through a cheering crowd of POWs and foreign workers. Relief lit up the faces of even the Germans. No more bombs – no more alarms for them. The worst of the war was finished as far as they were concerned.'

EDWARD WARD

No more war for them – that was how the prison guards felt now. Two years of accumulating defeat had steadily worn down the earlier arrogance of the Wehrmacht:

2 April 1945

'The German troops who cut short any ideas we may have had about getting home after the armistice in Italy in September 1943 had their tails well up. They were front-line troops full of fanaticism – or as they call it *fanatismus* – for the Führer. So were the Death's Head SS who shouted at us and brandished their tommy guns as we went, forty in a cattle truck to Germany.

'When we reached our permanent camp near Limburg we found ourselves under a regular colonel who maintained iron discipline in the camp, and the German guards were terrified of him. To give him his due, however, he was fair enough to us within his somewhat narrow limits. Both he and his security officer used to give "pep-talks" to the German guards once or twice a week. Because even then – and I'm talking of over a year ago – it was felt that the morale of the German troops needed boosting. Even then several of the guards were beginning to see which way the wind was blowing, and were coming across with scraps of news from the BBC, which they listened to at the risk of their lives. A slab of soap or a few cigarettes had just the same effect on them as it had had on the Italians.

'As D-Day came and the Allies swept across Europe the German guards saw more and more clearly which side their bread was buttered on, and showed themselves more and more willing to co-operate. But it wasn't until the last phase that they threw caution to the winds. At our last camp, from which we were rescued by the advancing American First Army, we were supposed to be in our huts by dark. But nobody paid the slightest attention to this rule. I used to wander round in the moonlight and chat to the guards. There was one who had lost several relatives in a raid on Cologne, in which his house had been destroyed. His seventeen-year-old son was in U-boats and was missing. He told me about all this and then, with his voice rising in fury, he said: "And who is responsible for this? The Party! Ach sie sind nicht Menschen, sie sind Bestien! (They are not men, they are beasts!) And as for Hitler – our beloved Führer – there is not a word in the dictionary to describe him. I was listening to your English news a few weeks ago," he went on, "and the speaker said the National Socialist Party must be stamped out and utterly destroyed. How right he is, *ach Gott*, how right he is!" The man walked away only to return in a few moments to add: "I suppose after the war we shall all be sent to work in Siberia. As a German it is not pleasant to think of this. But what else can we expect after what has been done by our leaders? I tell you I was on the Russian front myself and I saw things happen there which make me ashamed to call myself a German. I saw whole families torn apart from each other, herded together like cattle and sent here to work like slaves. You have seen them in Germany yourself. So why should we – God help us – expect any different treatment?"

'But the most remarkable thing of all was the change in the attitude of the German commandant. Only a few weeks before he had been telling his troops that they would be back in Stalingrad within a year. Now he openly stated that in his opinion Germany had lost the war and that he was going to do everything possible to keep us where we were until the American troops arrived.'

EDWARD WARD

∞

As Hitler's Reich dwindled, the prisoners were moved from one district to another – away from the liberating armies. Many died on these forced marches, many more suffered extreme privations. A South African sergeant, rescued at last by General Patton's forces, described how he and his fellow-prisoners had been made to march for forty-three days, in order to get away from Breslau as the Russians approached:

10 April 1945

'It's so nice and it's so exciting to be free again that I don't know how I'm going to talk, but I'll just tell you something about the march. I've got an entry in my diary dated Wednesday 24 January. "It's twelve degrees below, we have just had the order that we are to move from Breslau on foot." The next entry I've got is on Thursday 22 February. "We are now twenty-four miles from Leipzig. We have walked through snow, rain and quite decent weather for well over 200 miles. It has been a bit of Hell."

'On the first three days it was heavy going through about two feet of snow and nineteen degrees below. We carried on, on sleds for about five days and after that we went on to wheels. It was a ragged convoy. It has been a trail of thieving and hunger and grim physical effort. There were approximately 60,000 POWs on the way south-west from Upper Silesia, and the strain on the German administration has been too much. There were days of no rations whatsoever, days when we marched for an entire day on a little bit of black bread, and went to sleep that night in barns, cold, hungry, and not knowing what tomorrow might bring. We averaged about twelve miles a day, but there were some days when we marched as much as seventy miles in three days. The men are hungry beyond description and they loot and feed wherever they can. Potatoes, raw swedes, potato peels, even on one occasion I've known them to eat a dog. It shows you what the Germans treated us like. We reached here, Ziegenhain in western Germany, on 15 March. Hungry, tired, and miserable. The treatment here hasn't been – wasn't very much better, and you can imagine our relief when the Yanks pitched up at the gate and we were liberated. To be free again, to be able to smoke cigarettes. They've been awfully good, the Yanks, they've given us a lot.'

A SOUTH AFRICAN SERGEANT, NAME UNKNOWN

Among the men released were a Scottish padre and a British medical officer who, hearing of the plight of these prisoners, had obtained permission to leave their own camp and go to Ziegenhain. The padre described the conditions, when he reached the camp, as 'a bit upsetting':

10 April 1945

'The fellows were certainly, many of them, rather like skeletons, but the – as for a sort of depression or anything like that, well it just wasn't there. The welcome they gave us was marvellous and their spirits were very high indeed. They were lying around, some of them in what we call hospital – you would hardly recognise it as a hospital – but most of them were in the ordinary barracks and I didn't expect to have much of a welcome for my particular job as a padre. I didn't think they'd be wanting services or anything like that. But I had hardly got here before they were asking for services and we had quite a few. Well, the main question that the chaps always asked when we went around was, "What about parcels, sir? – what about parcels?" Well, we've been asking the same question in the Oflag for about six months, because as you know Red Cross parcels are what we live on. However, I tried to cheer them up, saying that we thought that the new lorry system would bring the parcels along, and I must say that was our main thought – parcels, would they be coming? Then after a day or two news began to come along that began to excite us a little bit. We heard from the German communiqué about the tremendous rapid advance, and when I went round the barracks last week I used to hear people ask me – they used to say: "What's it going to be, sir? Which is it going to be first? Is it going to be Parcels, Patton, or Peace?" Well, it's been Patton.

'As regards my own job I decided that I'd carry on with my Good Friday services – I had a service in the morning with our chaps up in the big tent. During the service we heard a bit of machine-gun fire and a certain amount of gunfire which was actually American tanks in the neighbouring village, but at that time we didn't know whether it was going to be the Americans who'd arrive or whether perhaps some column of SS or something like that would turn up. The Germans who'd been left – the better type – were equally anxious – we didn't know what was going to happen.

'Then I was told that the rest of my services would have to be indoors that day because we didn't want to give any signs of movement about the camp in case there should be some sort of activity, some fun and games. I went down to the gate at one time, and I met the German who was still nominally in charge. He told me that he thought there were German tanks on one side of the camp and American tanks on the other, and we looked like becoming a sort of battle area. So I went back then and started to have the service with the Americans inside their huts, and that's when we had a rather unusual type of service. On the third one I was in with the Americans and at three o'clock we were just finishing the service and were singing a thanksgiving hymn, "The Day of Redemption", and I heard a noise outside; we went out – the camp was seething with a mass of people weeping, cheering, laughing, and up the middle of the camp came an American jeep, and the first free Allied soldier that I'd seen for practically five years.

'I can tell you the services we had the rest of that day were Thanksgiving services. In the evening I wish you could have seen the fellows standing up on top of three-tier beds singing "God Save the King" at the end of the service: the first time I'd been able to do that – the Germans didn't allow it – for all these years. Fellows standing to attention with legs just like matchsticks – it was wonderful.'

CAPTAIN H. C. READ, CF

A few days later 20,000 Allied prisoners were liberated at one stroke when British tanks of the VIIIth Hussars reached Fallingbostel:

16 April 1945
'Twenty thousand Allied prisoners of war gained their freedom today when British tanks liberated two large prison-camps, Stalag 11*b* and Stalag 357. More than 10,000 of them were British or American, and the British troops included 600 men of the 1st Airborne Division captured at Arnhem last year, and many more who were taken at Dunkirk.

'This morning, when tanks of the VIIIth Hussars reached these two camps near Fallingbostel, thirty-five miles south-east of Bremen, they found that our troops (the prisoners) had already taken charge of the camp and interned their German guards. An airborne sergeant-major, an ex-Guardsman, was in command, and the British guards were as spick and span as any parade-ground troops. Their boots were polished, their trousers pressed, and their belts and gaiters blancoed. The British troops had taken over the German offices, and their liberators found clerks busy typing out nominal rolls on German typewriters.

'The prisoners had been running the camp since last Friday, when three-quarters of the German guards departed, leaving a skeleton force of sixty to carry on. For the past four days German and British troops have been on guard together, but this morning the Germans were disarmed.

'This afternoon, at Stalag 11*b*, I saw some of the 20,000, and learned from padres, doctors and NCOs how they'd been treated. They told me that in this camp there were 4256 British troops and 2428 Americans. Of these 6700, more than 1000 are in hospital suffering from wounds, injuries, or starvation, and I saw several thousand more suffering from starvation who should have been in hospital in any civilised country.

'Here in this camp I saw clear evidence of the German neglect and wanton disregard for the lives and health of their prisoners. Of the 4250 British prisoners, some 2500 have come into the camp in the last three weeks. The Germans have marched them from Poland, lest they should be set free by the Russian advance. Ten days ago in this camp there were 3000 other British and American prisoners who had made this terrible trek from Poland; but when the Second Army crossed the Weser, the Germans put these 3000 on the road again, and sent them marching back towards the Russians. They were determined to stop the 3000 being liberated, because they were airmen and paratroops.

'How far they'll be able to march I don't know, for I saw today the pitiable condition of those who have already made the nightmare journey from Poland. They certainly were exhausted at the end of that journey. I saw them in hospital – drawn, haggard, starved – starved beyond description – limbs like matchsticks, bodies shrunken till their bones stood out like knuckles.

'The doctor in charge of them said to me, "Nothing has kept these men alive except Red Cross parcels and their own spirit." But on that journey from Poland they had very few Red Cross parcels, and some got none.

'One padre who was captured at Calais in 1940 told me that this party had marched 400 miles in fifty-two days, and their rations, in the depth of winter, had been nothing but a bowl of watery soup and a couple of slices of Army bread per day. He had marched with 800 British and 6500 American airmen, many thousands of whom had been sent marching back again almost as soon as they'd finished their journey.

'An Australian gunner who'd been captured in Crete had marched even farther in far worse conditions – he'd come 500 miles from the other side of Breslau in two months – they'd started in January with snow on the ground and had been made to sleep in barns and unheated barracks, and one night he said they'd slept in the open. "Men with dysentery or pneumonia," he went on, "had to keep marching. If they fell out they were either shot or left to die by the roadside. In the end," he added, "we managed to get some farm carts and we carried the worst cases in these."

'I wish those people who think the Germans should be treated lightly had seen what I saw today. But I saw also something that was inspiring and encouraging. All this German oppression and brutality and starvation hadn't been able to kill the spirit and self-respect of these men of Arnhem, men of Crete, of Dunkirk and Calais, men of Bomber Command and the Eighth Air Force. They'd managed to rise above their sordid environment and today those of them who were on guard or on duty were as soldierly in their bearing as they were the day they were captured. They were proud that they had their own camp running when our tanks got there. They felt they had almost liberated themselves. And this afternoon they had the supreme pleasure of watching their German guards being marched away to our prison cage; and, as they watched, they cheered.'

CHESTER WILMOT

Other Arnhem prisoners were liberated by the US Ninth Army and celebrated their freedom by strolling to a nearby village, where they quickly established a typically British atmosphere:

17 April 1945
'How can I explain what that village looked like – it had become an English village – there were hundreds of British paratroopers lining its pavements – happy, smiling, giving the "thumbs-up" sign, some sunning themselves by the village duckpond, some playing around on bicycles. Two of them were trying to get a stubborn motor-cycle to

work. Most of them were parading the pavements in twos and threes – they were parading the village streets, just as you saw them walk out of an evening in England; clean-shaven, smart, walking in step, and this village had suddenly become more than just an English village, its pavements held a living cavalcade of our story in this war, because amongst the Red Devils – outnumbered by them but not outshone – were other British soldiers, and New Zealanders and Australians whose stories briefly told were the story of our part in the war. It was an American officer, I think, who summed up that spirit; he said "Prisoners? Gee, I thought they were troops going into the line." That was no exaggeration – they looked just like it – if you'd seen them today you would have been proud. But what I don't understand is where some of them got the blanco.'

ROBERT BARR

Some of our men had been liberated by the Russians: now we were able to return the compliment. At Wesuwe, near the Dutch border, Canadians found a prison camp filled with Red Army soldiers:

27 April 1945
'A British lieutenant-colonel is in charge, but the internal affairs of the camp are run by a Russian colonel who formerly commanded a division in Latvia and who is assisted by a major, a former Moscow journalist who speaks excellent English. When he took over the camp the British officer now in charge was sick and furious with what he found. He summoned five of the neighbouring German burgomasters to his office, ringed them round his desk and said: "I want every day without fail 800 litres of fresh milk, 500 eggs, meat, potatoes, delivered by you in your own carts beginning now. We have no water because we have no electricity. I want that electricity back in twenty-

four hours. It's twelve noon now. I want that electricity back by twelve noon tomorrow."

'The Germans laid seven miles of high-power cable in twenty-four hours and got him light and water, and he's been getting, from the rich countryside, the food he needs – particularly for the very sick.

'Scraggy, parchment-coloured men, motionless except when their coughing twists their bodies, have been spread out over the huts that the Germans used – and now there are forty or fifty in separate bunks in huts which contained 200 so close together that you could barely walk between them.

'There is a proper hospital where men with burnt faces or bent or amputated limbs can get proper treatment. But there are still not enough doctors. It was characteristic that when the Germans were preparing to evacuate the camp because the Canadians were almost all round it they should have taken away all but five of the forty-odd Russian doctors among the prisoners. They never had supplied enough bandages or other medical equipment, and they left none behind. After he left the camp the commandant ordered the people in the surrounding villages to shoot any Russians they might see trying to leave the camp. The commandant himself hid his uniform, disguised himself as a peasant, and remained in the neighbourhood. After the camp was liberated the English-speaking major led a patrol of the fitter men, armed with their former guards' rifles, to search the villages. They found the commandant, who kept protesting he was a peasant, but he's now wearing German uniform in his cell. They hope to take him back to Moscow for a properly organised trial. The little major said to me: "We will not shoot him. It is easy to shoot a man. But he must have a proper trial. We must show the world what is a German officer."

'It may seem a funny thing to say, but since I have seen for myself what some of these concentration camps are really like one of my main impressions has been how unconquerable is human hope. This major, for example, who had been in six of these camps in three years of captivity and finally was brought to Wesuwe to die, this major said: "Today begins a new day for us. We have prepared for this day. We have thought about the new life. The past is history – done, finished. Now we can begin." '

ROBERT DUNNETT

⁓

There was still hard fighting in Holland, which the Germans apparently intended to hold as one of the last pockets of resistance. However, the Canadian Army was fighting doggedly forward, and when the Arnhem prisoners were released at Fallingbostel they were able to hear that British troops were back again in Arnhem – and this time for as long as they needed to stay:

16 April 1945
'Arnhem. Today I drove into the smoking shell of that town, once one of the most beautiful in Holland. There was nothing there now but ruin, and a memory.

'It was fitting that it should be a British formation, the 49th West Riding Division, that should take Arnhem at long last and write the words "Paid in full" across another page of British history. Last September the world stopped breathing to watch this town. If the British Army had been able to link hands with the British 1st Airborne Division, which had landed round Arnhem, the Rhine would have been turned while the German armies were disorganised, and the armoured divisions would have poured into the plains of Hanover and Westphalia. But the effort was a bit too much for us, the weather was against us, and in fact we didn't have enough strength at the decisive place.

'I drove in from the south today, past powerful German forts and redoubts which had been shelled and bombed and burnt out by thousands of our rockets firing hundreds at a time. The town was a deserted, burning shell. I visited a British regiment, and saw about 200 German prisoners. Fires were blazing. Machine-guns chattered from the high ground north of Arnhem, and two or three German shells whistled into the town. An airplane engine, that had fallen from some British bomber, disintegrating high above, lay in a little park beside a canal. The whole thing was a dreary, disheartening sight – another of the destroyed towns of a beautiful continent.

Stanley Maxted with the BBC recording car in Schilberg in Holland. The sign on the wall reads 'With our Führer to victory', but the sign on the road is clearly where everyone is heading.

'A lone Dutchman, the first civilian we had encountered, came slowly down a long street. He shook hands. "You have come back," he said quietly. Just that. The British had come back, as they always do. I drove away. There were craters everywhere.

White tapes through the minefields. A British soldier who'd lost a foot on a Schu-mine. Two other soldiers being buried. Engineers making demolitions. Bulldozers, backing up a few feet, shaking their heads in roaring anger, and then tearing into the side of a broken house. A Martian ant-hill – a bedlam of men at war. Motor-cycles bouncing back and forth. Tanks and Bren-carriers dusting through to the next battle. Convoy leaders going crazy to get their convoys through. All the noisy, clanking machines and paraphernalia of war.'

MATTHEW HALTON, CBC

Farther north, at Zwolle, the Dutch people began to emerge from the captivity of German occupation, and it was the collaborators who now found themselves imprisoned:

17 April 1945

'When I arrived in the town they were busy putting the collaborators into the school that they had all known well for four years as the Gestapo prison. They said there were about 300 known collaborators in the town, and with typical Dutch thoroughness they were out to get them all. Many were young girls who had been too kind to the occupying forces. They were being marched along the winding main street with their hands up, and the staid population watched at places six deep along the way, under the huge, new Dutch flags hanging from every house and with brilliant orange favours in people's hats and lapels, blouses and hair.

'When the crowd threatened to surge across the road a little man in a blue suit with the Resistance armband on his left sleeve and an antiquated tin hat on his head jumped up and down shouting and fired his rifle in the air.

'A young man wanted to know if potatoes, bread and beans were rationed in England. Another if London had been badly damaged by bombs or by rockets for they'd seen V2s leaving from sites nearby, and one man said, "It was like a thunderstorm." A girl chipped in to ask – "Is Deanna Durbin still alive, and Shirley Temple?" '

ROBERT DUNNETT

CHAPTER XX
The German People

'I shouted "Anyone there?" No reply'

In the midst of this disaster which was overwhelming their nation, what were the feelings of the German people? Everywhere British and American troops were taking control: released prisoners stood in the streets, foreign workers downed tools and left the farms and factories. Great cities were ablaze, and German demolition squads added to the destruction. The Führer was silent and impotent. The great days of victory had gone for ever. The long dream of German domination was ending in visible ruin, in heaps of rubble and lines of prisoners, in German dead strewn everywhere, in anxious rows of white flags. What were the feelings of the German people?

8 April 1945
'We had come into the German kitchen not to fraternise, that strictly forbidden practice, but because we had seen a large radio set there and wanted to hear the BBC news at nine o'clock. It took us some time to find London on the dial and the announcer had already begun the bulletin when we brought his voice, loud and clear, into the room. The hotel family was already there when we came in. The old, white-haired man who watched us fearfully – I think the Germans had told him terrible stories of what we would do – his two not unattractive daughters, by no means frightened, and his grey-haired wife who sat knitting at the table. A woman friend was visiting them – one of the smarter women of the little town, with her hair caught up in a bright turban and wearing what looked to me like fully-fashioned silk

stockings. They – at least, the women – were ready and anxious to talk, but we made it pretty clear that we had come in only to hear the wireless.

'As we sat listening to the news about this battle area, I watched the reaction of this German family which had been engulfed in the fighting a very short time before, and could hear it going on now if we'd turned off the set. They were listening quite intently, understanding no English but catching the German place-names as Freddie Grisewood mentioned them. "Hanover," said the smart guest, "they're near Hanover." "Isn't that what he said?" she asked me. I said it was. And then the Weser was mentioned and, that being the local river, everyone heard it. Even the old man stirred himself from his gloomy apprehension. And then it was announced that the Americans were at or near Würzburg. "Würzburg? Where's Würzburg?" asked one of the daughters. The other got up and fetched a gazetteer from a shelf. She opened it at a map of central and southern Germany and the whole family pored over it, marking the places as they were mentioned. And as I watched them, a thought struck me. This was a recital from London of our success, of the growing and spreading defeat of their country, and yet there was not one sound or sign of regret on their faces, no shock, no despair, no alarm. They just picked up what was said, checked it on the map and noted it just as if they were a bunch of neutrals hearing all about somebody else. And indeed, I believe that that's what many of these front-line German people are. Neutrals in their own country. They seem to have lost the power of passion or sorrow. They show no sympathy for their army, for their government, or for their country. To them the war is something too huge and too catastrophic to understand. Their world is bounded by the difficulties of managing a country hotel – and there's no room in it for things outside.'

RICHARD DIMBLEBY

21 April 1945

'The vast bulk of the adult population as far as one can judge seem to be heartily glad of the chance to be out of it. But young boys and girls educated in Nazi schools can still be inspired by the patriotic screams of the old familiar voices. And it's to them that enemy propaganda seems now to be almost entirely directed. And so, cases are being found of boys of fourteen or fifteen trying to distribute pamphlets, of ill-written threats being pushed under civilian doors, of efforts being made to build up an adolescent guerrilla army. Every kind of trick may be expected before the end, because we've got to remember that, as the Wehrmacht itself throws in the sponge, we are faced with a harder and harder core of homicidal maniacs, to whom even their own people mean nothing whatever once they throw them over. To the Nazi, the German civilian who has surrendered deserves even less consideration than his enemy in the field. So we must be prepared for anything before the end. It isn't a question of sense or reason. Anything they can do to keep alive a few days longer, they're liable to try on. The war is becoming a colossal police operation – a siege of Sidney Street.'

DENIS JOHNSTON

For those deeply involved in the Nazi regime – the hard core – there could be no future. Trapped and desperate, they turned their hands at last against themselves, in many cases. The weapons of terror that they had wielded over a prostrate continent had now been torn from them: only the ultimate weapon remained – the razor, the revolver bullet, the phial of poison:

20 April 1945

'I went up a shattered stairway to the upper floors of Leipzig's Town Hall. Many rooms were damaged by shells, others almost untouched.

426

I went with two American soldiers who carried tommy guns at the ready, since we were the first to explore the inside of the building. In one room, which had been the Ober-Bürgermeister's Council Room, was a grisly spectacle. Three Volkssturmers lay sprawled, dead, over tables, with pools of blood on the floor – they had committed suicide. By the side of one was a bottle of cognac and a half-empty glass. He'd evidently needed courage. Most papers had already been removed, but otherwise all furniture in the rooms not hit by shells was intact and normal.

'After exploring the Town Hall, I went into the neighbouring building. In an air-raid shelter I found a small group of Germans who staff the Town Hall restaurant. They told me that the Ober-Bürgermeister and his wife and daughter had also committed suicide. Among these Germans was the caretaker of the Town Hall. He had the keys of the whole building. I took him over to the Rathaus, and asked which was the Ober-Bürgermeister's office. He took me upstairs to some doors which I'd found locked. He took a bunch of keys and opened the door. I shouted, "Anyone there?" No reply. I went into a luxuriously furnished, oak-panelled room. Seated at a large desk was Ober-Bürgermeister Freyberg, his hands on the table, his shaven head tilted back. Opposite, in the armchair, sat his wife; beside her, in the other armchair, sat his daughter, a flaxen-haired twenty-year-old, wearing spectacles. On the desk was a phial, with its stopper lying beside it. They were all dead. The caretaker said he thought they'd committed suicide yesterday, or perhaps the day before. He told me Freyberg had been Bürgermeister for about nine years, and though he'd been a party member, he'd wanted to declare Leipzig an open town, but had been overruled. On the wall, opposite the dead man, was a large oil-painting of Hitler. There was another locked door, leading out of this room – the caretaker opened it. Here Chief City Treasurer Doktor Lisso lay slumped on his desk. On a sofa, opposite,

427

lay his daughter, wearing hospital nurse's uniform. In an armchair sat Lisso's wife. Once again, on the table was an empty, unlabelled phial. By Lisso's side were two automatic pistols – but he had chosen poison.

'In an anteroom a dead Volkssturmer lay on the floor with twenty- and fifty-mark notes scattered round him – he, too, had poisoned himself. The caretaker seemed entirely unmoved by this terrible spectacle. We ordered the caretaker to lock up the doors again, and walked downstairs.'

EDWARD WARD

The general run of the civilian population, now concerned only to have the war end as quickly as possible, was all too willing to fraternise with the Allied troops. The official threats of underground resistance by 'Werewolves' appeared to have little substance:

3 April 1945

'The Germans don't like our non-fraternisation rule, and they don't like the way in which our troops are obeying these rules. In almost every German town that I've been in I've heard the same complaints from the population. They view us as liberators, they say, they hate to see us coming in as conquerors refusing to have any social contact with them. The civilians left behind in these towns claim invariably that they are the people who were never very keen on the Nazi regime. Their attitude is that they're more to be pitied than blamed; all they want is to let bygones be bygones and to celebrate with us.

'Now there are no doubt a number of Germans who really opposed the Nazis, but it's hardly likely that they're still at large when we enter a town. They've probably been under lock and key for a long time past. The people we meet are – well, the most favourable name

I can find for them is "opportunists". They see which way the ball is bouncing and they're acting accordingly. I've no doubt whatever that most of them cheered loudly enough when the Germans seemed to be winning. The attitude of these people makes our non-fraternisation policy more necessary than ever. They had to be told firmly that it is a two-way affair and that not only is a soldier forbidden to have dealings with them, they must not make any approaches to him.

'They accept the ruling very unwillingly, apparently on the basis at first that it's a security ban which will be lifted when the front has rolled forward a little. When they find that the rule is a permanent one, then they begin to show signs of resentment. They try to catch the eyes and the ears of our troops. Snatches of conversation on the subject are being made intentionally audible for overhearing. The Germans try to raise pity for themselves as the victims of devastation; they harp on racial and cultural similarities between themselves and the Allied troops. They make appeals for generosity and fair play. They do all they can to influence the sympathies of our men.'

FRANK GILLARD

31 March 1945

'As soon as they get over their fright and realise that we're not going to burn their villages down they stand on the side of the road and seem almost pleased to see us. We pulled up beside a farmhouse to change a wheel and out came a girl of about eighteen and offered us four eggs. At one village the children were waiting at the entrance, cheering and waving white flags. Frankly we found the whole business rather embarrassing. No one who remembers what the Germans did in Italy or France wants these demonstrations, and the officer who was driving with me agreed that the best thing was to preserve a formal politeness and then pass on.

'Frankly I thank my stars that it's not my job to decide on the correct course of action towards the Germans. And I think every British soldier feels the same way. If you're friendly to them, then they become embarrassingly welcoming. If you're tough with them, then somehow you yourself feel demeaned and degraded. Sheer hate is an emotion you can't cultivate for long. So we've agreed, and most of the troops we saw have too, that formal politeness, but nothing more, is our motto. These people we're now meeting are the small fry of Nazi Germany; all the party members and the big shots have fled to the East. And how we shall feel when we bump into them is a different matter.'

WYNFORD VAUGHAN-THOMAS

On the whole the villages were intact, except where there had been an attempt at local resistance. The condition of the industrial towns was very different: even where they largely escaped the fighting they had already been wrecked by air attacks. The fate of Leuna was typical of hundreds of others:

22 April 1945
'Acres and acres of twisted, rusted pipes – huge tanks ripped open – steel girders pointing to the sky. That is what had happened to the greatest petroleum-products plant in Germany, in spite of its being protected by more flak guns than there were defending Berlin.

'When we arrived, a couple of officers had the plant managers in the boardroom – they were checking production figures. The officers had their charts made up from aerial photographs. They would ask the managers, "What was your production on this date?" – the Germans would look at their records, and the answers were consistently within one or two per cent of the estimates that had been made in London.

The Germans had brought in a force of 4000 men just to carry out repairs. They would get the plant producing forty or fifty per cent of capacity, then would come another bombing and production would cease altogether. The German officials said that it had all been very discouraging.

'Leuna is an ugly monument to air power – it doesn't prove that bombers can win wars, but it does demonstrate that bombers can make it impossible for armies to move or for planes to fly.

'After a couple of weeks travelling in Germany, one gets the feeling that for the Germans this is a kind of delayed-action war. Their cities have been ruined and in many cases the destruction is complete. They have lost many dead and wounded. Most of their men will be in Allied prison cages when the war is over and it will be some time before they're home again; but in addition to all this the Germans will have no transport left. They've wrecked their bridges – the war has swallowed up their horses and their hopes – their factories are in ruins.

'For the rest of Europe the end of the war will mean some improvement in living conditions. For the Germans, things will get worse and worse. There won't be any bombers next winter, but there will be less food – fewer workers – the Germans will gradually realise that they've only started to pay the price. For Germany, the end of the war will be the beginning of great suffering and shortages of all kinds.

'One gets the feeling that here's a nation committing suicide. A city is completely surrounded and is asked to surrender – the local authority refuses and our troops start in. There is resistance from a couple of houses – tanks move up and cut the houses down. The Germans pull back nearer to the centre of the city. But they keep shooting; they did that for three days at Nuremberg and that city may be said to be dead. There are a few walls still standing and the cathedral spires are still there. But Nuremberg has been wiped out. Most of Bayreuth is gone too. Wagner's piano is still there, but part of the house has been knocked down. Rare books and fine manuscripts are trampled underfoot. There is an empty champagne bottle on top of the piano. The young lieutenant in charge of military government has written a letter to the Army asking for permission to put a guard on the place.

'There is no lack of looting in Germany. The foreign workers are interested in food and clothing and they will go after it right under the machine-gun fire. The other day a Pole found a suit of clothes in a box-car. As he carried it away he said, "This is my pay – five years' work." In Nuremberg a Russian walked down a street that was under small-arms fire. He carried a huge cheese – it must have weighed seventy pounds. He was interested in that cheese – not in the firing. As a new Burp gun opened up around the corner, an American corporal said: "Hey, Mack, do you know of any place around here where I can get some films developed?" There wasn't a building standing in the radius of a mile, but he was entirely serious.

'There are places down near the Czechoslovakian border where you can drive for sixty miles on a super highway and meet no traffic. You're never sure of where our forward elements are, and when you do find an outfit they're never sure just where they are in relation to other units. The tired driver of an armoured car said he remembered a town but that was about three days ago and he couldn't recall its name, but he'd had a glass of beer there – it was a dusty little place.

'In the larger cities there's occasional firing at night but not very much – the Werewolves aren't very active – at least not in the areas behind the First and Third Armies. The other night we were caught in a traffic jam leaving a pontoon bridge. There was a half-moon and the night was mild. A Strauss waltz came from a radio in a command car – the two lines of traffic did not move. A western voice said: "What's the trouble down there?" And a voice from the deep south answered: "There's a one-way bridge and the traffic is moving in three directions." '

EDWARD R. MURROW, CBS

In a small town south of Hamburg one correspondent was confronted by a shrine to the Nazi cult:

24 April 1945

'A month ago, we crossed the Rhine. I don't think that many of us who were in that crossing imagined that a month later we would still be fighting hard on the Elbe, many hundreds of miles to the east. Who would have imagined that the Nazis would force the German nation into what amounts to mass suicide?

'But standing here in the Nazi party meeting place in the little town of Buchholz, just south of Hamburg, you can easily see why the Nazis are acting as they are. If ever there was a nursery of fanaticism, here it is. This, to give it its official title, is the Hall of Honour of the National Socialist Party of the district of East Hanover. It's the most fantastic place I've entered for a long time. It's a modern building of neat red brick, standing back from the road in the middle of a small garden, and it's not large, it's about the size of a village hall. But the extraordinary thing about it is that it's not the normal party meeting place, rather the whole thing has an almost blasphemous resemblance to a small church or a chapel. It's got stained glass windows, but the sun shines in through SS men and soldiers rather than saints. There's a pulpit here for the local party leader rather than for the minister and, the final blasphemy, where the altar lies in a church there stands the life-size portrait of Hitler, flanked by none other than Himmler and Robert Ley. There's even a harmonium in the small gallery upstairs although the sort of hymns that were played on it are hard to imagine. All around the walls are paintings of the local party members and photographs of the Nazi old guard. Here, Julius Streicher, the Jew-baiter, leers down on us and here, surprisingly enough, is the photograph of the long-forgotten and unlamented

Ernst Röhm. The portrait of Hess, by the way, has been relegated to the basement.

'The whole place has the strained and furtive atmosphere of the meeting hall of a secret and fanatical cult, and you can easily imagine the local Gauleiter, whose portrait is everywhere on the walls with the inscription "To our beloved Stadtrat Telschau" and what a beauty he looks. Well, you can easily imagine him here haranguing his party members from the pulpit and whipping them up into a final state of frenzy.

'The people who built this hall with its heavy, far too Germanic furniture, its over-rich decoration, its endless portraits in savage bad taste, these are the people who, inevitably, will not admit the failure of this cult, who are going to pull the whole of Germany down about them to make a grandiose exit from this stage they've built for themselves here. They've even got music for it already. Rummaging about in the basement we found endless piles of National Socialist gramophone records and with the gramophone, slightly dusty from our shelling, all ready to play them on. Heavy, tramping, jackboot music it is, and in this empty Hall of Honour, the temptation is too great so we are going to try one. Here's one, the Hitler March, and listen to it.

[*Music plays.*]

'Shoo, that's enough of that, cracked and slightly out of tune, a fitting finale to the fantastic ceremonials that went on in this so-called Hall of Honour in the *Ostgau* of Hanover.

'Well, there's only one thing to do with this poisonous place, the nursery of the fanatics who are still costing the lives of our British soldiers one month after we'd smashed the last defences of Germany on the Rhine. The General commanding the Seventh Armoured Division, the famous Desert Rats, has issued the order. As soon as we've finished our recording this place is going to join the rest of the strong points in which the Nazis are still resisting – it's going to be blown sky high.'

WYNFORD VAUGHAN-THOMAS

cↄ◎ↄ

Town by town the Allied military authorities took control, and the citizens of Germany read the proclamations and learned to adapt themselves to a new order such as they had never anticipated. All visible signs of the Nazi regime disappeared. A strict curfew was imposed. Life became relatively peaceful again – but with the negative, exhausted peace of defeat. Here is a sketch of one such town – Sulingen, south of Bremen – during the first days of British occupation:

16 April 1945
'There's been no sign of "werewolf" activities in Sulingen. The walls of the houses opposite me are covered with proclamations laying down the way the townsfolk must behave. These proclamations are fairly stringent. There appears to be a strict curfew here for civilians. If civilians are found out after blackout, they must run the risk of being shot by our patrols if they look at all suspicious. And then there's a proclamation saying that all civilians with their handcarts, bicycles, and the rest, must keep off the road.

'And as for German motor-cars, well they'd been off the roads for a long time before our arrival. The Nazi party formations are of course all dissolved. All arms must be surrendered and all uniforms are prohibited. And this complete absence of uniforms, by the way, is the third striking thing. It's especially noticeable if you knew Germany before the war. I daresay these people must have their flags and their uniforms tucked away somewhere, but looking now at Sulingen, the only trace of the Nazi regime that I can see, frankly, is the short corduroy pants the boys still wear, relics of the Hitler *Jugend*. And by

435

the way, there's not even a propaganda poster left. In their place the only notices posted by Germans are rather half-hearted appeals on the doors of some of the houses. "Here Nine Children", one of them reads. And there's one that's irritated our American friends, because it says "Attention. Keep out. This house, the property of a certain American tobacco company". Well, needless to say, that ruse hasn't prevented the places being requisitioned where needed. Down the road are the offices of the military government, and one talk to the colonel there convinces you that, although all looks calm now on the surface at Sulingen, this little place fairly bristles with problems. There are the refugees, the Allied prisoners-of-war, the Russians and the Poles, they arrive in hundreds. And they've naturally been making free of the chickens and the foodstuffs on the surrounding farms. After all, they've been working like slaves on these farms for years, and they don't see now why they should go hungry. And yet you've got to keep a certain amount of restraint on them or else the whole structure of society here breaks down.'

WYNFORD VAUGHAN-THOMAS

CHAPTER XXI
The Cesspit Beneath

*'Cleanliness is a duty here, so don't forget to wipe
your hands'*

Along the shores of the Mediterranean, on the Russian front, and
in western Europe, the pride and power of the German Army
had been crushed. The Luftwaffe, once the terror of Europe, had
virtually ceased to have any military significance. The walls of Hitler's
Fortress were down, and out of the ruins came the great host of the
imprisoned and the enslaved, rejoicing in their liberation. But while
they emerged, in the random disorder of joyful surprise, there were
others who remained behind – the tortured dead, the feebly living
who were by now too weak to move. As Germany cracked open it
became abundantly clear that the Allies were fighting not only an
army but – behind that army – an underworld of secret police and
political terrorists, hardened and confirmed in practices of a vileness
that can never have been surpassed.

Of conditions in the concentration camps, and of the behaviour
of the Gestapo in occupied countries, we already knew a great deal. It
was perhaps forgivable to have hoped that some part of this might be
found to have been exaggerated, but the conditions laid bare by the
advancing Allies confirmed – and exceeded – the worst accusations
levelled at the Nazis' treatment of their victims.

In Holland, for example, at Zutphen, Canadians found ten bodies
loosely hidden under loose earth. They were the bodies of Dutchmen
who had been murdered with extreme brutality. The Canadians
compelled German paratroops to bury these mutilated corpses:

9 April 1945

'As the frightened paratroops looked on, Sergeant-Major Austin, cold with hate, bent over the dead men and showed me things much too horrible to describe. Some of these men had been tortured and then shot. Their hands were still tied behind them, but some hadn't even been shot. They had been tortured to death in unspeakable ways. The worst things you've ever read about in any account of Nazi atrocity were there. I saw and was sick.

'I don't know the names of these victims of the Master Race. There were no Dutchmen around, because there was a battle going on ahead and to left and right, and it's hard to get details during a battle. These men of the great Canadian Division are having sticky fighting for Zutphen and Deventer. But I knew the victims were Dutch resistants and that the murderers were the Gestapo.

'Some of the paratroops dug graves while others lay utterly exhausted on the grass after a gruelling battle. I looked them over and then spoke to one of them. I pointed to the ten Dutchmen and said: "What do you think of this?" The young, unshaven, red-eyed paratrooper rose to his feet and stood, shaking, at attention. "Das ist eine Schweinerei" ("It's a swinish thing"), he said in a trembling voice.

' "Who did it?" I went on. "Not us, not us!" he said. "We didn't do it! We are soldiers. The Gestapo did it." "Do you understand why the world hates your country?" I asked. And for the first time, in reply to that question, I heard a German say, "Yes, yes, I understand!" '

MATTHEW HALTON, CBC

That was German behaviour in Holland. Next, the treatment of foreign workers inside Germany:

14 April 1945

'Last Sunday a train steamed out of Brunswick Station. On board it there were 4500 prisoners and foreign workers, Frenchmen, Belgians, Russians, Poles, and even Germans. Men and women who had been working as Nazi slaves in the Hermann Goering Steel Works near Brunswick. Now, as the Allies drew near, the Germans tried to carry away their human loot, even though most of these 4500 were starved and sick. Their SS guards told them that they were being taken to another camp where they were to be gassed and cremated, but they didn't reach that camp. Yesterday, in the town of Celle, a Frenchman who was on that train told me what happened to them.

' "On Sunday evening," he said, "the train stopped in the yard at Celle, while the engine filled up with water and coal. Our carriages were left standing between an ammunition train and a petrol train, and we hadn't been there long when some Allied bombers came over. We heard them coming and we tried to get out of the train, but as we jumped down on to the tracks the SS guards opened fire on us with machine-guns. Then the bombs began to fall and they hit the train. The ammunition and petrol began to explode. Many," he said, "must have been killed. But those who survived tried to get away from the fire and explosions. Some of us," he went on, "reached shelter, but most of the rest were shot down by the SS guards. After it was all over, there were only 200 left out of the 4500, and we 200 were rounded up by the SS and herded into a stable – a filthy stable, and there we lay on straw that barely covered the manure underneath. Many of us," he added, "were wounded or burnt, but they left us there for four days without medical attention, food, or water. We were rescued only when the British came."

'Yesterday in Celle I saw most of the 200 survivors. I was taken round a hospital by a British doctor and a captain who were the first to find them. The men I saw were almost skeletons, and the doctor said he'd never seen men in such pitiable condition. They'd been starved for years, until their legs were no thicker than a man's wrist and their bodies were mere skin and bone. They must have been almost as starved as this when they boarded that train in Brunswick, and yet only the day before that most of them had been slaves in a German factory. They told us how the Nazis had put German criminals in with them to act as spies, and how these criminals had been given the privilege of supervising their work and of beating them on the slightest provocation.

'One Frenchman – a man who had been captured as a member of the Maquis – told me that when he came he couldn't understand German but when he didn't obey orders shouted at him in German he had been beaten. He and many others said that this was typical. And they told us how they had been forced to work on starvation rations and had been paid one mark a week – about sixpence. "And all we could buy with that," said the Frenchman, "was food that we give only to pigs."

'When these men were rescued by our troops they were too weak to move. They had to be carried on stretchers to German hospitals in the town; but our troops saw to it that these stretchers were carried by German civilians, and were carried through the streets so that the German people could see what their fellow Germans had done.

'Yesterday afternoon the doctor and the captain who'd rescued them were continuing this German education. I visited one of the hospitals with them and with four Germans. One, the local schoolmaster, who had been an ardent Nazi. Another – a man you might call a German country squire – who spoke perfect English. The other two, a man and his daughter, were members of the old Junkers Von Moltke family.

'Their reactions were interesting. The little Nazi schoolmaster tried to plead justification. "These men were criminals," he said. "We didn't treat all our foreign workers like this. Most of them were glad to come."

' "Yes," interrupted the squire, "those who worked on our farms were well treated, and had plenty to eat. The German people looked after the foreign workers, it is only the SS who have done this kind of thing."

'The Von Moltkes blamed the SS and the Party. But neither of them could see any connection between this and the support their military class had given to the Nazis. Even confronted with this evidence they could not see or admit Germany's guilt.'

CHESTER WILMOT

Deeds such as these, however, seem trivial by comparison with what was revealed at Buchenwald, at Belsen, at Dachau. First, Buchenwald – where the Americans compelled parties of German civilians to witness the iniquities that had been practised in the Third Reich:

17 April 1945
'The 21,000 inmates of the Buchenwald concentration camp near Weimar had something new and interesting to see today. It was ten or a dozen processions of German men and women, and youths and girls, being herded willy-nilly around the camp compound, through those stinking, infamous huts where forty men died every day, past the mound of the dead and through the camp crematorium.

'These sightseers, escorted by American Military Police and block leaders from some of the huts, were civilians from Weimar who'd been rounded up by the Americans and marched out to the camp just to let them see things for themselves so that there'll be no arguing in the months and years to come.

'It was a hot April afternoon, and the dusty compound of

Buchenwald stank. Some of the more stolid Germans just looked at those bodies and said nothing. Some of the women wept. Others fainted. Some wrung their hands and said they had no idea that all this had happened near their home.

'While those Germans were trudging around, American doctors and nurses and Army officers and GIs were grappling with the problem of rescuing the living. One of the first steps taken by the American Third Army was to move hospital facilities into the camp. It is estimated that there are at least 5000 sick. Forty of them are typhus cases. The remainder are suffering from starvation, tuberculosis and dysentery. Approximately 2500 are desperately ill. The doctors say that for many of them nothing more can be done than to alleviate the pain and suffering of their last days.

'The first thing has been to evacuate the sick from the huts where they had been left to die. The big SS Hospital outside the compound has been taken over and cleaned out. Ambulances were rushed into the camp from every army unit in the entire district to help clear the hutments as quickly as possible. Equally energetic steps have been taken to combat the spread of disease, to feed and clothe the inmates of the camp, and to administer the place generally. Every one of the 21,000 folk in the camp is being dusted with delousing powder. All foul clothing is also being gathered and burned.

'The main hutments where the prisoners lived without proper beds or bedding will be abandoned. Eighteen German army barracks are providing alternative accommodation. And, if that is not enough, any other likely German building will be taken over.

'Feeding is another great problem – not the lack of food, but the necessity for providing a suitable diet for men who have been systematically starved for years. The main food provided by the Germans for the prisoners had been a thin soup. The Americans have started out to build up from this point with a soup containing meat and vegetables. Also a ration of 300 grammes of bread per day has been increased to 750 grammes. In this way the diet will gradually be enriched until the prisoners can really face a square meal without disastrous consequences. All this food, by the way, is German – all captured stocks, with the bread supplied by German bakeries in the district. So is the clothing which is now being issued to the prisoners. Every bit of it is German.

'One of the greatest tragedies in the camp was the plight of 900 fatherless children – all boys, whose ages range from two and a half years to fourteen – boys whose fathers were once prisoners in Buchenwald, but are long since dead. These pathetic, ragged waifs, looking like little old men with yellow faces and shrunken cheeks, had been living in one hut, cared for by some of the older prisoners. A special child-welfare unit has been sent for to look after these children. And one of the first things done for them was to bring in supplies of fresh milk from local farms. Another thing was to make sure that the soldiers don't give them too much candy and make them ill. Another thing was to remove them at once to better quarters. The camp is being administered by the military government authorities with the aid of an international committee composed of twenty-one inmates – one representative for each thousand of the different national groups. The American Camp Commandant and his staff deal with this committee, whose members pass on the camp orders to their nationals, who provide the working parties for cleaning, maintenance and policing.'

ROBERT REID

What of the Germans who had lived *inside* the camp, as political prisoners? A citizen of the Danzig Free State, an anti-Nazi, spoke for them in a conversation with First Lieutenant Jack Hanson of the US Third Army:

CITIZEN: 'We used to wait every day for the Americans, and when we see that some German soldiers left this place we used to say well now it is the time the Americans will come and make us free. So we say we must see that we get guns and we must see that we can hold some prisoners, so they not can go any more to fight. So myself and four boys we go to the electric wire, going up to the guard and I say to the guard "Give over your rifle because I have here many men with rifles and if you don't give the rifle we shoot without looking." He give the rifle; I take that rifle and a machine-gun, going to another guard and there standing ten SS. These ten SS we take prisoners, we take away from them the rifles and so we got the camp. Give every political prisoner a rifle, guard the camp and waiting for the Americans. At four o'clock arrived the first American officer. We were very glad to see him because we didn't believe it that we are free. Just now when I talk I don't believe that I'm free. I see my wife – eight years I didn't see my wife, I didn't see my kids, and I'm very glad I can talk now to the American troops.

HANSON: Tell me how did they treat you here?

CITIZEN: Well, when I tell you that I think you never will believe it, or you might think I tell a story. The four years that I stay in the camp I get beat three hundred over my back.

HANSON: I see——

CITIZEN: Just for nothing – maybe I smoke cigarettes, or maybe I had organised a little bit of food or something like that, everything for that they beat us. We eating everything we used to find, we used to take perhaps of grass——

HANSON: Grass?

CITIZEN: Yes, we take grass and make salad from it because to have something – we used to think would have some vitamin to keep ourselves.

HANSON: Everybody in the camp as far as I can see is half-starved, do you agree with me on that?

CITIZEN: Yes, sir. You see it, I show it to you.

HANSON: That's right. I saw children here, how are they treated?

CITIZEN: The children was treated the same we are treated. We know – we used to say when the Americans come and we will build a new Europe we need these children, so we give the children the food we get, we took a little bit and give it over to that place where the children stay. The leader by the children is a Czech comrade, he was the leader, and we give it to him and he give it to the children, till they not die, they live, because we need these children, with the experience the children have in this camp, we need them to build the new Germany.'

 ⁘

To justify – or at least to palliate – the existence of these places, German civilians frequently asserted that only 'criminals' were sent to them. The assertion scarcely accounts for the presence of a British officer in Buchenwald. He was Captain C. A. G. Burney of Hay, Hereford, and he described his experience of fifteen months in the camp in a conversation with a BBC correspondent, Robert Reid:

REID: 'Who ran the place?

BURNEY: The place was run by the SS.

REID: What were they like?

BURNEY: Well, the best example you can get of what the treatment was like is the arrival here. Our arrival took place in the middle of the night, with a temperature of about fifteen below zero. We'd had our shoes and some of us had had our clothes taken away from us in the train to prevent us escaping, and when the doors were opened in the station, we were pulled straight out of the wagon by an SS man, given a hit over the head – I was pushed into a dog which bit my arm; another SS hit me again, kicked me in the backside, and then off I went.

REID: Now, were there many atrocities in this camp?

BURNEY: Yes. The means of execution were varied, and applied with great frequency.

REID: And on what basis did they do these executions? Was there any trial? Was it for any offence, or what?

BURNEY: Sometimes for no offence at all, sometimes for offences which they considered were offences but which no civilised person would consider an offence.

REID: Such as – ?

BURNEY: Running away. Anybody who escaped was automatically – if he stayed out for three days – was accused of pillage and was brought back and hanged.

REID: Now, what other means of execution had they?

BURNEY: They hanged; they shot, they had patent traps where you stood on a trapdoor which let off a bullet into your neck; they electrocuted; they injected with phenol, they injected with air, they injected with milk.

REID: Did you see any executions yourself?

BURNEY: No.

REID: Did you see any burials or any bodies?

BURNEY: I saw an enormous number of bodies. I must have seen thousands of bodies since I've been here.

REID: And where were they all buried – in the camp?

BURNEY: The normal way was cremation; there was the crematorium, and most of the bodies were cremated – but towards the end they ran out of coal and they had too many bodies.

REID: Was there any real community spirit inside the camp among the prisoners?

BURNEY: I can't say there was, frankly. If you wanted to be disgusted with humanity, all you had to do was to come and live in this camp. People were stealing, they were killing each other for a slice of bread, they were always quarrelling, there was always a lot of political intrigue. One group hated another and the other group hated the next and so forth.

REID: And did the German authorities attempt to foster this sort of feeling, or ill-feeling?

BURNEY: Yes, I should say they did.

REID: In what way?

BURNEY: By giving power to one group and by deliberately squashing another group. And that created jealousy between these various groups – the one that had power got a superiority complex and the one that hadn't got an inferiority complex.

REID: And how would you like to sum up your whole experience here?

BURNEY: Well, I couldn't politely say it over the microphone.

REID: But it has been shocking?

BURNEY: It's been shocking, but on the other hand it's so stunning it's almost unreal, and I think probably when one has been back among civilised people for a while one just forgets it.

REID: You feel as though you've been really out of civilisation, do you?

BURNEY: Oh yes, absolutely out of the world. Everything which happened here was without relation to anything which had ever happened before, and therefore one had a special year of life which just was somewhere else, in another world. It might have been on Mars.'

⟨oↄ⟩

Buchenwald was liberated – and destroyed – by the US Third Army. In the north the British 11th Armoured Division found scenes of similar degradation and bestiality in the concentration camp at Belsen:

19 April 1945

'I picked my way over corpse after corpse in the gloom, until I heard one voice raised above the gentle undulating moaning. I found a girl, she was a living skeleton, impossible to gauge her age for she had practically no hair left, and her face was only a yellow parchment sheet with two holes in it for eyes. She was stretching out her stick of an arm and gasping something, it was "English, English, medicine, medicine", and she was trying to cry but she hadn't enough strength. And beyond her down the passage and in the hut there were the convulsive movements of dying people too weak to raise themselves from the floor.

'In the shade of some trees lay a great collection of bodies. I walked about them trying to count, there were perhaps 150 of them flung down on each other, all naked, all so thin that their yellow skin glistened like stretched rubber on their bones. Some of the poor starved creatures whose bodies were there looked so utterly unreal and inhuman that I could have imagined that they had never lived at all. They were like polished skeletons, the skeletons that medical students like to play practical jokes with.

'At one end of the pile a cluster of men and women were gathered round a fire; they were using rags and old shoes taken from the bodies to keep it alight, and they were heating soup over it. And close by was the enclosure where 500 children between the ages of five and twelve had been kept. They were not so hungry as the rest, for the women had sacrificed themselves to keep them alive. Babies were born at Belsen, some of them shrunken, wizened little things that could not live, because their mothers could not feed them.

'One woman, distraught to the point of madness, flung herself at a British soldier who was on guard at the camp on the night that it was reached by the 11th Armoured Division; she begged him to give her some milk for the tiny baby she held in her arms. She laid the mite on the ground and threw herself at the sentry's feet and kissed his boots. And when, in his distress, he asked her to get up, she put the baby in his arms and ran off crying that she would find milk for it because there was no milk in her breast. And when the soldier opened the bundle of rags to look at the child, he found that it had been dead for days.

'There had been no privacy of any kind. Women stood naked at the side of the track, washing in cupfuls of water taken from British Army water trucks. Others squatted while they searched themselves for lice, and examined each other's hair. Sufferers from dysentery leaned against the huts, straining helplessly, and all around and about them was this awful drifting tide of exhausted people, neither caring nor watching. Just a few held out their withered hands to us as we passed by, and blessed the doctor whom they knew had become the camp commander in place of the brutal Kramer.

'I have never seen British soldiers so moved to cold fury as the men who opened the Belsen camp this week, and those of the police and the RAMC who are now on duty there, trying to save the prisoners who are not too far gone in starvation.'

RICHARD DIMBLEBY

Finally, Dachau – rivalling Auschwitz as the most notorious of Hitler's concentration camps, though nothing could surpass in horror what had already been disclosed at Buchenwald and Belsen:

1 May 1945
'I have just left Dachau with a mind confused between the joyous scenes of the liberation of 32,000 prisoners and the scenes of horror that remain, for Dachau is like the world's worst nightmare come true.

'Here briefly and baldly is what I saw today, Monday 30 April 1945. A hundred yards from the gates of Dachau concentration camp is a railway siding and on that siding I saw fifty wagons filled with emaciated bodies. They were the bodies of prisoners who had been brought alive from Buchenwald and had been on that train in that siding for three days without food or water. Those who tried to get out were shot down. Their bodies lay alongside the track.

'That was outside the camp – inside, in a moat-like river which runs alongside the barbed and electrified fence, I saw the bodies of 2000 prisoners who had been murdered by machine-gun fire, a few hours before the Seventh Army Americans reached Dachau. Farther inside the enclosure, I saw a long hut full of skeleton-like human beings, all dying and too weak to talk.

'Worst of all was the crematorium – a long brick building, with a reception room where the bodies, dead or alive, were taken in and stripped of clothing. Then came a shower-room, with jets in the ceiling and gratings in the floor, where the bodies were washed before being burnt. Then a charnel house in which I saw a pile of poor, wasted bodies stacked in neat orderliness, waiting to be burnt; and then the furnace room itself. On the walls of the crematorium was the notice in German "Cleanliness is a duty here so don't forget to wipe your hands", and beside the furnaces was an extraordinary mural painting of two headless SS officers astride bloated pigs.

'So much about the dead – what, then, about the living? As I said at the beginning, there are 32,000 of them still in the camp. And the majority will survive. As I went through the camp, gaunt, ragged men pressed forward to touch my hand. They were of all ages, young, middle-aged, and old, old men; some had only been in Dachau for a few weeks, others for eleven years, and they ranged from slave-workers of all nationalities to intellectuals and opponents of Nazism from all countries overrun by the Germans. In my brief visit I met and talked to one Englishman among all the thousands of Germans, Czechs, Poles, Russians, French, Belgians and Dutch.

'When the American troops stormed up to the camp and forced the Nazi Commandant and his SS guards to surrender, the enthusiasm inside the camp when they went through the main gates was wild and hysterical, and a battalion of infantry was required to restrain the liberated prisoners. They swarmed around the US soldiers, hugging and kissing them, and the countryside resounded to wild cheer after cheer which rose even above the crashing of gunfire.'

IAN WILSON

To comment on such scenes as these defies the vocabulary of human indignation and compassion. The perpetrators stand condemned by their own actions: of the victims, some at least were restored to the simple decencies of human life. While the doctors worked in Dachau to salvage what they could of health and self-respect from that vast wreckage of men and women, there was a different and happier scene reported from the West. Polish women soldiers, liberated earlier from a concentration camp near the Dutch border, prepared a dance for the Canadians who had rescued them. Many of the girls had contrived to make their national costumes out of material that the Germans tried to take away from them. Now, free once more from the nightmare that had threatened to engulf all Europe, they danced with their liberators:

1 May 1945
'Everything looks very Polish here – down at the bottom of the hall – it's one of the huts, just one of these thin-walled cold huts which make part of the concentration camp compound. Down at the bottom there is a white and red flag of Poland, draped right down the wall and a golden eagle on it, and between that, I'm sitting just with

my back to the platform where the music comes from, and between that flag and the music of the accordion, the dance has just broken up – the Canadian soldiers have let go of the Polish girls – some of whom are in national costume. The dance has broken up in laughter and in happy conversation. Now they're waiting for the next tune to begin, and here it comes. Now we're going to have a waltz, and the Polish girls are going to dance a waltz with the Canadians whom they're entertaining. There are British and Canadian officers here and Polish officers, and all the Polish girls are just beginning to swing into the waltz. Some of them are dressed in the white and red and black – very pretty costumes that they bring from Silesia and from Cracow and they're going round with their wide skirts swinging in the light of the candles – there's no electric light here – just candlelight, soft, soft candlelight going up the wooden roof and casting shadows across the floor and on to these pretty dresses.'

ROBERT DUNNETT

Perhaps that is the most fitting conclusion to a tale of cruelty which, in its unredeemed and unexampled foulness, must haunt the mind of Europe for generations to come.

CHAPTER XXII
The Last Fight

'I am in Berlin. Sidorov'

In the third week of April the wholesale collapse of the German Army in central Germany and the imminence of a link-up between the Russians and the Anglo–American forces made it certain that victory was near; but how near depended on the ability and the willingness of the Germans to continue fighting in isolated pockets of resistance. The framework of the Wehrmacht might be shattered beyond recovery, but substantial fragments remained in Norway, in Denmark, in Holland, in Czechoslovakia. There was the prospect of a final determined stand in Bavaria, and in the north the German Navy was fighting furiously to defend its principal bases:

30 April 1945

'Here in the north, there's still an army to be reckoned with; an army whose fighting power Himmler [*he had been appointed C-in-C Home Army after the 20 July plot*] may still regard as a bargaining weapon. We have smashed the German Army as a whole and its Air Force; but we haven't yet broken the power or the spirit of the German Navy. And it's now fighting hard in defence of its great ports and naval bases in the north. Even though the Navy has never been thoroughly pro-Nazi, it has been unquestionably loyal to the German High Command. In Kiel, Wilhelmshaven and the northern ports there are more than 100,000 German naval personnel – most of them with some training in the use of weapons; and they're being put into the land battle. We're meeting marines, sailors, and even submarine crews, and they're fighting well.

'Moreover, when Field-Marshal Busch became Commander-in-Chief North-West, he took over an area where the organisation and discipline behind the lines was still good, because the Navy still had the situation firmly in hand. Busch also found that in addition to the troops fighting south of the Elbe he had four other divisions that he could bring from Denmark. He thus had the core of a force to protect the naval bases; and the Navy was determined that he should use it to do so. This combination of circumstances has provided the Second Army with the immediate task of isolating and smashing this force, and of seizing the naval bases behind it. We can't afford at this stage of the war to pause in the task. So long as there are any pockets of resistance as well organised as this one, the Nazis may be encouraged to fight on elsewhere. And so here in the north the Second Army is striking at what amounts to Himmler's last hope.'

CHESTER WILMOT

In Holland, too, the fighting was extremely severe, and the Germans showed no willingness to surrender, even when they were cut off. On one occasion a Canadian Headquarters, at Otterloo, was nearly overrun when a thousand Germans tried to fight their way back to their own lines:

19 April 1945
'Down a road leading into Otterloo from the north came a column of men. A Canadian artillery sergeant challenged them when they came abreast of the gun lines. The reply was a vicious burst of Spandau fire. The battle of Otterloo was on. Ten seconds after the Canadian sergeant's challenge there was bedlam. Gunners jumped to their field

pieces and fired them over open sights at the oncoming Germans. When the enemy overran the guns the gunners dug themselves in and went on fighting from their slit trenches with Sten guns, rifles and pistols. Not a single gunner surrendered, and not a single gun was captured, but the Germans surged past the gun area and into Otterloo. If they could have penetrated the headquarters area, they might have been able to dash right across the corridor.

'They did not get through. A Canadian colonel firing from beneath his caravan killed two. His batman killed three. Nearly everybody in the headquarters has at least one notch to carve on his gun. Some have as many as ten.

'At the height of the battle, four Wasp flame-throwers trundled into the battle-torn village of Otterloo. They wheeled up to the road along which more Germans were pouring to join in the breakthrough attempt. Great tongues of flame spurted out. Terrible screams came from those who did not die instantly. In front of one flame-thrower this morning I saw 105 German dead, all terribly burned.

'The flame-throwers turned the tide. With 400 Germans dead and 250 taken prisoner, the enemy attack broke, and tonight remnants of the German force are being rounded up in the woodlands around Otterloo. Man for man these gunners and headquarters' soldiers had outfought the Germans. They killed more of the enemy than I have ever seen in such a small area.'

MATTHEW HALTON, CBC

◦◦◦

North of our original Rhine crossing German paratroops had fought hard to keep us from the North Sea ports, but by 22 April Bremen was under shellfire. The first shells carried a call to the city to surrender; as these failed to draw a reply, an ultimatum was telephoned to the garrison:

23 April 1945

'The telephone they used was found in the station at Achim, ten miles east of Bremen, when the 52nd Lowland Division took Achim this morning. This afternoon I was there when the ultimatum was phoned through. The stationmaster at Achim was asked to call up the stationmaster at Bremen, and then he handed over the phone to our intelligence officer. He spoke to a German lieutenant, who then went off to convey the message to the Bremen garrison commander, and to bring back a senior officer to discuss the ultimatum. We waited for over an hour. Then the phone from Bremen rang again. Not to tell us the reply, but to give us the friendly warning that the RAF was bombing Bremen, and to say that no senior German officer would come to the phone. Then the line went dead. The bombs had evidently cut it.

'We couldn't see much of the bombing because of the low cloud, but hundreds of Lancasters attacked the ack-ack defences and installations in and around the city. We've warned Bremen that yesterday's heavy raid is only a small foretaste of what is to come if they try to hold out, and already our heavy and medium guns are pounding away at the defences. Occasionally we're putting over a few more propaganda shells, filled with "free-passage" leaflets, for those who've had enough. And these appeals are being reinforced by loudspeaker vans blaring out across no-man's-land on the fringe of the city; but so far the Germans have shown no signs of cracking.

'No doubt, when Himmler visited Bremen in his special armoured train last week he tightened up the Nazi grip on this port. A Nazi chief has been installed to organise control of the SS, the Gestapo, and the local police, and to make sure that the garrison commander, General Becker, doesn't weaken. Civilians who've escaped say that already the local führer has sacked the burgomaster, who wished to surrender. Nevertheless the plight of the city is now serious; it's three-quarters encircled and the Germans control only two good roads leading out of it, and these only lead north into the peninsula which we've already sealed off between Bremen and Hamburg. Refugees say that inside Bremen there are about 300,000 German civilians; some 50,000 foreign workers and more than 20,000 troops are around the city. Civilians also say that they've been short of food in recent weeks, but their greatest problem now is going to be shortage of water. The city's local supply has been put out of action by bombing; and their main outside source, a pipeline from the Harz Mountains, was cut off today by us just before the RAF bombing began.

'Today they also lost their main source of fuel, an oil refinery at Achim which the 52nd Division captured this morning. The refinery and its storage tanks are hidden underground in a wood near Achim, and it was working until yesterday. In fact petrol and oil from this refinery moved the 15th Panzer Grenadier Division when it transferred from the south to the north of Bremen last week to counter the Guards' outflanking movement. There are, no doubt, other storage tanks in Bremen, but the loss of this refinery at this stage must be a considerable embarrassment.

'The Germans are now being driven steadily back into Bremen and the garrison of 20,000 may well be increased to 30,000 by the time all the units fighting outside the perimeter have withdrawn inside. There they'll have a very strong defensive position, for Bremen is very difficult to attack. It stands almost on an island in the flood plain of the Weser. On the south it's protected by a belt two miles wide which the Germans have flooded, and on the north-east and north the low-lying ground is laced with dikes and canals.'

CHESTER WILMOT

The city's formidable defences were unavailing. Four days later a BBC correspondent walked through the ruins of Bremen:

26 April 1945

'I am in the centre of the city of Bremen, if you can call this chaotic rubbish-heap in which our bulldozers are working as I speak, their men with handkerchiefs round their throats to avoid the flying dust, if you can call this rubbish-heap a city any more. There are walls standing, there are factory chimneys here and there, but there's no shape and no order and certainly no hope for this shell of a city that was once called Bremen. It's the sheer size of the smashed area that overwhelms you. These endless vistas down small streets to the houses leaning at drunken angles and this inhuman landscape of great blocks of flats with their sides ripped open, and the intimate household goods just blown out into the bomb craters. Well, I expected it when we came in, but still it's the scale that counts. Bremen by the look of it was a city of many thousand inhabitants, but once you are past the outer suburbs there is hardly a house intact in which these people could live, because they haven't even tried to live in them. Everybody has gone into those giant air-raid shelters, these great blocks of almost solid concrete that are dotted all over the ruins of Bremen. They stood up to the bombings well, and now, from the one opposite us, the people are coming out, to stare at the tanks and the bulldozers, and at the guns now rolling past us into the heart of the city. Some of these people are already starting to potter about in that seemingly aimless way that bombed-out people do among the dusty rubble. The foreign workers – there must have been thousands here in Bremen – are already on their way out; they go on tramping past our lads and waving to them as our jeeps and the lorries and bulldozers are coming to the city now in a steady stream. But the inhabitants of Bremen have got to stay in the ruins of their city. And they now have ample time to walk around us and see the results of total war.'

WYNFORD VAUGHAN-THOMAS

⟨◌⟩

On the Eastern Front Berlin itself was at last going down in the final throes of destruction. On 16 April RAF Mustangs, patrolling over the capital, met Russian Stormoviks in what might be described as the first operational link-up:

17 April 1945

'While we were still flying in towards the German capital someone reported aircraft on our port side – it looked as if we'd run into some trouble, and at once the whole wing changed course and headed flat out in the direction of the reported aircraft. It was rather hazy and for some time I couldn't see anything; then quite suddenly I spotted some aircraft almost dead ahead. There seemed to be quite a number of them, and they were flying in wide formation. Suddenly someone called up "They're Russians!" But we were still not sure and closed in towards them very cautiously. They'd obviously spotted us and seemed a bit wary too, and what seemed to me to be escorting fighters began to weave and do some tight turns – they were pretty manoeuvrable. Then all at once we were on top of the aircraft and saw that they were some of the Russian Air Force's famous Stormovik bombers escorted by Yak fighters. Recognition was mutual. At once we exchanged friendly signals and waved our arms in greeting to the Red pilots who waggled the wings of their planes. As we shot by we could see the Red Star of Russia on their wings and fuselage. And so, over the outskirts of Berlin, we met our Russian Allies for the first time.'

FLIGHT-LIEUT. PARTRIDGE, RAF

A week later Berlin was outflanked north and south, and the end was near:

22 April 1945

'Berlin, capital of the Reich that Hitler once boasted would last a thousand years, is living through its last hours in an atmosphere of confusion and panic. Russian and German pilots engage each other in ceaseless dogfights over the roofs of the city, while the air is filled with the thunder of Russian guns and the thud of their shells, which have already fallen right in the centre of Berlin in the Unter den Linden, the Potsdammer Platz, and the Leipziger Strasse. The air is filled, too, with desperate Nazi orders, threats and appeals, to a population that's either panic-stricken or sunk in complete apathy. That's the background to the dramatic statement shouted over the telephone by a Swedish correspondent to his paper in Stockholm. "This," he said, "is probably the last time I shall be speaking to you before the fall of Berlin." And what he said was underlined by the sound of Russian guns, clearly audible over the wire.

'When it became known that the Russians were advancing from the south as well as from the east, thousands of Berliners began a wild flight towards the west and north-west. Tank, infantry and Volkssturm reinforcements being rushed to meet the Red Army have found the streets of western Berlin filled with refugees. Trams and underground trains, strictly reserved for the transport of wounded, have been stormed by panic-stricken Berliners, who have literally fought their own wounded men for places in the cars. Hysterical scenes have taken place in underground stations as women and children of all ages have struggled in vain to find room on the trains. And those Berliners who remain in the city show no enthusiasm for fighting of any kind. Most of them spend their time in the air-raid shelters which are so full that nobody can sit down. Outside in the streets more and more prisoners of war and foreign workers are wandering about completely unguarded.'

NORMAN MACDONALD

26 April 1945

'The din of the street fighting can be heard three miles outside Berlin. The roads leading east are crowded with people. Some are Soviet citizens on the first stage of their way home out of German slavery. The rest are Berliners fleeing from the battle, seeking areas held by the Red Army. The Germans concentrated the best remnants of the Luftwaffe east and south-east of their capital, and threw in 1200 planes, including the Hindenburg, Udet and Germany Squadrons, to

Richard Dimbleby in front of the Brandenburg Gate in Berlin in July 1945.

defend the air approaches. They were engulfed by the might of the Red Air Force. The sky is sometimes quite overcrowded with aircraft acting in support of our ground forces. This is a typical conversation which I heard between a senior air officer on the ground and the commander of a formation in the air.

' "You're half a minute late over the target. Why?"

'And the reply: "I've been hanging around here waiting for the wave ahead of us to get out of the way." The commander's voice was heard a few seconds later, addressing the pilots of the other formation. "Petlyakovs, clear out and give us a chance, can't you? Your time's up."

'There has been some rain, which has helped to lay the dust. Oh, that Berlin dust! A westerly wind blew it towards our positions. It even blanketed the sun. From seven o'clock on a cloudless morning until noon we were enveloped in an unnatural gloom. We couldn't see for more than a few yards. The sun rose higher and higher, but its rays didn't penetrate to the ground. The truck drivers delivering ammunition to the forward elements had to switch their lights full on. It was simply impossible to tell that the sun was shining. The German Command are unable to do anything to save the situation, but they've been keeping up the fight. They divided the city into fortified zones, subdivided into sectors. All the tall buildings were turned into resistance centres, linked by communication trenches and passages. Guns, machine-guns and mortars stood at every street crossing.

'The enemy had every street under crossfire, and the many canals made serious obstacles. Their banks were heavily fortified. The Germans huddle near the houses, looking with puzzled expressions at the sky where the Red air fleets stream, and staring confusedly at the Soviet war machine thundering along the roads. Some Nazi, before our arrival, scrawled a slogan on the side of a house: "1918 will not be repeated." A Red Army man has crossed it out and written underneath, in Russian: "I am in Berlin. Sidorov." '

SOVIET WAR NEWS CORRESPONDENT

Reports that Hitler and Goebbels were staying to the last in the doomed city were at first received incredulously. Their decision to do so was apparently dictated by the hopelessness of further resistance. Having devastated their own country by protracting the struggle long after the issue was decided, at last even they were shaken out of their infatuation by the course of those momentous April days. The war was as good as over. In the heart of Berlin the Nazis made a last fanatical stand, but there was no prospect of their doing more than delay the Red Army:

30 April 1945

'Red Army forces converging on the heart of the capital are faced by an enemy who still fights with extreme fury. The Germans continue to feed men, tanks and guns into the inferno. They have fortified themselves inside half-ruined buildings. Each block interacts with its neighbours. There is only one way to approach these German strong-points, and that is by blasting a way through the walls of adjoining buildings. Mopping up has to be done with scrupulous thoroughness. Soviet tanks and guns are rolling down the streets of Berlin, three abreast towards the Unter den Linden and Alexanderplatz. Flashily dressed German girls and men in raglan coats and soft hats stand silently, shifting from one foot to another, staring at the Soviet tanks. Children shout "Hitler kaput!" with monotonous insistence, varying the chant with requests for a piece of bread.

'Soviet tommy-gunners convoy Volkssturm prisoners through the streets. One of Hitler's warriors has a beard to his waist; another, in dark glasses, steps high like a blind pony. A third stumps along on a wooden leg. He is frankly glad to be a prisoner. His reasoning is simple. Now the Russians have come, there will be order in Berlin. If there is order, then, naturally, there will be food, water and electricity – conveniences Berlin has lacked for a long time. The streets are strewn with SS badges, ribbons stamped with the swastika, torn-up Nazi Party cards, officers' shoulder-straps ripped out together with pieces of cloth. Drawn up along the pavements are perfectly serviceable cars – without any wheels. Before the Red Army appeared at the outskirts of Berlin the wheels of private cars were ordered to be turned over to the police, to prevent a wild rush from the city. An enormous dump of these wheels was found in the yard of a district police station.

'Berliners who have made their way through the firing line to the comparative quiet of the Soviet-held districts say that in the area still uncaptured mobs of people are looting the food stores and neither the police nor SS can stop them. A police battalion, sent to round up deserters, itself deserted almost to a man on the road.'

SOVIET WAR NEWS CORRESPONDENT

On Wednesday 25 April the US First Army linked up with the Russians at Torgau:

27 April 1945

'It was Lieutenant William Robinson's patrol of the 273rd Regiment that made the official link-up at Torgau last Wednesday afternoon between the eastern and western fronts. But there were several other First Army patrols active out there in the area east of the Mulde River which also succeeded in making contact that afternoon.

'For several days. General Hodges' troops had been waiting for this great moment. Pilots who came in from flights over the no-man's-land between the Mulde and the Elbe had been questioned and cross-questioned about what they'd seen. For hours on end men had been straining their ears at their radio sets catching snatches of Russian conversations. It was a very natural impatience, everyone was eager for the junction to take place.

'The First Army could, of course, have advanced beyond the Mulde River; there was no enemy opposition in front of these Americans which they could not have dealt with easily. But they were held back and very wisely so. We did, at one time, hold a substantial bridgehead over the Mulde; this was voluntarily withdrawn, not under any enemy pressure, but for very sound, if somewhat unusual, reasons.

'When these two mighty armies are driving towards each other with the common enemy in between them it's pretty obvious that, as the moment of junction approaches, there's going to be a considerable amount of uneasiness on both sides. Russians might find it difficult to recognise Americans, Americans might not find it easy to identify Russians. Moreover, a crafty enemy such as the German might well be expected to foresee the possibilities of the situation, and aggravate the dangers. Entirely through failure to recognise each other, clashes and skirmishes between the two friendly armies might occur, each thinking that the other was the enemy. Such armed encounters, of course, would be tragic.

'To eliminate all chance of such unfortunate occurrences, General Bradley very wisely halted his armies on an easily recognisable natural feature, on the west side of a clearly defined river line, there to await the arrival of the Russians. Our Allies knew exactly where we were; there was no question of confusion over map references, no risk of head-on collisions or inter-Allied battles. As a result the junction has taken place very smoothly and very happily, and that's a matter of great satisfaction to us all.'

FRANK GILLARD

27 April 1945

'In the picturesque medieval town of Torgau I saw 330 soldiers of the First American and the Red Armies throw their arms round each other's necks and kiss each other on the cheeks. I even had to undergo this greeting myself from a burly Ukrainian soldier.

'As I stood on a ramp on the west bank of the Elbe, the Russian soldiers in the town fired off mortars and rifles out of sheer joy: this most cordial of welcomes was a wonderful spectacle. The troops of each nation did their best to make the other understand what they were saying. (It's not so difficult as might be supposed.) The whole scene was one of the gayest fraternisation. A Russian lieutenant sat on a wall playing an accordion and singing Russian songs, and the Doughboys joined in. Drinks were passed round and everyone was happy.'

EDWARD WARD

CHAPTER XXIII

The Closing Scenes
'Now I will sign the instrument of surrender'

Somewhere in the inferno of Berlin Hitler was dead, or presumed to be dead. After the failure of Himmler's peace negotiations Admiral Doenitz proclaimed himself, on 1 May, as the new Führer. But who was Führer now no longer mattered. By the link-up west and south of Berlin Germany was divided. The surrender of all German forces in Italy and the speed of Patton's tanks sealed the fate of the redoubt in Bavaria [*the area of western Austria and southern Bavaria round Berchtesgaden known to the Nazis as the National Redoubt and the site for a possible last stand*]. In the north the British Second Army drove on to seize the remaining German ports and link up with Rokossovsky's Army:

3 May 1945
'The general surrender of the German forces opposing the Second British Army may now come at any hour; except in the pocket west of Bremen there is no longer any real opposition on General Dempsey's front, and pilots today reported that there are white flags flying from the houses fifty miles behind the nominal enemy line.

'It's been a day of surrender and negotiation for surrender by German officers ranging from commanders of regiments to commanders of armies. Last night two German divisions surrendered intact. Early this morning the commander of the Hamburg garrison, General Wolz, agreed not only to hand over unconditionally Germany's greatest port, but also personally to lead the 7th British Armoured Division into the city this evening. During the morning the 11th Armoured Division received word that the garrison of Neumünster, thirty-five miles north of Hamburg and only thirty miles from the great naval base of Kiel, was ready to give in. The Neumünster garrison also said that other troops on the Kiel Canal itself were anxious to surrender.

'But the biggest news of the day was the complete break-up and the attempted surrender of two of the German armies in Army Group Vistula, the group which has been opposing Rokossovsky and was defending the area north of Berlin. These armies had retreated about 150 miles since the Russian breakthrough on the Oder last month, and yesterday our columns cut right through the area where they were vainly trying to reorganise. Their fighting spirit was already broken, and they disintegrated at once.

'Today, their commanders, General Manteuffel of the Third Panzer Army and General Tippelskirch of the First Panzer Army, offered to surrender their complete forces to Field-Marshal Montgomery. This was refused, though we have accepted the personal capitulation of the two generals and many senior officers of Army Group Vistula.

'The official British attitude is that as these two armies are still engaged in fighting the Russians, we can't accept their surrender, and in any case their commanders are in no position to hand over the armies to us. And so tonight in the woods and villages between the Baltic and the Elbe there are tens of thousands of Germans from Army Group Vistula vainly trying to find someone who will accept them as prisoners. Their commanders have surrendered, their staffs have disintegrated; only those units still in direct contact with the Russians continue fighting – fighting rather than yield to the Red Army.

'The fact is that at all costs the Germans want to avoid surrendering to the Soviet troops. They know how great are Germany's crimes against Russia, and they know that the Russians won't forget.'

CHESTER WILMOT

On 3 May Hamburg radio station broadcast the dramatic announcement that British troops were marching into the city. Outside, at Lauenburg, a correspondent watched German troops coming out of Hamburg to surrender:

3 May 1945

'Since two o'clock this morning this endless stream of transport has been pouring through this town, under the white flags hung over the shattered houses by the inhabitants who are standing in the streets looking dumbfounded at this wreckage of the Wehrmacht that's going past us. For, make no mistake about it, this Army we see going by us is the most curious collection of wreckage you ever saw – improvised cars with people riding on the bumpers, half-track vehicles, thousands of them, going through in a steady stream, and to make matters even more fantastic they've got their own traffic policemen directing them, under British orders, standing on the corner waving listlessly on, as the thing goes steadily by us.

'These people are defeated soldiers – you can see it in their eyes. In the middle of them there comes a much more joyous note. We see a charabanc full of RAF released prisoners, cheering as they go by, and the Germans on the half-tracks looking glumly on.'

WYNFORD VAUGHAN-THOMAS

Later the same day the great news came through that British and Russian troops had met near Wismar:

3 May 1945

'The two great armies, British and Russian, have met. The Russians have set up a little wooden barrier across the road, they have got two smart guards mounted outside it, and around the barrier an international meeting is taking place. Everybody, the 6th Airborne, the boys who made the junction, have come out to see the Russians. The Russians have come out to see us. And around the barrier there has been a tremendous amount of handshaking and photographing, with the Russians posing as we photograph. There were some German prisoners trying desperately to get across the barrier. They got to the barrier, and the Russian guard gave a wink to me and said "Siberia". And everybody, I must say, has no pity for them at all. One of the 6th Airborne said: "It has been a long time but now it is here, and here we are with the Russians." The Americans have driven up; the French prisoners of war have got down and are shaking hands; the Russians have handed over Russian cigarettes, in fact the armies, American, British and Russian, seem to be meeting around here in the heart of Germany in view of the Baltic Sea. It's the end, the dead-end, of Hitler's Reich.'

WYNFORD VAUGHAN-THOMAS

And now the 'celebrities' of Nazi Germany began to appear among the host of prisoners the Allies were rounding up. One of the first was General Dietmar, the German radio commentator, who gave his last and most dispirited commentary on the war in an interview after he and his son had surrendered:

2 May 1945

'It was as a member of the German Officer Corps that Dietmar spoke. For the party men he showed a mixture of fear and contempt. "Hitler," he said, "would never have a strong personality in control of the Wehrmacht. The moment the German Chief of Staff began to think for himself or to show any initiative, Hitler stepped in to squash him!" Dietmar said that he often raised matters with Guderian, who time and again would say, "Yes, yes, but you know our difficulties."

'Of Himmler he said: "Ninety per cent of the officers of the German Army consider Himmler the grave-digger of the Wehrmacht. The other ten per cent are just youngsters – fanatical fools whose opinion doesn't count." He went on to illustrate his point by talking about the Ardennes offensive, mounted by Hitler. The intention was, he said, to cross the Meuse and swing northwards so as to cut off all the Allies beyond the river. But the operation was poorly prepared, and the Sixth SS Panzer Army, the mainstay of the attack, was grossly mismanaged by Sepp Dietrich, who had been placed in command of it by Hitler. The resistance was much too tough and well organised for the Germans. And when von Rundstedt went to Hitler to report this and to propose that they should be satisfied with the gains they'd made and should call a halt to the operation, Hitler flew into a temper and sacked Rundstedt, making him the scapegoat for the faults of the party men. And so, said Dietmar, we not only lost the battle here but we threw away the reserves we ought to have been cherishing for use elsewhere.

'In the same way Dietmar attributed the decline of the Luftwaffe to the bad training and the lack of foresight of the party men, who, he said, were constantly haggling about what sort of planes should be put into production, and never made up their minds. In the end Hitler took a vote of confidence among the flying personnel. Things have been so bad that his opposite number, the official Luftwaffe commentator on the German Home Service, had to be taken off the air.

'It is only very recently, said Dietmar, that the German people as a whole came to realise that they were totally defeated. Up to the last few weeks they really believed the propaganda and thought that at the very worst they'd be able to make some sort of compromise peace which wouldn't be too bad for them.

'The flying-bombs and V-weapons deceived nobody in the inner circles, Dietmar said, though they did give a big boost to the morale of the general public. Nobody who mattered ever thought that the V-weapon campaign would finish the war, or break the British, but they did think that it might weaken, to some extent, the British war potential.

'Although, he said, it was a perfectly natural thing that the divisions now falling back in southern Germany should withdraw into such a natural fortress area as the southern redoubt, Dietmar said that he had no definite knowledge of plans for a last stand, and neither had any of his friends; in fact, he thought the stand impossible.

'When the conversation turned on the awful atrocities which were being committed in the concentration camps all over Germany, his jaw sagged. He looked a grim, old man. Then he stated his case. The Officer Corps, he said, and the Armed Forces, were not fully aware and were not fully informed of what was going on. It was only when Himmler called a meeting of high-ranking generals, in order almost to apologise for what was going on, that the Officer Corps got some inkling of the true situation. Himmler said that it was the most difficult order he had ever been called upon to give, that this policy should be carried out, but that he'd been ordered himself to go ahead with it, and the generals interpreted this as meaning that the policy came from Hitler himself. Dietmar said that the generals couldn't make official protests. Each general's sphere of influence was clearly defined. If he stepped beyond its bounds to busy himself in matters outside his field, he was removed. The generals' answer, he said, was the bomb plot of 20 July, which unfortunately failed.

'Well, that's Dietmar's case, which no doubt we shall hear elaborated and argued again and again in the months to come. The weaknesses of it were put to Dietmar very forcibly this morning, and as I watched him I could see that on this subject here was one very worried German.

'We spoke a good deal, of course, about the alleged death of Hitler, and the appointment of Doenitz. He said that he accepts the fact that Hitler, by some means or other, has died. If the announcement is a swindle, said Dietmar, Hitler would never dare to reappear, for he'd be either branded as a coward or regarded as an impostor.'

FRANK GILLARD

Dietmar had come 'off the air' from Berlin. The fall of Hamburg put another well-known commentator out of business. On 4 May the familiar acid voice of Lord Haw-Haw was replaced by the voice of a BBC correspondent whose first broadcast from Germany had been made in a bomber over Berlin in 1942: now he spoke from William Joyce's studio in Hamburg:

4 May 1945

'This is Germany calling. Calling for the last time from Station Hamburg, and tonight you will not hear views on the news by William Joyce, for Mr Joyce – Lord Haw-Haw to most of us in Britain – has been most unfortunately interrupted in his broadcasting career, and at present has left rather hurriedly for a vacation, an extremely short vacation if the Second British Army has anything to do with it, maybe to Denmark and other points north. And in his place this is the BBC calling all the long-suffering listeners in Britain who for six years have had to put up with the acid tones of Mr Joyce speaking over the same wavelength that I'm using to talk to you now.

'I'm seated in front of Lord Haw-Haw's own microphone, or rather the microphone he used in the last three weeks of his somewhat chequered career; and I wonder what Lord Haw-Haw's views on the news are now? For Hamburg, the city he made notorious, is this evening under the control of the British Forces, and we found a completely and utterly bomb-ruined city.

'We thought Bremen was bad, but Hamburg is devastated. Whole quarters have disintegrated under air attacks. There are miles upon miles of blackened walls and utterly burnt-out streets, and in the ruins there are still nearly a million people and 50,000 foreign workers living in the cellars and air-raid shelters. Today you don't see a single civilian on the streets; as soon as we came in we imposed a 48-hour curfew, and there's a Sunday quiet over the whole city; all that stirs in the streets is a British jeep or an armoured car, or a patrol of British Tommies watching that the curfew is strictly enforced.

'The docks are even more devastated than the town, the great shipyards of Bloem and Voss are a wilderness of tangled girders, and in the middle of this chaos fourteen unfinished U-boats still stand rusting on the slipways. Work on them finally stopped two months ago; after that date Hamburg was a dead city.

'Rummaging through Lord Haw-Haw's desk we found a revealing timetable he drew up for his work, for 10 April 1945, and at the end of it is the glorious item: "1450–1510 hrs a pause to collect my wits." Well – he and the citizens of Hamburg have now got plenty of time to collect their wits, for tonight the sturdy soldiers of the Devons, the famous Desert Rats, are on guard over Haw-Haw's studios, the Allied military authorities are now running his programme, and instead of "Germany Calling" the colonel in charge gives you now the new call-sign of "Station Hamburg". This is Radio Hamburg, a station of the Allied Military Government. [*Same announcement in German*] And from Hamburg we take you back to London.'

WYNFORD VAUGHAN-THOMAS

The bombers of the RAF began the war by dropping leaflets; they ended it by dropping food. As the surrender of all German armies became imminent, a local truce brought some relief to the suffering people of Holland. On 29 April Lancasters flew over The Hague and other districts, dropping supplies to cope with the threat of starvation among Dutch civilians until land transport could be got through to them. The editor of the Netherlands News Agency flew in one of the Lancasters and described the mission:

29 April 1945

'The grocer called on the people of The Hague today – for the first time for years. True, it was Sunday; but this was definitely a case of "the better the day, the better the deed". He called at Rotterdam and Leyden as well. It was closing day too – not only because it was Sunday but also because the shops have had no food to sell for a long time.

'I was with the RAF delivery men on their rounds. We travelled in a Lancaster bomber, and as a result of the day's activities rations were provided for thousands of starving Dutch people, many of whom had not had a square meal for months. Our squadron, for example, carried sufficient food – forty-two tons of it – to feed one-fifth of the population of The Hague for one day. But there were other squadrons as well.

'Each of our aerial delivery vans carried food with which first-class meals can be produced. There were flour and yeast for bread-making; tins of meat and bacon, with pepper and salt and mustard to taste. The Dutch love for vegetables was met by tins of dehydrated potato, as well as bags of peas and beans. Sugar, margarine, dried milk, cheese, dried eggs and chocolate completed the order. Weeks of preparation and experiment had gone into the scheme, including the devising of special slings to ensure that in place of huge 12,000-pounders, each aircraft could drop 355 twenty-pound food bombs.

'We crossed the North Sea on our mercy mission shortly after midday and approached The Hague at a very low level. Our target area, the Ypenburg civil airfield south-east of the town, was clearly visible. It had been marked out by Pathfinders with green flares, and in the centre was a white cross surmounted by a red light.

'From the moment we crossed the Dutch coast, people in the fields and roads, and in the gardens of the sad little houses, waved frantically. But it was not until we were actually flying over The Hague that we saw what this manna from heaven really meant for the Dutch. Every road seemed full of people waving flags, sheets, or anything they could grab. The roofs of tall buildings were black with Dutch citizens welcoming us. On a barge we saw the Dutch tricolour bravely hoisted; across a large flat roof an Orange flag was colourfully stretched.

'The people were certainly overjoyed to see these huge bombers emptying their bomb-bays one after another on the target area, as thousands of food bombs fluttered out like confetti from a giant hand. And along the roads leading into The Hague were carts, perambulators and bicycles as the populace seemed to race to join in the great share-out. Unfortunately, owing to the recent spell of bad weather, we were just too late to give them their Sunday dinner, but with amazing enthusiasm the RAF aerial grocers today certainly delivered the goods.

' "These were the best bombs we have dropped for years," said Flight Officer [*sic*] Ellis, the bomb-aimer of our aircraft.'

H. G. FRANKS, NETHERLANDS NEWS AGENCY

A day or two later lorries began to pass through the German lines, bringing more food into Holland:

3 May 1945

'As we passed down the middle of the front the Canadian guns were firing, but all was silent as we passed through the deserted wreckage of the little town of Wageningen, and with rather a naked feeling we passed through our forward infantry positions, along a dead-straight cobbled main road lined with tall trees running between green fields and orchards in late blossom. We passed through a roadblock which the Germans had built and then broken up in the last few days to allow food convoys through. About 400 yards farther on the Dutch flag hung from a tree, and barrels of fats, tins of biscuits, boxes of meat, sacks of coal were laid out along the roadside for about two miles. Two armed SS men went up and down on bicycles. A British dispatch rider on his motor-bicycle, also armed, passed them. Dutch police from occupied territory in their black uniforms with high peaked caps talked to Canadian and British officers, and at the bottom of the road was a stout wooden barrier and smoke rising from houses beyond it. The German positions were there.

'The first lorry delivered its load at 7.30 in the morning, and by four o'clock in the afternoon over 1000 tons of food and fuel had been stacked under the tall trees lining the roads. Some 350 Dutchmen from occupied territory have been allowed through the lines by the Germans to load food on to their transport and drive it westward. The job is desperately urgent. Through a Dutch officer interpreter I learnt just how urgent.

'People in big Dutch towns have been keeping more and more to their houses. Some have on their doors notices saying "Any food left here will be welcome", but they have not the strength to go out looking for it. Lacking coal for power and pumping they have no proper water supply. The death-rate is still increasing, and they are unable to bury the dead. Lacking wood they are making paper coffins and stacking them in churches. One man said that hardly any of the city children born in the last three years have survived.

'The Dutchmen I saw at the food-control point were amazed at the quantity of food they saw, and at the quality and number of the vehicles bringing it in. All of these men looked sallow or pale and pinched. An officer who had been superintending the operation all day told me they were tremendously willing to work but they got tired very quickly, and it was only the enthusiasm of at last receiving food which enabled them to go on working for hours to get it through to the people needing it even more. As one lorry was being unloaded a little sugar was sprinkled on to the floor. To the Dutchmen who scooped it up and ate it, it was one of the biggest treats of their lives. One man speaking and waving his hand towards the west said, "You coming soon?" and then sadly, "But it is not good – all floods and Germans." Within the last week several thousand tons of food have already been made available to the Dutch, and from one man from Utrecht I learnt that air dropping had been generally very successful. This man estimated that perhaps eight per cent of the food had either been damaged, lost, or diverted. The dropping at Waalhaven near Rotterdam was a failure, because it landed in a mined area, and the butter dropped near Voorburg was spoilt, apparently because it had not been securely enough packed.

'One had only to see the drawn but smiling faces of these Dutchmen to realise what a tremendous thing it is for them to get this food and to see the supply and means of supply growing. Every lorry or aircraft that delivers food to Holland now may save several lives.'

ROBERT DUNNETT

The privations and suffering of the Dutch people, and of all the occupied peoples, were now virtually at an end: at least nothing further was to be added, for the Nazi beast was prostrate. On 4 May

War Report reached the climax for which it was designed when it broadcast a description of Field-Marshal Montgomery receiving the surrender of all German forces opposed to him. At one stroke he had liberated Denmark and still-occupied Holland, had gained control of what remained of the German Navy, and had signalled the final collapse of German military power:

4 May 1945

'Hallo BBC, hallo BBC, this is Chester Wilmot speaking from the Second Army front in Germany. This is not so much a description of what happened this afternoon, but the actual thing – recorded at Field-Marshal Montgomery's headquarters this afternoon – the full ceremony which took place when the German plenipotentiaries came to sign the instrument of surrender. I've just got to the transmitter and so I haven't had time to edit these recordings and will play them to you as we recorded them on the hill of the Lüneburger Heath this afternoon at Field-Marshal Montgomery's headquarters. There is an opening description of the arrival of the plenipotentiaries, and then you hear Field-Marshal Montgomery himself reading the terms of surrender. These are the recordings we made.'

'Hallo BBC, this is Chester Wilmot speaking from Field-Marshal Montgomery's tactical headquarters on a high windswept hill on the wild Lüneburger Heath near the River Elbe.

'It's ten minutes past six on Friday 4 May: the hour and the day for which British fighting men and women and British peoples throughout the world have been fighting and working and waiting for five years and eight months. The commanders of the German forces opposing Field-Marshal Montgomery's Twenty-first Army Group have come to this headquarters today to surrender. To make unconditional surrender. The plenipotentiaries are General Admiral von Friedeburg, Commander-in-Chief of the German Navy, who succeeded Admiral Doenitz in that post when Doenitz became the new Führer. With him are General Kinzel, Chief of Staff to Field-Marshal Busch; Rear-Admiral Wagner who is Chief of Staff to von Friedeburg; and another staff officer.

'They came here yesterday hoping to parley – to talk terms. But they were told to go back and return today with power to make unconditional surrender. They have come back through the lines again today, to make that surrender. And now we're waiting for them to come through the trees that surround Field-Marshal Montgomery's headquarters. And here they are now. General Admiral von Friedeburg is leading with Colonel Ewart, of Field-Marshal Montgomery's Staff; with him is the General of Infantry Kinzel . . . Rear-Admiral Wagner, and they're now walking up to the caravan which the Field-Marshal uses for his headquarters in the field. And now von Friedeburg is entering the caravan. He's gone inside, he stood for a moment at the door, saluted. He walked in.

'The four other Germans also saluted and they're now standing outside at the bottom step. They're standing underneath the camouflage netting screen, and ten yards away to their right is a Union Jack flying in the breeze, and they're just saluting Field-Marshal Montgomery under the shadow of that flag which is honoured by the troops to whom they're surrendering today.

'The caravan in which this final conference is being held is the caravan which the British troops captured from General Bergonzoli when they first destroyed an enemy army in this war, the army of Graziani in Cyrenaica in February 1941. In that caravan, souvenir of the first victory in this war, the discussions leading to our final victory are now taking place, and in a few moments Field-Marshal Montgomery and the German plenipotentiaries will move to a tent where the final ceremony of signing will take place.

'It's now twenty minutes past six, the discussions have been short and to the point. Admiral von Friedeburg has stepped down from Field-Marshal Montgomery's caravan; he is now walking over to the tent where the signing ceremony will take place with the other German plenipotentiaries, and Field-Marshal Montgomery is following behind carrying the instrument of surrender which they have agreed to sign. Now inside the tent, which is an ordinary camouflaged army tent, the five German plenipotentiaries are standing round the table, an ordinary army table covered with rough army blankets. Field-Marshal Montgomery enters, they salute, and he sits down.'

FIELD-MARSHAL MONTGOMERY: 'Now we've assembled here today to accept the surrender terms, which have been made with the delegation from the German Army. I will now read out the terms of that instrument of surrender. "The German Command agrees to the surrender of all German armed forces in Holland, in north-west Germany, including the Friesian Islands and Heligoland and all other islands, in Schleswig-Holstein, and in Denmark to the Commander-in-Chief 21st Army Group. This to include all naval ships in these areas. These forces to lay down their arms and to surrender unconditionally. All hostilities on land, on sea, or in the air by German forces in the above areas to cease at 0800 hours British Double Summer Time on Saturday the 5 May 1945. The German Command to carry out at once and without argument or comment all further orders that will be issued by the Allied Powers on any subject. Disobedience of orders or failure to comply with them will be regarded as a breach of these surrender terms, and will be dealt with by the Allied Powers in accordance with the accepted laws and usages of War. This instrument of surrender is independent of, without prejudice to, and will be superseded by, any general instrument of surrender imposed by or on behalf of the Allied Powers and applicable to Germany and the German Armed Forces as

On 4 May 1945, in the tent at his headquarters, Field Marshal
Montgomery, seated on the right, is reading the terms of surrender
of the German armed forces in northern Germany, Denmark and
Holland to the German plenipotentiaries. From the left, Rear
Admiral Gerhard von Wagner, war correspondent Chester Wilmot
who is standing and Admiral Hans-Georg von Friedeburg.

a whole. This instrument of surrender is written in English, and in
German. The English version is the authentic text. The decision of
the Allied Powers will be final, if any doubt or dispute arises as to the
meaning or interpretation of the surrender terms."

'That is the text of the instrument of surrender and the German
delegation will now sign this paper, and they will sign in order of
seniority and General Admiral von Friedeburg will sign first. . . . Now
General Kinzel will sign next. . . . Rear-Admiral Wagner will sign next.
. . . Colonel Politz will sign next . . .. And Major Friedl will sign now.

'Now I will sign the instrument on behalf of the Supreme Allied
Commander, General Eisenhower. Now that concludes the formal

surrender and there are various matters now, or details to be discussed, which we will do in closed session.

WILMOT: 'And now the discussions, of which Field-Marshal Montgomery spoke, are completed. The German generals have left the tent. They're moving through the trees to the visitors' camp where they will spend the night, as visitors in Field-Marshal Montgomery's headquarters. And the Field-Marshal himself has walked briskly across the grass square in front of his caravan, entered and closed the door behind him. The day's work is done. The triumph of the British armies in Europe is complete. Tomorrow morning at eight o'clock the war will be over for the British and Canadian troops, and for the airmen of Britain and the Commonwealth who came to liberate the occupied countries and to conquer Germany.

'Tomorrow morning their victory will be complete.'

CHESTER WILMOT

The formalities of surrender were completed, and then Lance-Sergeant Hugh Brown was given a message to transmit by radio to German headquarters:

5 May 1945

'Half an hour after the armistice was signed, and while the German delegates were still discussing details, a young Signals Sergeant at Field-Marshal Montgomery's battle headquarters was handed a rough sheet of paper, with thirty words in German hastily printed on it in ink. The paper was spotted with raindrops and the ink had begun to run; so much so, that some of the letters were indistinct. It didn't look like an historic document, but it was. It was a message for the radio station of the German headquarters from which the plenipotentiaries had come. It was a message telling the German Command that the armistice was signed. The English translation of the text read as follows:

"Have signed conditions inclusive of ships in same zone. Armistice as from 8 am 5 May. Please report receipt. End."

'That was all. But the operator, Lance-Sergeant Hugh Brown of Fulham, who's with me now, had some trouble in getting it through. Well, what was the trouble, Sergeant?

BROWN: Interference by Morse. I had to send the message three times before the German operator gave me the OK and repeated it back to me. The message finally got through at half-past seven.

WILMOT: And what signal procedure did you use to get it through? Ours, or theirs?

BROWN: Neither. I used international peacetime procedure with a few snatches of army procedure. The Jerry operator knew some of our terms and used them, and I used some of theirs.

WILMOT: Oh, so you'd worked German stations before?

BROWN: Oh yes. At Nijmegen during the Arnhem operation. I then called up the Germans and asked them if we could send some ambulances through their lines to get our wounded. They refused. But yesterday, when I called up the German HQ there was no question of them refusing. Their operator was very obedient and correct. But I could tell he knew the importance of the message he received.

WILMOT: How did you know that?

BROWN: His Morse was all over the place when he repeated the message back to me. His hand was obviously very shaky. My hand was shaking too, but – that's off the record! And today we've been sending the Germans orders. For my wireless operators this has been the greatest morning of the war. They've been busy sending orders from the Field-Marshal himself to the German Command we've been fighting for five and a half years – just the job!'

CHESTER WILMOT

Yes – just the job! Three more days were to elapse before the official announcement of unconditional surrender on all fronts, but it was felt appropriate that War Report should end when the British forces in Europe had reached their final objectives and stopped fighting. Its business had been to report their progress from D-Day to final victory, and the story ended with Lance-Sergeant Brown's contented comment – 'It's just the job!' – as he signalled Field-Marshal Montgomery's orders to the defeated Germans. For the last time, on 5 May, John Snagge said:

'That is the end of tonight's War Report,' and added: 'and the end of War Report. The war goes on, the BBC correspondents will be in the field until victory is won. But with the conclusion of the campaign on the Western Front, War Report completes its task.

'It began eleven months ago tomorrow, on D-Day, 6 June 1944, on the Normandy beach-head, and it has been broadcast 235 times. In the course of these months War Report has brought listeners the voices of members of all the fighting services, and of many nationalities; the voices of Dominion, American, and European correspondents, and the voices of the BBC correspondents, who, with recording and transmitting engineers, have followed the assaults on Germany and Japan. They are too many to mention, but here, in commemoration of their work, we report the names of BBC War Correspondents whose recordings and messages, written or spoken, have been the mainstay of this broadcast:

WAR REPORT

ROBERT BARR

DAVID BERNARD

GUY BYAM (*reported missing*)

RICHARD DIMBLEBY

ROBIN DUFF

ROBERT DUNNETT

FRANK GILLARD

DENIS JOHNSTON

PIERRE LEFEVRE

STEWART MACPHERSON

HOWARD MARSHALL

KENNETH MATTHEWS

STANLEY MAXTED

JOHN NIXON

CYRIL RAY

ROBERT REID

MICHAEL REYNOLDS

RICHARD SHARP

COLSTON SHEPHERD

PATRICK SMITH

MICHAEL STANDING

KENT STEVENSON (*reported missing*)

GODFREY TALBOT

WYNFORD VAUGHAN-THOMAS

EDWARD WARD

DOUGLAS WILLIS

COLIN WILLS

CHESTER WILMOT

IAN WILSON

CHAPTER XXIV
Unconditional Surrender

'Defeat with humiliation'

To round off this report of the campaign which led to Germany's defeat it fell to Chester Wilmot to describe the concluding moments:

8 May 1945

'When General Jodl signed Germany's unconditional surrender, the night before last, this was the climax of four days of peace negotiations. During this time, the Germans did their best to split the Allies and obtain terms. The final surrender developed directly from the negotiations which led to the armistice on Field-Marshal Montgomery's front last week. After signing the instrument surrendering the forces in the north-west on Friday, Admiral von Friedeburg went on to SHAEF to see General Eisenhower next day.

'Doenitz and Keitel, the chief of the High Command, then still hoped that, even if Eisenhower would not accept the surrender of all the German armed forces to Britain and America alone, they might achieve almost the same end by surrendering these forces piecemeal – hence the surrenders in Italy, the north-west, and then in southern Germany. They hoped to persuade Eisenhower to accept the piecemeal capitulation of the forces facing his troops, until they had brought peace to the whole of the western front. They could then, they thought, carry on the war against Russia, withdrawing their armies on the Soviet front gradually back through the British and American lines. That hope was shortlived. Eisenhower demanded surrender to all powers unconditionally, and Jodl was in no position to bargain, though he did try to haggle. By forcing the German Government and High Command to sign an instrument of unconditional surrender, the Allies have gained a far greater victory than seemed possible a month ago. Then it appeared that Germany would just disintegrate and that we should have to mop up each individual pocket, but now we have obtained written admission of defeat from the established Government and from those very military leaders, Doenitz and Keitel, who have fought the war right through. The pockets will not have to be mopped up for we've concluded an agreement with the Government and the Command which has power to issue the order to lay down arms, and which now that it's admitted defeat is willing to do what it can to maintain order and restore normal life in Germany. And so by this we've gained not only a great military triumph but also a tremendous political victory.'

CHESTER WILMOT

8 May 1945

'I don't think you can realise the completeness of the German defeat until you've been to Flensburg, the present seat of the Doenitz Government and of Keitel's High Command.

'In the streets civilians were going about their normal business with expressionless faces, but the crowds outside the food shops were much larger than those gathered to read Doenitz's proclamation about the end of the war in the north-west. Neither the civilians nor the ordinary troops any longer care.

'All this wasn't surprising, but I did expect that somehow the atmosphere at the High Command Headquarters would be different; but this was the scene. A rather dirty Marine barracks housed the Headquarters and the Government; outside it, eighteen scruffy sentries, as dirty and dishevelled as the troops in the town. In the car park beyond the gate there were a dozen big staff cars, replicas of those great sleek black Mercedes in which the Nazi leaders have swaggered through the capitals of Europe. And now, here they were in the last bolt-hole, their shining black surfaces hastily camouflaged with paint that had just been slashed on, and with branches of trees tied on so that they looked like Macduff s men who carried Birnam wood to Dunsinane.

'Here in these cars was the end of Nazi glory. The only evidence that this was the High Command's Headquarters was a small sign painted in black on the torn-off bottom of a camouflaged boot-box. It bore the letters "O.K.W." [*Oberkommando der Wehrmacht – High Command of the Armed Forces*].

'British officers who had been inside told me that the interior is just as dirty and decrepit. It has the same atmosphere of defeat and despair. Yesterday a British officer tried to deliver a message to Field-Marshal Keitel. He found him in a poky room at the end of a long passage, no sentries outside the door – three Germans lounging at the window at the end might have been sentries. He went in through an outer office, pushing his way past typists and clerks, through a small door and into Keitel's office, a room twenty feet by fifteen. Keitel sat at a small table in full uniform with his Field-Marshal's baton beside him. Behind his chair was a photograph of Hitler; on the wall in front was a large school map of Europe which Hitler conquered but couldn't hold down. Here in this miserable little room, a far cry from the great chancelleries of Europe where he so often laid down terms, sat Keitel himself. Here, and in another office which Doenitz used, the German Führer and the Chief of the High Command had come to the fateful decisions of the past few days. The power and glory of the greater Reich, the pomp and pageantry of Hitler's empire had been reduced to this. Only the glittering uniforms remained. During yesterday afternoon Keitel was handed the text of the surrender terms which Jodl had signed at SHAEF, a document which meant not even peace with honour but defeat with humiliation.'

CHESTER WILMOT

June 1944–May 1945

A Chronology

The following chronology mainly covers North-West Europe, but includes some more important events from other theatres of combat.

1944
June

4	Rome entered
6	D-Day landings in Normandy
8	Bayeux liberated
12	Churchill visits the Normandy beach-head
13	First V1 flying-bombs fall on London
19	US forces liberate Saipan
27	Cherbourg liberated

July

3	Minsk, Siena captured
9	Caen captured
17	Rommel wounded
18	British and Canadian forces break through east of the Orne
20	Attempt to assassinate Hitler fails
26	Lvov liberated
27	US forces break through west of St-Lô
31	Avranches and Brest-Litovsk captured

August

1	Warsaw rising begins; US troops enter Brittany

3	Rennes captured
9	St Malo and Le Mans captured
12	German retreat from Normandy begins
15	Allied landings in south of France
19	Falaise gap closed; Paris rising; Florence liberated
21	US forces cross the Seine
25	Liberation of Paris; and of Marseilles
30	Rouen captured
31	Russians enter Bucharest

September

1	Eisenhower takes over direct control of ground forces; Dieppe falls
2	German Gothic Line in Italy broken
3	Liberation of Brussels; and of Lyons
4	Antwerp captured, docks intact
8	First V2 rockets land in England; Ostend, Liège liberated
9	Sofia liberated
10–17	Churchill and Roosevelt meet in Quebec
12	Le Havre captured
15	Siegfried Line breached; Helsinki liberated
17	Airborne landings at Eindhoven, Nijmegen and Arnhem
18	Brest captured
22	Boulogne, Rimini captured
25	British troops withdrawn from Arnhem
30	Calais captured

October

9–18	Churchill visits Moscow
14	Athens entered
20	Belgrade entered; US troops land in Philippines

21   Aachen surrenders

24–26 Battle of Leyte Gulf

November

1   Landings on Walcheren

12   *Tirpitz* sunk

20   Belfort captured

22   Metz captured

23   Strasbourg captured

28   Antwerp reopened to shipping

December

5   Ravenna taken

16   Germans begin Ardennes offensive

18   North Burma cleared of Japanese

26   Bastogne relieved

27   Budapest surrounded

1945

January

1   British offensive opens in Burma

17   Warsaw entered by Russians

18   Cracow captured

23   Russians reach the Oder

27   Russians reach Auschwitz

February

4–11   Yalta Conference

4   Belgium finally liberated

6   Oder crossed by Russians

13   Bombing of Dresden

16   US landings on Corregidor
19   US landings on Iwo Jima

March

1   Mönchen-Gladbach captured
4   Manila liberated
5   Cologne entered
7   Bridge at Remagen captured and US troops cross the Rhine;
        Mandalay entered
17   Iwo Jima surrenders
23   British troops cross the Rhine
27   Last V2 rocket falls on Britain
28   Last V1 falls on Britain
29   Russians enter Austria
30   Russians enter Danzig

April

1   US landings on Okinawa
10   Hanover captured
11   Essen captured
12   Roosevelt dies; succeeded by Truman
13   Vienna liberated
14   Arnhem re-entered
20   Russians reach Berlin
21   Bologna liberated
22   Stuttgart captured
23   Allies reach the Po; UN conference opens in San
        Francisco
26   Bremen surrenders; US and Russian troops meet at Torgau;
        Milan liberated by partisans
27   Genoa, Verona liberated

28   British troops cross the Elbe; Mussolini executed by
           partisans

29   Venice, Munich entered; Germans sign unconditional
           surrender in Italy, to take effect 2 May

30   Hitler commits suicide; Turin entered

May

1   Doenitz takes power in Germany; Goebbels commits suicide

2   Berlin surrenders to Russians; British and Russian troops
           link at Wismar; Trieste captured; Rangoon entered

3   Hamburg entered

4   German 1st and 19th Armies surrender to US forces; US
           5th Army crosses Brenner and links up with US 7th Army

5   All German forces in Holland, North-West Germany and
           Denmark surrender to Montgomery

7   Jodl signs unconditional surrender in Rheims

8   VE-Day; unconditional surrender signed again by Keitel in
           Berlin; German troops in Norway surrender

9   German troops in Channel Islands surrender

12   Prague liberated

The war against Japan continued until August. The main events were:

August

6   Atomic bomb on Hiroshima

8   Russia declares war on Japan

9   Atomic bomb on Nagasaki

15   Japan announces surrender

September

2   Japanese surrender signed

Glossary

Bailey bridge	bridge made in prefabricated sections
bangalore torpedo	long thin tube filled with explosive, used for blowing gaps in barbed wire
bazooka	hand-held American anti-tank weapon
bren	British light machine-gun
buffalo	armoured amphibious personnel carrier
Churchill	British slow heavy tank
Dakota (C47)	American transport aircraft
DR	dispatch rider
duck (DUKW)	amphibious truck
E-boat	fast German light naval craft
Element C	German metal beach obstacle
FFI	Forces Françaises de l'Intérieur
flak	German anti-aircraft artillery
Hamilcar	large British glider
hedgehog	German anti-tank obstacle
Horsa	British glider
LCM	landing craft, mechanised
LCT	landing craft, tank
Lightning (P38)	American twin-boom fighter aircraft
LST	landing ship, tank
Maquis	French resistance forces in the countryside
Marauder (B26)	American light bomber
MCN, MCO, MCP	BBC mobile field transmitters
MTB	motor torpedo boat
Mulberry	artificial harbours off Normandy coast
Mustang (P51)	long-range American fighter

Nebelwerfer	German multiple mortar
OP	observation post
Panther	German heavy tank
piat projector	infantry anti-tank (clumsier British version of bazooka)
QRM	wireless interference
RAMC	Royal Army Medical Corps
RASC	Royal Army Service Corps
R-boat	German light naval craft
RE	Royal Engineers
REME	Royal Electrical and Mechanical Engineers
SHAEF	Supreme Headquarters, Allied Expeditionary Force
S-mine	small deadly German anti-personnel mine
Sherman	American heavy tank
SP	self-propelled gun
Spahi	Algerian cavalry
Spandau	German light machine-gun
sten	cheap British submachine-gun
stencil	duplicating machine for typescript
telediphone	dictaphone working off a telephone line
Thunderbolt (P47)	American fighter
Tiger	German super-heavy tank
Todt organisation	forced labour battalions working under German orders
tommy cooker	small portable smokeless stove
Typhoon	British tank-busting fighter
werewolf	notional member of stay-behind parties the Nazis were thought to have organised to continue fighting after formal defeat; werewolves turned out to be mythical

The War Correspondents

It is inevitable that many of those whose voices became so familiar on War Report are now dead. Two of them, indeed, were killed in the war: Kent Stevenson in a raid on north-west Germany just over two weeks after D-Day; and Guy Byam, whose full name was Guy Byam-Corstiaens and whose reports had all the marks of a great future in broadcasting, in a raid on Berlin in February 1945.

Of those who feature most prominently in the preceding pages, Chester Wilmot was an Australian who went on to write what is perhaps still the best single-volume survey of the war in the West, *The Struggle for Europe*, and was tragically killed, aged forty-two, in the Comet airliner which disintegrated over the Mediterranean in January 1954. Richard Dimbleby became one of BBC television's best-known personalities as presenter of *Panorama* and commentator on state occasions; he died in 1965. Robert Reid, still remembered by many for his description of General de Gaulle entering Notre Dame under a hail of bullets (see p. 227), was News Editor of the *News Chronicle* and a freelance broadcaster; he died in 1974. Stanley Maxted was a Canadian, who had joined the BBC earlier in the war as a War Correspondent from CBC radio; after the war he returned to the USA for the drier climate and subsequently died there. Howard Marshall had been a well-known commentator before the war and was the BBC's Director of War Reporting. After the war he was Director of Personnel and Public Relations for Richard Thomas and Baldwins and died in 1973.

Frank Gillard stayed with the BBC, a familiar voice as a broadcaster, becoming Managing Director of BBC Radio before retiring in 1970.

He became heavily involved as a consultant in National Public Radio in the United States and then became a co-founder of the BBC's Oral History Project, recording interviews with retired staff for more than twenty years. He died in 1998. Wynford Vaughan-Thomas too continued to be a familiar voice as a broadcaster and commentator on radio and television, and wrote a number of successful books. He died in 1989. Robert Barr moved after the war to television, where he made documentaries, including the first-ever TV documentary, 'Germany under Control'. He went on to become Executive Producer of series such as *Z-Cars* and *Spy Trap* and a popular scriptwriter. He retired to his beloved Isle of Bute and died there in 1999. Robert Dunnett was Publicity Officer for BBC Scotland and covered the 1947 royal tour of South Africa before resigning to freelance and subsequently become PRO for Scottish Gas. He died in 1990.

Stewart MacPherson was well known on radio after the war as a commentator and question-master for such programmes as *Twenty Questions* and *Ignorance is Bliss*. He returned to Canada at the end of the 1950s and became director of programmes for a television station in Winnipeg, where he died in 1995. Edward Ward, who had been captured in North Africa and was liberated in time to cover the last month of the European war, continued as a freelance foreign correspondent all over the world; in 1950 he succeeded his father as the seventh Viscount Bangor. He died in 1993. After the war Godfrey Talbot was appointed the BBC's Royal Correspondent in 1948 and became one of the most familiar voices on BBC Radio and Television, as he travelled the world with the royal family on state visits. He wrote a number of books on this period of his life. He died in 2000 at the age of 91.

It has not been possible, in the space available, to refer to all those who contributed to War Report, or indeed to the editors, administrators and engineers who were working on this side of the

Channel in the war. But we record here the complete list of all those of the BBC staff whose work as correspondents, recording engineers, transmitter engineers, and drivers carried the day-to-day burden of spoken news, often to the danger of their lives. Some of them were in theatres of the war which are not reported in these pages; but their material found its place in War Report. Their names are printed here according to the regions in which they mainly worked.

WESTERN FRONT
Correspondents

ROBERT BARR

DAVID BERNARD

GUY BYAM

RICHARD DIMBLEBY

RUPERT DOWNING

ROBIN DUFF

ROBERT DUNNETT

ALFRED FLETCHER

FRANK GILLARD

DENIS JOHNSTON

PIERRE LEFEVRE

STEWART MACPHERSON

HOWARD MARSHALL

STANLEY MAXTED

ALAN MELVILLE

RICHARD NORTH

CYRIL RAY

ROBERT REID

E. COLSTON SHEPHERD

MICHAEL STANDING

KENT STEVENSON

WYNFORD VAUGHAN-THOMAS

EDWARD WARD

DOUGLAS WILLIS

COLIN WILLS

CHESTER WILMOT

IAN WILSON

Recording Engineers

C. D. ADAMSON

W. R. ARNELL

F. J. COOPER

W. S. COSTELLO

D. H. FARLEY

J. C. FONVIELLE

S. GORE

H. L. HAYHURST

W. H. E. LINDOP

T. A. MELLOR

R. E. PIDSLEY

H. O. SAMPSON

H. F. L. SARNEY

S. UNWIN

G. F. WADE

J. B. WATSON

MICHAEL REYNOLDS

PATRICK SMITH

GODFREY TALBOT

Transmitter Staffs

C. F. R. ABBOTT

F. A. CORMACK

W. H. E. FLINT

J. H. GILMAN

G. D. HERRIN

R. W. HOWARD

W. A. JACKSON

W. H. E. LINDOP

T. G. MAY

E. P. METCALFE

R. L. S. NEWMAN

J. OATES

J. SHALLCROSS

A. E. SNOWDON

J. T. STOCKING

P. H. WALKER

A. E. WINDSOR

Recording Engineers

C. C. CARLYON

DOUGLAS FARLEY

STANLEY UNWIN

G. W. WADE

HERBERT WALDEN

Rome Staff

R. C. ASHTON

G. F. BERESFORD

EDWARD BONONG

R. W. LESLIE

ARTHUR PHILLIPS

BURMA

Correspondent

RICHARD SHARP

Recording Engineer

EUGENE GIROT

ITALY

Correspondents

REGINALD BECKWITH

FRANCIS HALLAWELL

JOHN NIXON

BALKANS

Correspondent

KENNETH MATTHEWS

Index